T0319469

RETHINKING
SOVEREIGN DEBT

RETHINKING
SOVEREIGN DEBT

*Politics, Reputation, and Legitimacy
in Modern Finance*

Odette Lienau

HARVARD UNIVERSITY PRESS
Cambridge, Massachusetts
London, England
2014

Library of Congress Cataloging-in-Publication Data

Lienau, Odette, 1978–

  Rethinking sovereign debt : politics, reputation, and legitimacy in modern finance / Odette Lienau.

    pages cm

  Includes bibliographical references and index.

  ISBN 978-0-674-72506-5

  1. Debts, Public—Case studies.   2. Debt cancellation—Case studies.

I. Title.

  HJ8015.L54 2014

    336.3'4—dc23   2013020190

For my parents and Aziz

Contents

RETHINKING
SOVEREIGN DEBT

Open Questions in Sovereign Debt

SOVEREIGN DEBT markets have demonstrated incredible resilience despite a century of dramatic political and economic upheaval. Among the most remarkable aspects of the contemporary debt regime is the degree to which expectations of borrowers remain relatively uniform even in the face of such major shifts. These basic expectations resolve into one background rule: sovereign borrowers must repay, regardless of the circumstances of the initial debt contract, the actual use of loan proceeds, or the exigencies of any potential default. This is not to say that countries always pay; certainly, they do not. But the background rule remains, and it sets the standard by which creditors and others form their reputational judgments and against which sovereign borrowers are evaluated and chastised.

This repayment norm helps to immunize the debt regime from serious challenge and to stabilize the massive sums at stake. In particular, it buttresses our avoidance of prickly questions about fairness and appropriateness in the international economic arena. Several troubling queries in recent decades include: Should a black-African-led South Africa really be expected to repay apartheid era debt? Or, given that Saddam Hussein was a dictator who used funds for the oppression of a majority of Iraq's population, would it be appropriate to require future Iraqi generations to pay for his iniquity? More generally, who counts as the "sovereign" in these debt situations—is sovereignty just the legal shell for whoever happens to control a territory, or does it imply underlying principles of legitimate representation or public benefit? And how might all this fit into assessments of a country's creditworthiness?

Notwithstanding such questions, the repayment norm exerts a particular kind of power in international economic relations by shaping expectations of appropriate action in the area of sovereign debt. The rule is strengthened by its popular identity as a market principle, with effects that can be identified and measured but that ultimately cannot be changed. A study commissioned by the United Nations Conference on Trade and Development (UNCTAD) noted,

> one of the major policy concerns that has deterred some transitional regimes from repudiating "odious" debt from the previous regime is that of reputation in the capital markets; a transitional regime may be concerned that creditors will not in the future provide access to funds, because they are unable to distinguish the exceptional political decision to repudiate debt due to its odiousness from the general creditworthiness of the regime.[1]

The narrative shaping such decisions suggests that without the background rule of consistent repayment, reinforced by the disciplining mechanism of reputation, lending to many sovereign states would disappear. International debt markets in the absence of a clear cross-border enforcement mechanism would be too risky, requiring more information on sovereign borrowers' subjective repayment proclivities than would be worthwhile for any creditor to collect. Although the repayment norm is most starkly applied in situations of regime change and transitional justice, its expectations filter into the prospects and bargaining positions of debt negotiations more generally. If repayment is expected *even* in such extreme circumstances, then debtors should *certainly* bear the burden in other situations that might emerge. By policing the boundaries of the sovereign debt regime—and ensuring that such issues remain marginal—this rule keeps the core flow of capital safe and relatively free of controversy.

In this volume, I argue that the market narrative supporting the repayment norm is overly simplistic and in some respects entirely wrong. It forgets to ask key questions about the relationship between sovereign debt, reputation, and legitimacy over the last century—questions that have surprising answers embedded in the historical development of modern finance, with significant ramifications for how we approach debt markets in the future. How have we come to think that the norm of sovereign debt continuity—the rule that sovereign states should repay debt even after a major regime change and the related expectation that they will otherwise suffer reputational consequences—is more or less unavoidable for a working international financial system? Is it possible to think of an alternative approach—or find one historically—in which odious debt ideas and selective debt cancellation might be incorporated into a functioning debt market grounded in reputational assessments? And if so, why hasn't such a system developed, especially given the politicized discussions of sovereign legitimacy that have taken place alongside the development of modern finance?

The framing of repayment and reputation as a market principle—one that disciplines debtors and creditors alike—discourages this type of questioning in part by propagating the following three assumptions. First, although creditors may assess a specific borrower's political characteristics through the lens of sovereign risk, judgments about a borrower's repayment decisions are not shaped by politics per se. Rather, they are simply the best objective assessment of a given set of material facts. Second, the mechanism of sovereign reputation itself is similarly free from subjective and historically variable political judgments. And third, all rational creditors are expected to respond in basically the same way to particular market events—especially those events that challenge the principle of continuous repayment. Therefore, it is not necessary to study the historically conditioned identities and interests of particular creditors to understand how capital markets, as a whole, will respond to any given sovereign action. These assumptions of political neutrality, reputational stability, and creditor uniformity support an assessment that the basic contours of the sovereign debt regime are effectively unchangeable.

In the following pages, I contend that, far from being the stable and all but inevitable market principle we sometimes imagine, the debt continuity norm is intrinsically political and historically variable. It has been shaped over the last century by political actors, broader ideological shifts, and changing public and private creditor structures. To begin with, any discussion of sovereign debt is rendered intelligible *only* by quietly incorporating a definition of "sovereignty" that is necessarily normative. Depending on the theory of sovereignty implicitly or explicitly adopted in international economic relations at any given time, the practices of sovereign debt and reputation may diverge significantly. Furthermore, creditor uniformity cannot simply be assumed, and in fact different creditors may interpret—and historically *have* interpreted—the same politicized debt repudiation in opposing ways. A close look at the post-World War I cases of the Soviet Union and Costa Rica suggests how, under conditions of market competition and ideological flexibility, creditors can make rational reputational judgments in favor of post-repudiation lending. The absence of similar cases later in the century resulted not from rigid market certainties but instead from changes in creditor interactions and broader norms of sovereignty. These shifts in turn followed from choices by actors such as the World Bank, globalizing private banks, and the US government.

What might this theoretical instability and historical variability mean for the repayment norm today? A strict rule of sovereign debt continuity after regime change is hardly necessary for workable reputational assessments in international capital markets. Alternative approaches, incorporating ideas of illegitimate debt and allowing for limited cancellation, emerged historically and could function more fully in the future. Thus scholarly and popular discussions of sovereign debt have the potential to be much more wide-ranging than their current contours imply. That said, the norm is deeply embedded in international finance and can't simply be argued away, and it is more powerful than much conventionally enforceable treaty law at shaping international actions. Indeed, on difficult issues like debt repayment after regime change and potentially illegitimate debt there is no multilateral treaty in force, even despite several efforts. Legal scholars and activists have attempted to resuscitate ideas such as a formal doctrine of "odious debt," according to which a fallen regime's debt need not be repaid if it was not authorized by and did not benefit the underlying population.[2] However, efforts to alter the repayment standards run up against already powerful practices of debt continuity—something of a global soft law in hiding—that have the predictability and compliance pull of conventional law if not its external trappings.

To think seriously about altering the current framework, then, it is necessary to recognize its theoretical supports and historical foundations. In this introductory chapter, I aim to lay the groundwork for such an understanding. I begin by filling out the analytical problems with the conventional approach to sovereign continuity in debt and reputation, and identify opposing "statist" and "non-statist" ways of thinking through the question. I then highlight how we can study both the historical variation in this norm and its political underpinnings through the issue of odious debt. This introduction also provides an overview of the historical arc of my argument, which underscores that other approaches to debt continuity emerged in the early twentieth century and suggests how they were covered over by broader political and financial trends in the latter part of the century. Finally, I discuss the role of power and interest in the long-term development of a norm that, over time, has exercised significant power in its own right.

Problems with the Conventional Wisdom

The assumptions of neutrality, reputational stability, and creditor uniformity that underpin the repayment norm are, if not entirely mistaken, at least greatly oversimplified. Although I expand on this claim more fully in chapter 2, a quick overview is warranted up front. To begin with, one of the most puzzling elements of the conventional narrative is the notion that the sovereign debt regime's repayment rule could be apolitical. The mere mention of sovereign debt invokes one of the most politically controversial concepts in global affairs and international law: sovereignty. And perhaps unwittingly, a very distinct political theory of sovereignty supports the current system of international lending. In discussing arguments that the post-2003 Iraqi regime should be freed of Hussein-era debt, a *Financial Times* leader noted, "The principle [being attacked] is sovereign continuity—the idea that governments should honor debts contracted by predecessors. Without this, there would be no lending to governments."[3] Sovereign continuity means that the same "sovereign" remains, and thus is subject to the same contractual obligations, regardless of any internal political changes. It effectively derives from what I call throughout this book a strictly *statist* conception of sovereignty—the idea that the content of and changes in a state's internal structure, interests, and popular support are irrelevant to its status as a legitimate sovereign and thus to its external relations and obligations. While this statist vision has deep roots in global affairs, it is heavily contested in legal and international relations theory, and indeed it has been subject to debate and alteration over the twentieth century and into the twenty-first. In particular, the possibilities of democratic sovereignty or a sovereignty legally bound by constitutional norms are some of the *non-statist* concepts of sovereignty that have gained considerable traction in the international arena. An international economic regime more attuned to these alternative, non-statist concepts should be much more hospitable to something like the odious debt idea mentioned above—and thus more amenable to noncontinuity and debt cancellation under certain circumstances. Indeed, I suggest that the necessity of a statist repayment rule for continued sovereign lending is a contestable claim. But what is perhaps most puzzling is the way in which, in the face of these multiple alternatives, a statist political theory has become so thoroughly embedded in the sovereign debt regime that its deeply *political* character effectively disappears.

Turning to reputation does not in and of itself provide a sufficient answer. Just as the rule of continuous repayment depends on a particular vision of legitimate sovereignty, the reputational mechanism supporting this rule takes the same implicit theoretical approach. The determination of *which sovereign* a reputational assessment attaches to is necessarily infused with a background, historically informed political judgment: Should a recently anointed democratic government, flush from the overthrow of a dictator, be assessed as a new, untested sovereign? Or is it evaluated as a continuation of the previous regime? The statist and non-statist approaches suggest very different responses. In short, the call for a reputational assessment does not on its own necessitate the adoption of a statist political theory. It is entirely possible to maintain the importance of reputational assessments in general while accepting that debt repudiation should *not* result in a lending hiatus in all cases. Far from leading in a mechanistic way to the repayment-as-market principle conclusion, reputational judgment itself is fairly flexible. This plasticity suggests that the category of "excusable default"—sovereign defaults justified by major events such as natural disasters and thus having only modest reputational repercussions—may be broad enough to include principled *political* defaults under certain circumstances.[4] It also deepens the puzzle of how the very notion of a working reputational mechanism became so thoroughly intertwined with a statist insistence on debt continuity that the possibility of alternatives faded away.

Perhaps this all leads to the final key assumption of the market principle story—that rational creditors will respond in basically the same way to market events, and in particular will respond in the same hostile way to events that challenge the rule of continuous repayment.[5] Certainly, the norm of sovereign continuity provides something of a windfall to creditors as a whole; it means that states will be expected to repay debt that might have been subject to cancellation under alternative sovereignty frameworks. But even accepting this windfall, what would account for the *conceptual* strength of a statist approach relative to all others? Part of what is interesting is the absence of any acknowledgment that non-statist concepts are entirely consistent with making reputational judgments. Is it possible that creditors coordinate to suppress the very idea that non-statist approaches are possible, including in academic and broader policy discussions of sovereign debt? This would be quite a feat of deliberate collusion—one for which there does not appear to be evidence, though such findings undoubtedly would be newsworthy. I find it more likely that contemporary creditors, and those that write about them, have been similarly conditioned to understand the rules of repayment and reputation according to a fairly narrow political theory.

But even the initial assumption of a shared creditor interest in universal repayment is problematic, and is not fully supported by the historical record. To begin with, it is not entirely clear that all creditors would oppose nonpayment in all instances. This could be the case if, for example, a creditor accepted as plausible the argument that a successor regime constituted a new sovereign, worthy of modest and appropriately priced investment, rather than an intransigent continuation of the previous regime. Such a stance would effectively indicate a reputational assessment consistent with a non-statist concept of sovereignty. While a creditor would hardly be keen to hear such an argument from its own debtor, it might be more receptive to such an argument from a new potential client, particularly in the context of a competitive market.

Furthermore, there are historical instances in which creditors respond in entirely different ways to the same debt repudiation. The Soviet repudiation of tsarist debt, perhaps the most notorious default of the twentieth century, is generally proffered as an exemplar of the reputational risk associated with repudiation, for example in Michael Tomz's important work on reputation in sovereign debt markets.[6] Read as such, it would support the repayment rule's status as a uniform and historically stable market principle. However, as I argue in chapter 3, this reading, based principally on the fact that the new regime was unable to float bonds on the international capital markets, overlooks key elements of the historical record. In fact, while creditors of the previous tsarist regime remained very hostile and insistent on repayment, several newer American banks actually sought to facilitate long-term bond issues by the new Soviet government in the 1920s. These banks were halted not by a reputational assessment—indeed they were impressed by the Soviet Union's reliable payment of shorter-term trade credits—but rather by the US government's *political* hostility to the regime. A closer look at both the theory and history of creditor interaction thus demonstrates that the existence of a relatively uniform creditor approach to sovereign reputation cannot simply be assumed but has to be explained.

What does this mean for the solidity of the sovereign debt regime, including its bulwark rule of repayment and its coordinating reputational mechanism? It is true that settled expectations and market practices have developed, which shut off questions of sovereign legitimacy that might reasonably be at the center of international lending. An equilibrium of sorts has been reached, and any countervailing pressure has thus far been insufficient to produce a real shift. But this does not foreclose the possibility that there are several potentially stable market norms—or multiple equilibria—that could yet develop or that might have developed historically under different circumstances.[7] The fact that the current system looks to many like an immutable market principle, with seemingly consistent creditor reputational assessments, constitutes a puzzle in itself. So far, we have yet to see a satisfactory explanation for this puzzle.

Odious Debt as Sovereignty in Practice

Even if the market principle assumptions underpinning the contemporary norm of sovereign debt continuity do not hold, where does that leave the repayment rule as a practical, historical matter? For any given sovereign borrower, international debt practices can still seem an extremely unyielding edifice. Nonetheless, the theoretical instability does point to the possibility of empirical study and encourage a closer, more critical look at the historical record. If we know that the current approach is inherently political and necessarily historically shaped, there should be a way to identify the assumptions and assessments that underlie a particular moment in international finance.

Even acknowledging the plausibility of empirical study, asking how the practices and reputational underpinnings of debt continuity interact with historically grounded ideas of legitimate sovereignty remains quite difficult in practice. The issue of sovereignty is notoriously slippery and does not easily lend itself to concrete examination. And accepting that a contested concept such as sovereignty plays an important role in any discussion of sovereign debt and reputation does not in itself grant access to its workings. Usually, the question of who might constitute the legitimate sovereign in economic relations remains in the background and is largely forgotten. States enter into and threaten to default on international contracts fairly regularly, and the particularly *political* character of sovereign debt is rarely raised by either party.

There are certain types of debt repudiation, however, that bring these background matters to center stage. Central here is the issue of odious debt, which in the most common formulation arises when an illegitimate regime contracts debt that is not authorized by and does not benefit a nation's people. This idea helps us think through questions of politics and authority in sovereign debt, and makes observable—or operationalizes, in the preferred language of social science—the idea of sovereign legitimacy underpinning the debt regime at a given moment. The classic legal doctrine of odious debt, first developed after the Spanish American War of 1898 and formalized by Alexander Sack in 1927, states that sovereign state debt is "odious" and should not be transferable to successors if the debt was incurred (1) without the consent of the people, *and* (2) not for their benefit.[8] This doctrine directly counters the norm of sovereign continuity in two ways, corresponding to the two prongs of the doctrine. It first suggests that some form of popular consent may be relevant to the existence of binding debt obligations, contradicting the statist theory of sovereignty that underlies sovereign continuity. Alternatively, it highlights the centrality of a debt's *purpose* by noting that any binding sovereign obligation must be entered into for the purpose of benefiting the underlying people.[9] As a whole, it remains fairly conservative—a creditor can expect to be paid so long as the funds are either authorized by the people or are incurred for the public benefit.[10] Were the doctrine to be adopted more broadly, it is likely that most sovereign debt incurred in the contemporary era would still be binding most of the time.

Although Sack's formulation is the one cited by scholars as "the doctrine of odious debt," multiple permutations are possible when we consider the many available theories of governmental representation and legitimate state purpose.[11] Indeed, recent scholarship on the idea of odious debt has frequently focused on how it might be altered and applied as a contemporary doctrine.[12] For the purposes of this book, however, the key point is that all versions of an odious debt idea challenge the dominant statist vision of sovereign continuity in international economic relations. If we are concerned with the existence of a stronger representative link between a state and its people, then the idea of certain types of principled debt cancellation makes sense; it seems philosophically and legally problematic to expect a state's people to pay back debt that they did not authorize and from which they derived no benefit. In other words, an application of non-statist visions of sovereignty to international economic relations suggests that debt should *not* be continuous in some cases. Conversely, if we subscribe to a strictly statist approach to sovereignty, then it logically follows that all debt should be repaid, even if it is "odious," because popular consent and benefit are irrelevant.

The idea of odious debt also gives us some traction in analyzing the historical record, by hinting that challenges to the norm of sovereign continuity and uniform debt repayment might be more likely in times of regime change. Although the enforcement of any sovereign debt necessarily rests on a theory of sovereignty, usually this remains a background issue. However, when a regime changes, the incoming regime frequently seeks to distinguish itself from its predecessor, and may consequently seek to free itself of the predecessor's debt obligations on the basis of right. Sack distinguished between proper "national debt" and the "personal debt" of a previous regime, and argued that only the former should continue to successors:

> If a despotic power incurs a debt not for the needs or in the interest of the State, but to strengthen its despotic regime, to repress the population that

fights against it . . . [t]his debt is not an obligation for the nation; it is a regime's debt, a personal debt of the power that has incurred it, consequently it falls with the fall of this power.[13]

Broadly speaking, regime change constitutes those moments at which a new agent claims to represent a nation's people. The most extreme transformation involves state succession, in which there is a change of sovereignty over a given territory, as in the case of decolonization. A change in government administration stands at the opposite pole, in which there is a legitimate change in leadership within an existing political and constitutional framework.[14] For the purposes of this book, a regime change—or government succession—is the intermediary action, in which there is no alteration in the most basic form of sovereignty (which remains vested in the same territory and people), but where there has been a significant change in the political and constitutional structure and associated practices.[15] The idea of odious debt thus provides some guidance as to the types of claims states may make in using non-statist concepts to problematize the norm of sovereign debt continuity. It also hints at the times that states are most likely to make such claims. In short, this framework helps us think through ways to study how modern debt practices developed toward a relatively narrow approach, that is, to so uniformly expect a statist continuity practice despite other possible alternatives.

Broader Politics and Creditor Competition in the Last Century

Even if the issue of odious debt offers some guidance as to when challenges to sovereign continuity might arise, it leaves open the questions of which historical period is most relevant for an empirical study and which factors are likely to be most influential in shaping understandings of sovereign debt. It also does not address how these elements might interact and the way in which power and interest, so central in the development of global practices, play into the narrative.

To begin with, the dilemma of where to start a historically grounded investigation is never easy. This is especially true here, where different ideas of sovereignty have existed in political and legal thought and practice for a very long time. In this book, I begin the discussion in the early twentieth century, when questions about legitimate and illegitimate forms of rule familiar to contemporary audiences became more prevalent on a global scale. The idea of odious debt itself developed in part out of admittedly self-interested US actions following the Spanish-American War of 1898. The Spanish Crown argued that the United States should assume debts that the Crown had contracted on behalf of Cuba. The United States refused, insisting that the debts were contracted by the previous Spanish regime in its own interests, which were distinct from and even in opposition to the interests of the Cuban population. As such, the United States argued, the debts were illegitimate and should not be transferred to the Cuban population or its new US protectors.[16]

As the early twentieth century progressed, such non-statist conceptions of self-determination and popular sovereignty spread more widely. The aftermath of World War I involved a major overhaul of organizing principles in international relations, including the beginnings of decolonization and a tentative universalization of the basic animating ideas of the American and French Revolutions. In particular, different visions of self-determination became ideals accessible, at least in theory, to all people for the first time. The new normative framework was promoted by such ideologically divergent figures as Woodrow Wilson and the early leaders of the Soviet Revolution. This rejection of imperialism and internal forms of absolutism at the international level, along with the more global application of ideas of sovereign equality, poses the strongest historical starting point for questions of political legitimacy in modern finance. In other words, the widespread emergence of non-statist approaches to sovereignty in the early twentieth century presses the issue of how these concepts were received and developed in the realm of sovereign debt and reputation. And the strengthening of such frameworks by the late twentieth century makes even more puzzling the question of why the norm of sovereign debt continuity, grounded as it is in contrary ideas of sovereignty as physical control, remained dominant in contemporary finance .[17]

Moving to the second question of which elements might be most influential in actually shaping these sovereign debt practices, I argue that two interacting factors are especially important for understanding how non-statist odious debt ideas emerged briefly and then declined in the decades since World War I, allowing continuity norms to develop the veneer of a market principle. First, I contend that the *ways in which creditors are consolidated or competitive* in their interactions and risk interpretations affect the degree to which non-statist approaches are accepted in sovereign debt. To the extent that creditors view each other as part of the same group and so have a consolidated interpretation of risk, a strictly statist insistence on continuity is likely to be dominant. In times when creditors are more competitive and they consider *each other* to be significant risks, sovereign debt norms should be subject to greater contestation. Thus, although creditor uniformity is not a theoretical given—contrary to what is frequently assumed—the degree of creditor uniformity at any particular historical moment remains a relevant factor. As the second key element, shifts in *broader norms of sovereignty* in the international arena affect the to which we consider odious debt ideas plausible in international economic relations. A strictly statist framework of sovereignty dominant in the world at large will support a similar approach in the area of debt, whereas non-statist sovereignty norms might problematize the rule of continuity. Although they are not central in every instance, broader political and legal understandings of sovereignty (be they statist or popular), political ideology, and insistence on principle are neither epiphenomenal nor merely "cheap talk." Rather, they can play a central role in conditioning the initial assumptions and ultimate responses of key actors in any sovereign debt interaction. Given the multiple historical forces that shape these elements, it is difficult as a matter of general theory to make predictions on the balance between them. However, the basic character of this relationship is presented schematically in Table 1.1:

TABLE 1.1. Interaction between Creditor Risk Interpretations and Norms of Sovereignty

		Broader Concepts of Sovereignty in International Relations	
		Statist Concepts Dominant	Non-Statist Approaches Resonant
Creditor Interaction / Risk Interpretations	**Consolidated** (Less flexible; likely to insist on continuity)	Norm of debt continuity stronger *(Mid-twentieth century)*	Ambiguous (Depends on strength of non-statist concepts)
	Competitive (More open to borrower claims)	Norm of debt continuity likely (Any default or repudiation likely made on different grounds)	More flexible treatment & acceptance of odious debt ideas possible *(Post-WWI)*

An Overview of the Historical Record

What does this mean for thinking through the development of sovereign debt norms over the course of the twentieth century and into the twenty-first? The background ideas of political legitimacy grounding any sovereign loan or any reputational assessment come to the fore through claims of illegitimate debt. Although instances of debt repudiation are not numerous, they do suggest that the continuity norm is not predetermined and also highlight how creditor interaction and broader conceptions of sovereignty make flexibility more or less likely at certain historical junctures.

In this book, I begin the historical narrative in the tumult following World War I, which accompanied a rise in the non-statist concepts of sovereignty that should resonate with more flexible debt practices. This greater ideational openness in the early part of the twentieth century converged with an injection of fresh competition into the international credit markets due to the emergence of new American banking houses. As surplus American capital sought investment outlets overseas, these relatively young US financial institutions—supported by expanding US political interests—began to fight for a piece of the credit market previously dominated by British and French banks. These ambitious new creditors were less concerned by losses imposed on their established competitors, and remained more open to gaining a potentially reliable client even at the expense of a commitment to strict debt continuity.

The two early twentieth-century cases presented fully in chapters 3 and 4 illustrate how these emerging principles and market structures resonated in the world of debt claims. In 1918, the new Soviet Union annulled the foreign loans contracted by the tsarist regime, arguing effectively that they constituted personal debts of the Tsar and not legitimate debts of the new Soviet Republic and its people. Although this alienated European and especially French debt holders, several New York banks that were newer to international lending actually attempted to facilitate the issuance of Soviet securities in the face of resistance from their own government. In 1920, Costa Rica repudiated the debts entered into by the previous dictator Federico Tinoco, after returning to constitutional rule following a two-year aberration. US Chief Justice Taft, ruling in an arbitration between Costa Rica and Great Britain, distinguished between debt contracted for "personal" as opposed to "legitimate government" purposes, and held that only the latter could exist past the downfall of a regime. Perhaps surprisingly, the Costa Rican regime was not cut off from the international capital markets as a result of its repudiation or

Justice Taft's decision. The victors of World War I also seemed to reference an odious debt idea when they included the repudiation of Polish
debt in the Treaty of Versailles in 1919. The treaty repudiated the debts
that Germany had contracted on behalf of its colonies, particularly on
behalf of Poland to fund the settling of ethnic Germans in Polish land.
The Reparations Commission took the standpoint that "it would be unjust to burden the natives with expenditure which appears to have been
incurred in Germany's own interest."[18]

This ideational and material background shifted in the post-World
War II era, as I discuss in chapters 5 and 6. Creditors were harmed badly
during the defaults of the Great Depression. In the cautious postwar
economic recovery, they developed closer ties with each other through
international financial institutions such as the early World Bank, private banking integration, and global loan syndications. Creditors became more consolidated in their interpretation of threat through these
interactions, such that questioning the doctrine of sovereign continuity
under any *particular* circumstance seemed more like an assault on the
rights of creditors *generally*. As to ideational elements, the concept of
popular sovereignty and the efforts to distinguish legitimate and illegitimate government that dominated post-World War I discourse subsided
in the destruction of World War II. Although the new United Nations
did support local sovereignty and self-determination, these terms during
the Cold War emphasized a norm of nonintervention and ultimately
leaned toward a statist viewpoint. In short, a closing in what constituted
the interests of creditors was matched by a narrowing of the discourse
surrounding sovereignty and sovereign debt.

The cases reflect this mid-twentieth-century trend, and the era did not
follow up on the potential turning point of the post-World War I period.
The People's Republic of China repudiated the debt of its predecessors,
but remained marginalized in the international credit markets for decades. A repudiation of many foreign financial contracts followed the
1959 Cuban Revolution, and a similar sidelining resulted in that case as
well. The remainder of the Cold War era saw few claims of right associated with an odious debt idea. Even following major social revolutions in
Nicaragua and Iran in 1979, as well as after a series of democratizations
during the 1980s' debt crisis, countries ultimately adhered to the principle of debt continuity. The statist approach to sovereignty in sovereign
debt, which came under question in the early twentieth century, had
reconsolidated its dominance.

The increasing breadth and depth of financial integration since the
1970s has arguably made "international finance" a more singular force

than in previous eras. Still, the post-Cold War decades have also shown a degree of movement toward greater flexibility in repayment norms, as I discuss in chapter 7. In the ideational arena, concepts of democracy and constitutionalism and more substantial attention to human rights have made headway. Although a definitive claim cannot yet be made, it is possible that the post-Cold War era and the beginning of the twenty-first century has witnessed a new opening in the sovereign debt regime's notions of sovereign legitimacy and continuity. The idea of odious debt has regained some of its earlier traction, and scholars and social activists have focused on the potentially problematic foundation of a portion of the developing world's debt today. As for the creditor interaction factor, a shift to greater use of bonds rather than bank financing has disaggregated creditors somewhat. In addition, new sources of capital such as south-south flows and sovereign wealth funds have disrupted the north-south financing divide of the late twentieth century. However, countervailing financial trends exist—notably the rising importance of credit rating agencies and credit default swaps, all of which can unify the inherently multiple voices of capital into a single chorus. In short, the credit market structure is more ambivalent in its effect. But some possibility still remains that the historical trend over the last hundred years is more U-shaped than unidirectional.

Power, Interest, and Norms in Sovereign Debt

Students of international relations may raise the question here of how power and interest factor into into this historical narrative. As a general matter, I agree that actors in the global arena use "power" to further "interests." However, this formulation frequently is too indeterminate to be especially useful, especially for understanding the development of long-term practices rather than for explaining singular events. In particular, it misses the role that norms themselves—expectations of appropriate behavior shared by a community of actors—have in shaping how interests are formed and how actors' capacities are deployed. Understood most broadly, the work of a norm such as sovereign debt continuity exists through both the expectation or standard itself as well as the ways in which we understand and speak approvingly about it and the actions that reflect and reinforce it. Indeed, I view expectations, discourse, and action as a mutually reinforcing package that develops over time and that therefore tends to evade ahistorical explanation.

To begin more specifically with questions of interest, part of my argument is that it is hard to know in advance what an actor's interest is likely to be at any given moment. For example, one might say creditors are generally self-interested and concerned with making a profit. However, this does not necessarily indicate what they will interpret as the right course of action at a particular historical juncture. Certainly, as I explain in greater detail in chapter 2, it does not suggest that all creditors always insist on uniform debt continuity. Indeed, the wildly volatile trends in what is considered rational, possible, or prudent in international financial circles bear testimony to this uncertainty.[19] It is also possible that certain creditors have interests beyond pure profit and actually embrace particular visions of sovereign legitimacy.

Even assuming a profit motivation, I argue in part that larger, historically conditioned structures of creditor interaction are relevant to shaping interpretations of interest and rational action. Individual creditors may well have created these larger structures—including institutions such as the World Bank, instruments such as syndicated loans, formal and informal rules, and so on—to support their own interests at a particular time. But the longer-term consequences of these frameworks tend to go well beyond the founders' initial objectives as they take on a life and dynamic of their own. Farther down the road, these structures can in turn shape how the same or subsequent actors interpret their interests, roles, and identities in ways that would not originally have been foreseen. Thus, there is a necessary and mutually constitutive interaction between actors and broader institutions and norms—between agents and structures—that affect how interests are formed and understood.[20] This book takes a long view of the development of debt continuity in part to understand this mutual construction.

Claiming that power matters is similarly indeterminate and overlooks a parallel dynamic. To begin with, multiple forms of power may be at work in a particular interaction. First, there is the understanding of power as the material capacity of a particular actor to shape the actions and payoffs of other actors and thus affect outcomes in its favor.[21] Certainly, such power is manifest in the international arena, as demonstrated by the bribes and threats that sway states toward or against particular actions. However, identifying the powerful actors at any given moment is unlikely to result in a full explanation—even setting aside the above-mentioned difficulty of identifying their *ex ante* interests in the first place. Different actors at different times may have completely divergent understandings of how the same capacities translate into actual possibilities for action. For example, counting gunships is unlikely to be directly helpful in explaining why certain countries are most likely to have their way in issues of money and finance, though there may still be an indirect relationship. Modern gunships now are considerably more powerful than they were in 1902, when the British and German navies sank Venezuelan ships and bombarded Venezuelan ports in part to enforce monetary compensation claims.[22] While they would theoretically be as effective against a poor and underdefended state today, this material capacity is no longer likely to be as useful in enforcing monetary claims, due to intervening shifts in what is considered plausible or acceptable action. This is not to say that power understood in this way does not matter, or that powerful actors are not more capable of shaping outcomes than nonpowerful actors. Rather, physical power controlled by a given actor is an insufficient explanation for any set of outcomes without additional understanding of how it is situated in a particular context.

Relatedly, this definition of power as the material capacity of a specific actor is incomplete. Another more diffuse but no less effective form of power can exist through shared ideological structures or discourses— ways of thinking and talking about things in a particular community (such as the international financial community). If a given set of norms seems reasonable, plausible, and *normal,* then any actions that resonate with these expectations will meet with little resistance or comment. Conversely, practices that counter these expectations will be treated as radical and may be resisted. Over time, actors are more likely to make choices in line with these norms, further strengthening their shaping effect. The discourse and actor practice thus are mutually constitutive and reinforcing, making the norm appear so natural that other alternatives become difficult to comprehend. In this way, the norms themselves have a less visible power that can nonetheless affect outcomes and payoffs as effectively as any set of material capacities.

In this book, I seek to explain the foundations for the norm of sovereign debt continuity, which exerts this more diffuse power in international economic relations. The way in which we think and speak about debt continuity acts as a kind of global soft law, shaping expectations of appropriate action for borrowers and lenders alike and structuring key moments in debt relations today.[23] This is not to say that there is a direct causal link between these broader ideational frameworks and the outcome in any given exchange. However, they enable and promote particular outcomes and make contrary approaches seem implausible. In this book, I seek to understand how the norm of sovereign debt continuity—which is *always* a key factor shaping contemporary debt interactions—gained power in modern finance to the near exclusion of other possible approaches.[24]

Conclusion

The norm of uniform repayment across all sovereign debt, regardless of its provenance, rarely seems puzzling to those working in the international economic field. Despite an absence of any conventional legal rule on the topic, the implicit acceptance of debt repayment and its reputational supports as a stable market principle covers over any lingering questions about the practice. However, the assumptions undergirding the market principle status of the norm are hardly unproblematic. Far from being neutral and historically uniform, sovereign debt practices implicate inherently political ideas and are located in necessarily variable historical contexts. Indeed, such dry inquiries as "is there a reputational effect in sovereign lending" would fail to be sensical without some embedded vision of sovereignty—one of the most contested concepts in international relations today. But the norm of sovereign debt continuity has been so woven into the practice of international finance that it is rarely even questioned, and its controversial political character has all but disappeared in mainstream discussions.

The very solidity of this norm begs the questions of this book: How did sovereign debt continuity rise to such prominence in modern international finance, despite its incongruence with ideas of governmental rule that also spread throughout the globe over the last century? Have approaches emerged that unify ideas of illegitimate debt with working reputational assessments, and under what circumstances? The fact that the continuity norm has been more variable than it first appears invites further study of how the current system developed. Moments existed in the post-World War I era from which alternative frameworks might have developed, and I suggest that both creditor interactions and broader norms of sovereignty shaped the emergence and outcomes of such cases. These two elements also affected the reduced flexibility in sovereign debt and reputation in the decades that followed, and are relevant for thinking about how to structure economic governance in today's unsettled sovereign credit markets. The issue of odious debt offers some guidance as to when we might see this usually hidden question of political legitimacy in international finance rise to the surface, and also helps us perceive more clearly how certain material and ideational structures might support one norm over another in the sovereign debt regime.

In discussing these contrasting approaches in the debt arena, I highlight the political choice inherent in the alternatives: a statist theory of sovereignty necessarily underpinning debt continuity, and non-statist concepts underlying certain allowances for debt discontinuity. While I encourage normatively inclined readers to think through these ethical questions—as I discuss in the final chapter, the policy issues are complex to say the least—the book's primary purpose is not normative argumentation per se. Rather, I contend that the historical contexts in which odious debt might be an issue offer windows into how market structure and broader ideologies privilege one approach over another in any given instance. Studying these cases across time and in relation to one another sheds light on the historical and political foundations for the contemporary norm of sovereign debt continuity and its reputational supports. It also casts empirical doubt on the suggestion that the practice of debt continuity is a historically uniform or inevitable market principle. This uncertainty should disquiet anyone interested in the foundations and ramifications of contemporary international financial practice.

2

Theoretical Underpinnings of Modern Finance

And from what book of history has it been read or heard . . . that a
king paid the debt of another king? And no mortal ever discharged
the obligations of his enemies.

— ATA-MALIK JUVAINI, thirteenth-century chronicler of the Mongol
  Empire, *Genghis Khan: The History of the World Conqueror*

THE NORM of sovereign debt continuity is so regularized in international economic relations today as to become largely unremarkable and taken for granted. We tend to dismiss—or even fail to
see—the possibility of alternative approaches to sovereign debt and reputation. This dismissal, it seems, derives at least in part from intellectual
path dependence. Without a closer look at the theory or the history, it
is easy to suppose that current debt practices are the only ones available
and truly workable in a functioning international capital market. And
without fully acknowledging the degree to which theories of sovereignty
are deeply contested, it is also easy to assume that these practices are
ideologically neutral and therefore largely unobjectionable, even if they
may lead to troubling consequences.

While most of this book presents a new narrative of how debt continuity overcame other possibilities to become dominant over the last century, this chapter fills out the theoretical background for my argument. I
begin by more fully dismantling the assumptions of political neutrality,
reputational stability, and creditor uniformity underlying any claim that
blanket debt repayment is a baseline rule for a functioning international
capital system. I highlight how conceptions of sovereignty act as principal-agent theories in international relations, and emphasize that these
necessarily politicized concepts are essential for any workable sovereign
debt market. I also demonstrate how the mechanism of reputation is

sufficiently flexible to incorporate alternative non-statist approaches, and argue that—far from assuming creditor uniformity—we should *expect* to see some elasticity in creditor behavior given the complex dynamics at play in debt markets.

In the second part of this chapter, I look more closely at what multiple ideas of sovereign legitimacy really would mean if brought into the international debt regime, and where these ideas come from. If we accept that debt mechanisms are indeed more open to non-statist approaches, what is the range of possibilities? I take this opportunity to draw out the ramifications for sovereign debt contracts of four alternative visions of sovereignty with deep roots in political philosophy and international law. Finally, this chapter addresses how to think about case studies in understanding ideas of sovereign legitimacy in debt and reputation, building on the discussion in chapter 1 of how odious debt offers a practical window into these broader questions.

Some readers may already accept the basic openness of market principles and reputational mechanisms in sovereign debt, the possibility of coherent debt practices drawn from divergent theories of sovereignty, and the feasibility of a careful historical study of these questions. This chapter is written especially for those who remain unconvinced.

Addressing the Conventional Approach

There is an easy supposition that the theoretical underpinnings of the contemporary sovereign debt market, including its expectation of continuous debt repayment, are fairly stable. I noted in introducing this book that the seeming inevitability of this baseline draws support from the assumption that the basic rule is politically neutral, supported by a clear reputational mechanism, and obliged by uniform creditor appraisals. But each of these conceptual bulwarks for the statist approach is deeply problematic.

Indispensable Politics: Sovereignty as the Missing Agency Question

By necessity, the controversial and highly politicized concept of "sovereignty"—which carries with it overtones of legitimate, or at least internationally acknowledged, rule—stands at the center of any discussion of the sovereign debt regime. As I noted in the introductory chapter, a particular political vision of sovereignty is *already* deeply embedded in the lending regime. The strict rule of repayment depends upon a distinctly statist concept of sovereignty, which assumes sovereign continuity within the same territory and insists on the irrelevance of changes in internal rule for sovereign identity. Indeed, there is no way for sovereign lending to exist without the unspoken adoption of one or another idea of sovereignty. To the extent that a sovereign debt contract exists at all, enforceable against future generations of a state's people, it must at least implicitly rest on an underlying theory of the relationship between that country's government and its people. The fact that we choose to leave the nature of that relationship entirely unstudied does nothing to diminish its importance.

Perhaps unsurprisingly, financial writers tend to take a dim view of any impulse to define sovereignty—and therefore implicitly sovereign legitimacy—in the arena of international debt. The *Financial Times* preferred a more "pragmatic" approach for post-2003 Iraq, arguing that "instead of embarking on a theological discussion of whether the debt contracted by Saddam Hussein is legitimate, creditors should swiftly reduce the country's debt-service obligations to manageable proportions."[1] The dominance of this ostensibly matter-of-fact approach has helped to address particular instances of debt restructuring, but leaves embarrassingly undertheorized very basic questions. Who actually constitutes the ultimate principal in a sovereign contract? If it is the people, what type of governmental authorization is needed to make such a contract binding? The seemingly abstract discussion of legitimacy in fact fills an important and surprising gap in our practical understanding of sovereign debt contracts. Whereas a relatively clear theory of agency and authority is central to the modern practice of domestic contract law, the dominance of short-term pragmatism has left us with long-term practical confusion in the international realm.

It would help if we recognized that different theories of sovereignty in fact act as alternative theories of agency in the international context, whether or not they are expressly recognized as such. Any valid domestic contract made on behalf of another entity is at least implicitly (and frequently explicitly) grounded in a theory of agency. And any theory of agency identifies the nature of the relationship between the agent—who acts or enters into the contract—and the principal, the entity against whom the contract is ultimately enforced. Agency theory specifies the conditions under which a principal will be forced to perform on the contract made by the agent. Usually the agent must be retained or acknowledged by the principal for its actions to be respected. For example, if a Chief Financial Officer (the agent) enters a contract on behalf of a company and ultimately the underlying shareholders (the principal), then the company is likely to be liable for that contract. However, any so-called contract made by a deranged junior employee who has taken the company hostage is unlikely to be respected—unless the resurrected company later has the opportunity to affirm the contract—because there is no legitimate agency relationship in this scenario. This assumption of consent and ultimate ownership also underpins the expectation that the principal (the shareholders, collectively) will be the residual claimant in any financial restructuring or bankruptcy proceeding, receiving only the leftovers once bona fide creditors have been satisfied.

If the relative simplicity of this distinction between legitimate and illegitimate domestic contracts falls apart when we move to the realm of transnational sovereign debt, it is in part due to the lack of a clear theory of agency in the international arena. The confusion would be as bewildering in domestic contract law if we insisted upon the validity of all debt contracts undertaken on behalf of "The Coca-Cola Company" without specifying who could act on behalf of Coca-Cola and under what conditions. Just as we assume a definition of who counts as "Coca-Cola" to distinguish between legitimate and illegitimate Coca-Cola debt contracts, we would need a definition of who counts as "Ruritania"—that fictional country of law school exams—to distinguish between legitimate and illegitimate sovereign contracts signed in Ruritania's name. In short, what is missing from the current discussion of sovereign debt is a clear idea of who counts as "sovereign" in a sovereign contract.

This is where the seemingly abstract discussion of politics and sovereignty becomes immediate and concrete. Different theories of sovereignty effectively constitute different theories of agency in the international realm, with divergent ramifications for whether or not a sovereign contract is legitimately enforceable. A theory of agency specifies the nature of the relationship between the agent—who acts or enters into the contract—and the principal, against whom the contract is ultimately enforced. Similarly, a theory of sovereignty specifies the nature of the relationship between the sovereign government—the agent who acts or enters into a contract—and the principal, the people against whom the contract is ultimately enforced. Just as different theories of agency will result in differential enforcement of domestic contract obligations, different conceptions of sovereignty should result in differential treatment of sovereign contract obligations. Or from an alternative perspective, calling any given sovereign contract "legitimate" necessarily implies and reinforces a particular idea of sovereignty, and thus validates the mode of rule upon which it rests.[2]

In short, the current system of sovereign lending already, and necessarily, rests on a concept of sovereign legitimacy that takes the role played by agency theory in domestic contract law. It serves as an unacknowledged support in the otherwise somewhat mysterious act of complex, agent-based sovereign contract-making—that is, the conversion of a fleeting promise by an individual or group of individuals into a permanent obligation for an entire population. Failing to discuss the concept of sovereignty underlying sovereign debt contracts does nothing to eliminate this political choice entrenched at the very core of international economic law. It only leaves the system's analytical foundations unclear and undertheorized. Even if particular creditors do not deliberately choose one political theory over another, they participate in a collective practice that depends upon and reinforces a profoundly political judgment.

The Indeterminacy of Sovereign Reputation

Turning to reputation or creditworthiness does not escape from this foundational puzzle. An implicit determination of legitimate sovereignty is just as embedded in any reputational assessment as it is in the appraisal of a sovereign debt contract's basic validity. And although an insistence on the strict rule of repayment seems to assume that only one analytical angle is possible, in fact the reputational mechanism is flexible enough to incorporate a range of statist or non-statist approaches, including approaches that would allow for debt cancellation. Given the variety and different placement of creditors, it would be surprising for only a single sovereign reputational assessment to emerge.

THE POSITIONAL ASPECT IN REPUTATION

This is not to reject the importance of reputation itself. Indeed, reputation, broadly understood, has been put forward as a key driver for compliance with international legal agreements by multiple scholars.[3] The specific question of why states comply with international debt contracts has been taken up most extensively in economics and international political economy, where arguments exist between those who contend that debt repayment results from a fear of direct retaliation, and those who argue that it follows from concerns about reputation.[4] While an extensive literature review is not necessary, the evidentiary support for a general reputational effect in the debt arena does seem strong. Michael Tomz's in-depth analysis, perhaps the leading account of sovereign reputation in international political economy, highlights the centrality of reputational factors in ensuring continued cooperation between creditors and sovereign borrowers. Tomz argues that creditors consider both payment record and the situational context of repayment to develop beliefs about a borrower's type—that is, whether it is a "lemon" that will default without justification, a "fair-weather" that will repay only when times are good, or a "stalwart" that repays in good times and bad. This belief on the part of international investors in turn constitutes the borrower's reputation, which guides creditors' risk assessments and lending decisions.[5]

Tomz provides a compelling argument for the centrality of sovereign reputation generally, and even explicitly builds political or governmental change into the model. He highlights that the inevitability of governmental change makes reputations in sovereign debt "fragile," in that investors will recognize that a new government may have a different policy preference than previous governments. They may therefore downgrade or upgrade a state's reputation as a whole, depending on the actions of the new governmental actor.[6] In this presentation of political change and reputation, however, Tomz accepts the basic statist understanding of reputation as continuous across (though also changeable by) different regimes. He does not consider the possibility that a new regime might constitute a new sovereign altogether, in need of a fully separate reputational assessment. As such, he neglects the even deeper way in which the content of reputation depends on broader contexts that change across time, place, and creditor. He falls more neatly in line with the suggestion that the rule of repayment, as the core of debtor cooperation in the sovereign debt regime, serves as something akin to a uniform and ahistorical market principle due to the mechanism of reputation. Tomz thus overlooks the ways in which the practice of assessing sovereign creditworthiness may well be contingent upon the assessor's position and ideological inclinations.

But as Ashok Vir Bhatia points out, the limited predictability of sovereign economic and political behavior, as well as the absence of widespread robust statistical testing, "leave[s] the task of credit ratings assessments poorly suited to formulaic straightjackets."[7] Market research into sovereign creditworthiness necessarily blends objective analysis with subjective debate. Even in theoretical studies from economics and finance, there have been questions as to the degree to which reputation-formation and perceptions of credibility are fully uniform and "rational" in the traditional sense. Robert Frank, for example, has highlighted how emotion plays a key role in the formation of reputation, apart from any objective or material determinants.[8] James Forder points out that definitions and perceptions of "credibility" are not a given across different professional groups.[9] Academic economists and central bankers, for example, have very different views on the importance and definitions of "credibility," and Forder contends that this has ramifications for the ways in which credibility as a concept can be abstracted for the purposes of both academic studies and policy proposals. Jonathan Mercer draws from the insights of psychological theory to suggest that reputation-formation fundamentally links to a human tendency to attribute only negative or undesirable outcomes to another actor's character or reputation. Desirable positive outcomes, on the other hand, become associated with the other actor's situational context and thus a "good reputation" can never really develop.[10] And Rachel Brewster considers the limits of existing reputational models in international law, disaggregating and temporalizing both the "state" and the external audience for state actions in ways that parallel several of the conceptual claims in this book. In particular, she emphasizes the shifting nature of how domestic actors value the reputation of the state that they represent, and also focuses on the degree to which external actors account for governmental and issue variability in ascribing reputational consequences to state actions.[11]

These studies of the foundations of reputation question whether it is constant and objective in the sense assumed by much economic, political, and legal analysis, and suggest that we should be looking for something *other* than uniformity in creditor action. It is not generally agreed upon that reputation is a stable factor with contours that do not vary across time, context, or creditor. Even accepting creditors' basic profit orientations, then, more attention should be paid to their relative economic positions and larger social contexts. While creditworthiness may be uniformly important, its particular *content* vis-à-vis principles of sovereign continuity or odious debt will still be embedded in a historically contingent economic and ideational framework.

The Politics in Reputational Judgment

Privileging a conceptual framework that assumes plurality rather than homogeneity encourages a closer look at how different approaches to legitimate sovereignty and debt continuity would lead to conflicting reputational assessments. Just as any claim about the validity of sovereign debt links to a claim of who constitutes the "sovereign" in sovereign borrowing, any claim about sovereign reputation implicitly rests on an underlying political and legal theory. In particular, while a state could never develop a *positive* reputation after a repudiation on the basis of an odious debt principle, it is an open question as to whether a *negative* reputation should necessarily result. A creditor or other international economic actor could reasonably understand that the willingness of a new regime to repay a loan depends on the degree to which its population benefited from or authorized the loan.[12] If a previous obligation was used to oppress the population or was entered into in order to facilitate corruption, then a subsequent regime's willingness to repay this debt may not have much bearing on its readiness to pay legitimately contracted or publicly beneficial loans in the future.

Any acceptance of an odious debt idea, which might highlight the importance of authorization and/or public benefit, thus suggests the presence or plausibility of non-statist approaches in sovereign reputational analyses. If such an argument were made and accepted by a creditor after a regime change, the incoming regime would be treated not as a "lemon," in Tomz's typology, but rather as a new or unseasoned borrower. Conversely, a statist concept of sovereignty, supportive of the continuity norm, would not distinguish between legitimate and illegitimate debt in assessing a new regime's repayment record as part of a creditworthiness analysis. In fact, a strictly statist approach would be *most* hostile to repudiation on the basis of something like odious debt, given that there is no acceptable economic reason for the default.[13] Shifting perspectives somewhat, the degree to which an implicit or explicit reputational assessment accepts or rejects an odious debt idea operationalizes the concept of sovereign legitimacy underlying reputation for any given creditor. The reputational interpretation and financial treatment of a borrower as new/unseasoned rather than as a lemon indicates the acceptance of a more open approach to sovereignty and debt continuity on the part of that creditor, and an alternative politics in this area of international finance.

Thus, while I agree that "reputation matters," such an assertion on its own is indeterminate for a range of politically, legally, and financially pressing questions, given that the meaning of reputation itself is more open than usually acknowledged. It also fails to recognize the historical possibility that creditors may implicitly accept a non-statist perspective on debt continuity—that is, the prospect that they would make reputational assessments that do *not* insist on debt continuity in all cases, while still considering creditworthiness analyses an important tool for capital markets. While many discussions of sovereign debt thus implicitly set aside (or exogenize) the actual theoretical content of sovereign reputation, I begin by endogenizing the idea of sovereign reputation itself and so locating it within broader theoretical and historical contexts. Certainly, the fact that reputation aligns equally well with statist and non-statist approaches only makes more puzzling why the norm of debt continuity became prevalent in modern international finance.

Further Unpacking Creditor Interest

Related to the conjecture that there exists a uniform idea of reputation and a market principle of consistent repayment is the assumption of a unified "creditor interest." I noted in the introductory chapter that too quick a recourse to "interest" and "power" tends to result in overly simplistic and ultimately indeterminate explanations. Interest depends upon particular circumstances and identities that may shift over time, and power has multiple facets, including as the often less-recognized power exerted by norms themselves. Still, as a general matter, capital market lenders might be expected to have a strong preference for maintaining sovereign debt continuity, given the sizable distributional consequences at stake. What I call a strictly statist account of sovereignty, in which the *fact* of state control is sufficient regardless of the internal mechanism of control, supports the repayment of debt despite concerns about internal governmental illegitimacy. Disregarding any expectation of internal rule of law, legitimate borrowing purpose, or democratic legitimacy as a factor in lending and repayment would allow occasional windfalls to creditors. In asking why a statist norm of repayment has become so regularized as to appear inevitable, one immediate possibility therefore rests with the interest and significant persuasive capacities of previous generations of creditors.

Such a hypothesis, while initially plausible, still offers an insufficiently nuanced view of creditor interests. In particular, this "creditor power" hypothesis fails to recognize that while creditors may at times have shared interpretations of interest and threat, tending toward debt continuity, such consolidation is not inevitable. At certain historical moments, creditors may well identify other lenders as primary threats, and look more favorably upon potential borrowers. In such situations, sovereign lending practices are likely to be more receptive to sovereign debtor concerns. To add nuance to the "creditor interest" argument, I suggest that the degree to which creditor interactions are competitive or consolidated—rather than creditor power in general—may affect the degree to which the rule of continuous debt repayment is stable.

We often speak of "creditors" as if they were a single roving pack, and to some degree this rings true. Leaving aside public creditors for a moment, most creditors have analogous goals—to recoup investment expenses and make productive use of their capital—and are generally privy to the same types of information and analysis. Frequently, creditors will respond similarly to similar situations even in the absence of any collusion. However, it would be a mistake to ignore the fact that they—like all actors—are embedded in a collective world and are therefore both social and strategic. Their interpretations of default or repudiation should thus reflect both their general social proclivities and their strategic positions vis-à-vis other creditors. As such, I disagree with Tomz and others who may argue that, in all instances, "If a government defaults without adequate justification, it acquires a lemonlike reputation not only in the eyes of current investors, but also in the estimation of other individuals and institutions around the world."[14] Or more precisely, I argue that investors and institutions can differ significantly on what counts as "adequate justification" in ways that have not been identified previously.

In fact, there is little reason to expect that creditor interests in the arena of sovereign debt will be entirely uniform, given that they respond to two principal sources of risk. First, creditors as a whole face the threat of default and repudiation, and in this sense have a shared perspective vis-à-vis sovereign debtors. Debtors, however, are not the only, or even the most pressing, source of risk for creditors. Other lenders constitute a second threat, as a healthy credit market is driven partially by competition between suppliers of credit for the same borrowing client. The prospect of losing clients to competitors thus represents a second central problem for creditors.[15]

How might this framework interact with questions of sovereign legitimacy to strengthen or weaken the norm of repayment in international debt? As long as major creditors identify nonpayment of loans as the central threat in the sovereign debt market, then a hegemonic insistence on the payment of *all* debt, including potentially "odious" debt, makes sense.[16] This effectively adopts and strengthens the purely statist political framework of sovereignty that coincides with such a practice. This creditor approach should be more likely to emerge when the market is consolidated, that is, when the underlying material and social structures of creditor interactions encourage more unified interests and risk interpretations. In this case, creditors consider their own fate to be intertwined with that of their fellow creditors, and the perceived threat of creditor competition and client poaching recedes while that of sovereign state default becomes more dominant. As such, they will be more hostile toward debtors who refuse to pay previous loans and less solicitous of the views of potential borrowers. Borrowers facing a limited set of intermediaries for capital will have little recourse but to accept the terms set by these creditors working together. In a consolidated context in which the interest of one is the interest of all, creditors will have little incentive to accept claims based on a non-statist view of sovereignty. Even if one creditor considered the odious debt argument valid, its relationship with other creditors, including the discontented debt holder, could prevent its acceptance of a more flexible approach. Although it is difficult to place a monetary value on the exclusive adoption of a concept, the ascendance of a statist political theory in the sovereign debt regime—with its occasional windfalls to creditors—effectively grants a conceptual monopoly as financially valuable as any other monopoly. Over time, this conceptual monopoly can gain the appearance of naturalness or inevitability, including to creditors themselves, achieving the stable status of a market principle. Such a status would eventually make alternative approaches seem impracticable and thus shape the underlying theoretical context of sovereign lending in the long run.[17]

However, this naturalization is hardly inevitable. We can imagine that in a market with more competitive creditor interactions, in which creditors view not only the sovereign debtor but also fellow creditors as risks, the preferred approach should not be so uniform. In this case, creditors may be more anxious to protect their links to existing clients and to lure new clients away from potential competitors. While the holder of a particular debt instrument will prefer a strictly statist repayment framework as to that instrument, other creditors hoping to attract the same borrower may be more flexible. A new creditor, in the hopes of displacing a competitor, may be indifferent as to whether a prospective client pays that competitor's arguably illegitimate loan obligation. This underlying desire could reasonably lead to a weaker insistence on the norm of sovereign continuity and a more flexible perspective on who counts as the "sovereign" in sovereign debt. So long as a potential borrower looks like a good credit risk overall, a new creditor—considering the new regime an unseasoned borrower rather than a lemon—may be willing to extend credit even after repudiation.[18] Thus, a more competitive credit market should be more lenient toward sovereign governments that repudiate arguably illegitimate debt.

How would this dynamic play out in practice? Creditors do incorporate the possibility of political instability and regime change when assessing country risk. In this context, lenders may pay attention to sovereign legitimacy if they believe that the debt contracts of less oppressive regimes will result in higher rates of repayment even in the absence of accepted odious debt ideas. However, creditors as purely financial actors have no foundational need for a discussion of whether sovereign borrowers are internally legitimate. Under the statist background norms of the current financial system, lenders are entitled to the repayment of all debt. Therefore, they are unlikely to consider independently any explicit questions of sovereign legitimacy, at least to the extent that they are principally profit-motivated. Non-statist alternatives in the debt regime are likely to remain in the background until pressed by a sovereign government, either upon repudiation or when seeking to borrow after a repudiation or default. As such, a creditor's receptiveness to borrower government claims may well mediate the relationship between ideas of sovereign legitimacy, market competition, and practices of debt continuity.

Starting from the premise of uncertain and potentially conflicting creditor interest, the contingent features of any given historical moment—or any given country case—should mediate the degree to which creditor interactions are competitive and thus receptive to alternative approaches presented by borrowers. For example, as I highlight in the Soviet Union case in chapter 3, broader economic problems and a difficult market might heighten the belief that competitors (rather than valuable borrowers) constitute a principal risk. Similarly, the borrowing capacity or market power of a potential sovereign borrower can alter this calculus, deepening rifts between creditors in a given case. Geopolitical struggles often provide the backdrop for overseas lending, and competition or cooperation in the political arena could also condition what is considered risky or logical in the economic realm. By contrast, expanded social and financial links between creditors, which could emerge through geographical integration and creditor cooperation in syndicated bank loans, for example, can enhance the degree of consolidation at any given moment. As a historical matter, each of these dynamics has been relevant to the construction of sovereign reputation over the last century.

In short, although creditors *may* proceed jointly with regard to a particular debt event, this is not always the case. Nor is it necessarily the case that creditors should deliberately think and act together to strengthen a norm of debt continuity across many decades. Rather, they are more likely to take steps that serve particular short-term purposes, which when aggregated result in overall patterns of creditor interaction that can help to either strengthen or diminish statist debt practices over time. And the debt continuity norm, once emerged, may in turn affect creditors' interpretations of their interests in a cyclical manner. Similarly, if a noncontinuity norm were to become dominant, that would also shape creditors' assessments of their own and other creditors' interests and likely actions. Thus, questioning the idea of a monolithic creditor interest in sovereign lending only makes more apparent how the sovereign debt regime's repayment rule, reputational underpinnings, and implicitly statist political ideology are more contingent than they initially appear. Two alternative logics exist for creditor preferences, depending on the nature of their interactions and interpretations of risk. The dominance of one or another logic remains a question of historical investigation rather than theoretical presupposition.

The Multiple Roles of Public Creditors

Of course, this analysis may change somewhat for public creditors, who have distinctive goals and concerns stemming from their more explicit dual role as both financial players and broader norm-propagating actors. Although international creditors are frequently discussed as a single category, public creditors' particular motivations and organizational structures can affect their lending purposes and interactions.[19] While the nuances of this difference come through more clearly in my historical narrative, three distinctive features bear upon the debt continuity norm and should be applicable to other issues of international economic governance as well: Public creditors are generally less focused on competition, more explicitly public-minded, and more concerned with the "power of the purse" than with profit. While these features are not equally relevant to all public creditors, highlighting them in advance helps to identify the pressures at work over the last century.

One of the central characteristics of a public as opposed to a private creditor is its different approach to competition, and especially its lower competitiveness relative to market actors. In particular, the publicness of these lenders obviates the way that market competition, absent any contrary consolidative pressures, encourages efforts to solicit and retain borrowers. The classic public actor is established not out of a profit motive but rather to instantiate some broader goal or idea of the public good.[20] As such, public lending results in a different relationship with debtors and with the sovereign credit market as a whole. With regard to their potential borrowers, these creditors' ideological perspective and relative lack of concern with profit will make them *less* inclined to court potential borrowers by giving greater credence to their independent viewpoints and claims. They may be less willing to think seriously about the degree to which reluctance to make payments on previous, arguably illegitimate debt actually predicts the likelihood that comparatively legitimate loans will be repaid in the future. Although public creditors (as with most explicitly political actors) should want to keep borrowing countries within their policy circle, they may be less likely to moderate their own outlook or ideological position as a result of borrower pressure. In short, the legitimacy claims and other substantive arguments of a borrower could, paradoxically, fall on less receptive ears.

In addition to this basic motivational difference, public creditors are rarely part of a very large market of similar actors, with similar goals, providing similar services. Because of their distinct and sometimes highly individualized goals in lending, any competition between public creditors that does exist will take on a different cast. Public lenders (and public actors more generally) will be less concerned with the actions of other creditors as competitors for the same borrowers, although they may view such creditors as a threat to their own policies or goals and challenge them on this front.[21] As I discuss in the following chapter, this was the case to an important degree in successful US governmental efforts to prevent American banks from financing the Soviet Union after its debt repudiation at the end of World War I. The normative position taken by public creditors may be enhanced and eventually naturalized if there is little competition from alternative, private sources of funding—as was the case with World Bank lending in post-World War II international finance. Such oligopoly will make public creditors even less open to borrower claims, and thus can further close off the potential for borrowers' assertions about sovereign legitimacy to make any headway.

Whereas general publicness tends to minimize the way in which competition can make creditors more open to borrower claims, the more overt public-mindedness of such actors cuts in both directions. Public creditors have a unique dual role in international lending, as both participants in the broader credit market and as norm-generating and norm-enforcing actors in their own right. This explicitly social outlook may involve an *ex ante* commitment to ensuring that public resources benefit a state's underlying population, or to promoting the rule of law or more democratic forms of sovereignty. In this case, a public creditor's position as a noncompetitive and even monopolistic or oligopolistic actor would be overshadowed by a deeper commitment to particular political values. This is the case for certain contemporary creditor countries, such as Norway, which have taken the lead in propagating odious debt ideas, as I note in chapter 7. On the other hand, a commitment to imperial projects or to an ideologically based economic policy vision (such as communism or capitalism) could undermine attentiveness to questions of legitimate sovereign statehood, as I discuss with regard to the mid-twentieth century and the Cold War in chapter 5. In short, rather than understanding these actors as creditors whose outlook is somewhat modified by their public characteristics, in some cases it may make sense to focus on them first as public actors whose credit activities serve larger public goals.

Finally, the power of the purse, which holds public creditors accountable to their funders, may well shape their ultimate viewpoints.[22] This power is likely to be especially strong because the interests of borrowers are less of a countervailing force. Whereas a private creditor balances the demands of its own investors (generally for higher rates of return) with those of its borrower clients,[23] public creditors may be less concerned with the independent views of debtors due to the noncompetitive dynamic noted above. While this funding element can reinforce the public-mindedness just discussed—after all, those who launch and fund a public creditor presumably do so for a social purpose—this effect is hardly absolute or permanent. Although a public creditor's founding members formulate its initial goals, they may also establish a funding structure that renders the creditor dependent on external actors whose interests are in tension with those original goals.[24] As I discuss in chapter 5, this analytical framework helps to make sense of why the early World Bank ultimately adopted a strictly statist approach for its own lending and creditworthiness analyses.

In short, to speak of creditors as a single group in sovereign lending is not only historically problematic but also theoretically untenable. Although greater uniformity may exist at particular moments, the competitive pressures on private creditors and the unique characteristics of public creditors mean that these moments should provoke additional investigation rather than simply solidify preexisting assumptions. Neither creditor uniformity, nor the mechanism of creditworthiness, nor a claim of political neutrality is sufficient explanation for the market principle expectation of continuous debt repayment. This leaves us with unanswered questions as to how sovereign debt and reputation can be understood as a theoretical matter, and why it has been framed in particularly narrow ways as a historical matter.

Alternative Sovereignties and their Ramifications

If the norm of debt continuity cannot be accepted as a neutral market principle with which all reasonable people must agree, nor does it emerge from the idea of rulership itself. In the current international system, the mechanisms of sovereign rule are tied to, and perhaps hidden by, the trappings of statehood. But imagine a world of personalistic rule, in which "sovereigns" exist not as states but rather as human beings with definite, if unpredictable, mortality. A conquering sovereign in this world might take over a rival's territory, neutralize his descendants, destroy his monuments, and otherwise banish memories of the previous rule. If the creditors of the deposed ruler approached the new sovereign requesting payment of the previous regime's debt, they might be as likely to leave without their heads as with their principal plus interest.

While this hypothetical is somewhat extreme, it is far from a fantasy, as versions of such personalistic dominion have existed throughout human history. An incident recorded by thirteenth century Persian chronicler and Mongol bureaucrat Ata-Malik Juvaini highlights how expectations of *noncontinuity* might seem reasonable under these alternative forms of rule. When Mengü (grandson of Genghis) was elected Great Khan by an assembly of Mongol princes in 1251, the debts of his predecessor and first cousin Güyük were presumptively erased, notwithstanding the family connection and the relatively orderly nature of the succession.[25] A discussion of appropriate debt practices resulted from an appeal by certain of Güyük's creditors, whose "cause was lost" but who nonetheless approached the new ruler, "partly hoping for his justice and partly despairing." Juvaini notes that "all the functionaries of Court and Pillars of State were of [the] opinion that there was no obligation to pay the amount due . . . and that no mortal would have cause to object." After all, "from what book of history has it been read or heard from reciters that a king paid the debt of another king? And no mortal ever discharged the obligations of his enemies." That Mengü ultimately did compensate the creditors for the debts of his predecessor was considered—far from the creditors' right—evidence of the new Great Khan's generosity and noble character.[26]

The financial context of the Mongol era differs radically enough from our own that few direct lessons can be drawn from this anecdote. But it is telling that economic advisors of civilizations past might have scorned the expectation that a new government—particularly one antagonistic to the previous regime—should make good on all its predecessor's debt. Episodes in later centuries, several of which I discuss at length in this book, suggest continuing distaste for discharging the obligations of enemies. The restored Mexican republic repudiated the debts of the French-supported Hapsburg emperor Maximilian in 1867, "on the ground that they were contracted for the purpose of combating the constitutional government."[27] In 1868, the fourteenth amendment of the US Constitution voided outstanding civil war debts "incurred in aid of insurrection or rebellion against the United States."[28] The Costa Rican and Soviet repudiations discussed in chapters 3 and 4 similarly reject the idea of paying the debts of another. These episodes highlight how, as the meaning of "sovereign" becomes less personalistic and more associated with abstract statehood, the idea that debt can permanently attach to a governmental entity becomes plausible. But they also demonstrate that pressure can build to authenticate the legitimate character of the borrowing regime in question.

At the center of the debt continuity norm, then, is neither market discipline, nor the idea of governmental rule per se, but rather the ephemeral and multifarious idea of sovereignty itself. Although financial writers might use the term "theological" dismissively in referring to contemporary discussions of debt legitimacy, in many ways the term is fitting.[29] Political theorists have pointed out that underlying the modern structure of international relations is a secularized theology or metatheory of the sovereign state.[30] Just as theology deals with the nature of god and its relationship to man, this secularized theology of the sovereign state specifies the nature of the state and its relationship to the people. Principal among these theological exports has been the idea of a unitary and omnipotent god, transformed into the absolutist or "command" theory of a unitary and omnipotent sovereign state. But, as the following discussion makes clear, this statist politics of sovereignty, a version of which underlies the doctrine of sovereign continuity, is not the only possible approach to sovereignty or sovereign contracting. Indeed, the Western philosophical tradition grounding current international relations provides a range of competing ideas based in popular, rule-of-law, and outcome-oriented theories. And these alternatives, all of which have found defenders through the last century, may well fit more comfortably with our current sensibilities.

Who Can Sign? The Statist Roots of Contemporary Debt Contracts

Where does the statist idea of sovereignty embedded in current lending norms come from, and how deep does it go? In this absolutist conception, the sovereign is simply the juridical body that has ultimate control and authority over a given people and territory, and that issues commands within that territory in the form of general laws and sui generis orders. This sovereign is functionally similar and juridically equal to other sovereigns, and the structure and legitimacy of its internal constitution, culture, and stage of development are conceptually irrelevant to its external relations. This framework conceives of the sovereign state as a secularized deity—the supreme power within its realm, subject to no law or higher authority and equal only to other states. It might also be understood as the latter-day incarnation of an absolutist, divine, or militarist conception of rulership, updated to fit modern definitions of states as territorially bounded.[31]

In Western political theory, Jean Bodin provided perhaps the first of these explicit accounts, by defining sovereignty in the sixteenth century as "the highest power of command" and "the absolute and perpetual power of a commonwealth."[32] This tradition was carried forward by Thomas Hobbes and Benedict de Spinoza, both of whom considered the sovereign as constituting the supreme law-making authority, free from limitation on its actions.[33] In this view, it does not matter how the governmental entity claiming sovereign status gains control. It may do so by liberal democratic means, by other constitutional means, or by force alone—the strictly statist requirements for sovereign action pay little attention. As Bodin makes explicit, "If [power is taken] by force, [the government] is called a tyranny. Yet the tyrant is nonetheless a sovereign, just as the violent possession of a robber is true and natural possession even if against the law, and those who had it previously are dispossessed."[34] Although Hobbes distinguished between sovereignty by force and sovereignty by voluntary institution, he insisted that "the rights and consequences of sovereignty are the same in both."[35]

This tradition carries into legal and constitutional theory as well, as represented by the classical positivism of John Austin, who understood law as the command of the sovereign backed by force.[36] And in his formulation of positivist international law in 1912, Lassa Oppenheim similarly rejected the moral foundations and judgments implied by natural law accounts.[37] In denying the relevance of internal culture, religion, or political form, he sought to organize international law on the basis of sovereign equality and state consent. Or in the preferred metaphor of international relations theory, this account of sovereignty conceives of the state as a "unitary black box" whose internal machinations are irrelevant to its foreign interactions.[38]

This principle of recognizing sovereign governments on the basis of command or effective control was accepted as a central principle of modern international law by early members of the Permanent Court of International Justice. For example, J. B. Moore, a prominent American jurist and member of the Court, wrote in the early 1900s,

> The origin and organization of government are questions generally of internal discussion and decision. Foreign powers deal with the existing *de facto* government, when sufficiently established to give reasonable assurance of its permanence, and of the acquiescence of those who constitute the

state in its ability to maintain itself, and discharge its internal duties and its external obligations.[39]

This essential commitment to disregarding internal differences and the possibility of internal coercion is enshrined in the basic legal principles of twentieth-century international relations—equal sovereignty and the doctrine of nonintervention, as highlighted in Article 2 of the UN charter. International or "external" sovereignty in this statist approach is thus based on effective control and recognition by the community of states. As a consequence, it pays little attention to the potential internal dimensions of sovereignty.[40] The central contours of this statist framework have remained fairly stable into the turn of this century.[41]

How would this paradigm translate into a theory of agency or authority to enter into contracts? The answer here is relatively straightforward: whoever exercises control may sign the sovereign contract. And because the state's population is not considered the "principal" of the state in any true sense, no real agency problem exists. The core relationship between the people and the government is not characterized as one of principal and agent but rather, in the language of John Austin, as one of "sovereignty and subjection."[42] The people under this theory of sovereignty are ultimately "subjects" of the state, who are subject to the commands and obligations of whichever government successfully controls them. This political theory should look familiar to those working in international capital markets today: regimes that rule by force, exploit local communities, and violate their own laws may still enter into international agreements under statist norms.

Who Can Repudiate? The Rise of the Eternal Sovereign

So, we know that even widely disparaged governments may enter into internationally binding obligations according to statist political thought. But the second key question is whether a successor regime *must* be bound by that prior regime's actions under this approach or whether, in the alternative, the successor still has a presumed right to disclaim the debt. There are two opposing answers to this question even within the statist framework, which in the Western tradition corresponds to a split between late medieval thought and the high modernism of the Scientific Revolution.

The first approach, associated with late medieval political theory, insists on the eternal nature of the state apart from any changes in actual rulership, and thus considers sovereignty to live forever. In the early and high Middle Ages, the Christian conceptual universe had been divided into the eternal/transcendental and the temporal/profane realms. While a ruler derived legitimacy from the eternal divine, he himself was a temporal being. With the shift away from this dualist aspect of the late Middle Ages, however, space emerged for an intermediate arena in which earthly beings—such as states—might yet have eternal duration. Thus, previewing more contemporary jurists and financial actors, the late medieval legal theorist Baldus di Ubaldi argued, "A realm contains not only material territory but also the peoples of the realm . . . And the totality or commonweal of the realm does not die, because a commonweal continues to exist even after the kings have been driven away. For the commonweal cannot die . . . it lives forever."⁴³ Although Bodin is rightly cited as an early modern political theorist for insisting that sovereignty may be claimed by undisguised force rather than through divine blessing, on the question of sovereign continuity he hearkens back to this earlier age. Bodin considered both sovereignty and the status of the "sovereign" to be perpetual, transferring to whoever gains effective control of a state's territory.⁴⁴ Jens Bartelson emphasizes that this combination of state continuity with ruler discontinuity is an essential aspect of what he calls the "proto-sovereignty" of the late medieval era. "The body politic could be accounted for as something ontologically separate from the existence of the ruler within it, yet as something continuous, transcending the life of the ruler in time and space." He emphasizes the importance of this move, in which "we witness the first steps towards a theory of inalienability, which implies a set of rights well separated from those of the individual king."⁴⁵ Along with these inalienable rights of the eternal state, it would seem, can come inalienable obligations. In this premodern framework of the eternal state, sovereign obligations might remain even in the case of major regime change. Although medieval scholars intended this vision of sovereignty to be secular, to many contemporary political theorists it retains "a whiff of incense from another world."⁴⁶

Despite this particular historicity and provenance, the doctrine of sovereign continuity is very much alive in practice today. Echoing Baldus in the fourteenth century, J. B. Moore in the early twentieth clearly links the status of sovereign to the theory of sovereign sempiternity, and then to the continuity of contractual obligations:

> Changes in the government or the internal policy of a state do not as a rule affect its position in international law. . . . though the government changes, the nation remains, with rights and obligations unimpaired. . . . The principle of the continuity of states has important results. The state is bound by engagements entered into by governments that have ceased to exist; the restored government is generally liable for the acts of the usurper.⁴⁷

The *Financial Times* continues the trend into the twenty-first century in its insistence—without irony—that we avoid "theological" discussion and simply accept the eternal nature of states for the purposes of enforcing debt obligations. At least in contemporary international financial circles, the innovation of late medieval jurists lives on.

Notwithstanding its remarkable resilience, the theoretical innovation of unbroken sovereignty did not stand alone in the early modern tradition of Western political thought. The opposing approach, associated with Hobbes and the high modernism of the Scientific Revolution, insists more explicitly on the sovereign's absolute right to do as it pleases, which would include contract repudiation. Although he shared Bodin's indifference to competing forms of internal rule and the mechanism of gaining sovereign power, Hobbes very explicitly considered his work to stand upon a more materialist conception of the universe. Drawing inspiration from the revolution taking place in the natural sciences in mid-seventeenth-century Europe—and keenly aware of the ravages wrought by the religiously inspired Thirty Years War—Hobbes rejected both religious foundations and any Platonic idea of eternal essences in formulating his political vision. He insisted instead that "every part of the universe is body, and that which is not body is no part of the universe."[48]

Perhaps unsurprisingly, he took a fairly materialist view of sovereign existence and power, including in times of succession. Unlike the late medievalists and Bodin, Hobbes did not consider that sovereignty could exist forever, ungrounded from actual rulership. He was especially concerned with clarity in sovereign succession *precisely* because without this the choice would be uncertain, and "then is the commonwealth dissolved" and "the multitude [left] without any sovereign at all."[49] Hobbes joined this materialism with an insistence on the sovereign's indivisible right to determine the means necessary to promote the interests of the commonwealth and its subjects. Thus sovereign power is absolute, "as great as possibly men can be imagined to make it."[50] This is not to say that the sovereign cannot constrain its own actions and encourage stable interaction by promulgating laws and binding itself through contracts. Although Hobbes was primarily concerned with the prospect of civil disorder and internal constraint, this ability to bind would presumably extend to the realm of external contracts as well. However, these constraints would always be contingent and subject to repudiation on the basis of sovereign status and power alone.[51]

While Hobbes is rightly considered foundational to modern thinking about sovereign states, an adoption of his strictly materialist approach in sovereign lending would entail a radical departure from today's dominant practices. The debt continuity norm in modern international finance owes its existence to older, more religiously grounded strains of thought in the Western philosophical tradition. In its legal and normative expectation that states never die, the contemporary economic framework adopts the version of continuous statism associated with Bodin and late Medieval scholars. In this view, each new ruler or regime is not granted a clean slate on which to make decisions (or build a new reputation), but rather is assumed to be the reincarnation of an indefinitely ongoing sovereign existence.

An Alternative Authorization Grounded in the People

Perhaps the most vocal competitor to a statist politics of sovereignty today is the idea of popular or democratic sovereignty. This broader ideology, which has become increasingly prominent over the last century, has markedly opposed consequences when translated into the sovereign debt regime. In this framework, sovereignty ultimately lies with a "sovereign people," whose authorization provides legitimacy to the state and its external interactions. Both the sovereign state and the laws it promulgates are valid only if they reflect the consent of the underlying population. The mechanism by which this consent finds expression is not specified, and may be direct or through representation. We can even imagine, at the outer edges of popular sovereignty, the possibility of a consensual monarchy. The key is that the state as a secularized deity has been dethroned, and now is subject in some way to the ultimately sovereign people. Under this approach, not all states are properly or equally "sovereign" simply by virtue of their territorial command. The evaluation and recognition of true sovereignty—and therefore of valid sovereign obligation—requires the consideration of a regime's internal practices.

Jean-Jacques Rousseau stands as a central thinker in this approach. Writing in the mid-eighteenth century, he conceived of a "sovereign will" founded in a social contract as providing a form of government "by means of which each one, while uniting with all, nevertheless obeys only himself and remains as free as before."[52] Emmanuel Joseph Sieyès followed in insisting on the unity of the nation with the people in the context of the French Revolution. "The Third Estate [the order of the common people as distinct from nobility and clergy] thus encompasses everything pertaining to the Nation, and everyone outside the Third Estate cannot be considered to be a member of the Nation."[53] Thomas Paine, also reflecting upon the French Revolution and equating the nation with the larger public, commented, "Monarchical sovereignty, the enemy of mankind, and the source of misery, is abolished; and sovereignty itself is restored to its natural and original place, the nation."[54] The commitment to basic self-legislation found expression in the work of Immanuel Kant as well, although Kant understood self-legislation primarily as "freedom from tutelage" in the realm of thought.[55] This attentiveness to the relevance of a state's internal makeup also resonates with the Liberal school of international relations theory, which explains the international behavior of states on the basis of their internal characteristics.[56]

The idea of a sovereign government as fundamentally grounded in the consent or authorization of the people has translated fairly smoothly into an admittedly controversial principle of international law. In this view, a sovereign state may be legally recognized—and thus capable of valid international action—only if the state is constituted by popular means. Woodrow Wilson in particular is associated with this discourse of international interaction, due to his stated commitment to the principle of self-determination in the League of Nations and his own administration's refusal to recognize governments claiming sovereignty by force.[57] While still grounded in the limitations provided by state structures and territorial boundaries, this approach resonates with the Cosmopolitan school of political theory and international law, which puts individual rights at the center of any legitimate polity or legal system. It is manifest in the emerging language of international judicial decisions and foreign policy, which Ruti Teitel analyzes as "humanity law."[58] The strong version of this approach presents a vision of consent, sovereignty, and human rights that is in deep tension with a statist concept of sovereignty as command. Modern day champions of a Wilsonian ideal of sovereign legitimacy, such as Michael Reisman, continue to promote this view of a "new constitutive, human-rights based conception of popular sovereignty."[59] Some legal scholars, such as Thomas Franck, have gone so far as to insist that contemporary international law in fact contains an emerging right to democratic governance.[60]

This democratic or popular framework of sovereignty suggests a unique relationship between the people and state legality and legitimacy. Unlike the statist conception of sovereign as command, in which law is imposed by force on a subject people, here the people themselves are sovereign and thus exist prior to the law. Rousseau makes clear that the people acting as sovereign are free even from the constraints of their own prior laws, as "it is contrary to the nature of the body politic that the sovereign impose upon itself a law it could not break."[61] Sieyès distinguished between a government and the underlying people or nation that provides the authorization for governmental action. "Government can exercise real power only insofar as it is constitutional. It is legal only insofar as it is faithful to the laws imposed upon it. The national will, on the other hand, simply needs the reality of its existence to be legal. It is the origin of all legality."[62] Thus, law and valid government action exist, but in a very different form than that found in other approaches to sovereignty.

How would this paradigm translate into a theory of agency or authority to enter into contracts? Authority should derive from the sovereign people—now properly understood to be the principal in any sovereign contract—either acting directly or through their representatives. Government officers act as their agents, and so long as they act according to the roles assigned to them or the mechanisms established by the underlying people, they have authority to bind the sovereign nation. In this framework, the people are subject only to those contracts that their authorized agents have entered, once they have been constituted as "sovereign."

In this approach, sovereign obligations, properly understood, do not exist unless they have actually been properly authorized by the population. A regime change in which a democratic sovereign government comes into being after a period of rule by other means would effectively constitute the first appearance of a legitimate sovereign government. The previously existing government would not in fact have comprised a proper sovereign state, but only a private form of rule imposed on the underlying and disempowered sovereign people. Therefore, regimes that rule by force would not be able to enter into international agreements that bind the population after their fall. And if sovereignty is conceived under this more democratic or popular framework, creditors who lend to such regimes cannot expect to be repaid after a regime change. This is not necessarily to say that all previously existing obligations would be repudiated. On the contrary, they would likely be evaluated by the newly empowered sovereign on a pragmatic basis. However, this pragmatic approach is very different from that implied by the doctrine of sovereign continuity, which presumes the perpetual nature of any sovereign obligation on the basis of strictly statist assumptions about sovereignty.

Sovereign Authorization Delimited by Law

Although the tension between strictly statist and popular conceptions of sovereignty is perhaps most well known, an intermediate alternative relevant through the last century exists in what might be called "rule of law" or constitutional sovereignty. Like popular sovereignty, this school pays attention to internal modes of legitimation in recognizing valid sovereign action. However, it does not require that this internal authorization ultimately come from the underlying people. The sovereign state exists and is both empowered and limited by its internal constitution or rule of law, whether or not it is democratic. Thus, an internal rule-of-law or constitutional framework that denotes a nonconsensual monarchical or other nondemocratic political order would be sufficient to authorize—and render presumptively binding—sovereign action.

This concept of sovereignty is not as well developed into a coherent school of political theory as strictly statist or popular sovereignty. However, it relates to Max Weber's basic insight that the use of force is not a means specific to states alone, and that therefore force cannot be the sole defining characteristic of statehood. Writing in the early twentieth century, Weber thus modified the basic definition of a sovereign state to include the element of legitimacy; a state in this view is "a human community that (successfully) claims the *monopoly of the legitimate use of physical force* within a given territory."[63] Unlike democratic or liberal theorists, Weber himself did not insist on any substantive internal requirements for this ultimate legitimacy, and considered that different types of domestic regimes would be consonant with legitimate statehood.[64] Perhaps the paradigmatic legal theorist working in this approach was Hans Kelsen, who sought to identify and understand law as "pure"—a separate and internally coherent order independent from politics and morality.[65] Kelsen follows John Austin in separating valid law from moral questions, but differs in that he does not consider law to be ultimately reducible to force. Rather, the promulgation of acts and statutes by a sovereign government can only be identified as legally valid within the context of that state's own internal norms or legal rules, which in turn build from the basic norm *(grundnorm)* or constitution of that polity. This basic norm itself "cannot be derived from a higher norm," but instead "constitutes the unity in the multitude of norms by representing the reason for the validity of all norms that belong to this order."[66] Kelsen sought to provide law with the clearest possible "decision rule," emphasizing law as an autonomous and internally coherent order and thus granting it objectivity and stability. In so doing, he hoped to insulate it from the subjectivity and uncertainty inherent in the concept of law as sovereign command—whether the sovereign be an individual ruling by force or the people as a whole. In this, Kelsen foreshadowed Hannah Arendt's political commitment to a constitutional system of checks and balances, as well as her concern about the instability and potential extremism that could arise in both absolutist rule and pure popular sovereignty.[67]

The rule-of-law or constitutionalist conception of sovereignty as determined and limited by internal norms or rules of law can translate into the international realm as well. In this framework, international law and international affairs would remain interested in questions of internal state legitimacy. However, this approach would not investigate the substantive democratic legitimacy or internal human rights compliance of governments. Rather, it would focus on ensuring states' commitments to a more *procedural* vision of rule of law in both the domestic and international spheres. Conservative early twentieth-century American lawyers, including Supreme Court Justice (and former president) William Howard Taft, were at the forefront of this rule-of-law approach in the international arena.[68]

How would this paradigm translate into a theory of authority to enter into external debt contracts? Authority should derive from a vision of the sovereign as constituted and limited by law, so a government actor could act on behalf of the state as a whole, including its people and territory, as long as it follows the domestic legal framework. Even the government official who originally promulgated the law under which he or she acts must then stay within its purview, as *any* actor is ultimately subject to the law itself. Kelsen presents this dynamic of law-making authority and subjection to law as follows: "Only a competent authority can create valid norms; and such competence can only be based on a norm that authorizes the issuing of norms. The authority authorized to issue norms is subject to that norm in the same manner as the individuals are subject to the norms issued by the authority."[69] Given this fundamental commitment to rule of law (or basic constitutionalism) as such—as distinguished from an adherence to liberal democratic constitutionalism, for example—neither the particular internal form of the state nor the substantive content of rules and laws are important. So long as internal rules are followed, the appropriate government official can act as an agent for the sovereign state, thus binding the territory and population under that state's legal framework.

Under this approach, sovereign obligations exist and are continuous if they have been validly authorized under the internal legal framework, even if that internal framework is distasteful according to some moral standards. If the proper internal rules were followed, the sovereign obligation stands whether the previous regime was autocratic or democratic. Thus, a regime change in which a democratic government comes to power after a period of rule by other means should not alter the existence of a sovereign obligation, so long as that obligation was validly incurred under the internal rules of the previous contracting regime. Therefore, even a nondemocratic regime may enter into international agreements that bind the underlying population, so long as it specifies and then follows its own laws. And if sovereignty is conceived through this rule-of-law framework, then creditors who lend to nonrepresentative regimes may still expect repayment if they carefully respect that regime's internal constitution and rule of law. In short, this conception of sovereignty modifies somewhat the strictest doctrine of sovereign continuity. Sovereign obligations persist, regardless of regime form or regime transformation, so long as the internal rule of law in place at the time of the contract is respected by both parties to the contract: the sovereign government and the external contracting party.

Sovereign Action as Outcome-Oriented

The three schools discussed above present visions of sovereignty that are ultimately process oriented—they interrogate the relationship between the ruler and the ruled in a given state and underscore the procedures of sovereign contracting that this relationship entails. However, a discussion of the political concepts underlying sovereign debt may also focus on the *outcome* of such contracts. An outcome orientation in sovereign contracting would require that valid sovereign action be in the interests of the state, broadly understood. This orientation is not at all exclusive to any one of the three different procedural schools of sovereignty discussed above. Indeed, the internal procedures by which a sovereign action is decided or acted upon are conceptually unrelated to this approach; the action could be undertaken according to absolutist or democratic means, either following or disregarding the internal rule of law. What matters instead is attentiveness to the ultimate outcome or intended beneficiary: a given sovereign state itself, rather than those who act in its name.

This outcome orientation is, at least potentially, entirely complementary with either of the statist, popular, or rule-of-law accounts. Indeed, each of these process-based approaches may be understood as part of the larger metaparadigm of statehood characteristic of the modern era, which conceives of sovereignty as limited to an established (if expandable) territorial boundary. This geographical groundedness counters earlier ideas of a personalized sovereign ruler unifying an essentially private domain of otherwise disconnected territories. The modern concept of sovereignty not only grounded sovereign statehood in a given geographic realm, but also attempted to strip the now explicitly *public* state from its association with rulership as private ownership.[70] In place of the language of personal domain, modern discourse substitutes the language of commonwealth, public protection, and state interest. Hobbes, who insisted on there being no distinction in the basic sovereign rights of an "instituted" as opposed to an "acquired" sovereign, still postulated the initial existence of the sovereign state itself in terms of the security and order of the underlying commonwealth. Bodin, among the most absolute of the traditionalist thinkers, shared this language of the sovereign state as "commonwealth" rather than disconnected private domain. The concept of modern statehood as linked to internal responsiveness is even clearer in the popular and rule-of-law visions of sovereignty.

Several thinkers of the early to mid-modern period thought fairly explicitly about the relationship of sovereignty to sovereign debt through this model of basic responsiveness to underlying public interest. Previewing arguments afoot today, they warned that sovereign debt or "public credit" could make government officials overattentive to the needs and desires of creditors, and also enable them to embark upon understudied misadventures. This dependence would render the state less responsive to true public need and neglectful of the greater national interest. Sieyès, one of the key thinkers in the school of popular sovereignty, was hostile to the entire idea of sovereign debt and favored instead building public finance on a system of taxation. In fact, one of his central political writings on the French Revolution focused on the centrality of instituting a tax law. This law of taxation would allow the power of money to "be merged with and, so to speak, made to be identified with the nation so that it can never serve anything other than the general interest."[71] He considered the rejection of public credit so fundamental to a truly responsive constitutional government that he self-consciously called his proposed tax law nothing less than a "constitutional law of taxation."[72] This is not to say that Sieyès favored an immediate repudiation of the monarchist debt; in fact, he felt it should be repaid on practical grounds.[73]

This concern with the potentially detrimental effects of sovereign debt on a nation's core responsiveness to public need was not limited to Sieyès, the paradigmatic popular sovereigntist. The monarchist David Hume famously claimed in 1752 that, "either the nation must destroy public credit, or public credit will destroy the nation."[74] Istvan Hont has highlighted how Hume's deep suspicion of sovereign debt financing

drew from his concern for national security in the face of potential international disorder. Hume felt that public credit tended to sacrifice the
nation's long-term strategic interests for the short-term concern of maintaining financial stability, and also to embolden government officials
to embark on capricious escapades. Hume was "quite ready to counsel
sacrificing the property of thousands (he estimated that Britain had approximately 17,000 foreign and domestic creditors) on the altar of the
nation's national security interests," and felt this much preferable "to the
horrible political crime of sacrificing millions for the temporary safety
of creditors."[75]

As Sieyès and Hume make clear, the argument that sovereign debt
may be inherently antithetical to public responsiveness and the national
interest is not a distinctly contemporary contention. Today's concerns
about lost economic sovereignty are not at all new, and are in fact almost as old as the modern conception of statehood itself. The claim
that a sovereign state, however it is internally constituted, should be
attentive to the national interest, does not need to reach the extremes of
Sieyès and Hume. This "outcome orientation" could result in a separate
requirement that government action should be responsive to the public
needs of a state, whether those are defined in statist, rule-of-law, or
popular terms. This impulse might be operationalized in a requirement
that valid sovereign debt at least ostensibly serve the public interest of
the state, as distinct from the merely personal interest of a ruling elite
masquerading as a modern officialdom.[76] Indeed, the second prong of
the odious debt doctrine as imagined by Alexander Sack—that debt
may be considered odious if it does not benefit the underlying population—offers such an example.

Caveats and Normative Ramifications

Three caveats are important before going any further. First, this discussion should not be misunderstood as either an attempt to provide
anything close to a sufficient interpretation of the thinkers mentioned
or a comprehensive overview of theories (or theorists) of sovereignty.
The four paradigms highlighted here, which resonate across political
theory, law, and international relations, demonstrate how different ideas
of political legitimacy result in divergent expectations about government
competence for sovereign contracts and the subsequent continuity of
those contracts. However, the theorists within each approach disagree
with each other in myriad ways and may on some questions have more

in common with scholars I have categorized as belonging to a different school. Furthermore, theories of sovereignty could be organized along different dimensions altogether, or divided into a more detailed categorization. The key is that the implicit or explicit adoption of one as opposed to another politically contested vision of sovereignty will result in very different understandings of what is rational, appropriate, and reputationally enforceable. A summary of this analytical structure is presented schematically in Table 2.1.

The second and related caveat is that, although this discussion highlights the politics at the center of sovereign debt, it should not necessarily be taken as a normative assessment of either these ideas of sovereignty in their own right or their appropriateness for international finance. Certainly, a sharper framework for talking about sovereign legitimacy enables clearer political and moral debate, and I will touch upon policy questions in this book's conclusion.[77] However, I intend my categorization to serve two principal purposes that are analytically prior to policy argument. First, the discussion gives lie to any descriptive contention that a working sovereign lending system can possibly be apolitical and neutral. Indeed, the dominant continuity norm is deeply indebted to a vision of the state with roots in a particular (and contested) political philosophy. And second, these categories can be used as analytical building blocks to enable an empirical assessment of why one as opposed to another political philosophy holds sway in international debt finance today. Conceiving of these schools as "ideal types" helps to identify historical variation in the conceptual framework that underlies sovereign debt over time. In the historical discussion of the following chapters, I use them as such to underscore the shifting claims and outcomes in sovereign debt and reputation through the last century.

And, finally, it is important to point out that any sovereignty concept has both an internal and an external dimension. I have focused primarily on internal sovereignty, or the "fundamental authority relation within states between rulers and ruled."[78] However, these internal relations are in turn linked to an external dimension of sovereignty, or "a fundamental authority relation between states which is defined by international law."[79] To enter into an internationally enforceable contract, a sovereign must exist in both dimensions. It must have sufficient standing or recognition internationally to be considered a valid sovereign actor, able to make acknowledged promises on behalf of a state. It must also have the necessary relationship with the underlying people and territory to allow it to extract the resources (natural, financial, or human) to perform on a

TABLE 2.1. Sovereignty Frameworks and their Ramifications

Framework	Internal Sovereignty	External Sovereignty	Related Explanatory Framework	Ability to Make Binding Contracts
Statist Sovereignty (*Two versions*)	Relationship of command. Government is supreme and stands above the law. Premoderns & Bodin (continuous/eternal sovereignty); Hobbes (discontinuous/ material sovereignty)	Government is recognized if it has effective control over a territory, regardless of the internal mechanisms of control. Oppenheim	The state is understood to be a "unitary black box" whose internal machinations are irrelevant to foreign interactions. Waltz	Minimal requirement for competence/agency; even those that rule by force and fail to follow their own law may make international agreements. Continuous: Agreements bind successors. Discontinuous: Sovereign retains repudiation option.
Rule-of-Law Sovereignty	Government is both created/legitimated and limited through rule of law. Weber; Kelsen; Arendt	Government is valid/recognized if it exercises control through law/legal mechanisms. Taft	Internal respect for rule of law/constitutionalism may affect foreign relations (variants of Liberal theory).	International acts are valid and binding if they follow internal requirements for competence or ratification, even if those mechanisms are nondemocratic.

Popular Sovereignty	Government must reflect the consent or choice of the ultimate "sovereign," the underlying people. Rousseau; Sieyès; Paine	Government is valid/recognized if it is popularly authorized. Wilson	The internal governmental form or local interests are central to understanding state action (variants of Liberal theory, i.e., democratic peace). Kant	Sovereign action is internationally valid if the government is popularly authorized. Basic rule of law/constitutionalism alone is insufficient to bind if it does not reflect the people's underlying consent.
Outcome Orientation	Process of internal rule is irrelevant so long as it produces acceptable outcomes.	Government is externally valid/recognized if it produces positive outcomes for the state's population. Sieyès; Hume		Minimal agency/competence requirements. Sovereign contract/action is valid and binding if its (intended) outcome benefits the public.

contract or repay a debt. Although these two elements are conceptually separate, in practice they frequently reinforce each other. A sovereign actor with a strong and clear relationship with the underlying people and territory should have fewer problems gaining international recognition and entering transnational contracts than a sovereign actor with only a tenuous link. However, the reverse channel of influence can also work: international recognition and capital may allow a government with only a tenuous internal link to strengthen its relationship of domestic control. In short, the recognition and enforcement practice of any sovereign debt regime both depends upon and reinforces a given sovereignty paradigm. The doctrine of sovereign continuity, a central philosophical support for the current sovereign debt regime, rests on and gives force to a statist conception of legitimate sovereignty. Laying bare the theoretical claims implicit in sovereign debt practices can thus sharpen our historical analysis of the lending system and provide the groundwork for more clear-eyed assessments of its ramifications.

Case Studies in the Historical Narrative

Considering theories of sovereignty may well be analytically important, but how can we study the historical development of these concepts in actual debt practices? If a politics of sovereign legitimacy is indeed implicated in every debt interaction and reputational assessment, the universe of potential cases is virtually limitless. Although the following chapters unfold in roughly chronological order, they do not constitute anything close to a complete history of the sovereign debt regime. Instead, I construct a genealogy of how debt continuity norms associated with a statist discourse dominated over other plausible alternatives in modern debt and creditworthiness. As such, I make use of historical events and cases insofar as they help us understand the contingent factors that enabled or disabled more flexible approaches to debt continuity.

In selecting cases to study over the last century, I have focused particularly on those in which we might *expect* to see resistance to debt continuity—and then asked whether or not any such resistance materialized or resulted in an actual repudiation. In chapter 1, I suggested that the issue of odious debt best highlights the questions of this book, and also that debt repudiations would be most likely to occur in situations of regime change. Therefore, I take a look at those regime changes most likely to result in odious debt claims. One possible set involves social revolutions, which explicitly reject the legitimacy of the previous regime and frequently seek to refashion the social and economic as well as the political structure of the state. As such, regimes resulting from social revolutions would reasonably be expected to repudiate the debts of the previous regime, particularly those debts used for projects that the new regime finds objectionable.[80] Another range of cases includes postdictatorial democracies, which do not necessarily seek to rework the entire foundations of the state, but do aim to place the nation on a more representative political footing. They could be expected to repudiate debt that has been lost to corruption, or debt associated with contracts signed due to political favor.[81] I have for the purposes of this book laid aside the question of postcolonial regimes and state succession, in part in order to limit the potential universe of cases but also because a separate body of law and treaty interpretation has emerged with regard to state succession.[82] As such, while these cases provide helpful background they are as a whole less appropriate for thinking through the mechanisms supporting debt continuity more generally. I also do not consider postmonarchical or postimperial regimes, which may consider their predecessor governmental forms inappropriate for a new historical period but still tend to claim continuity with the history (as well as the wealth and glory) of the previous regime.[83]

Within this universe of potential cases, my approach focuses on the contingent historical factors that enable or disable certain possibilities at key historical moments. In studying a particular country case, therefore, my goal is not dispositively to explicate state or creditor action. Rather, it is to understand how discursive frameworks and material conditions construct behavioral pathways and thus render certain decisions more or less likely. In one phrasing, this approach "is less directed toward answering the question 'why' than the question 'how,' or, more specifically, 'how possible'."[84] In other words, while some projects focus on why actors select one path over another, this approach focuses instead on the prior issue of how a potential choice is constructed or closed off. In effect, a state's ultimate reason for taking a particular decision is less central, while the conditions that make that decision conceivable or plausible constitute the core of my study.

As such, different country cases play very different roles in the study and thus are given varying weight and space in the analysis. Through the case studies of the Soviet Union and Costa Rica in chapters 3 and 4, I argue that the early twentieth century constituted a potential turning point in the debt regime—an open moment in how ideas of legitimate statehood and sovereign continuity fit into international debt and reputation. These deeper case studies reveal the possibility that an alternative discourse and practice could have been adopted more widely. This is not to say that state and creditor decisions emanate directly from these larger structures; this gives insufficient weight to the agency of particular decision makers and social groups. Rather, the focus is on how an action taken by a particular state—and perhaps a particularly brave or foolhardy state—was enabled by broader circumstances and in turn could have enabled further flexibility going forward.

The openness that these two cases reveal about the early twentieth century raises questions about why additional cases did not materialize in the mid- and late twentieth century. In chapters 5 and 6, I highlight how new material and ideational circumstances emerged in ways that undermined the early twentieth-century potential. Part of the historical puzzle for my analysis is precisely the *absence* of cases that pose a serious challenge to the dominant discourse and practice. While my interest in studying this lacuna undermines the plausibility of a pure case study method, these chapters highlight several situations in which a challenge to the statist framework was either attempted or would have been most likely to occur. Just as state action can underscore the enabling potential of broader material and ideational frameworks, partial state action or the absence of state action where it might otherwise be expected can illustrate how a particular context closed off certain possibilities.

In thinking through these cases as manifestations of a particular practice or as potential turning points, I ask three sets of questions: First, to what degree are principles or claims presented and actions taken that challenge the dominant discourse and practice? Although such articulations will frequently be made by states themselves, this is not necessarily the case. Given that norms are expectations of appropriate action shared by a community of actors, other "members of the community" may well provide arguments that enable states to act in ways that shift the long-run practices. Second, what is the immediate argumentation or response by other relevant actors for a given issue? Such actors may include interlocutors in a particular claim or dispute, external decision makers, and other relevant figures. Such a response may be hostile, receptive, or may vary across actors. The nature of the response is important as well. Are interlocutors hostile to the formulation of a claim, its practical effect, or both? Part of the claim may be rejected (i.e., the existence of a right to repudiate) while another part is implicitly accepted (i.e., that after repudiation a state should be treated as an "unseasoned borrower" rather than a "lemon"). Finally, what is the longer-term reaction of the relevant actors (i.e., creditors and government actors who serve as gatekeepers), and to what degree is their response uniform? In the case of sovereignty and odious debt treatment, is creditor willingness or unwillingness to lend a response to an assessment of creditworthiness (which implicitly suggests a theory of sovereignty, as I discuss above) or are there other issues involved?

As should be clear from the foregoing, the particular characteristics that are relevant for any given country's experience are likely to vary across case and historical period. Just as the uniform repayment norm itself is more complex than it first appears, its historical study escapes easy simplification. I have identified creditor interactions and broader norms of sovereignty as key in shaping possibilities in sovereign debt and reputation. However, the particular historical contours of these factors—and the ways in which specific actors react to these larger structures—are necessarily specific to time and place.

Conclusion

Mainstream approaches to international finance implicitly assume that it is theoretically untenable and impracticable to suggest alternatives to the current expectation of consistent repayment, or to ask about ideas of sovereign legitimacy underlying debt and reputation. These suppositions act as a bulwark against real engagement with proposals to alter the global debt regime in any significant way. However, the political theory and expected economic practice surrounding sovereign debt are not as unvarying as they initially appear. The assumptions of political neutrality, reputational stability, and creditor uniformity do not hold. And different concepts of sovereignty suggest alternative plausible approaches to debt obligations. As the following chapters emphasize, this theoretical openness is joined by historical variation. The dominant norm of debt continuity is not an ahistorical market principle but rather has been actively constructed and supported by changing market structures and broader political ideologies over the last century.

Although efforts can be made to cordon off the political realm from international business and finance, politicized concepts and arguments eventually tend to slip through. Given that the international debate surrounding sovereign legitimacy is unlikely to die down, it makes sense for those involved in the international economic arena to address the question of sovereignty head-on rather than risk being blindsided farther down the road. In the following chapters, I highlight how these questions of state legitimacy, reputation, and debt continuity have come to life in the concrete experiences of states, their creditors, and the other global actors that play a role in the sovereign debt arena. And these past experiences should offer some insight into how sovereign debt issues—at their intersection with questions of reputation and politics—are likely to unfold into the future.

3

Costly Talk?
Reinterpreting the Soviet Repudiation

Our own debts we pay and shall continue to pay, but we have
no desire to pay anybody else's debts . . . So long as we desire to
maintain trading relations with the rest of the world we are bound
in our own interests to carry out our obligations.

—LEON TROTSKY, 1923 Interview

THE SOVIET REPUDIATION of tsarist debt in 1918 has been presented as a cautionary tale—perhaps the most important cautionary tale—in support of the force and reputational basis of the debt
continuity norm. In this chapter, however, I contend that any such account
relies on an incomplete reading of the historical record. A closer look at
the repudiation and its aftermath underscores the indeterminacy of sovereign debt and reputation, and highlights the possibility of making a reputational judgment in favor of lending even after a politically motivated
debt cancellation. It also emphasizes the degree to which competitive creditor interactions and emerging political ideas made the early twentieth
century a potential turning point for the sovereign debt framework.

World War I—the precursor to the demise of tsarist rule—was called
the Great War for good reason. As a result of its upheaval, the balance
of global economic and political power shifted drastically. The United
States expanded its reach over formerly European spheres of influence,
and the centers of capital accumulation and distribution shifted as prewar European financial cities faltered under the weight of war debts and
economic uncertainty. The normative principles that had shaped international interactions came under significant pressure, and increasingly
vocal colonies and nationalities demanded greater recognition. It would

be surprising if the realm of sovereign debt remained entirely untouched by this upheaval. Indeed, major international actors championed new ways of understanding sovereign statehood and, perhaps more importantly, suggested that these approaches should eventually apply not only in the West but across the globe. This, in conjunction with changing patterns of economic interaction and competition, provided an opening in how debtor states, creditor states, and private creditors might view the possibilities in sovereign debt going forward.

This moment of flexibility found a material manifestation in the Soviet debt repudiation. Russia had been a major international borrower since it first turned to Western financial markets in the middle of the nineteenth century, and its outstanding public debt on the eve of World War I was £930 million, constituting half of national income.[1] In the preceding five decades, Russia had undertaken major financial campaigns to update infrastructure, and had also contracted debt to strengthen the imperial regime against rebellion and to fight (and lose) the Russo-Japanese war in 1904–1905. Many of the infrastructure and especially railroad bonds had been floated with the active interest of Western allies—particularly France—who were especially eager for Russia to bolster its military and transport capacities in light of their tensions with Germany and Austria-Hungary. These funds, however, paled in comparison to the war debts undertaken by the Tsar's regime after the onset of European fighting in 1914. By the end of the war in 1918, Russia's public debt reached £3385 million.[2]

Continuities between autocratic imperial Russia and its successor regimes have been much commented upon, both in scholarly writing and in the popular press. Nonetheless, it is a serious understatement to say that the Bolshevik Revolution of October 1917 marked a major shift in Russia's domestic and foreign policy. Perhaps more importantly, and reflecting changing ideas about popular sovereignty, it constituted a repudiation of the previous mode of Russian politics. I begin this chapter by highlighting the competing visions of sovereignty at play in the World War I and postwar era, which challenged strictly statist approaches to global politics and provided a potentially emancipatory language for debt as well. The new Russian regime used this emerging vocabulary to justify its debt repudiation and so stake out an alternative framework for lending. In hinting at another path, it did not reject the centrality of maintaining global capital flows per se. Indeed, Trotsky himself noted the importance of maintaining a state's creditworthiness for continued international engagement. Rather, it argued for a modified—and discontinuous—theory of sovereignty within the existing global credit framework.

If the debt continuity norm were as uniform as it initially appears, then creditors of the time should have consistently rejected the possibility of further lending after such a massive disruption in debt payment. But this is not in fact what happened. In the third section of this chapter, I consider how the new regime's erstwhile allies—now its major public creditors—expressed less concern with undoing the concrete financial consequences of the repudiation than with suppressing the emancipatory discourse associated with the Soviet action. Far from being a reputational judgment separated out from political ideology, the breakdown of debt negotiations ultimately resulted from disagreement *not* on repayment amounts but rather on which political principle would underscore the final write-down. And though all creditors opposed the Russian repudiation, the vehemence of a creditor country's antagonism certainly correlated with its exposure. Had World War I alliances followed a different pattern, it is entirely plausible that the Russian repudiation might now stand for a different precedent in international finance. Furthermore, as I discuss in the final section of the chapter, Russia's inability to float long-term bonds after its debt cancellation did not result from a uniform reputational interpretation of the repudiation among *private* creditors either. In fact, there was again significant variation among creditors in their animosity, with some new American banks even expressing interest in assisting Russian bond floats in the 1920s. Major Western political actors—including a US government motivated by ideological anticommunism—barred these nascent developments, insisting upon an older, statist vision of "civilized" global diplomatic and financial relations. These governmental decisions undermined the potential for the Soviet case to entrench new ideas in lending and to provide an alternative framework for creditworthiness in debt.

Thus, if the Russian repudiation can be read as a cautionary tale, it is not one about the apolitical reputational consequences of adopting a non-statist approach in light of uniform creditor responses. Rather, the moral of the story deals more with how historically embedded sovereignty norms, creditor interactions, and political ideologies may have spillover effects in the sovereign debt arena.

A New Language of Sovereign Legitimacy

To an important degree, the political order maintained by the nineteenth-century European powers rested upon what I have termed a statist approach to sovereignty. For the small group of countries within this "civilized" order, a state's internal form of political organization and the degree to which it might be considered legitimate was considered irrelevant to external status, obligations, and interactions. Although differences in internal rule sometimes engendered public opposition and early humanitarian impulses—for example in British disapproval of domestic oppression in tsarist Russia—this did not extend to legal or policy commitments to particular domestic forms. This statist premise in foreign policy connected to what Arno Mayer calls the "Old Diplomacy" of European annexations, protectorates, and spheres of influence.[3] These traditional interests, furthered by closed-door diplomacy and secret treaties (concluded silently in part to undercut negative public opinion), undermined alternative commitments to popular rule or independent domestic legal frameworks.

Although this approach remains present today, the early twentieth century saw competing political theories emerge. For the first time, the notion of valid sovereign statehood shifted away from conceiving of local populations, including those outside of Europe, as passive subjects of either humanitarian concern or external control. From opposite ends of the political spectrum, both Woodrow Wilson and Vladimir Lenin presented visions of popular self-determination as a new universal ideal for legitimate sovereignty. Legal activists pressed for a vision of legitimate statehood, along with a reformed international arena, grounded in neither pure prerogative nor self-determination but rather in a strict commitment to the rule of law. Another emerging approach, also opposed to strictly statist traditions, focused not on the processes of domestic rule but on the intended outcome of government action as beneficial to the local population. And, of course, the traditional statist vision, interwoven with concerns about maintaining a "civilized" international realm, remained a contender to these alternatives. As demonstrated by the Soviet and Costa Rican cases of this and the following chapter, these more flexible notions of sovereign statehood found early twentieth-century expressions and could have emerged more fully as sovereign debt practices progressed.

The Rise of Self-Determination

One key conceptual development that emerged out of World War I was the idea of "national self-determination." While this vision did not yet take root in international law, it increasingly shaped the formulation of both local goals and international responses. The concept has been called "Janus-like" by Antonio Cassese for good reason, suggesting as it does multiple potential meanings.[4] On the one hand—as in the Wilsonian vision of constitutional democracies—*internal* self-determination can mean the empowerment of individual citizens to determine their collective political fate. On the other, *external* self-determination involves the rejection by a local populace of governance by external powers in favor of some (not necessarily democratic) form of domestic rule.[5]

Although both versions were certainly present, external or national self-determination became an undisputed centerpiece of political thinking in the decades following World War I.[6] The cause of national self-determination received support from multiple sources as the World War drew to a close. Lenin in March 1916 completed his *Theses on the Socialist Revolution and the Right of Nations to Self-Determination.* Linking national movements to class struggle, Lenin argued that national self-determination was a universal principle. This principle was of course intended to support a borderless international socialism, and in practice the Soviet Union sacrificed the hopes of its formerly subject populations to peace with the Central powers and breathing room for its own fragile regime in the Treaty of Brest-Litovsk.[7] However, even after leaving the war, the Soviet regime continued to publicly argue on behalf of open diplomacy, self-determination, and popular say over foreign policy.[8]

Soviet ideological support for national self-determination, along with its rejection of annexation and punitive indemnities as valid war aims, worried Wilson and only deepened his own commitments. Concerned that the "voices of humanity" would be channeled in unwise directions, Wilson insisted that a just vision "ought to be brought under the patronage of its real friends."[9] Although Wilson's initial dedication to self-determination derived from the American tradition of internal consent of the governed, it extended to more external forms. In considering the organization of postwar Europe, Wilson contended that the desires of local populations should be expressed in the new state system. Relatedly, he argued for the protection of national minorities from the whims of larger state actors. Certainly, Wilson was unaware of the full ramifications of presenting self-determination as a universal ideal. As Wilson himself said in 1919, "When I gave utterance to those words 'concerning self-determination' I said them without the knowledge that nationalities existed, which are coming to us day after day . . . You do not know and cannot appreciate the anxieties that I have experienced as a result of many millions of people having their hopes raised by what I have said."[10]

The European colonial powers remained, unsurprisingly, acutely aware of far-flung local independence movements and were initially resistant to self-determination of any sort. Arno Mayer highlights that they acceded to it as a postwar political ideal only after considerable pressure, again in no small part due to the specter of international socialism. Calls to nationalism could serve as potentially effective bulwarks against the even more menacing foes of internal and foreign Leftism. Opinion-makers such as *Le Temps* made arguments along these lines, imagining European leaders to be at a crossroads: "One [was] the way of the nationalities. The other the way of classes. . . . Peace of nations or Bolshevism, between these two perspectives a choice [must] be made."[11] Whatever the misgivings, ulterior motives, or second guesses of the US and European powers, the universalized ideal of external self-determination took root. Although not yet incorporated into positive international law, and certainly undermined by the continuation of colonial practices, it drastically altered the discursive framework of international relations and thus the expectations and claims of local populations. Adopting Wilson's language, Algerian, Vietnamese, and Tunisian nationalist movements among others strengthened their arguments for self-government.[12]

The appearance of external self-determination on the international scene was accompanied by seemingly improved prospects for *internal* self-determination as well. While the concept of popular rule had emerged as a practicable political idea with the American and French Revolutions, the early twentieth century saw its first promulgation as a potentially universal ideal. Although Woodrow Wilson eventually curtailed his espousal of self-determination as democracy, he did initially suggest that popular governance might be appropriate—in good time— for the world at large. In speaking of the League of Nations Covenant in 1919, Wilson stated, "The fundamental principle of this treaty is a principle never acknowledged before . . . that the countries of the world belong to the people who live in them, and that they have a right to determine their own destiny and their own form of government and their own policy."[13] Some support for popular rule also made it into Wilson's Fourteen Points, in which point six advocated that Russia and formerly Russian territory be given "an unhampered and unembarrassed opportunity for the independent determination of her own political development and national policy."[14] Countering Republicans such as Theodore Roosevelt and Henry Cabot Lodge as well as his European allies, Wilson framed American war aims not as unconditional victory over Germany but rather as the promotion of democracy and the promulgation of a new form of international order.[15] Although the idea of self-determination as democratic governance was not fully accepted on a global basis, the explicit adoption of broader popular control and benefit as relevant to legitimate rule was revolutionary. Publicizing these principles and insisting on "the people" as the fundamental locus of sovereignty further undermined the notion that individuals were merely subjects of rulers and appendages to territory.

Well-Being and the Rule of Law

Yet a further refutation of sovereign absolutism involved emerging understandings of valid political rule on the basis of beneficial *outcomes* for the target population. In February 1918, Wilson argued that "every territorial settlement in this war must be made in the interest and for the benefit of the populations concerned, and not as part of any mere adjustment compromise of claims amongst rival states."[16] The Soviet Revolution's slogan of "Peace, land, bread" similarly marked a substantive and popularly oriented outcome as the end of political action, and as such constituted a clear break from much previous political ideology. While the new League of Nations Mandate System allowed traditional colonial powers to continue administration of foreign jurisdictions, such administration was now for the "well-being and development" of mandate populations.[17] Antony Anghie's work on the interwar period highlights the risks involved in such an open-ended ideal, arguing that "the broad phrase 'well-being and development' was interpreted principally in economic terms," and that "a form of economic development that was disadvantageous to the mandate territories was instituted by the system as a result."[18] Still, much of the discourse and settlement following World War I made explicit the notion that foreign territories should—at least in their stated goals—be administered to serve the interests of their inhabitants. In short, the early twentieth century witnessed the development of an understanding of valid sovereign authority as based on beneficial outcomes for the relevant population. This helped to undermine a strictly statist understanding of sovereignty as pure command and subjection.

Another effort to reshape sovereign action in the World War I era—and one especially relevant to the Costa Rican case in chapter 4—involved the effort of international jurists, many of them American, to develop clearer legal frameworks for international relations. This effort challenged the nineteenth century's more overt balance of power approach to politics, which posited a sovereign government largely unfettered by external (or internal) legal constraints, and which came under even greater attack after the disorder and violence of the Great War. In its place, jurists and politicians sought to construct international institutions such as the League of Nations and the Permanent Court of International Justice. Augmenting this commitment to international legalism, these jurists aimed to establish a framework of arbitration treaties that would mitigate or at least judicialize international conflict going forward. Although this approach to sovereign action depended on the *initial* consent of states, it then insisted that the resulting rule of law should shape and constrain future state action. This legalist approach is distinct from a moralist framework, which would conceive of domestic or international law as an embodiment of deeper morality rather than a mechanism for order and the rule of law more narrowly understood.[19] Although the primary projects of early twentieth-century legalists were directed toward the international level, they connected to a commitment to the rule of law more generally. Certainly, the idea of enabling and constraining governmental action on the basis of legal rules involved a significant departure from conceiving of sovereign statehood on the basis of command and control alone.

Early Expressions in Sovereign Debt

Perhaps more so than at any other time in history, then, the world following the Great War turned partially away from nineteenth-century tenets that framed sovereignty as command over (often foreign) subjects and territory. Instead, major international actors promulgated multiple political ideals in which the interests and even the voices of local populations should be taken into account. Although these ideas had not been internationally sanctioned previously, they had inspired certain sovereign debt events prior to this period. In particular, ideas of national self-determination, understood as freedom from explicit external control, had emerged in several earlier situations. In repudiating the debt of the Hapsburg emperor, who had ruled Mexico between 1863 and 1867, the Mexican government in 1883 rejected the validity of the external "pretender" to legitimate rule. A scholar writing soon after pointed out, "A large part of those debts has been created to maintain that usurper in his place against the legitimate authority and all of them were most scandalously usurious."[20] The US repudiation of Spanish debt on behalf of Cuba in 1898 took a similar tone. US commissioners argued that the loans were not contracted for the benefit of the Cuban population, nor through their consent, but rather according to the interests and authority of the Spanish Crown.[21] And the Treaty of Versailles itself followed such precedents in repudiating debts that the German and Prussian governments had contracted in association with their control of Polish territory.[22] The Reparations Commission, by highlighting that the funds were inappropriately borrowed to colonize the territory and diminish its "Polish" character, incorporated into this key international treaty a conceptual shift away from the traditional nineteenth-century vision of valid sovereignty.[23] Nationality-based ideas of local control had evolved into a possibility accessible to all.

It is perhaps not surprising that Alexander Sack's doctrine of odious debt was formalized in the 1920s, drawing as it did from the example of these cases and resonating with non-statist ideals declared as universal at the time. As legal scholars have pointed out, Sack did not seem to consider his view to be a radical departure from emerging, generally accepted legal doctrine. Rather, he framed his formulation as merely a summary and consolidation of different strands in understanding unacceptable sovereign debt contracts.[24] He considered that debt would be "odious" if it was not contracted for beneficial purposes *and also* failed to receive the consent of the population affected. This implicitly presents either outcome-oriented or consent-based conceptions of legitimate sovereign action as alternative foundations for identifying valid sovereign debt. Reflecting ideas in the early twentieth century, it conceives of local populations as explicit beneficiaries or authorizers of sovereign action. Perhaps most importantly, Sack understood his doctrine to be a narrow exception to the general rule of sovereign continuity.[25]

Although at the time it merited little discussion or condemnation, Sack's formalized doctrine of odious debt is now considered a risky departure from mainstream practice. The doctrine is not a widely accepted element of current international law or financial practice, which has instead solidified around the expectation of sovereign continuity, and arguments about odious debt repudiation today can generate suspicion if not outright hostility. It is conceivable, however, that things might have developed in a different direction. Multiple concepts of sovereignty and valid sovereign decision making emerged and remained in play in the early twentieth century. These new discursive frameworks altered the conditions of political possibility by suggesting that not all sovereigns or sovereign actions are equally legitimate. A natural enough next step would translate this shift into the international financial arena—in part by adopting an idea that not all sovereign debts are equally legitimate and therefore equally continuous. In short, had events taken an alternative course through the twentieth century, the sovereign debt regime at the turn of the twenty-first might look quite different.

Repudiation as Political Emancipation

The actions of the incoming Soviet regime both manifested and further catalyzed the new thinking emerging out of the Great War in ways that would seem surprising today. One noteworthy aspect of contemporary post-regime change debt negotiations is the reluctance of successor governments to make claims along the lines of odious debt, even when plausible conditions exist for doing so. Despite the revival of interest in the idea—and even in spite of its explicit invocation by international policy makers arguing in favor of write-downs—negotiating teams themselves have consciously steered clear of any such claims on the basis of principle.[26]

The Soviet articulation of its reasons for repudiation could not differ more starkly from this nonconfrontation. In February 1918, the Bolshevik government cancelled the debt of its predecessors, causing uproar among both its private and public creditors. The decree specified that "state loans concluded by the Government of the Russian landlords and the Russian bourgeoisie . . . are hereby repudiated" and that "all foreign loans, without exception, are absolutely repudiated."[27] The decree itself did not provide much elaboration beyond this, and indeed there was little time for negotiation with creditors during the civil war that ensued. The Western powers financially and militarily supported anti-Bolshevik factions, and newly communist Russia and its foreign adversaries only began debt discussions in 1921–1922, after the end of serious fighting.

A series of diplomatic notes between 1921 and 1923, and most importantly a May 1922 memorandum issued after a diplomatic conference on monetary economics at Genoa, Italy, provide perhaps the clearest articulation of Russia's reasons for repudiation. The Soviet delegation drew from emerging post-World War I ideas, particularly those of sovereignty as discontinuous under some circumstances and as grounded in legitimate consequences or popular support. And, far from rejecting the central mechanisms of international capitalism wholesale, new Russian elites openly accepted the importance of creditworthiness for continued cross-border relations. They suggested only that the reputation of a new regime should be de-linked from that of its predecessor, and thus not analyzed punitively after the repudiation of illegitimate debt but rather allowed to develop on its own. And while the new regime rejected any obligation to pay as a point of legal and political *principle,* it actually expressed willingness to negotiate partial debt recognition—especially the payment of pre-World War I debt contracted for infrastructure such as railroads—as part of a broader agreement involving new credits. In essence, it argued for the compatibility of principled debt cancellation with functioning capital markets, and used ongoing postwar debates about sovereignty to formulate an alternative starting point for non-statist discussions of debt.

The Language of Popular Right

While the new Russia certainly considered economic emancipation central to true revolutionary change, its debt negotiations relied on principles of *political* emancipation that resonated more generally in the Western world. It argued that emerging political thought included "a principle of right, namely, that revolutions which are a violent rupture with the past carry with them a new juridical status in the external and internal relations of States."[28] This discontinuity of states should, it followed, lead to a discontinuity in state obligations. "Governments and systems of government which have emerged from a revolution are not bound to respect the obligations of Governments which have lapsed."[29] In a 1923 note to US Secretary of State Charles Hughes, reprinted in *Pravda,* it stated,

> Mr. Hughes, who is the representative of the educated classes, must know that "obligations" can refer only to one and the same person, unless such obligations are formally transferred to another person. So for instance, America is not obliged to pay to France Germany's debts. While Soviet Russia . . . is infinitely further from the Russia of Nicolai Romanoff and Alexander Kerensky, than the America of Mr. Hughes is from the Germany of Mr. Ebert.[30]

The Soviet government highlighted precedent for this idea in earlier regime changes, pointing out that Russia spoke to "an assembly of powers among which many count in their history more than one revolution." Citing in particular the US repudiation of Spanish and British treaties upon taking control of their former territory, it explicitly pointed out that "more than one among the States represented at the conference of Genoa have in the past repudiated debts and obligations contracted by it." Russia additionally argued that this practice had "been elevated to the rank of a doctrine by eminent lawyers," and asserted its refusal of any compulsion to assume responsibility in conformity with such precedent.[31]

Beyond a simple assertion of right on the basis of sovereign discontinuity alone, the Russian delegation claimed the mantle of the French and American revolutions by arguing for a distinction between more and less popular regimes. It noted that, "the French Convention, of which France considers herself the legitimate successor, proclaimed on the twenty-second of September 1792, that 'the sovereignty of peoples is not bound by the treaties of tyrants.'"[32] Just as this declaration had prompted revolutionary France to repudiate the treaties and debts of its predecessors, the Russian government sought to reject the obligations of an onerous ruler on behalf of the masses. In a statement conveyed to the Allies in October 1921, the government contended that no people could be expected to pay the price of "chains fastened upon it for centuries" by a political system it had succeeded in replacing.[33]

While it is difficult to imagine the tyranny and depredation of Stalinism as emerging from a moment of emancipation, there was little disagreement about the undesirability of the previous regime. Indeed, the British government had long expressed discomfort with the absolutist excesses of the Tsar, and Woodrow Wilson was uneasy about entering World War I in alliance with a monarch diametrically opposed to American principles of popular rule.[34] Articulating the views of progressive thinkers like himself and Wilson, David Lloyd George in 1919 described the old Russian order as "inept, profligate and tyrannical." According to Lloyd George, it "had been guilty of exactions and oppressions which were accountable for the ferocity displayed by the Revolutionaries" and had received its just desserts.[35] Thus, although the Western powers were opposed to the economic ideas of the Soviet revolution, they could hardly deny the repellent character of the previous regime.

Degrees of Legitimacy and Pragmatic Repayment

Notwithstanding seeming consensus on the injustices of tsarist rule, the new Russian regime suggested that it might nonetheless accept responsibility for certain debt obligations as a gesture of goodwill and in the context of a broader economic agreement. Although the new regime stated that it would not "subscribe blindfold [sic] to propositions which are too onerous,"[36] it took care to separate out and highlight especially arduous claims raised by the Western powers. Thus, although the core Soviet argument focused on debt discontinuity in light of tsarist illegitimacy, it also suggested that the intended *outcome* of loans might affect debt continuity. In particular, it distinguished between the claims based on World War I debt and losses suffered during the civil war—which even the White Russian tsarist supporters would also have balked at—and the prewar tsarist debt.

As a starting point, the Russian memorandum to the Genoa participants rejected the validity of claims made by Western powers on the basis of their economic losses suffered during the Russian Revolution and Civil War. The Soviet regime argued that the destruction wrought by such great popular movements constitute the equivalent of a "force majeure," and pointed out that even the Tsar's government refused to pay indemnity to its own or foreign citizens after the revolution of 1905–1906. The Western powers, as post-1906 creditors to Russia themselves, were well aware of the imperial government's ability to obtain funds despite this refusal. The Soviet delegation also suggested that, if claims arising from the civil war were to be included, its own counterclaims for damage caused by foreign intervention and blockade were better grounded.[37]

The new regime most vehemently repudiated the World War I debt that had accumulated by 1918 on the basis of its "quite specific origin."[38] According to Moody's, the external war loans of the Russian government amounted to £810 million, overshadowed by internal war loans of £1635 million but almost reaching the amount of the entire £920 million prewar state debt.[39] The Western powers had eagerly offered loans to tsarist Russia during World War I as part of the military alliance against the Central powers, and especially to strengthen Russia's involvement on the eastern front and so take pressure off their own troops on the western front.[40] The Communist Party, accurately assessing the Russian population's unwillingness to continue fighting for an Eastern European empire, had opposed Russian participation in the war and made clear its intention to withdraw from fighting.[41] By the signing of the Treaty of Brest-Litovsk, in which the Soviet government ceded a considerable portion of the empire to end formal hostilities with Germany, Russia had suffered over 1.7 million military deaths.[42]

In its memorandum, the new Soviet regime emphasized that the debts were extinguished in part "by the very fact that Russia having dissociated herself from the war and having taken no part in the division of its resulting advantages could not take its expenses on her shoulders."[43] On this point, most of the Russian factions fighting the civil war seem to have agreed. Even the White Russian supporters of the tsarist regime considered any Western insistence on full debt repayment unjust, due to Russia's absence at the Versailles discussions to end the war and the subsequent lack of consideration for Russian interests in the peace treaties.[44] On the issue of war debts, then, the civil war armies supported by the Western powers did not take a very different view in practice from the Bolshevik regime. Even so, a British-American consortium was willing to issue a significant loan to the anti-Bolshevik Russian government based at Omsk in late 1919.[45]

Perhaps surprisingly in light of its initial wholesale repudiation of "tyrannical" debt, the Russian delegation did not deem the *pre*war debt of the Tsar's regime to be as problematic. It criticized the civil war and World War I debt claims as onerous in their substance and, in the case of the war debt, unsustainable in practice. The prewar debt, however, was not considered illegitimate per se but only *presumptively discontinuous* in light of a new and fundamentally different sovereign regime. While unwilling to compromise in advance on this claim of principle—and so give up an important bargaining chip—the Russian delegation indicated willingness to acknowledge this debt as part of its concessions in a more comprehensive agreement. In an October 1921 statement conveyed to the Western powers, it specified that it would conditionally recognize tsarist state loans contracted before 1914 with other governments and their citizens.[46] Both the May 1922 memorandum and the earlier statement made particular note of "small bondholders" and the "small foreign owners, whose property has been nationalized or sequestered, and whom the Russian Government intended to include among the claimants of justice and the good foundation of whose claims it recognized."[47]

It noted that postrevolutionary regimes such as France had eventually agreed to refund a portion of the previous regime's debt. However, it pointed out that this was purely pragmatic or "political opportunism."[48] The French claim of right and the legitimate precedent remained, even in the eventual practical accommodation with capital markets at the turn of the nineteenth century. Similarly, the Soviet delegation expressed readiness to make partial payment in the context of a larger agreement on government credit. It "declared itself disposed conditionally to renounce its counter-claims and accept the engagements of the former Government in exchange for a number of concessions on the part of the powers, the most important being real credits placed at the disposal of the Russian Government amounting to a sum to be determined in advance."[49] In effect, it expressed willingness to turn back the financial clock to 1914, rejecting the civil war and war debt claims but assuming the Tsar's prewar debt obligations in return for additional funding and a recognition of the *principle* of debt discontinuity.

Questioning Sovereign Continuity in Creditworthiness

The Soviet regime took a similarly pragmatic stance on the issue of new sovereign borrowing and investment. Far from denouncing the reputational mechanism so central to international capital flows as oppressive or unacceptable, the new Russian elites spoke very directly to the question of their future creditworthiness. They explicitly rejected the idea that repudiation of the Tsar's debt would have any bearing on how it might treat its own obligations. The incoming regime considered ungrounded "the suspicion which it is sought to impute to the attitude of the Russian Government as regards future creditors of Russia" on the basis of initial debt repudiation:

> Repudiation of debts and obligations contracted by the ancient regime, abhorred by the people, cannot in any manner prejudice the attitude of Soviet Russia, issue of the revolution, toward those who would come with their capital and their technical knowledge to help its revival.[50]

The new regime effectively argued that it should be considered not a "lemon"—an unreliable borrower even in good economic times—but an "unseasoned borrower," in the terminology used by Michael Tomz.[51] Leon Trotsky, in a 1923 interview, underscored that treatment of a predecessor's debts did not foreshadow the regime's likely future actions. He also directly acknowledged the importance of maintaining the regime's own reputation in facilitating continued economic relations:

> Our own debts we pay and shall continue to pay, but we have no desire to pay anybody else's debts. . . . You ask where is the guarantee that we shall not later refuse to pay our own debts. All I can say is that such an act on our part would be simply suicidal. So long as we desire to maintain trading relations with the rest of the world we are bound in our own interests to carry out our obligations.[52]

Interestingly enough, some private financiers would later explicitly point to the Soviet government's creditworthy record of repaying its own trade debt in their efforts to extend longer-term credit to the regime. If indeed the new Soviet regime was discontinuous with the Tsar's rule—as the Russian delegation argued had been the case with its own and the French and American revolutions—then preceding obligations should also be discontinuous, leaving a clean slate for the new government. Far from being a rejection of the importance of creditworthiness in economic relations, the new regime argued that it was simply a modification of political ideals within the same financial framework.

In short, when it finally came time to articulate its position on debt repudiation and recognition, the new Russian regime did not take an absolutist position on actual debt payment. It expressed willingness to negotiate for partial debt recognition as a practical matter, and fully accepted that it would need to rebuild its own reputation, but rejected the requirement to pay as a point of principle and out of compulsion. It presented a series of arguments that drew from discourses of sovereignty as basically discontinuous, and as grounded in legitimate consequences and even popular support.[53] In doing so, it formulated a starting point for discussions of sovereign debt that were grounded in ongoing post-World War I debates and that could have built a foundation for future shifts.

Cheap Talk? The Intransigence of Principle

Unsurprisingly, the initial response of Russia's creditors to the debt repudiation was unreservedly hostile. Its war allies, many of whom were also creditors, led the condemnation. Immediately following the publication of the repudiation decree, the representatives of every country with diplomatic missions in Petrograd issued a protest against the loan nullification.[54] Private creditors and investment analysts were similarly critical. In his survey of interwar investment literature, Tomz points out that "analysts invariably denounced the outcome as a 'flagrant case' of 'voluntary repudiation' and singled out Russia as 'the outstanding example of bad faith to foreign security holders.'"[55] He cites a vice president of Fitch as saying, "Any nation that deliberately defaults in the payment of its foreign debt finds its credit gone . . . its reputation for honesty is destroyed and later borrowing impossible except upon ruinous terms. . . . Russia, at the present time, is an example of a nation in this position."[56] That the new regime was unable to obtain any real foreign credit as a result of its repudiation is openly acknowledged.

One question that has been overlooked, however, centers on the relative importance of the *voluntary repudiation* as opposed to the *financial default* aspect of the Russian decision. Tomz notes that post-World War I investors differentiated between "willful repudiation and unavoidable defalcations" and highlighted the Russian repudiation as the paradigmatic example of the former.[57] The new regime's decision to repudiate as opposed to simply default rendered Russia's intransigence crystal clear, relieving creditors of any uncertainty about its intentions. But did the discursive context of the Soviet decision do any more than this? It is common to hear that "cheap talk" should be distinguished from "costly signals" in assessing the intentions of actors in a strategic game. In the case of debt negotiations, a borrower can relatively easily make a promise to pay (cheap talk) whereas actually following through with repayment is more difficult (a costly signal).

In the Russian case, then, we might expect that the language of principle added only a supplementary or even an entirely extraneous discursive layer to the objective fact of nonpayment. To the contrary, I argue that the interactions of the new Russian regime with its public creditors in the early 1920s undermine this expectation, emphasizing the historically contingent aspect of broader norms and ideology in debt and reputation. Although many countries defaulted on debt in the interwar period, what made the Russian case distinctive and especially problematic was its explicit embrace of repudiation on the basis of political principle. Given the perceived importance of Russian economic revival for Europe's financial rehabilitation, the Soviet regime would likely have obtained additional credits even while in default. The fact that the new government faced major economic obstacles to immediate debt repayment was openly acknowledged. Had the regime taken a different route—permanently discontinuing payment on the stated basis of economic reasons rather than claims of principle—the story of the Russian debt default might now read very differently. Far from being cheap talk, the new regime's insistence on a non-statist approach proved to be extremely costly in shaping its interactions with public interlocutors. Thus, instead of being apolitical and neutral, any reputational fallout that did exist resulted largely from political antipathy to the principles declared in the Soviet action.

Contrary Principles

Just as the new Russian regime insisted on repudiation as a point of principle, its interlocutors insisted on fidelity to a statist principle of contract acknowledgment, separate from—and more important than—the question of how much tsarist debt would actually be recouped. The Allied powers presented their own conditions for financial negotiations most clearly in a May 2, 1922 memorandum to the Genoa Conference, the Russian reply to which is discussed above. Most importantly, they insisted that "the Russian Soviet government recognizes all public debts and obligations which have been contracted or guaranteed by the Imperial Russian government or the Russian Provisional government or the Soviet government itself toward foreign powers."[58]

This *recognition* of obligations proved to be central for the Western powers, who framed it as a basic principle of "civilized" interaction. The subcommission on debts at the Hague Conference in 1922 noted that the Soviet government should be forced to "submit to the general law which governs relations between civilized states, and to recognize the obligations accepted by preceding governments."[59] In discussions with Soviet representatives in February 1922, the British prime minister Lloyd George contended that the Western powers' conditions were "only [those] on which every civilized government conducted its affairs."[60] The US government, while recognizing the right of revolution, decried the Russian "repudiation of the obligations inherent in international intercourse and . . . defiance of the principles upon which alone it can be conducted."[61] Like his West European counterparts, US president Coolidge insisted on "the sanctity of international obligations."[62] Nongovernmental creditors used a similar language of principle to register their objections.[63]

A fundamental tension thus emerged between two sovereign discourses—that of long-standing "civilized" sovereign continuity (and thus debt continuity) on the one hand, and that of newer ideas of valid sovereignty as potentially discontinuous and grounded in broader consent and benefit. The Soviet delegation was only willing to pragmatically acknowledge debts if its own government was first declared valid and legal. The French representative at the Genoa Conference made explicit the alternate view, namely that such *timing* was backward and unacceptable. As reported in the *New York Times,* the French responded that the Russian reply "provided no recognition of debts without formal recognition, whereas the French point of view was that recognition of debts should be given first."[64] As contemporaneous American commentators noted, "This difference of views on a question as formal and technical as the principle of legal liability is more important than it might appear to be."[65] Their commentary further stated, "In all the negotiations conducted so far on the subject of the Russian debts, the question at issue has always been whether or not the Soviet government is *legally liable* for the prewar and war debts of Russia."[66] More so than is usually acknowledged today, the debt disagreement between the new Soviet government and the Western powers centered not so much on financial particulars, but rather on the underlying legal and political theory upon which essentially the same financial outcome was to be based.

Debt Recognition as Cheap Talk

While the Western powers considered the principle of debt recognition central, they showed considerable flexibility on actual payment. In pointing out the importance of theories of legal liability for the 1922 conferences, American commentators noted, "Recognizing the legality of obligations is, however, a very different matter from paying such obligations."[67] In the 1922 discussions, the British government insisted that the new regime announce its *theoretical* acceptance of repayment to satisfy creditors, even if this did not translate to practical financial obligations. As Stephen White points out, "Until the [Russian] government acknowledged (but not necessarily paid) its debts, [Lloyd George] feared that the business community could not be brought whole-heartedly to accept any arrangements with that country."[68]

The record suggests that a Russian successor regime, of any ideological persuasion, may well have successfully rebuilt its credit by recognizing if not paying the tsarist debt along these lines. A new government in 1918 or 1922, facing huge economic crises, could have politely and plausibly claimed duress and discontinued payment. Russian agricultural and industrial capacity had been destroyed by fighting in both the Great War and the civil war, and a subsequent drought and major famine threatened approximately fifteen million people with starvation.[69] Indeed, analysts of the 1920s considered that actual debt *payment* would prove difficult if not impossible for some time. As noted in 1926, "It is readily admitted by both sides that Russia has at the present time no paying capacity whatever. . . . Until the process of Russia's economic restoration at least to the prewar level of operation is somewhere near completed there can be no question of any debt-paying capacity."[70] An earlier study by the same authors pointed out that the Russian economic system had been "weakened by the war and the revolution [and] completely shattered during the period of communist experimentation,"[71] and that serious questions surrounding the domestic budget and foreign trade would have to be addressed for any fulfillment of debt obligations.[72] In an address to the American Society of International Law on the question of recognition, a commentator highlighted again that the issue at stake was really legal and political rather than financial: "Russia cannot be expected to pay [the debts to the US government and its citizens] within the next twenty years, so that the only practical question is whether the Soviet Government must admit the validity of this claim and promise to pay it before we recognize that government."[73]

In light of the acknowledged difficulties of repayment, the memorandum presented by the Western powers during the 1922 Genoa economic conference ultimately stated that the Allied powers would not insist on immediate payment of war debts.[74] Reporting on general agreement at the conference, the *New York Times* noted that "some postponement in the payment of the Russian debt undoubtedly would be authorized." It suggested that "the question of a moratorium probably would develop during the discussion of the experts," but reported that even in advance of any real negotiation on time frames, "France at present is disposed to granting Russia a five years' moratorium."[75] The article also noted a report that the Russian delegation had requested a fifteen-year moratorium, on which the French had not commented but which, it seems, even they did not immediately reject.[76]

The Genoa Memorandum ultimately went further than a moratorium on debt payment, noting that the Western powers would consider the eventual adjustment of war debts as part of any "arrangement concluded between the Allied and Associated Powers for the liquidation or rear- rangement of war debts."[77] And indeed, a 1924 American economic anal- ysis of Russia's payment capacity noted that during the 1922 conferences *"it was generally conceded that new loans would have to be extended to Russia.* With credit Russia might succeed in rehabilitating her shattered economic system and regain financial solvency."[78] With its considerable natural resources and potential for industrial capacity, Russia should certainly have had the eventual ability to repay loans. However, that capacity would have to be redeveloped, probably with foreign assistance and over a considerable length of time. The same study suggested that, even if Russia regained its pre-World War I economic activity, its trade balance would be sufficient only "to cover the interest charges on a re- construction loan of about 1,400 million roubles, allowing for no mar- gin of income above interest obligations. No interest payments would be possible on either the war or the pre-war state debt, nor could any interest or dividends be paid to foreign holders of Russian industrial securities."[79] The study acknowledged that it might eventually be possi- ble for the new regime to make payment on prewar debts, but that this would depend on the resumption and expansion of trade to a consider- able degree.[80] Indeed, in December of 1921, British, French, and German representatives laid out a tentative plan for an international syndicate to promote reconstruction in Russia.[81] This presumably would have in- corporated the various debt write-downs, payment postponements and additional credits—amounting to significant cancellation—that could have been acceptable to the Soviet regime as a practical financial matter.

It is interesting to ask whether White Russian leaders would have ac- ceded to a very different practical financial outcome had they come to power. Barring a significant reapportioning of postwar territory and reparations receipts, it is unlikely that *any* Russian regime would have embraced full payment of the war debt. A White Russian government would likely have balked at paying civil war damage claims—as did the Tsar—particularly given that Western states would have participated heavily in bringing any White Russian or liberal government to power during the civil war. This leaves payment of the prewar imperial debt, which even the Soviet government ultimately seemed willing to pay in re- turn for an extension of further credit. The Bolshevik regime repudiated the tsarist debt in principle, but was willing to negotiate upward to partial compensation in practice. Any new non-Bolshevik government would have *recognized* the tsarist debt in principle, but then negotiated downward to a lower payment in practice—of course, in exchange for a new infusion of funding.[82] In short, the final outcome of any long-term repayment and refunding agreement with Russia's creditors may not have looked markedly different.

In all likelihood, an acknowledgment of the debt claims by *any* new regime would not have translated into substantial payment obligations for some time. Interwar investment experts, such as the vice president of the American Academy of Political and Social Science, recognized that—barring a clear voluntary repudiation—"it is not a simple matter to distinguish between defaults of interest or principal which result from bad faith and those which sometimes arise out of economic circumstances beyond the power of the borrower to control."[83] Even if the new regime never intended to repay more than the prewar debt, a decision to switch from the language of repudiation to that of economic default would have been far more effective in serving its pragmatic interests, if not its ideational goals. Contrary to general understandings of discourse and debt, a decision to *acknowledge* debt (in principle if not practice) would have been cheap talk in the early twentieth-century Soviet case.

From this perspective, the Soviet insistence on the language of repudiation as a point of principle and legal right was incredibly costly. In adhering to its conceptual framework, the new regime undermined its access to foreign credit and to crucial reconstruction resources. The Russian delegation dismissed the idea of acknowledging the Tsar's debts *in principle* as a precondition for further discussion and insisted that any recognition of claims would have to be mutual. It asked Western states to "cease to hold toward Russia language held between conqueror and conquered, Russia not having been conquered," and continued that "the only language which would result in a common agreement was that which is the language held between States negotiating on a footing of equality."[84]

Such discursive audacity proved unacceptable to Russia's immediate interlocutors, even if the final financial outcome may not have differed greatly. Although new ideas of sovereignty had emerged in the international arena of the early 1920s, their acceptance and application remained tentative in both the political and economic realms. The Western powers at Genoa constructed a reply to the Russian delegation that recapitulated their own statist position, including the centrality of debt acknowledgment, and went even further to require several changes in the

Soviet legal system.[85] A British Foreign Office minute commented that its own negotiating position asked "everything—or practically everything—and offers nothing in return," and that the object of the British foreign policy leaders' stated position was merely to "make it appear that they are not primarily responsible for the failure of Genoa."[86]

Creditor Disunity and the Possibility of New Lending

The inability to come to an agreement on the Russian debt during the 1920s' economic conferences constituted a particularly harsh blow to future international capital markets. State and state-guaranteed securities were the predominant Russian issues placed abroad, with public debt constituting about 75 percent of overseas Russian issues in 1913, down from a high of over 90 percent in the early 1890s.[87] More importantly, Russian securities constituted an important bloc of the issues in European capital markets as of 1914, particularly in Paris. It is hardly surprising that creditor governments and private investors called for an acknowledgment of this particular financial obligation as well as for Soviet acceptance of the general principle of debt repayment. That said, it is also possible to imagine that this might have heightened pressure on the Western powers to enter into a more pragmatic grand bargain involving simultaneous political recognition and partial debt payment.

Despite the lack of any ultimate agreement, it would be inaccurate to present the 1918 repudiation as evidence of a uniformly statist insistence on debt continuity, based on a clear reputational interpretation of major debt cancellation. Although the repudiation did undermine Russia's access to international credit, the response across both public and private creditors actually varied to some degree according to previous Russian exposure, with several new American players expressing interest in facilitating additional lending. Furthermore, the mechanisms by which more extensive financing failed were not purely market-based. Particularly in the United States, the opposition of state authorities—due to political and normative considerations—proved crucial. Far from demonstrating how uniform reputational assessments support the norm of debt continuity, a closer look at the creditor response to the Soviet repudiation exposes the centrality of ideology and historically contingent creditor interactions. It also highlights the conditional capacity of creditors to acknowledge non-statist claims in sovereign debt and embrace the possibility of post-repudiation lending.

Varied European Hostility to the Soviet Repudiation

Notwithstanding a relatively high degree of transnational cooperation, pre-World War I international finance displayed distinct patterns of capital export resulting from geostrategic affinities, private competition, and varied interest and experience. This differentiated involvement in prewar lending had consequences in the postwar world. In particular, the British and French cases demonstrate that although the overall response to the Russian repudiation was hostile, creditor interactions and risk interpretations remained disaggregated, with reactions diverging along the lines of earlier exposure.

Much of this was on display in the discussions at Genoa, which the three wartime allies attended with very different goals.[88] France, Russia's primary pre-Revolution creditor, proposed that the conference should focus narrowly on sanctions for repudiating the prewar debt.[89] The United Kingdom, by contrast, was more concerned with stabilizing broader economic relations and deepening trade ties. While European countries in general were hostile to further Russian credit extensions, the different approaches taken by France and Britain in particular emphasize the ambiguity of lessons learned from the Soviet case. They suggest that creditor variation in the treatment of arguably odious debt is possible, and that historical uniformity is far from given. These cases also support an attentiveness to internal domestic politics and their refraction of larger normative or ideological considerations, reiterating the insufficiency of overly general understandings of debt and reputation.

A STRONG FRENCH OPPOSITION

Four-fifths of Russia's direct government debt held abroad was in the hands of French investors by 1914,[90] and perhaps more so than any other country France suffered financially as a result of the Russian repudiation and the subsequent failure to come to an agreement. By World War I, French investors held over 11 billion francs of Russian securities, including 9 billion francs owed by the Russian government. The French government, at least in part to support its alliance with Russia after 1887, had actively supported the placement of these securities on the Paris bourse.[91] These securities were held across French society; investors such as industrial workers, shopkeepers, and peasants presented 1.6 million individual claim declarations after the war.[92] Russian investments constituted a quarter of all overseas French ownership, and an even larger proportion of the foreign capital lent by smaller investors.[93] The syndication structure of French loans to Russia also broadened the effect of the repudiation. As the war approached, major financial houses increasingly included provincial banks in loan syndicate contracts. These contracts, in the case of railway bonds and shares, developed to include multiple railway issues in a single loan agreement.[94] The holding of Russian securities was thus spread not only across class levels but also geographically.[95] By the eve of World War I, the involvement of French capital in Russian public financing was deeply and broadly entrenched.

Perhaps unsurprisingly, the French reaction to the Russian repudiation in 1918 was extremely hostile. French commentators recognized the role of their own leaders in pressing Russian securities, and in some cases called upon the government to take greater financial responsibility for its role.[96] However, most of the public's hostility remained oriented toward the new Soviet regime. This focus was bolstered through the 1920s by émigré and prerevolutionary Russian business owners, who were very active in France and established associations to ensure that their views were not forgotten.[97] Trade and investment relations did relatively little to mitigate this finance-based antagonism. Although France eventually returned to trading with Russia in the early 1920s (following Great Britain), and made some efforts to promote French exports during cooler periods in Anglo-Soviet relations,[98] it never came anywhere close to its extensive level of prewar Russian involvement. Of the over three hundred and thirty operating concessions signed by the Soviet regime between 1920 and 1930, only a dozen were French.[99] The French government's antagonistic attitude undermined a number of peace overtures and potential diplomatic ententes that might have otherwise been more successful. In late 1918 and 1919, despite agreement between the British War Cabinet and President Wilson to respond more positively to civil war armistice possibilities with the Soviets, the French remained opposed "to [making] any pact with this criminal regime."[100] Similarly, French opposition was partially responsible for derailing Lloyd George's efforts at Genoa.[101] More so than other Western powers, France insisted that Russia acknowledge the validity of tsarist debt in principle before any serious financial negotiations took place.

The fact that French capital did not play a prominent role in post–World War I Russian investment may have had much to do with the scarcity of funds in postwar France. France had borrowed significantly from Great Britain and the United States, and the war devastated much of its own capacity for wealth generation. French investors had resold many of their best securities, and public opinion was hostile to returning to foreign issues in general.[102] Still, the refusal of the Soviet regime to acknowledge the debts of its predecessors remained a major thorn in French international relations going forward.[103] Importantly, it shaped French interaction with its allies, encouraging France to intercede if the United States or Great Britain appeared to stray from the principles established for Soviet relations in the early 1920s. When five million dollars of Soviet gold arrived in New York in 1928, the State Department acquiesced to a French demand that it enforce a 1920 US policy prohibiting the acceptance of such gold.[104] The French ambassador also blocked attempts by a US financier to advance the Soviet regime $40 million in consideration of a Russian mining concession of formerly French ownership.[105] France's policing of Soviet relations thus helped to maintain an appearance of uniformity in the face of actual creditor divergence.

THE MORE MODERATE BRITISH APPROACH

As the unparalleled creditor nation before World War I, Great Britain had a significant stake in a statist debt system in its own right and might reasonably be expected to deplore any sovereign repudiation. The government had sent considerable funds to tsarist Russia during the war, as well as to the White armies during the Russian Civil War.[106] The return of these funds certainly would have ameliorated Britain's postwar financial situation. Nonetheless, British investors were far less enmeshed in prewar Russian securities than their French counterparts. The long-term British economic response, while still negative, was less hostile and was partially driven by competing commercial interests and broader political and anticommunist ideology. Furthermore, Great Britain's close diplomatic relationship with France is more important than usually acknowledged in its ultimate treatment of the new Soviet regime.

London banking houses such as Baring Brothers and N. M. Rothschild & Sons began issuing Russian securities after the Napoleonic Wars and became major issuers after the Crimean War. However, British investors began to pull away from Russian issues after 1875, in part as a result of Anglo-Russian disagreements in the Middle East.[107] Even after political relations improved at the turn of the century, British banking houses took a dimmer view of the sustainability of Russian securities.[108] While British banks did join in additional Russian issues, their participation was largely symbolic.[109] One estimate suggests that of the £3,763.3 million of long-term publicly issued British capital investments overseas on the eve of World War I, only £110 million remained in Russian investments. While a considerable amount, this is dwarfed by the £1,780 million of publicly issued capital going to territory within the British empire and even by the £756.6 million going to Latin America.[110] Thus, as the

Great War approached, British capital, which had been put to use largely in the British Empire and in the Americas, was not as deeply entrenched in Russian securities as it might have been.

Perhaps as a consequence, British hostility did not reach the heightened level seen in France. Recognizing this different dynamic, Prime Minister Lloyd George wrote to Winston Churchill in a 1919 message about the latter's aggressive stance in the Russian Civil War: "The French are not safe guides in [the matter of Russian relations]. Their opinion is largely biased by the enormous number of small investors who put their money into Russian loans and who now see no prospect of ever recovering it. I urge you therefore not to pay too much heed to their incitements."[111] The British government, which by the Genoa Conference in 1922 claimed Russian war debts of about £650 million, had little expectation of recovering its own debt and was generally more amenable to the renegotiation of debt claims.[112] However, its commitment to the French alliance stiffened its negotiating stance, particularly on the issue of private property claims.[113] While Germany signed the separate Treaty of Rapallo during the Genoa Conference, to considerable British and French consternation, it is difficult to imagine that Britain would have done something similar given this closer alliance. Indeed, the Rapallo breakthrough, which included Germany's renunciation of compensation for nationalized property, weakened Western Europe's joint leverage and encouraged the Soviet delegation to seek additional bilateral agreements, particularly with Great Britain.[114] Although Great Britain ultimately proved unwilling to negotiate bilaterally, it is interesting to consider the counterfactual. Had Lloyd George stayed in power, would a separate British agreement have been possible in the absence of the French link or French intransigence?

Indeed, British domestic politics proved central in shaping ultimate attitudes toward the Soviet regime, and the political winds changed after the demise of Lloyd George's coalition government in late 1922. The Foreign Office under George Curzon was far more anticommunist as a point of political ideology (a characteristic Curzon shared with Winston Churchill), and less likely to look favorably upon the Soviet government for reasons independent of any objective financial calculus. Curzon was also far more suspicious of long-standing Russian geopolitical and economic interests in central Asia, perhaps partially on account of his experience as viceroy of India. Curzon's effort to exclude the Soviet delegation from the Lausanne Conference, which dealt in 1922 and 1923 with Near Eastern questions including Black Sea access, resulted in Lenin rejecting a deal that had been successfully negotiated with regard to British interests in Russo-Asiatic Consolidated, representing about a quarter of British property nationalization claims.[115] Furthermore, labor unrest in 1920s Europe, the growing transnational links of socialist groups, and the concomitant rise of anticommunist rhetoric made the British government and the public at large more negatively inclined than they otherwise might have been toward Soviet economic arguments.[116] If a newly *liberal democratic* (rather than Leninist) Russian regime had repudiated debts on similar grounds, on the basis of principle and reciprocity, its negotiating positions might have received more consideration from the British government.

In the absence of any broader agreement, major long-term financing remained elusive. For another decade and a half at least, and through ups and downs in Anglo-Soviet relations, arguments made in favor of extending credit were met with reminders of repudiation and confiscation during the revolution.[117] However, pressure did exist for improved relations with the Soviet Union, much of it deriving from the importance of trade to the United Kingdom and from the dismal employment numbers in the years after World War I. Although those industries in potential competition with Russian imports dampened any uniform enthusiasm for increased trade and credit availability, disagreements emerged between London financiers and industrialists centered in the British Midlands. Difficult economic conditions through the 1920s intensified rivalry with other economic powers and made the Russian market even more important. Decrying the suspension of commercial relations in 1932, the president of the Machine Tool Trade Association noted that "Russia is the only country in the world which is engaged on a wide scheme of industrialisation and consequently it is from Russia alone that large-scale orders for industrial plant are available."[118] The usually anti-Soviet *Spectator* considered that Germany and America were "eager enough to snatch Russia's orders that might be keeping British workmen employed."[119] British politicians argued that Germany had used its credit position to Russia to increase trade and so build its industrial capacity, and that Britain should extend loans to offset such competition. Interestingly, at least one politician making this argument explicitly highlighted the *creditworthiness* of the Soviet Union in the fifteen years since the end of the civil war, noting in 1935 that, "after the crisis of 1931 Germany defaulted widely on her foreign commitments. Russia, on the other hand, has repaid in full."[120] In emphasizing the creditworthiness of the new Russia—perceived as paying its *own* debts in full if not that of its predecessor regimes—this hinted at a discontinuous, non-statist approach to understanding sovereign reputation.

Although no formal long-term bond lending became available from British markets, and trade credits were much more closely linked to particular expenditures than were previous railroad and municipal bonds, the Soviet Union was able to gain significant development financing through this method alone. British companies were also increasingly willing to return to Russian investments, even concluding agreements to export "stolen oil." Particularly in the 1930s, British capital flowed in this way into the Soviet regime, repeating its early twentieth-century interest in oil extraction and mining.[121] The British government brought up the long-standing question of tsarist-era claims during May 1930 commercial negotiations, but by then had less bargaining power than before. Whereas earlier even the extension of export credits had been made conditional, by the end of the 1920s the Soviet Union had secured sufficient credit to reindustrialize, and there was less pressure for it to grant further concessions.[122]

GERMANY AND THE EUROPEAN COUNTERFACTUAL

While the rising German state had played an increasingly important role in pre-World War I European finance, France and Great Britain were much more important creditors to tsarist Russia. Germany's lesser exposure, in conjunction with the more amicable end to war hostilities and its pressing need to redevelop economic capacities, moderated Germany's post-World War I relations with the Soviet regime. The bilateral relationship was not burdened by the issue of intergovernmental war debts, and although Germany briefly served as Russia's main creditor after a post-1875 worsening of Anglo-Russian relations, it was far less enmeshed in pre-1914 Russian investment. German Chancellor Otto von Bismarck had imposed a ban on Russian securities in 1887, enabling France to become the dominant Russian creditor and dampening lending to Russia even past an 1894 Russian-German trade agreement.[123] By 1914, out of a total of 23.5 billion marks of German long-term foreign investment, Russia accounted for only 1.8 billion marks.[124]

After World War I, Germany was certainly the most eager in Europe to resuscitate its economic relationship with Russia, with some attempts to trade even during the Russian Civil War in 1919.[125] This relationship picked up after the 1922 Treaty of Rapallo, in which the two parties reciprocally renounced war claims and losses, and in which Germany agreed to renounce compensation for nationalized property so long as the Soviet regime did not grant compensation to other nationals.[126] Germany became a major trading partner of the Soviet Union in short order, and the ability to trade with the new Russia—and particularly to develop and export major industrial manufacture—likely played a role in the revitalization of Germany's industrial capacity.[127] Much of the available capital in Germany during the 1920s went west to reparations payments, and granting any early credits may also have been limited by Allied disapproval of explicit advances to the Soviet regime.[128] However, Germany over time did begin to extend significant trade financing to the Soviet Union.[129]

Interpreting history through counterfactuals is inevitably tricky, but thinking through alternative trajectories can shed light on what in fact proved central at a given moment. Had the former World War I Allies reached a broader intergovernmental agreement, Western European financial relations with the new Soviet regime may have been more moderated—even without any acknowledgment of the tsarist debt. While a general agreement proved elusive, even in this failure differences surfaced in the responses and latent openings to the Soviet regime. Given the great interest in resuscitating the Russian market, especially in Great Britain, the absence of intervening political and diplomatic variables might have led the British and French paths in particular to diverge even more. Thus, although the European reaction to the repudiation was negative, gradations in response emerged due to both previous Russian exposure as well as domestic political ideologies and exigencies. Such variations, which at points hinted at the possibility of non-statist financial relations, could have gone even further under different circumstances.

Disagreement in American Capital

Given the extreme financial difficulties of the European powers, and especially of the formerly dominant British and French capital markets, the importance of the United States in any return of capital to the new Russia was clear relatively early. The *New York Times,* reporting at the 1922 Genoa Conference, noted that "the insistence of the Soviet on foreign financial aid as a necessary condition to Russia's salvation serves to turn all eyes toward the United States, for it seems to be recognized that effective succor for Russia is impossible without the participation of American capital."[130] At the center of this stood the US government, which acted as a gatekeeper to private American capital and had been a creditor to the previous Russian regimes—both directly and also through its extensive lending to Great Britain and France. As such the actions of the American government and other major financial actors, effectively at the core of European debt circulation, were central to how the Soviet economic story unfolded.

It is common to think of a particular country's financiers as a unified group with largely shared interests. This expectation may well hold in certain contexts, and plays out to some degree in the French case. However, I argue that the US situation after World War I counters the idea that "finance" or even "American finance" necessarily acts with one voice in sovereign debt and reputation. There was significant disaggregation among US creditor institutions in their interpretation of the risks involved in continuing relations with the new Soviet regime after repudiation. Although many of the older European-linked financial houses shied away from Soviet financing, other institutions—along with many major industrial actors—expressed greater interest, and even actively attempted to facilitate the issuance of long-term Soviet securities. This element of the story, necessarily overlooked by studies from political science or economics that rely heavily on final bond issue numbers, suggests that the failure to lend more extensively and openly did not result from a uniform interpretation of Soviet creditworthiness following the repudiation. Rather, to an important extent it had more to do with obstacles posed by US government policy and broader political ideology.

Opposition from Establishment Financiers

Perhaps the most significant long-run economic shift resulting from World War I was the rise of the United States as a major international player and a key creditor. The United States initially achieved its financial position due to Europe's fiscal need during World War I. However, the postwar world saw the United States emerge as a fully fledged international creditor nation in its own right. The new Soviet regime understood very well that this presented an opportunity to obtain financing and technical expertise from new sources, and made significant efforts to woo American business.[131] While it successfully obtained sufficient short-term credit and technical aid to trade and redevelop infrastructure, American financiers differed in their interest in facilitating longer-term credits and loans for Soviet Russia. Those financial institutions that had been more exposed to prerevolution Russian finance tended to be most prominent in speaking against the extension of both long-term financing and diplomatic recognition. In particular, major East Coast banks that had prewar links to Europe were the most hostile to financing the new regime, frowning even upon the extension of anything beyond the shortest-term trade credits.

Prior to 1914, US financial institutions primarily focused on import financing and domestic investment,[132] and they remained minor players in international finance compared to their British, French, and German counterparts. US foreign investment stood at $3.5 billion in 1913, only about 2 percent of national wealth (compared to numbers of $19.5 billion foreign investment and 25 percent of national wealth for the United Kingdom).[133] Moreover, the United States as a whole was a debtor nation by about $3.7 billion. World War I shifted American interest overseas to a considerable extent, and left the United States a net creditor by $12.5 billion. Although intergovernmental war debt made up over $9 billion of this amount, private lending that had picked up during the war continued afterward on a more aggressive scale.[134] Of a piece with the relatively limited US involvement in international lending prior to World War I, American investment in pre-1914 Russia was minor, especially when compared to European investment.[135] A US Department of Commerce study after the war also noted that "half a dozen large American concerns hold practically all of American claims against Russia."[136] This lack of prewar involvement, in conjunction with the fairly shallow US ties with the tsarist government, could have made the United States more fertile soil for Russian borrowing even in the absence of any agreement with largely European bondholders.

Still, many of the most established American financial institutions were wary of lending to the Soviet regime after the repudiation, and continued to insist that the new regime should accept the obligations of its predecessor. Although these banks were far less exposed than their counterparts in Paris or even London, they tended to have strong links with continental financial centers and did participate in European-led bond syndicates. In the late nineteenth century and early twentieth century, closer business ties and faster telecommunications resulted in considerable integration among the main financial centers, and securities were frequently simultaneously floated in several major exchanges.[137] Certain New York banks established close links with the London capital market and to an important degree these banks were integrated into wider European networks. J. P. Morgan in New York worked closely with its London counterpart; Kidder, Peabody & Co. was the exclusive agent for Barings; and August Belmont & Co. served as the Rothschild agent.[138] Kidder Peabody had participated in Russian government bond sales since 1889 and was more involved than any other US bank. J. P. Morgan had been heavily courted by the tsarist government and did subscribe to an 1898 bond sale along with Kidder Peabody, August Belmont, and the National City Bank (Citigroup's early precursor).[139] He came close to arranging several New York-led securities issuances and was a syndicate member for a Russian railroad loan, but ultimately considered Russia too unknown and never engaged in larger-scale Russian financing.[140] Two more US-based institutions also had been involved in prewar Russia. National City Bank had over $22 million in Russia assets at the time of the revolution,[141] and New York Life Insurance had Russian investments of over $26 million by 1913, including state bank deposits and state and state-guaranteed railroad bonds.[142]

Perhaps as a result of these links and in response to the related losses they did incur due to the revolution, these financial institutions tended to be the most hostile to Soviet financing. The president of National City Bank, as head of the Committee for Protection of Creditors, encouraged the State Department to delay relations with the Soviet regime until after the resolution of creditor claims.[143] When other financial institutions attempted to move beyond approved short-term financing arrangements, J. P. Morgan, National City Bank, and anticommunist citizens' groups wrote formal complaints to the US government.[144] Some members of Congress believed that these tsarist debt holders were so powerful that they were responsible for American troops remaining in Russia through most of 1920, well after the final outcome of the civil war became clear.[145] In any case, these creditors supported and helped to police the established policy, strengthening the illusion of a unified front against financing the Soviet regime.

ATTEMPTS AT NEW LENDING

This hostility to postrevolution Russian borrowing was *not* universal, however. In particular, a new range of banks rose to challenge the American financial institutions that had dominated US-based international finance prior to 1914.[146] Some of these, which had not participated significantly in previous Russian business, pushed the envelope in extending financing to the Soviet regime—at first through major trade credit and then even attempting to facilitate longer-term loans. These forgotten efforts, which would not be evident in the historical bond float data, challenge the view of a uniform response to the Soviet repudiation. They further suggest that these institutions implicitly worked within a non-statist financial framework more permissive of post-default lending, and might have entered into long-term lending had a different set of political circumstances prevailed.

These up-and-coming institutions in international finance, including Chase National, Guaranty Trust, and Equitable Trust, initially began by extending trade credits from short- to medium-term and by granting substantial spending limits. Chase National Bank was among the most prominent and aggressive of these institutions, with a Chase vice president serving as president of the American-Russian Chamber of

Commerce. Chase began its more substantial efforts at Soviet involvement in the mid-1920s by providing financing for cotton shipments, the most important US export to the Soviet Union until it was surpassed by manufactured goods in 1928.[147] Chase had initially provided financing of $2 million for the cotton syndicate, which was backed by a Soviet state guarantee, and then increased its financing to $15 million and finally $30 million in 1926. Equitable Trust, reassured by a 50 percent guarantee by the Soviet state bank, also began financing for Moscow around this time. National City, a previous Russian creditor, was unhappy with Chase's entry into more significant Soviet financing, although it could not actually prevent these actions by its major competitors.[148]

Likely buoyed by the successful extension of these larger trade credits, Chase along with the Amalgamated Bank of New York, the Amalgamated Bank of Chicago, and the Bank of Italy in San Francisco (soon to develop into the Bank of America) decided to go even further. These banks, led by Chase, attempted in 1928 to actually facilitate the sale of longer-term Soviet government-backed railroad bonds in the US—securities very similar to those that had made up a significant portion of the prewar tsarist-era debt. The central obstacle to the project was that the US government opposed the issuance of long-term loans of this type. As such, the $30 million bond issue was technically authorized in Moscow, but—as promoted in a January 1928 *New York Times* advertisement—coupon payments of principal and interest could be made in dollars through the participating American banks, and the bonds could be purchased by mail in the United States[149] The State Department interpreted this bank participation as an unsubtle attempt to sell Soviet bonds in the United States.[150] It had received protests from a range of organizations, including the New York Life Insurance Company, which held significant prewar Russian railway securities. New York Life argued that the Soviet regime was being assisted "to realize on the credit of the Russian railways, while at the same time repudiating the earlier obligations of the same railways."[151] Under subsequent State Department pressure, the Bank of Italy withdrew immediately and Chase and Chicago Amalgamated eventually stated that they would not make payment on the coupons. Chase optimistically wrote to the State Department that they would withdraw from the scheme "until further advice of any change in policy."[152]

In another less direct effort to provide longer-term financing to the Russian regime, W. A. Harriman asked the State Department about the possibility of floating a $25–35 million loan on the American market. This loan would formally be extended to a German export company, which would in turn use the credit for Russian financing. The Department responded negatively, noting, "in its essence, the proposed transaction would be Russian financing and in effect the flotation in the United States of a loan for the purpose of making an advance to the Soviet regime."[153] The State Department also undermined a 1927 attempt by the financier Percival Farquhar to issue in the United States $20 million in bonds with which the Soviet government could purchase German goods and a 1926 effort by the New York Trust Company to discount Russian obligations endorsed by German firms and the German government.[154] In its response to the New York Trust Company, the government used its standard language to indicate that it "would not view with favor" the proposed Russian financing.[155] A 1928 attempt by Farquhar to extend a $40 million advance, to be financed through a loan flotation, was similarly rebuffed.[156]

The American Locomotive Sales Corporation also inquired about the possibility of granting to Soviet agencies credit of five years or more, which would likely be financed through securities sold to the public. Interestingly, it specifically emphasized the *creditworthiness* of the Soviet regime, noting that US bankers and manufacturers extending mid-range credits found that Soviet agencies "have lived up scrupulously to the terms of every agreement and transaction," and that when large credits were extended by German and British manufacturers, "the payments on such credits were made punctually when due."[157] Although the State Department allowed American Locomotive to extend longer-term credit for railroad equipment purchases, it insisted that it "would not view with favor any financial arrangement which involved the sale of securities to the public."[158]

Another interesting instance, though more deeply subterranean as an attempted loan, involved a 1928 arrangement between the Soviet regime and Averell Harriman (associated with Guaranty Trust) to liquidate a manganese concession Harriman had held since 1925.[159] The initial concession itself aroused the ire of other Western governments when it came to light, with Great Britain arguing that Harriman had received the 1925 concession "for the purposes of establishing the fact that a big American concern had taken the properties which belonged to foreign concerns and thereby recogniz[ed] the right of the Soviet Government to nationalize property."[160] In August 1928, Harriman agreed to a compensation payment for the estimated $3.5 million initial investment along with an additional $1 million for a total of $4.45 million. This payment, however, was not immediate but would involve the transfer of 20-year bonds at 6–7 percent interest to be arranged by Chase National. The US

consul in Riga, Latvia, called the supplemental amount a loan, and the
State Department also viewed it skeptically, noting that "it would appear
that Harriman and Company has advanced to the Soviet Government
a sum of approximately $1,000,000."[161] However, the Department de-
clined to investigate further, given that the agreement was presented as
compensation for the original concession.

These financiers and industrial manufacturers did take additional risks
to move beyond their competitors in postrevolution Russian financing.
However, they were not alone in hoping for better economic relations
and easier credit for the Soviet Union. In particular, as in the British
case, the poor economic situation and the threat of overseas competition
during the 1920s made Soviet opportunities more attractive to many. As
early as 1919, the National Association of Manufacturers declared that
"many thousands of [US] manufacturers would be in a position to do
business with Russia,"[162] and American cotton dealers were especially
enthusiastic about the increased availability of bank financing for Soviet
purchases in the mid-1920s. The head of the largest brokerage, which
unsuccessfully lobbied for more significant shifts in the government's
Russia policy, noted, "These purchases have come at a time when our
own textile industry has been passing through the greatest depression
perhaps in its history. . . . We have found a sorely needed outlet in Russia."[163] These actors were keenly aware that Soviet business might easily
go elsewhere in the absence of cooperation and credit from the US government. Indeed, as Antony Sutton amply demonstrates in his three-vol-
ume study of Western assistance for Soviet economic development, many
major manufacturers extended credit on their own and "statements that
the Soviet Union developed without foreign financial assistance are seen
to be manifestly untrue."[164]

In short, the American financial and business response to the Soviet
repudiation was far from uniform. Some actors, in particular those with
prewar involvement in European-led financing, were noticeably hostile.
But other financial institutions were far more interested in extending and
facilitating credit, and were supported in this orientation by the competition for major business resulting from economic conditions in the United
States. This differential interest in new lending points to competing interpretations of the meaning and import of repudiation, and, in particular,
of Russian creditworthiness. Each American effort at postrepudiation
Soviet financing, which might have otherwise deepened into a more extensive financial relationship, was stopped by ultimately nonfinancial
obstacles. In particular, US government policy and larger political issues
between the United States and the Soviet Union stood in the way.

POLITICAL IDEOLOGY AND CIVILIZED LAW

We often make a distinction between political actors and financial actors in assessing the reaction to a major economic event. While this distinction is valid and important, it is easy to miss significant interrelations if any such analysis is too deeply bifurcated. Through the 1920s, US government policy was incredibly important in shaping the American financial response to the Russian Revolution and repudiation. While maintaining an official policy of neutrality with regard to Soviet trade relations, the government blocked a number of important and potentially pivotal longer-term financial transactions. The reasons for this included a concern with Soviet propaganda in the United States, anticommunist ideological opposition to the Russian regime, and a normative commitment to principles of debt continuity associated with "civilized international law." Ignoring the important government role in the inability of the Soviet regime to obtain credit—apparent in government correspondence with American business—skews the lessons of the case for thinking broadly about debt and reputation.

The Soviet Union did not receive diplomatic recognition from the United States until 1933, well after international lending had fallen into disrepute with the onset of the Great Depression. In the decade and a half prior, the State Department had effectively instituted a policy against advancing American capital to the Soviet regime. The Securities and Exchange Commission, now the federal government agency tasked with regulating securities offered to the public, was not founded until 1934, sixteen years after the Soviet repudiation. State laws relevant to issuing securities similarly provided little bar to Soviet lending.[165] Instead, the State Department enforced its policy according to a March 1922 statement or informal ruling. The key portion of this "Statement for the Press on Flotations of Foreign Loans" noted,

> The flotation of foreign bond issues in the American market is assuming an increasing importance and on account of the bearing of such operations upon the proper conduct of affairs, it is hoped that American concerns that contemplate making foreign loans will inform the Department of State in due time of the essential facts and subsequent developments of importance. . . . The Department will then give the matter consideration and . . . endeavor to say whether objection to the loan in question does or does not exist.[166]

The statement acknowledged, "The Department of State cannot, of course, require American bankers to consult it," but averred that, "in view of the possible national interests involved," the government should have the opportunity to provide its opinion. A fairly regularized procedure evolved around this language, and there is no evidence to suggest that banking houses ever failed to submit potential loan issuances to the State Department.[167] According to a commentator writing in 1928, "the banking house receives a reply within a few days and even within a few hours. The need of a quick response becomes more pressing as the competition of British and Continental banking houses for international loans becomes keener."[168]

In line with this process, the State Department enforced its goals primarily through voluntary correspondence with American financiers. On loans to the Soviet government in particular, Secretary Kellog summarized the policy in 1928:

> The department objects to financial arrangements involving the flotation of a loan in the United States or the employment of credit for the purpose of making an advance to the Soviet Regime. In accordance with this policy the department does not view with favor financial arrangements designed to facilitate in any way the sale of Soviet bonds in the United States. The department is confident that the banks and financial institutions will cooperate with the government in carrying out this policy.[169]

This policy was reiterated in response to a senator's inquiry into Russia policy, confirming that the government viewed "with disfavor the flotation of a loan in the United States or the employment of American credit for the purpose of making an advance to a regime which has repudiated the obligations of Russia to the United States and its citizens and confiscated the property of American citizens in Russia."[170] In rejecting the attempted $25 million loan issue by W. A. Harriman & Co. in 1926, the State Department used very similar language. It indicated that it "would not view with favor" the transaction, which it considered to be a loan flotation to a regime which "has repudiated Russia's obligations to the United States and to American nationals."[171] In a similar 1927 response to a request from the American Locomotive Sales Corporation about the possibility of issuing Russian securities for sale to the US public, the State Department responded as follows:

> The Department has objected . . . to financial projects involving the flotation of loans in the American market, and to banking arrangements not incidental to the sale of American commodities to the Soviet regime, which, as you know, has repudiated the obligations of Russia to the United States and its citizens, and confiscated the property of American citizens in Russia. . . . The Department . . . would not view with favor any financial arrangement which involved the sale of securities to the public.[172]

In conjunction with clear State Department policy on the Soviet regime, the US Treasury also refused to accept and assess Soviet gold at its assay offices. In an April 1921 note, the State Department indicated in response to a Treasury inquiry that it could "not give any assurance that the title to Soviet gold will not be subject to attack, internationally or otherwise."[173] This policy, which was reasserted on several occasions through the 1920s, made it difficult for the regime to maintain gold reserves in the United States, which otherwise may have facilitated its obtaining more credit on better terms. When Chase National Bank and Equitable Trust attempted to present $5 million in gold to the US assay office in New York, as agents of the National Bank of Soviet Russia, the Treasury refused to accept it.[174]

Despite the disunity in business and financial circles about long-term credit for the Soviet regime, the government itself constructed a relatively unified American front. This US policy was influenced by political concerns about a propagandistic revolutionary Russia, and also by normative commitments to the continuity of sovereign property obligations. In its 1927 response to the American Locomotive inquiry, the State Department noted that it aimed

> to exercise pressure . . . to the end that this regime may eventually come to realize the necessity of abandoning its interference in the domestic affairs of the United States and of recognizing the international obligations devolving upon it with respect to the indebtedness of Russia to the United States and its citizens, and with respect to the property of American citizens in Russia.[175]

It stated that, given this aim, it should follow "that the Department view with disfavor all financial arrangements, whether in the form of bond issues or long term bank credits . . . which would result in making financial resources available to the Soviet Government."[176] Indeed, like Great Britain, the United States was periodically caught in the grip of anticommunist and thus anti-Soviet sentiment. Almost immediately after the 1918 Russian Revolution, and no doubt partially in response to Lenin's "Letter to American Workers" of August 20, 1918, the American government became especially concerned with the possibility of rising communist sentiment among the working classes. The Senate established a subcommittee on Bolshevik propaganda, New York state troopers stormed the preliminary commercial bureau established by a Soviet representative, and the US attorney general launched an offensive against suspected radicals and their sympathizers.[177] Although this first Red Scare died down after the US withdrawal from the Russian Civil War and the reestablishment of trading relations, hostility and suspicion remained in US government and business circles and in segments of the general public. The concern about communist propaganda, along with debt recognition, remained at the top of the American agenda for Soviet relations for some time.

The government's accompanying pronouncements on credit policy and recognition ultimately reiterated a strict vision of sovereign debt continuity. In calling the Soviet regime an "outlaw state" and decrying its repudiation of the previous regime's debt, the United States drew upon the statist tenets of international law dominant through the nineteenth century but still very present into the twentieth. It minimized the relevance of alternative non-statist political conceptions also afoot, which it had relied upon itself in the Cuban context after 1898. These statist ideas of "civilized international law" were most associated with the highly legalized State Department. Robert Lansing, Woodrow Wilson's secretary of state during the Soviet rise to power and the architect of the US approach, was certainly deeply grounded in this establishment framework, as a founder of the American Society of International Law and the former principal legal advisor at the State Department. Historian Katherine Siegel suggests that "[Lansing's] legal background was not conducive to friendly relations with the Soviets, whom he thought had done little but flout international rules."[178]

While this debt and nonrecognition policy was initiated during the Wilson administration, which propagated a similar nonrecognition policy for nonconstitutionally formed Latin American governments,[179] it was continued by subsequent administrations. Although Warren Harding had campaigned in part against Wilson's "idealism" and even promised to take a different approach to the Soviet Union, his state and commerce secretaries ultimately held the line on Russia policy. His secretary of state, Charles Hughes, served on the US Supreme Court both before and after his tenure in Harding's cabinet, and took center stage in maintaining a Russia policy drawn from fairly traditional visions of international law. Emphasizing the continuing importance of debt recognition as a legal and political issue, Hughes in 1923 noted that "the fundamental question in the recognition of a government is whether it shows ability and a disposition to discharge international obligations. . . . It's a question of principle."[180] This stance aggravated those advocating for Soviet recognition, such as former governor of Indiana James Goodrich, who considered Hughes's "technical lawyer" perspective unproductive.[181] Commerce Secretary Hoover, notwithstanding his work to facilitate Soviet trade and eventually commercial credits, shared Hughes's basic principles on this point. As Siegel suggests,

His litmus test for recognition was one issue: debts. . . . Central to Herbert Hoover's outlook, and a reflection of his Quaker upbringing, was a passion for cooperation and voluntarism, whether among nations abroad or businesses at home. Soviet Russia, in his view, had showed it would not cooperate with the maxims of international law by its repudiation of foreign debts and nationalization of properties.

Siegel argues that Hoover's emphasis on debt recognition suggests that he was less caught up in anti-Soviet ideology and more upset by Moscow's refusal to conform to what he considered "civilized international behavior."[182]

What emerges from the historical record is that the US foreign policy establishment had a clear vision of what did and did not constitute appropriate American lending behavior to the Soviet regime—a much clearer and more unified vision than that presented by financial institutions themselves. This was not driven by its narrow pecuniary interests alone, as the US government's own claims seem to have been significantly satisfied by the sale of Russian property on American soil.[183] Concerns about the political character and international intent of the new Russian regime, along with a strict adherence to the continuity of state obligations as a point of principle, nonetheless made the US government an essential player in determining the financial consequences of the Soviet repudiation. Far from playing a secondary role, anticommunist ideology and political-legal sentiment crucially shaped the response to the Soviet debt repudiation, making the creditor outcome appear to fall much more in line with a uniformly statist reputational assessment than in fact was the case.

The Untenability of Assuming Creditor Uniformity

Given the devastation of Europe during the First World War, it is not surprising that the new Russian regime would turn to the United States in particular to obtain financing for its post-civil war revitalization. But in line with statist expectations of creditworthiness, the Soviet Union was unable to borrow significantly after its repudiation—not only in the European markets but also in the relatively new American market. If we consider only quantitative financial data on new debt issues during the 1920s, the reputational interpretation of the Soviet repudiation seems to have been consistently negative. No new sovereign or railroad securities of the type so prevalent in tsarist financing are listed, and many investors and commentators were vocally wary after such a major financial upheaval. Even without any creditor collusion or embargo, we might conclude that the politically willful new Russia—even more than other defaulting countries—had difficulty financing on the basis of a tarred reputation alone.[184]

While aspects of this analysis may be true, taking a closer look at the Soviet case suggests a different story. It is easy to forget that financial data (like all data) is already predigested to some degree, giving only the final outcome and covering over any preceding efforts or disagreements. Looking more carefully at the historical record indicates that creditors exhibited divergent interpretations of the Russian action. In Europe, France was the most hostile and the least willing to extend financing, likely reflecting its more significant exposure to earlier Russian borrowing. London, although a major capital center, was less involved in prewar lending to Russia and displayed greater flexibility. Little ultimately came of this, however, due to both its closer relationship with France and its significant anticommunist sentiment domestically. The United States is perhaps the most interesting case. While some lenders did treat the new regime as a financial pariah, others were surprisingly open. They started with relatively minor financing, as would befit a new and untested borrower, but then exhibited interest in facilitating longer-term loans. In this they were blocked not by their own reputational interpretations, which seemed to develop positively over time, but rather by the hostility of external governmental actors and the broader anti-Soviet social environment.

While it remains unclear how an alternative path might have developed, these efforts by American financial actors to move into long-term Soviet debt issuances were significant as important potential turning points. Had these overtures been allowed to proceed, there is little reason to believe that the Soviet regime would have been any less punctilious in this debt payment than they were in their careful and remarked-upon respect for trade credits. With this background, we can imagine that post-repudiation debt financing may not have appeared so alien in subsequent cases over the twentieth century. These instances therefore illustrate not only the disaggregated reputational risk interpretations implicated in the financial response to the Soviet repudiation, but also the role played by US government policy in maintaining the façade of a unified front. Due to concerns of domestic propaganda and civilized international law, as well as considerable political antipathy toward the regime itself, the government effectively monitored American institutions for compliance with a "no long-term credit" rule that obscured the creditor disagreement actually in existence.

The Forgotten Potential of the Soviet Repudiation

Contemporary discussion of the Soviet Union is deeply colored by the Cold War experience and by the knowledge of the regime's repugnant actions over the course of the twentieth century. It is now difficult to imagine the October Revolution carrying forward the banner of popular sovereignty unfurled by the American and French revolutions. It is similarly difficult to think of the Russian repudiation as a potential turning point for the sovereign debt regime. However, the repudiation itself was very much framed in the language of principle, and the subsequent negotiations—more so than is usually realized—centered as much on the legal-political theories of any possible grand bargain as on the actual financial outcome. The new regime effectively articulated an alternative conception of sovereignty for sovereign debt, which emphasized the idea of sovereign *dis*continuity in creditworthiness and suggested that public benefit should factor into assessing a debt's validity. Although the initial repudiation was absolute, in subsequent negotiations the Soviet regime actually indicated a willingness to acknowledge and repay a portion of the debt but held fast to the general principle of debt cancellation. This insistence on claims of right was especially problematic for the regime's immediate interlocutors—its erstwhile allies—who might have been willing to facilitate and encourage financing if the previous debts had been *acknowledged* in principle, even without being substantially repaid. The Soviet approach of repudiation, in contrast to one of quiet default, proved to be not an instance of cheap talk but rather a very costly decision on the part of the new regime.

Thus, while the Russian repudiation is frequently read as a cautionary tale, it also stands as a potential turning point and incubator for new practices and norms in sovereign debt. The reasons it did not become a stronger precedent have more to do with historical circumstance than with any necessary, ahistorical, and apolitical rules of reputation in sovereign lending. The Western powers' normative commitment to sovereign continuity in the Soviet case was caught up in anticommunist antipathy to the new regime, particularly in the British and American cases, making it difficult to disentangle this political aversion from a measured response to sovereign debt claims. Had the new regime been an (ultimately liberal) revolutionary government in the mode of the earlier American or French revolutions, it is possible that historical events might have unfolded differently.

Even as things developed, there was less consistency in creditor response than is usually acknowledged. Whereas the French response was extremely hostile, the British response was more measured; it might have been even more lenient if not for the Anglo-French relationship and anticommunist domestic sentiment. As for the crucial absence of American capital, the documentary evidence supports the argument that American government policy during the 1920s constituted a "virtual loan embargo," which effectively restricted long-term financial and commercial credit to the new Russian regime.[185] This virtual embargo was not created or enforced by bank collusion; indeed, this was not necessary and likely would not have been possible given varying bank interests. Instead, it was monitored by a government shaped by its own political concerns and normative visions. This in turn influenced the larger environment for lending, and quietly covered over the precedential potential of the Soviet case for shifting the norms and practices of the sovereign debt system going forward.

4

Costa Rica, Public Benefit, and the Rule of Law

> All the circumstances should have advised the Royal Bank that this
> . . . was for personal and not for legitimate government purposes.
> —US CHIEF JUSTICE WILLIAM HOWARD TAFT, *Tinoco Arbitration*

WHILE THE Soviet debt repudiation displayed all the political drama, financial consequence, and diplomatic tension a post-World War I newsroom could possibly wish for, on the other side of the globe Costa Rica undertook a similar action on a much smaller scale. The Costa Rican debt repudiation of 1920 has been largely forgotten in political science and economics, but features fairly prominently in international legal literature. Unlike the Soviet case, the Costa Rican repudiation was not a revolutionary rejection of multiple centuries of previous rule. Rather, it involved the denial of a brief authoritarian aberration in otherwise constitutional rule. The cases are similar, however, in using ideas of valid sovereign action that gained prominence in the World War I era to challenge the dominant statist insistence on sovereign debt continuity. And, as with the Soviet example, the Costa Rican repudiation and the subsequent creditor response suggest that there is more flexibility than is usually acknowledged in the norm of debt continuity and in the concept of sovereignty that could underpin a functioning debt regime. The fact that similar patterns are detectable in such radically different contexts only serves to make them more notable.

As with the Soviet case, Costa Rican arguments with regard to the repudiation rested on non-statist claims about political legitimacy, resonating with emerging ideas in early twentieth-century international relations. And these claims were not immediately rejected by the major creditors of the day. Although Great Britain, whose citizens' interests were most immediately at stake, responded with a narrowly statist interpretation of sovereign contract, the United States took a more neutral stance. Costa Rica's action was in fact validated by US chief justice and former president William Howard Taft sitting as arbitrator in what is popularly called the *Tinoco* arbitration. This decision, which is considered the leading arbitral authority on sovereign recognition—the practice of recognizing a sovereign state or government and thus granting it international legal status—is somewhat confusingly claimed by advocates of both sovereign debt continuity and an odious debt doctrine. I suggest that in fact it provides a novel combination of both rule-of-law and outcome-oriented aspects of sovereignty, offering a challenge to strictly statist approaches and allowing for repudiation in some cases.[1] I also note that the long-term consequences of the repudiation for Costa Rica's financial standing were relatively minimal, indicating that even at a purely reputational level this early twentieth-century precedent could have served as a turning point in sovereign debt norms. Finally, I look at the competitive 1920s economic and geopolitical context of the Caribbean, suggesting that this background may have encouraged variation among creditor countries and expanded the range of approaches to debt continuity considered plausible or desirable. As with the Soviet case, the Costa Rican example demonstrates the flexibility of sovereign debt norms and suggests that the early twentieth century might have provided a foundation for alternative approaches going forward.

Sovereign Legitimacy and Creditor Disagreement

The story of the 1917 Costa Rican coup, though unique in being relatively brief, parallels narratives that became alarmingly common in Latin America and elsewhere through the twentieth century. General Federico Tinoco, Minister of Defense at the time, overthrew Alfredo González Flores in January of 1917. González had lost significant support over his three and a half years in office, and Costa Rican elites in particular opposed his decision to institute property taxes and a progressive income tax in response to World War I trade difficulties.[2] Following the coup, Tinoco established a new cabinet and held elections of questionable validity in April 1917, initially garnering the support of domestic business interests and the acquiescence, if not the enthusiasm, of the broader population.[3] However, less than one year after coming to power, the Tinoco government had become increasingly repressive, and its financial and militarization policies diminished any local support it may have had.[4] Two and a half years of domestic unrest, counterrevolutionary activity, and uncertainty as to American and British intentions proved to be too much pressure. Tinoco entered into negotiations that led to his resignation on August 12, 1919, and his government fell the following month.[5]

Although regular elections and direct voting were not established in Costa Rica until 1912, the country had achieved considerable political stability relative to its Latin American neighbors.[6] After the restitution of constitutional government and the December 1919 election of Julio Acosta, the restored regime sought to expunge the Tinoco contracts from Costa Rica's debt. When the Costa Rican Congress passed the "Law of Nullities" (No. 41) to repudiate Tinoco's contracts, it distanced itself from the aberration of military rule and repudiated the dictatorial regime's political and financial legacy. The Costa Rican Congress did not intend this as a rebuff to international capital flows or to broader trade and investment. Rather, the language of the nullification decree and subsequent interactions mark out the possibility of an international economic framework resting upon non-statist visions of sovereign legitimacy.

Restoring Legitimate Government in Sovereign Contracts

The Costa Rican Constitutional Congress's initial repudiation and the country's arbitral presentation three years later make clear that, like the new Soviet regime in 1918, Costa Rica laid its claim on the basis of right. Regardless of the potential consequences of the action—of which the government was well aware—it persisted in distancing itself from what was considered a dictatorial usurpation. In fact, the decree was not uniformly supported and was reenacted by the legislature to override President Acosta's initial veto.[7] Acosta emphasized Costa Rica's positive international reputation just prior to the veto, noting, "As a happy exception, amongst the small countries of this Continent . . . our country has cultivated the most cordial international relations, and has imposed on itself the most trying sacrifices to comply, even in critical times, with the obligations created by foreign debts."[8] He expressed concern that enforcing Law No. 41 with regard to the British claimants would rupture this positive standing vis-à-vis Great Britain in particular.

Notwithstanding the hesitation of the executive, the constitutional congress went forward with the enforcement of the decree. The Law of Nullities "declared absolutely null and without legal value from their origin" both Tinoco's own constitution and "all the contracts celebrated between the Executive and private individuals, with or without the approbation of the Legislative Power" during his rule.[9] The law marked a clear challenge to the idea that sovereign debt contracts should be enforceable against a successor regime. In arguing that not all debts are created equal, Costa Rica's claims echoed the justifications of valid sovereignty at play in the World War I era, resonating in some cases with the arguments put forward by the Soviet Union. Both in the initial repudiation and in the subsequent arbitral argument, Costa Rica distinguished between legitimate rule and that of a usurper, highlighted the importance of genuine governmental purpose, insisted on adherence to internal laws, and maintained the ultimate authority of a rightful sovereign government to decide on the validity of its contracts.

THE EXISTENCE OF A VALID GOVERNMENT

Part of the Costa Rican argument lay with the fact that Tinoco had militarily usurped a constitutional republic that, by the standards of the day, reflected the popular will. In the repudiation law, the constitutional congress emphasized that the coup had replaced the previous republic with "an illegitimate and arbitrary regime which deprived citizens of all their political rights under the Constitution and their laws" and that the crime of military rebellion against the constitutional regime could not "produce legal effects nor in any case create the basis of legal rights."[10] In its presentation during the 1923 arbitration with Great Britain, Costa Rica pointed out that the 1871 Constitution "had never been legally displaced and continued in force in Costa Rica."[11] It suggested that the Tinoco regime "born of rape and treason . . . was predestined to a career of lawlessness and treachery," listing the decrees Tinoco enacted in violation of the constitution to effectively grant himself dictatorial powers.[12]

In addition to asserting that the Tinoco regime was illegitimate as a result of its usurpation, Costa Rica contended that the government was not even sufficiently established as to justify de facto recognition by other powers or by business interests. In making this claim, which would further render the regime's contracts presumptively null, it argued that the nonrecognition policy adopted by the United States should be taken as evidence of the regime's nongovernmental character.[13] In particular it noted that the usual practice of the United States was "to give recognition to the *de facto* status of a government when it can be regarded as established with the general consent and support of the people of its country and capable of performing its international obligations." This ostensibly nonideological policy (notwithstanding Woodrow Wilson's explicit wish to support only constitutional regimes) made the US decision against recognition all the more "authentic" as evidence of the regime's nongovernmental character.[14] Costa Rica further argued that the companies at issue would have been put on notice of this fact, given that their own governments failed to recognize the Tinoco regime.[15]

In addition, Costa Rica asserted that the Tinoco regime's contracts had violated particular laws of the republic and even had violated its own (questionably constitutional) laws. In the initial 1920 repudiation decree, the constitutional congress specifically highlighted that in addition to being "intrinsically null and of no value and effect" certain Tinoco contracts had violated more specific provisions in the previous fiscal law.[16] In the presentation of claims to the arbitral tribunal, Costa Rica argued that Tinoco had violated his own constitution by arrogating to himself the office of president, and by attempting to give several of the contracts that had been signed the status of law.[17] This conception of valid sovereign action as strictly defined and delimited by law was actually adopted in the arbitral decision, discussed later in this chapter, making attentiveness to *domestic* law a possible challenge to sovereign debt continuity in international law.

Legitimate Government Purpose and the Primacy of Sovereignty

As with the new Soviet government, the Costa Rican Congress made an effort to distinguish between more and less legitimate debt expenditures on the basis of their ultimate purpose. The new Soviet regime had not only generally relied on the oppressive nature of tsarist rule, but also specifically denied the validity of the World War I debt and Russian Civil War compensation claims—debts that had been incurred to serve the Allies' own strategic goals rather than to meet the needs of the broader Russian population. In a similar vein, Costa Rica contended that a major agreement for the Amory oil concession was not signed in the best interest of the country. It pointed out that the very same British oil company had made an offer on more favorable terms for Costa Rica to the legitimate González administration, but that the offer had been rejected prior to the Tinoco regime. Costa Rica suggested that "the explanation of the [Tinoco regime's] acceptance of their less advantageous later offer is found in the fact that, as they well knew, they were dealing with an irregular and illegitimate regime, and the advantages which should have been secured to the public were diverted to other channels."[18] It further argued, "It is common knowledge that the terms of the Concession Agreement were inequitable and unfair to the national interests of Costa Rica and the course of the events and proceedings resulting in the making of this Concession Agreement confirm the suspicion of official malfeasance which its terms suggest."[19] Although developing an oil concession might generally be a legitimate public purpose, the particular circumstances of the Tinoco agreement raised questions as to whether it was negotiated primarily for the public good. On a smaller scale, the Costa Rican government made a similar argument about a loan extended to benefit Tinoco and his brother, which seemed to serve no genuine governmental purpose and therefore raised the particular ire of the restored regime.[20]

While the constitutional congress ultimately did validate certain of the governmental measures undertaken by the Tinoco regime, it maintained that these affirmations were exceptions to the general principle of repudiation, undertaken in accordance with good faith and public policy.[21] In this, the Costa Rican decision was similar to the ultimate Soviet argument, which insisted on repudiation as a point of principle but indicated a willingness to pay certain claims (particularly those of small bondholders) in the context of a larger agreement. Although it was eventually willing to submit particular claims to the arbitral tribunal, Costa Rica also insisted that the country itself was the final arbiter on the invalidity of the Tinoco regime's claims:

> The nullity of all the acts and proceedings of the Tinoco regime was definitively settled by a decree of the Constitutional Congress of Costa Rica, which was the highest and ultimate authority having jurisdiction upon that subject, and its decision on that question, made in the exercise of the sovereign rights of the people of Costa Rica, is not open for review by any outside authority.[22]

It further pointed out that, with regard to the particular claims before the tribunal, at least one of the business claimants, upon accepting a charter to do business in the country, had already agreed to decide matters in Costa Rican tribunals and to renounce the power to invoke foreign laws.[23]

In line with the argument distinguishing Tinoco-era contracts from those of the earlier constitutional regime, Costa Rica continued to make payment on pre-Tinoco debt throughout this controversy. Moody's Investor Services noted that in December of 1916, on the eve of Tinoco's January 1917 takeover, Costa Rica's public debt was just under $21 million, resulting from two bond series issued in London, Paris, Hamburg, and New York.[24] Neither Moody's nor diplomatic or press coverage describes a default on either debt issuance at or after the time of the controversy.[25] Although the Costa Rican Constitutional Congress dismissed President Acosta's concern that the repudiation decree would sully the country's creditworthiness, it remained committed to paying non-Tinoco debt, in line with the expectations of a non-statist reputational mechanism.[26]

Creditor Disunity in the Immediate Response

Accepting the debt continuity norm as a market principle suggests that creditors should uniformly reject claims for discontinuity and should also decline to lend after financial disruptions, even despite major regime changes. But, as in the Soviet case, Costa Rica's main diplomatic interlocutors, the United States and the United Kingdom, did not offer a unified response. Great Britain decided to pursue claims on behalf of two British companies, insisting on the continuity of obligations even while acknowledging the usurpation of constitutional rule. The American administration, on the other hand, had actively refused to recognize the Tinoco regime and chose to remain neutral on the Costa Rican repudiation.

WOODROW WILSON'S INSISTENCE ON CONSTITUTIONAL REPUBLICS

Woodrow Wilson's declared commitment to self-determination and constitutional government, which I discussed in the previous chapter, found a foreign policy outlet after the Tinoco coup. To support this ideal, Wilson had established a policy of not recognizing governments in Central America that came to power through unconstitutional means. In addition to a genuine concern with constitutional and preferably self-determining government, Wilson hoped that this approach would help to break the Central American "cycle of violence," in which governments rose and fell with alarming regularity.[27] In line with this policy, the United States withheld recognition of the new Tinoco regime in Costa Rica, publicizing in Central American capitals that it would "not give recognition or support to any government which may be established unless it is clearly proven that it is elected by legal and constitutional means."[28] It also actively discouraged US companies from entering into business in the country, issuing a press release to advise that it would "not consider any claims which may in the future arise from such dealings, worthy of its diplomatic support."[29]

The Wilson administration maintained this policy despite the concerted lobbying of both the Tinoco government and the powerful American-owned United Fruit Company and its founder, Minor Keith.[30] Such lobbying may in fact have been counterproductive, as Wilson personally disliked these elite Americans in Costa Rica, considering them unpatriotic and even asking the Department of Justice to consider prosecuting Keith.[31] Wilson also maintained the nonrecognition policy in the face of resistance from within his own administration. The policy was unpopular in the cabinet due to the geopolitical context of World War I, and Wilson may have been the only member of his foreign policy team that wholeheartedly supported it. His secretary of state, Robert Lansing, urged the recognition of the Tinoco government in light of concerns about German interest in the vulnerable Caribbean basin.[32] Although Wilson's nonrecognition policy was not able to forestall all political and economic relations with Costa Rica, it did eventually help to weaken the Tinoco regime, in part by throwing the local economy into disarray.[33]

The United States did not support the military removal of Tinoco, but did indicate a degree of acquiescence by extending recognition to Costa Rica again upon the return of the previous regime's representatives. Having welcomed the return of the constitutional republic, the United States chose to remain neutral upon the passage of Law No. 41 and the nullification of the Tinoco regime's acts. This decision was no doubt buttressed by the absence of any strong US claims affected by the decree. A range of agreements, including those involving American interests, had been signed or ratified during the Tinoco administration. But in diplomatic correspondence with the State Department, the US consul indicated that four countries—not including the United States — were most affected by the nullification of foreign concessions.[34] It briefly appeared that there might be an American oil concession at stake in the Costa Rican legislation, which could have encouraged a different response. However, this never materialized, and the United States ultimately did not take sides on the nullification issue.[35] The American delegation in San José kept the State Department informed of developments, including the British actions in particular, but refused to support the British demand for arbitration on the validity of the Amory concession.[36]

RELUCTANT NONRECOGNITION AND A
DECISION TO PRESS BRITISH CLAIMS

Great Britain took a very different approach after the Costa Rican repudiation. At the insistence of the United States—a key wartime ally— Great Britain had also withheld official recognition from the Tinoco regime. However, British Foreign Office telegrams indicate that the British approach to recognition during World War I, particularly with regard to Costa Rica, was "really that of the United States and not [Britain's] own invention."[37] Notwithstanding their government's decision, and thus potentially forfeiting diplomatic protection if things went awry, several British companies took the risky step of extending their economic involvement in Costa Rica under Tinoco. Two transactions gained particular significance after the repudiation decree. First, British interests through an American front company purchased the "Amory concession" for oil exploration. Second, the Royal Bank of Canada provided a line of credit to Costa Rica under Tinoco's control.

In post-Tinoco diplomatic correspondence with Costa Rica, the British government rejected both the importance of its own nonrecognition policy and the relevance of governmental legitimacy for a regime's ability to sign contracts. In insisting that a regime had this ability by virtue of its control over the country, Great Britain effectively espoused a traditionally statist conception of sovereignty for sovereign contracting. It contended,

> The recognition or non-recognition of a Government by another is a question of judgment and policy on the part of a country and has nothing whatever to do with the actual existence of a de facto Government, it being the legitimate right of a foreign country or of its subjects or citizens to deal with the ruler of a country or with a Government actually recognized by the acquiescence of the Nation, in order to acquire a part of the public domain, or private properties which may have been confiscated, and as a principle, the acts of a de facto Government must be considered as valid by the legitimate Government upon the restoration of the latter, although the acts of the former may be considered by the restored Powers as those of a usurper.[38]

It further argued that the Amory company had invested large sums of money, and asked what would be done by the Costa Rican government to "maintain in full the legitimately acquired and valid rights" of the British subjects. The British government specifically contended that the Costa Rican action was "in so far as it affects the rights of foreigners in Costa Rica . . . contrary to the well-established principles of International Law."[39]

Although other countries' interests were affected, it seems that only Great Britain decided to pursue its claims. It did so aggressively, threatening a commercial boycott that would have significantly undermined Costa Rica's important coffee export industry.[40] In one of the last hurrahs of European gunboat diplomacy in the Western hemisphere, it went so far as to station a warship in Costa Rican waters.[41] Although President Acosta made an effort to compromise by agreeing to arbitration in early 1921, the Costa Rican Congress initially insisted that the British bank claim be brought in Costa Rican courts.[42] When the two countries eventually signed an arbitration treaty in March 1923, they disagreed again on the selection of who should hear the dispute.[43] Finally, President Acosta secured British agreement by suggesting the newly appointed US chief justice (and former president) William Howard Taft as sole arbitrator.[44]

As with the timing of the Soviet Revolution, Tinoco came to power at the height of World War I, during major shifts in the larger framework of international relations. Emerging ideas of non-statist sovereignty appeared not only in Costa Rica's own arguments but also surfaced in foreign policy approaches such as the US nonrecognition policy. This thinking encouraged the American administration to part from its British allies in its treatment of post-Tinoco Costa Rica and its response to the repudiation decree. Whereas Great Britain insisted on the continuity of obligations even in the face of an acknowledged coup, the United States remained neutral. Costa Rica's willingness to accept an American judge as arbitrator attests to the potency of this disunity between frequently allied creditor nations.

Establishment Validation and a Muted Creditor Response

While debt repudiations frequently elicit a response from creditors and other market actors, the Costa Rican case is unique in also giving rise to an arbitral award considered foundational in modern international legal practice. Unlike with the Soviet Union, the restored regime's decision to submit its disagreement to external review raised the risk of an unfavorable finding. But it also opened the possibility for a validation of its claims by a neutral adjudicator. Although arbitral awards do not have binding precedential value, they do grant an establishment imprimatur of sorts, and so can mark out actions and analytical frameworks as plausible and worthy of acceptance in international practice. For a government unilaterally repudiating a previous regime's contracts, both the risk of denunciation and the possibility of acquiescence would have had great import.

Justice Taft made his award in October of 1923, ultimately deciding in favor of Costa Rica on both the oil concession and line of credit claims, but in a somewhat roundabout way. He did not entirely subscribe to the argument of either party, providing instead an intermediate approach that incorporated attentiveness to internal law and appropriate governmental purpose as elements of enforceable sovereign action. In the portion of the *Tinoco Case* most frequently cited in international law textbooks, and seemingly in line with the statist British presentation, Justice Taft held that the Tinoco regime *was* indeed the sovereign government of Costa Rica, and that Great Britain's nonrecognition policy did not bar suit by British companies.[45] On the other hand, Taft's finding for Costa Rica is employed as possible precedent for solidifying non-statist approaches to debt continuity generally and even for resurrecting the formal odious debt doctrine, which explicitly asserts that the debts of an illegitimate government may fail to bind a state after that regime's downfall.[46] The fact that Taft settled on an intermediate approach, challenging strict practices of debt continuity—seemingly with no negative consequences for Costa Rica—deepens the empirical question of why only the statist element of this arbitral award found its way into sovereign debt norms over the course of the twentieth century.

A Conservative Foundation

It is rare for debtor states to be as bold as either the Soviet Union or Costa Rica in their economic dealings. In most cases, countries prefer the safer route of taking steps considered defensible by responsible international parties, even after a major regime change. Although a particular state's creditors and counterparties would hardly approve of any unilateral repudiation, debtor states contemplating such an action welcome any form of international acquiescence. Justice Taft's decision, representing as it does a fairly unadventurous approach that nonetheless departs from strict debt continuity, provides one possible route.

The *Tinoco* decision is characterized principally as a case about the recognition of sovereign states in international law, and as standing for a relatively conservative "effective control" test as to what constitutes a sovereign government. On the question of whether the Tinoco regime comprised the government of Costa Rica, Taft agreed with Great Britain: the Tinoco regime, at least for the majority of its tenure, was in de facto control of the state. This assessment accorded with the dominant statist principles of international law at the time, and continues to have resonance today. In his decision, Taft quoted J. B. Moore on sovereign continuity:

> Changes in the government or the internal policy of a state do not as a rule affect its position in international law. . . . though the government changes, the nation remains, with rights and obligations unimpaired. . . . The principle of the continuity of states has important results. The state is bound by engagements entered into by governments that have ceased to exist; the restored government is generally liable for the acts of the usurper. . . . The origin and organization of government are questions generally of internal discussion and decision. Foreign powers deal with the existing *de facto* government, when sufficiently established to give reasonable assurance of

its permanence, and of the acquiescence of those who constitute the state in its ability to maintain itself, and discharge its internal duties and its external obligations.[47]

Taft pointed out that for two years Tinoco and the legislative assembly ruled Costa Rica without serious revolutionary activity and with the apparent acquiescence of the people, despite the country's economic despondency.[48] He discounted the importance of other states' failures to recognize the Tinoco government, which Costa Rica presented as definitive evidence of the regime's nongovernmental character.[49] Taft concluded that, although a nonrecognition policy might have evidentiary weight as to a regime's status, it was not dispositive. He thought this was particularly the case given that the policy was "determined by inquiry, not into [the regime's] *de facto* sovereignty and complete governmental control, but into its illegitimacy or irregularity of origin."[50] This de facto control requirement continued the statist approach grounded in the international legal practice of the nineteenth century and before.

Justice Taft's decision thus explicitly countered the idea of a valid sovereign government put forward by Woodrow Wilson's nonrecognition policy, which acknowledged only those states formed by constitutional means. Any criticism of Wilson's policy, if Taft meant it as such, was not explicit. The arbitral award accepted that the decision of whether or not to recognize a foreign regime was a matter of national policy, in which different countries and presidential administrations might follow contrary courses of action.[51] However, it contended that the international legal principles of sovereign recognition were separate from any national political decision to challenge the legitimacy of another country's government. In this assertion, Taft took a step toward insulating international economic relations from the emerging ideas of non-statist sovereignty that might shape the preferences of particular states.[52]

The Rule of Law as a Facet of Effective Control

Notwithstanding the statist foundation of the *Tinoco* decision, ultimately Justice Taft concluded that the Amory and Royal Bank contracts were not enforceable. Given the determination that a valid government existed after the coup on the basis of "effective control," such a finding might appear incongruous. Although Taft agreed with Great Britain that the Tinoco regime embodied the government of Costa Rica, he did not therefore conclude that the regime's contracts were internationally valid. It is on the basis of this ultimate decision for Costa Rica that contemporary proponents of the odious debt doctrine embrace Taft as a predecessor. In deciding for Costa Rica on both the oil concession claim and the Royal Bank claim, Taft adopted a rule-of-law conception of sovereignty in line with the early twentieth-century legalist trend that I discussed in the previous chapter.

Although Taft's decision hardly instantiates a commitment to popular democracy, a closer look reveals that the effective control requirement is not entirely statist or absolutist. Whereas under a purely statist approach the *fact* of control is sufficient to define valid sovereign action, Taft paid attention to the *mechanism* or procedure of control in his formulation. In this intermediate framework, a sovereign government's international action is valid and binding on successor governments only if it has followed its own internal legal requirements for competence or ratification. Again, although this theoretical structure does not mandate any particular set of internal laws—for example liberal democratic constitutionalism—it does insist on the primacy of respecting legal and constitutional requirements. As with the statist school, such basic constitutionalism is not concerned with whether governmental mechanisms are democratic or grounded in popular consent, but it does conceive of a sovereign government as both constituted and constrained by law.

As such, Taft's framework does not ultimately support the continuity of sovereign obligations in *all* cases. If an international contract is signed in contravention of a government's own internal laws, then that contract may risk repudiation by a subsequent regime. Although this intermediate approach to sovereignty and valid sovereign action does not go so far as to insist on popular consent, it does promote both internal and external transparency by requiring that any laws in existence are in fact followed. In what might have been an unwelcome development for many twentieth-century government elites and creditors had it been fully adopted, Taft's award effectively maintains that even a dictatorial regime must live up to the laws on its books for its actions and debt contracts to be internationally enforceable.

This interesting theoretical framework, in which Taft essentially adopts a rule-of-law approach to sovereign continuity, emerges from his decision on the Amory oil concession. Taft states that the validity of the concession is "to be determined by the law in existence at the time of its granting," namely the law of Costa Rica under the Tinoco government.[53] In line with the de facto control rule of recognition, Taft considered irrelevant the fact that the Tinoco government itself had emerged in contravention of the previous constitution and counter to democratic principles. He made no reference to any larger claim, such as inherent popular ownership of a country's natural resources, and de-linked the validity of state action from the underlying legitimacy of the state. Having established this formalist framework, however, Taft's decision follows it strictly. His ultimate finding for Costa Rica on the Amory oil concession rested on an assessment of Tinoco's own governing laws, and in particular on the legislative approval requirements of Tinoco's 1917 Constitution.[54]

Attentiveness to the technical requirements of internal rules thus is central to this approach. The Amory concession contract had been signed by Tinoco's Minister of Public Works and John M. Amory & Son, a technically American firm that was an agent for British Controlled Oilfields, Ltd.[55] As part of the Amory enterprise, Costa Rica had exempted the British company from a range of national and local taxes and tax increases. As a result, Taft points out that the grant of this concession "involved the power to approve laws fixing, enforcing or changing direct or indirect taxes."[56] This taxing power, however, was among those enumerated by the Tinoco Constitution as belonging exclusively to the congress sitting *jointly,* and thus including both the Chamber of Deputies and the Chamber of Senators.[57] Notwithstanding this requirement, the Amory concession had been approved only by the Chamber of Deputies. Rejecting Great Britain's urging of a modified construction of the constitution, Taft found, "As the Chamber of Deputies was expressly excluded from exercising this power alone, Article X [of the concession contract, which granted the tax exemption] was invalid."[58] Taft also refused to separate out the tax exemption clause from the remainder of the concession, considering the fifty-year exemption, "one of the great factors of value in the contract."[59] In refusing to limit or rewrite the contract, Taft invalidated the Amory concession as a whole.[60]

Abstracting from the particular facts and rule of the case, the *Tinoco* decision on the Amory concession makes a critical theoretical move for thinking through the continuity of sovereign obligations. The foundation of Taft's framework initially seems very statist: a sovereign state government exists when it has de facto control of a country. Considerations of legitimacy drawn from a strong understanding of individual rights or democratic consent are set aside. Taft takes a similarly formalist view of the relevant law for a sovereign state contract as being the law in force at the time of the contract. However, the Amory concession decision sets a limit on *every* sovereign government's power, forcing any regime, whether dictatorial or democratic, to actually abide by its own laws in entering internationally enforceable sovereign contracts. In this, Taft steps away from understanding law in the stark terms offered by

John Austin, as merely the command of the sovereign backed by force.[61] In its place, Taft formulates a vision of "effective control" that privileges established rules over both force and democratic ideals, validating an approach that mitigates a narrowly statist idea of sovereign contract obligation.

Governmental Purpose and Valid Sovereign Action

Justice Taft declined to enforce the Tinoco regime's contracts not only due to rule-of-law concerns but also by suggesting outcome orientation as an element of valid sovereign action. This reflected several of Costa Rica's own arguments and also resonated with broader political ideas of sovereignty emerging in the post-World War I era. In particular, Taft's decision on the Royal Bank's monetary debt claim implied that a sovereign debt contract may not be internationally enforceable unless it intends to serve a legitimate governmental purpose. Taft presented this as a separate and additional requirement, regardless of a regime's internal governmental form or of whether internal rules are actually obeyed. Thus, under the *Tinoco* framework, a sovereign contract not designed to serve the underlying state might be invalid *even if* it followed the relevant internal legal procedures.[62]

The facts of the Royal Bank claim make clear that, under Taft's framework, the legitimate governmental purpose requirement cannot exist only on paper. The Royal Bank of Canada had furnished $200,000[63] of funds to Tinoco in the regime's last days, ostensibly to fund the "representation of the Chief of State in his approaching trip abroad" as well as for four years advance remuneration to Tinoco's brother as the ambassador to Italy.[64] Taft used a contextual approach to determine that these funds were not actually grounded in valid governmental objectives, and thus were not the debt obligations of Costa Rica after the fall of the Tinoco regime. In the quote most used by proponents of resuscitating an odious debt doctrine, Taft found against Great Britain and the Bank because "all the circumstances should have advised the Royal Bank that this [loan] was for personal and not for legitimate government purposes."[65] The relevant circumstances for determining the private as opposed to the public nature of the credit included a transaction full of irregularity and informality, and a lack of underlying legal authority for the initial credit fund. Filling out this narrative, Taft highlighted the "most unusual and absurd course of business" involved in paying salaries four years in advance, and pointed out that the bank knew that this money was to be used by the Tinoco brothers for their personal use.

Taft denied that either the Royal Bank or Federico Tinoco "could hold [the Costa Rican] government responsible for the money paid . . . for this purpose."[66]

As further evidence of the private rather than the public nature of the funds, Taft pointed to the fact that the popularity of the Tinoco regime had disappeared by the spring of 1919 and that the movement to end that regime continued gaining strength until Tinoco's resignation.[67] However, Taft does not regard the political disorder and lack of control as indicating the absence of a de facto government, which might suggest that no competent regime existed when the Royal Bank claim was signed. Instead, Taft presents the context as part of the evidence that the loan was unlikely to serve valid state interests. After enumerating the sinking popularity of the Tinoco regime among other factors, Taft holds that "all the circumstances should have advised the Royal Bank that this . . . was for personal and not for legitimate government purposes."[68] The decision presents the existence of a legitimate government purpose as central, with the extreme circumstances acting as supporting evidence of its absence.

Taft also makes an important point on the issue of a creditor's knowledge regarding a loan's ultimate purpose. The remedy of debt repudiation may not be available under Taft's framework unless the lender knew about the illegitimate nature of the debt contract itself, that is, that the end uses were not designed to serve the interests of the underlying public. According to the *Tinoco* framework, if a lender makes a loan in good faith, it should be able to collect on that loan despite its ultimate ill use. However, Taft seems to allow for the possibility of constructive knowledge as well, or the idea that a creditor may be held to the level of knowledge obtainable through ordinary care and diligence. This idea that a party "knew or should have known" of relevant facts or conditions is used in domestic contract law to prevent willful ignorance and a failure of due diligence.[69] Moving to the level of international sovereign contracts, this would place the burden of proving good faith on the creditor claimant rather the sovereign debtor—certainly a step away from strictly statist norms of debt continuity. With regard to the Royal Bank claim, Taft states, "[the Bank] must make out its case of actual furnishing of money to the government for its legitimate use."[70] Again, he suggests that evidence of knowledge can derive from the background conditions of the loan, stating that "all the circumstances should have advised the Royal Bank" that the loan at issue would be used for illegitimate ends.[71]

Justice Taft himself, in introducing non-statist elements into his arbitral decision, would hardly have intended this framework to undermine fully functioning international capital markets. Perhaps the most widespread and somewhat caricatured view of Taft in American politics is as "a stubborn defender of the status quo, champion of property rights, apologist for social privilege, inveterate critic of social democracy."[72] While his ideological approach was less simplistic than the purely big business caricature, he is certainly among the most establishment-friendly of 1920s' American establishment figures. Property protection stood at the core of Taft's judicial ideology and, during his time as Chief Justice in the 1920s, he was particularly concerned about populist attacks on property rights and on the judiciary.[73] Still, Taft did seem to be guided by genuine capitalist beliefs rather than short-run pandering to particular capitalists. Although Taft's policy and judicial decisions generally favored business interests, his core orientation was to the market as a point of principle.[74] As such, he would have been attuned to the distinction between a pro-market framework and an approach that favored a particular creditor. He objected strenuously to widespread economic change, and presented the validation of Costa Rica's action in the *Tinoco* arbitration as a fairly unobjectionable and market-friendly requirement that sovereign contracts comply with internal laws and serve a legitimate government purpose. In this, he echoed and supported emerging twentieth-century ideas that the rule of law should be incorporated into all levels of legitimate sovereign state interaction, and translated these ideas into the international economic arena.

A Muted Response and a Procapital Perspective?

Despite the British antagonism over the Costa Rican action, there seemed to be few long-term ramifications for Costa Rica. Indeed, the repudiation and subsequent arbitral finding received minimal attention at the time and is little remarked upon in historical studies. Most Western legal commentators in the 1920s seemed unperturbed by Taft's arbitral award for Costa Rica. The *British Yearbook of International Law* only covered the basic discussion on sovereign recognition, minimizing the precedential importance of the actual finding. It said only that "on the merits of the British claims the Arbitrator's decision was on the whole favorable to Costa Rica, but this part of his opinion is of less general interest."[75] The *Wall Street Journal* reported Taft's decision for Costa Rica on both the bank note and the oil concession claims, without any additional editorialization.[76] Costa Rica faced unrelated creditor pressure on a more quotidian dispute with French bondholders in 1923.[77] Still, by 1924—two years after the legislation repudiating Tinoco's debts and one year after

Justice Taft's arbitral award—Costa Rica was able to issue new and unrelated bonds and eventually regain its financial footing, strengthening its economy by the late 1920s.[78] In short, the nullification decree did not significantly hinder Costa Rica's long-run financial flexibility or seem to undermine its ability to attract investment or capital.

Indeed, Costa Rica did not intend its nullification decree to be a radical action. As highlighted by the post-Tinoco Acosta administration, the country took pride in its international reputation and had a history of repaying previous obligations.[79] The Costa Rican Congress took care to distinguish between the debts of the Tinoco regime and those of the previous constitutional republic, treating the international contracts signed during these two periods differently. In contemporary economic and political science discussions of interwar defaults, Costa Rica's nullification decree is not treated as a major challenge and receives little attention. The Tinoco regime itself never issued foreign securities—perhaps in part due to the nonrecognition policies of the Allied countries, which were home to the major early twentieth-century financial centers.[80] As such, all of Costa Rica's foreign bonds had been issued by pre-Tinoco administrations, and were thus considered valid by the reinstated constitutional government. The bases upon which Costa Rica repudiated, including the tyranny of the previous regime and the importance of public benefit for valid sovereign obligations, were similar to those of the Soviet repudiation. And, like the Soviet Union, Costa Rica did not frame these principles as necessarily antiliberal or anticapitalist.[81] Indeed, they presented them as ultimately continuous with the Western heritage of liberal constitutionalism and with a fairly conservative respect for the rule of law, ultimately even submitting their disagreements to arbitration.

Given that both the Costa Rican government and Justice Taft were hardly revolutionary in their self-perception and rhetoric, it is perhaps unsurprising that the response to the Costa Rican case was relatively mild. Creditors and their governments were not consistently hostile to the action or the subsequent arbitral decision. They failed to interpret the nullification law or the arbitration as a threat to creditor and investor interests as a whole, perhaps in recognition of their different—and generally nationally based—economic interests. The ability of these early twentieth-century actors to take a more pragmatic approach to sovereign debt continuity supports the idea that there is more variation than we usually acknowledge in this norm. It further deepens the questions of how context shapes what is considered rational and neutral in sovereign lending, and of which subsequent historical developments made this more flexible approach less likely to take hold.

Competition in the Caribbean as an Enabling Context

The Tinoco coup and the subsequent repudiation and arbitration took place in the twilight of imperial competition in the Caribbean, at the dawn of American hegemony, and in the context of British-American economic and geostrategic rivalry. This underlying competition surfaced in interactions between Costa Rica, the United States, and Great Britain with regard to the repudiation, and was deepened by American concerns about oil concessions and the Panama Canal. Although British companies and officials viewed the Costa Rican action negatively—and expected the United States to view it similarly—this larger context moderated the US view. This is not to say that US officials, or Justice Taft, based their decisions on a desire to assist creditors and companies in the region, many of which were American. Even if they had wished to support a pro-creditor approach in general, the disaggregated context of sovereign lending in the early twentieth century would have mitigated against any oversimplified understanding of market rationality or creditor interest. Rather, an awareness of competing European interests in the region would have made a broader range of sovereign borrower actions more acceptable. In particular, diplomatic correspondence suggests that Costa Rican arguments and actions that had the effect of undermining British involvement in the Caribbean received a more cordial reception than they might have otherwise.

Economic and Geopolitical Competition

A significant portion of early twentieth-century American foreign economic policy involved supporting US banks in their efforts to break into areas already supplied by European powers and their financiers. During this period, American capital sought investment outlets and struggled against the market dominance of British, French, and German banking houses. Indeed, as president, Taft had been active in this program.[82] These initial efforts failed in part because of the relative immaturity of US capital markets, but also due to the intransigence of other interests.[83] Although the United States was relatively stronger in Latin America, particularly after World War I, British capital continued to prevail through most of the 1920s.[84] While US investments in Latin America doubled to $3 billion between 1924 and 1929, British investments dominated the region throughout this time period.[85] The US rise as a creditor nation accelerated after World War I, but the United States still had not solidified a hegemonic status and viewed British economic interests in the region with some suspicion.

This economically competitive context was only enhanced by geopolitical considerations. While the United States viewed Great Britain and other Western European nations as an economic risk, US support for overseas investment was matched by geostrategic concerns. The Roosevelt, Taft, and Wilson presidencies were committed to opening foreign markets as an independent goal, but also aimed to use private capital as an instrument for promoting stable and solvent governments in areas of geopolitical concern.[86] As early as 1823, the Monroe doctrine asserted that the newly independent Latin American countries constituted part of a US sphere of influence, and declared that any European attempts at control would be viewed "as the manifestation of an unfriendly disposition to the United States."[87] US interest in the Caribbean only deepened when it launched its overseas empire in Cuba, Puerto Rico, and the Philippines after the Spanish-American War.[88] The 1904 Roosevelt Corollary to the Monroe Doctrine went even further, claiming an international police power in the Western Hemisphere to correct any "chronic wrongdoing" or disorder resulting from any "general loosening of the ties of civilized society."[89] As part of his corollary, Roosevelt hoped to prevent intervention by European powers claiming to protect their national interests in the Caribbean.

The central preventive policy of this larger strategy involved the promotion of stable and solvent Caribbean governments and the limitation of new European economic interests in the region, including new loans that might lead to more European gunships in the Western hemisphere.[90] Taft and then Wilson continued the rough trend of this policy in their "dollar diplomacy," which repaid European loans with American money and established customs receiverships to guarantee this debt.[91] This increasing American political concern with the Caribbean was further magnified by the development of the Panama Canal. The United States had entertained the possibility of building a transisthmian canal well before the turn of the century, but initially devoted more energy to preventing other powers from building and controlling any such canal.[92] As the turn of the century approached, however, the United States began considering more seriously the possibility and strategic implications of a transisthmian shipping route. The Canal was ultimately opened in 1914, but much of the project was completed under the Roosevelt administration, with Taft deeply involved as secretary of war.[93] American attentiveness to the risks posed by European and particularly British involvement in the region would likely have made any economic or legal-theoretical framework that undermined British interests appear more plausible and rational to US diplomats stationed in Central America and even to Taft sitting as arbitrator.

Undermining a Uniform Approach in Costa Rica

While this underlying rivalry provided an important backdrop in its own right, these issues emerged even more directly with regard to the Costa Rican repudiation. Great Britain had reacted strongly to the nullification decree, and rejected the idea of bringing its dispute before Costa Rican courts. It requested US support in pressing its claims internationally, pointing out the two countries' shared interests in the region and beyond. In asking for support in the Costa Rican matter, the British ambassador noted to US Secretary of State Charles Hughes that "to admit the validity of confiscatory legislation of this character would create, to my mind, a most dangerous precedent, apart altogether from the question of the interests involved. We should in fact be accepting in Costa Rica that to which we so strongly object in Mexico."[94] In his response, Secretary Hughes indicated that the United States would not object to any arbitration agreed to by Costa Rica, but considered that the British claimants had fair access to Costa Rican courts. He further noted that the purging in such courts of Tinoco-era appointments, about which the British were concerned, was only a return to the earlier judiciary organized according to Costa Rica's proper constitutional principles.[95] Perhaps surprisingly, the United States thus declined a unified creditor position, providing some leeway for the alternative approach provided by the Costa Rican example and Taft's subsequent arbitral decision.

In fact, as part of the general policy of limiting European involvement in the region, the United States had been particularly wary of allowing the development of British oil concessions in Costa Rica, the latter being "of unusual interest because of its relation to naval bases and the proximity of Costa Rica to the Panama Canal."[96] The State Department had aimed to prevent German and British companies from obtaining oil concessions under Tinoco's predecessor.[97] This policy seems to have been largely successful; except for the Amory concession signed by the Tinoco regime, oil interests at the time of the repudiation were entirely American.[98] British companies had been unable to gain a foothold in Costa Rican oil exploration despite earlier efforts, and very likely took advantage of the opportunity presented by the new Tinoco government to gain extensive rights in the Amory concession.

Defending the nullification decree to the United States, Costa Rican politicians certainly tried to emphasize this aspect of the British claims. The president of Costa Rica's Constitutional Congress pointed out that the Amory concession was obtained "where Americans were restrained from entering the Costa Rican field" and suggested that British interests had used an American front company "as a wartime policy . . . to avoid attracting American attention."[99] The United States, it seems, needed little convincing. Indeed, there is some intimation that the American consul in San José may have even encouraged the repudiation decree, particularly with regard to the Amory concession. Certainly the British government thought this was the case and made its concerns known to the US secretary of state. In his reply, Secretary Hughes did not in fact deny that this occurred, asserting only that Washington did not "authorize or approve" the consul's actions and, in any case, did not formally know of the concession's British parentage until several months after the fact.[100] Although by the 1923 arbitral award there had been sufficient exploration to determine that Costa Rica in fact had very little oil wealth,[101] these broader economic and geostrategic rivalries undermined the easy adoption of a uniform approach. They made the Costa Rican action and the arbitral decision's ultimate theoretical framework more plausible, rational, and appealing to the United States in particular.

The Shared Openness of Opposing Cases

The two post-World War I cases presented in this and the last chapter are so notable for their differences that it is easy to overlook their important similarities. The Soviet repudiation was part of a major social revolution and the attempted launch of a wholly new social order. Although the regime eventually modified and moderated its approach to the tsarist debt, there was no denying the newness of the political moment or the radical nature of the regime's break with the past. By contrast, the Costa Rican repudiation was framed as an ultimately conservative if principled action, as a return to constitutional order after a brief period of unrest. Furthermore, the political and economic inclinations of the repudiating regimes were very different and elicited dissimilar responses. The October Revolution was explicitly based on a rejection of economic and political control by either an absolutist monarchy or a liberal market state, whereas the Costa Rican overthrow of the Tinoco dictatorship explicitly embraced the constitutional and liberal values espoused by the West. Russia had been a major prewar economy and the repudiation had serious ramifications for other countries. Economically, Costa Rica was only one of many small Latin American countries, and the repudiation had no systemic effect; additionally, the initial nullification law itself was targeted to a brief period. Looking at these differences, it would be surprising for the Soviet and Costa Rican cases to share many similarities at all. Indeed, these distinctions no doubt account for the very different international reaction—incredibly vocal for the former and relatively minimal for the latter.

Nonetheless, both cases are important in highlighting the possibility of alternatives to the norm of sovereign debt continuity and deepening the question of why such alternatives failed to take hold. They also suggest the existence of an open moment for the contemporary sovereign debt regime, including its reputational supports, in the post-World War I era. As with the Soviet case, the Costa Rican repudiation and Justice Taft's subsequent arbitral finding are now cited by odious debt advocates as an important precursor for the idea that not all sovereign debts are equally legitimate. Indeed, neither the Soviet Union nor Costa Rica framed its decision as a simple default or a request for debt forgiveness. Rather, both based their claims on principled arguments about the proper nature of valid sovereignty and sovereign action. They contended that the debts of the previous regimes had been illegitimate—due to the nature of the regimes themselves and to the particular circumstances and intended outcomes of the contracts. And whereas some creditors and governments reacted very hostilely to the repudiations, the response was not uniform. In the nature of the claims made and in the varied response of both immediate interlocutors and later potential creditors, the Soviet and Costa Rican cases evince greater flexibility than would be predicted by an ahistorical market principle. They also point to the importance of political ideas and actors in shaping debt events, and suggest that historically contingent contexts are crucial in framing our interpretations of debt continuity.

These early twentieth-century cases raise questions as to why similar possibilities in debt and reputation did not emerge later on. In doing so, they hint at the relevance of creditor competition and broader political ideas in enabling such flexibility. International lending to sovereigns had emerged as a major financial activity in the late nineteenth century, and European and American banks competed for a share of this market through the 1920s. Partly as a result of such competition, financial institutions and their home countries disagreed on the proper responses to these challenges to debt continuity. In the Soviet case, a more disaggregated creditor context enabled attempts by new US banks to finance the Soviet regime, although these efforts were only partially successful. In Costa Rica, the US government acted with a view to its national creditors and investors, and as a geopolitical player in its own right. This moderated any statist approach it might have taken in the conflict of Great Britain—its main Caribbean competitor—with the newly restored Costa Rican government. This period also saw traditional ideas of sovereignty in the larger international arena come under attack from both liberal and Left perspectives. Alternative discourses of governmental legitimacy, taken up by divergent political figures such as Woodrow Wilson and Vladimir Lenin and by institutions such as the League of Nations and the Permanent Court of International Justice, made the Soviet and Costa Rican claims resonant if not fully accepted. These country cases tapped into the emerging discourses, although they came up against opposing ideas of civilized international interaction and, in the Soviet case, virulent anticommunism.

As I argue in the next chapters, the elements of creditor competitiveness and of openness in the meaning of legitimate sovereignty actually weakened as the twentieth century progressed. Cross-border lending effectively halted during the Great Depression, and when sovereign borrowing reemerged after World War II, it took on a very different cast, with fewer players involved and a more consolidated form of interaction. The ideational context also changed, and the post-World War II principles enshrined by the United Nations, accepted by financial institutions, and defended by a wave of postcolonial states were closer to statism than to forms of sovereignty more concerned with internal rule and public benefit. This shift had important consequences for normalizing a statist framework of sovereign continuity in sovereign debt and reputation for the next fifty years.

5

Public and Private Capital in Mid-Century Repayment Norms

The limit of risk-taking in the Bank's lending operations should be set in such a way as to facilitate the Bank's role as a borrower in the capital markets of developed countries.
—IBRD/IDA Internal Memorandum (1968)

ALTHOUGH SOVEREIGN STATES desperately needed long-term capital to rebuild their economies in the years following World War II, private finance was initially not forthcoming. The London-centered financial system that had globalized the world economy through much of the nineteenth and early twentieth century suffered crippling blows during the First World War. It definitively lost its preeminent financial role in the decline of international trade and capital flows during the interwar period and World War II. While private lending in the United States increased dramatically during the 1920s and to some degree competed with older London and European houses, this source of capital also dried up during the Great Depression. Private finance was hard to come by for sovereign states, particularly the less economically developed and less politically mature among them. As a result, a new international capital recycling mechanism had to be found, and it fell to public creditors such as the US government and the new International Bank for Reconstruction and Development (the IBRD or the "Bank," which later expanded to the World Bank Group) to actively intervene and fill the gap.[1]

These public actors would have been ideally situated to reformulate the rule of sovereign debt continuity to take into account ideas of sovereign legitimacy emerging after World War I. However, they ultimately led in the opposite direction, helping to regularize a strictly statist framework as the conventional and "neutral" approach, solidifying its appearance as an ahistorical market principle. In this chapter, I consider what might account for the closure of these earlier possibilities and the normalization of statist practices. While the Soviet and Costa Rican cases hardly would have been sufficient in and of themselves to launch an opposing rule, they did carve out space for further potential challenges. Was the ultimate mid-twentieth-century rejection of this alternative path simply the return of a more or less unavoidable trajectory in sovereign debt and reputation? Certainly not. The disappearance of this earlier potential, like the emergence of the earlier historical cases, was shaped by creditor interactions and broader sovereignty norms specific to that moment. In particular, I argue that decisions taken by the early World Bank, in conjunction with the choices of other public actors like the US government, moved contemporary understandings of responsible lending and acceptable sovereign action in a statist direction.

The first section of this chapter takes a closer look at the World Bank's role. I suggest that the Bank's early concern with the views of private finance, its interpretation of political neutrality, and its consolidated or oligopolistic relationship with market creditors strengthened a statist approach to sovereign lending and repayment. While the Bretton Woods institutions were established explicitly to limit the international power of private finance and to become "instrumentalities of sovereign governments and not of private financial interests,"[2] the Bank's initial funding mechanisms—oriented toward Wall Street actors that were avowedly *non*competitive with regard to sovereign lending—significantly shaped its interpretation of creditworthiness requirements and its treatment of sovereign debt continuity. Furthermore, in the context of broader midcentury norms of sovereignty, the Bank's mandate to remain politically "neutral" took on a statist cast. Developing and postcolonial countries themselves did not present a strong case for alternative understandings of sovereign legitimacy, particularly given their concern with limiting international scrutiny of their own governments. Despite efforts to influence sovereign lending through the UN in cases such as apartheid South Africa and colonialist Portugal, the ultimate failure to establish limitations on the basis of internal sovereign characteristics further entrenched statist continuity as the ostensibly apolitical default position.

I also consider the role played by the massive outflow of American public capital after World War II. Although this capital provided some soft competition for the World Bank's approach, it did not ultimately challenge the Bank's underlying political framework or its normalization of sovereign continuity in the debt regime. US (and Soviet) preoccupations with the Cold War sidelined any commitment to extending particular principles of sovereign legitimacy into international economic governance. And, in combination with a broadly statist idea of political neutrality, the antileftist political ideology of the United States rendered any challenge to the norm of debt continuity even more difficult, particularly given the leftist bent of many political transformations. This larger international context helped shape the response to two major regime changes during this period—that of the People's Republic of China in 1949 and the Cuban Revolution of 1959. Thus, the creditor structures, political actors, and broader ideologies of the post-World War II era did not move international financial norms and reputational mechanisms toward non-statist ideas of selective debt cancellation. Instead, they laid the foundations for a reconsolidation of debt continuity in the second half of the twentieth century.

Public Credit, Private Capital, and Political "Neutrality"

In its later years, the World Bank has become an intermittent target for critics of economic globalization, who accuse the organization of betraying its stated commitments in order to further the interests of financiers.[3] One of the great ironies of the World Bank's close working relationship with private creditors does indeed lie in the fact that a major impetus for its establishment was to create a publicly oriented international bank free from the influence of Wall Street. While the Bank's genuinely public outlook is beyond doubt, its early history necessarily affected the ways in which Bank staff carried out this commitment and continue to see their role. In particular, both the close interaction of the Bank with private creditors and the general norms of mid-century international relations shaped its interpretations of appropriate behavior for responsible state borrowers, with consequences for how we think about sovereign debt today. Due to almost-immediate funding problems, the early IBRD established its goals and decision-making procedures with a close eye on the private banking community, which in effect was oligopolistically organized with regard to sovereign lending after World War II. These epistemic and financial links resulted in a narrowed definition of sovereign creditworthiness for its own borrowers, and connected to a strict insistence on sovereign debt continuity. As a consequence, the Bank helped to limit the midcentury possibilities for alternative approaches to sovereign debt and reputation that had been raised in the post-World War I era. In addition, the Bank's early interpretation of "politically neutral" lending—which largely fell in line with broader sovereignty norms in the international arena—further normalized the statist framework.

The IBRD as the Inheritor of the Logic of Sovereign Lending

Understanding the early IBRD is especially important because the practices and the logic of sovereign lending became bifurcated after World War II. The US government, which had lending outflows considerably higher than those of the IBRD, conceived of sovereign financing in terms of its larger foreign policy goals, which were driven by concerns for a stable and secure Europe and later by apprehension of the Soviet Union.[4] The Bank, as a longer-term development agency charged with its own financial maintenance, incubated a finance- and development-driven system that explicitly dealt with issues of creditworthiness. Because of this bifurcation, and the relative inattention of the United States to questions of reputation or sovereign legitimacy, the IBRD-driven system effectively maintained a monopoly on the analytical framework for "normal" sovereign debt. As a result, the Bank's ultimate understanding of how ideas of sovereign legitimacy might apply to debt continuity and creditworthiness became the dominant vision for the remainder of the century.

This bifurcation into roughly "geostrategic" and "economic" arenas for sovereign lending followed a split in the geographic focus of these two public actors, at least in the first decade and a half of the Bretton Woods era. For the first fifteen years of the IBRD's existence, its area of focus differed considerably from that of the American government. The US concern with European reconstruction and then the Cold War affected its early financial and military aid; its sovereign lending was directed first toward Western Europe and the "rim" nations of Central and Northeast Asia and later to South Asia, Indochina and the Philippines, as well as Turkey and Iran. The Bank shared the South Asian focus, and India and Pakistan became major borrowers, but otherwise tended to focus on the Latin American and African countries.[5] Therefore, the first half of the Bretton Woods period saw the "free world" split, in terms of sovereign lending, with political and military concerns dominating one area while economic development concerns dominated the other. Thus the United States and the Bank each had a fairly free hand in their own sphere, and large swathes of the borrowing world—particularly Latin America, Africa, and South Asia (at least early on)—remained virtually untouched by early US government funding.

Although other international economic links, such as trade, aid, and foreign direct investment (FDI) eventually became important, many of these channels were not open in the immediate post-World War II decades. Trade barriers remained high, and aid was limited by the funds available in the United States and in other, war-torn industrialized countries. Although Europe saw a major increase in FDI fairly soon after the war, American and later European companies were not initially interested in direct investment in most of Asia and Africa.[6] This lack of willing suppliers matched an ambivalence on the part of many developing countries as well, which remained concerned about ceding control to foreign enterprises. As such, although IBRD funds were not abundant, they remained a key transnational economic link for many postwar countries, carrying the Bank's voice farther than it might have reached otherwise.

Studying the IBRD in the post-World War II period thus helps to make sense of policies and analytical approaches that remain relevant in recent decades. The idea of the World Bank—later along with the International Monetary Fund (IMF)—as a leader or initiator for broader private lending probably does not apply in the first two decades of its existence. But the post-World War II era effectively laid the groundwork for the Bank's activities in the 1970s and beyond, when it became a major player and gatekeeper in international finance. This earlier gestation period also solidified the Bank's relationship with major actors in the private capital markets, who returned to direct international lending in the 1960s and especially the early 1970s.[7] While the United States' Cold War concerns and practices have diminished in importance, the analytical frameworks adopted by the early Bank proved more long lasting. The IBRD effectively served as the incubator for contemporary sovereign risk analysis after the disappearance of private finance from international lending during the Great Depression, and its viewpoint was adopted more widely—and with significant ramifications—as the twentieth century progressed.

A Financial System Free of Wall Street

In conducting preparatory work for the Bank and the IMF, Harry Dexter White, then special advisor to US Treasury Secretary Henry Morgenthau Jr., submitted an April 1942 "Proposal for a United Nations Stabilization Fund and a Bank for Reconstruction and Development of the United and Associated Nations." White's proposal noted that the end of World War II would require a mechanism, among other things, "to supply the huge volume of capital that will be needed virtually throughout the world for reconstruction, for relief, and for economic recovery. . . . Clearly the task can be successfully handled only through international action."[8] There was significant support for a development bank, with plans for such an institution submitted by delegates from not just the United States and European countries but from throughout the world.[9] As the proposals developed, it was thought that the Bank portion of the plan should encourage private finance to return to the international capital system, albeit in a modified form. A memorandum by Secretary Morgenthau accompanying a US draft proposal in late 1943 noted: "The most important of the Bank's operations will be to guarantee loans in order that [private] investors may have reasonable assurance of safety in placing their funds abroad. In this way it is expected that the international flow of capital in adequate volume will be encouraged."[10] The massive foreign bond defaults during the 1930s, including many sovereign bond defaults, had effectively made "international" an unpopular word on Wall Street.[11] The private financial sector had developed a distinctly national orientation in the 1930s, which strengthened in the 1940s and remained dominant into the 1960s. New York underwriters floated only $4.2 billion in foreign issues between 1955 and 1962, compared to $126.5 billion in national issues.[12] Morgenthau, White, and others in the US Treasury involved in early Bank planning recognized the importance of private capital flows in international economic relations, and also understood that private finance might be hesitant to return.

Still, some reservations accompanied this recognition, as the interwar financial crisis had hardly endeared Wall Street to Washington. The US government during the 1930s and the first part of the 1940s was acknowledgedly hostile to the New York financial community, and blamed the bankers for much of the interwar economic crisis.[13] As such, the Bank's government founders were far from interested in giving private finance the control over international lending it had previously commanded. As Richard Gardner has noted, the New Deal Treasury sought to "make finance the servant, not the master, of human desires—in the international no less than in the domestic sphere."[14] Morgenthau himself claimed that his principal objective as secretary of the treasury was "to move the financial center of the world from London and Wall Street to the United States Treasury, and to create a new concept between nations in international finance." In Morgenthau's address to the final session of the Bretton Woods Conference in 1944, he stated that the new institutions would "drive . . . the usurious money lenders from the temple of international finance."[15] Some major commentators of the time went further, hoping that cross-border lending would be conducted at an explicitly international level. One important tract argued that "the functions of investment promotion and protection should be lodged in various agencies representing the world community and having world-wide jurisdiction."[16]

Indeed, early discussions of the Bank and the IMF even included proposals to enable the institutions' direct involvement in debt restructuring, which would have granted them significant power over borrowers but also might have undermined the effect of bondholder intransigence. White's initial drafts contained provisions that would not "permit any defaults on foreign obligations. . . . without the approval of the Fund"[17] and prohibited the Bank from lending to countries in default in the absence of an agreement "to renew service of the defaulted debt on a basis worked out by a special committee appointed by the Bank for that purpose."[18] Although there was no guarantee that this power would have been used to tip the scales in favor of debtors rather than creditors, such provisions were motivated by frustration with bondholders. White felt that a special committee "could approach the problem with a great deal more objectivity than could be true of a bondholders' committee. . . . It could in its recommendations take a broader point of view."[19] This meant that "a loan could be forthcoming if the defaulting government accepted the committee's recommendation of terms of adjustments irrespective of whether the bondholders did or did not."[20] Interestingly, another exception to the proposed rule against lending to countries in default would be if "the defaulted loan was made between two Allies in a common war," hearkening back to the arguments made by the post-World War I Soviet regime to France and Great Britain.[21] Although these provisions do not speak to debt continuity per se, they do indicate open acceptance of the fact that not all debt would (or should) be repaid prior to the resumption of lending. More importantly, they suggest an attentiveness to political context that, especially in light of the hostility toward private finance, could have incorporated ideas of illegitimate debt over time. Ultimately, White's proposals for Fund and Bank involvement in debt adjustment were rejected in part due to concerns about how countries in default, particularly in Latin America, might interpret the provisions. According to a US Treasury official, Secretary Morgenthau "did not wish to be a party to any debt-collecting arrangement smacking as clearly of dollar diplomacy."[22]

Arguably, however, the arm's-length approach finally adopted, combined with ambiguity in the new Bank's goals, did even less than White's proposal might have done to alter the playing field or to highlight governmental and developmental purpose in debt negotiations. Although

part of the impetus for the Bank's creation was to guarantee the independence of international lending from the caprices of private finance, over
time both the capacity and the desire of its management to maintain this
separation diminished. Coming out of the Bretton Woods negotiations,
the Bank itself was established with less than a perfectly lucid mission.
While the development bank was clearly a public actor, the definition of
the public it should serve or the concept of public good that might act as
its guidepost remained indistinct. In fact, it was uncertain whether an
international bank would even be discussed at Bretton Woods. To the
chagrin of many, much of the conference focused on the amalgamation
of British and American plans into a joint statement on the International
Monetary Fund.[23] Although the Bank featured in early US proposals, it
had dropped to secondary importance by the Bretton Woods Conference
in July 1944. Furthermore, the balance of reconstruction as opposed to
development in the Bank's operations was left open. There was some
pressure at the conference, particularly from developing countries, to
emphasize the centrality of development, and indeed evidence suggests
that White considered development important to the future Bank's mission.[24] However, the lead actors eventually indicated that reconstruction
was their primary goal. In his opening remarks to the first meeting of the
Bretton Woods Commission on the Bank, John Maynard Keynes stated,

> It is likely, in my judgment, that the field of reconstruction from the con-
> sequences of war will mainly occupy the proposed Bank in its early days.
> But, as soon as possible, and with increasing emphasis as time goes on,
> there is a second primary duty laid upon it, namely to develop the resources
> and productive capacity of the world, with special attention to the less
> developed countries.[25]

What emerges from early Bank history is that, although its founders
hoped that international development finance would not be subject to
private interests, they did not specify what vision of the public good
might stand as an appropriate bulwark. Nor did they establish clear
mechanisms, such as an independent debt adjustment committee, that
might have acted as an institutional counterweight to creditors. As a
group, the founders espoused a general commitment to reconstruction
and development and to postwar political neutrality, but were less clear
about what these conventionally held ideas of economic progress might
mean in practice. This was accompanied by inattentiveness to the political and social ends and intended beneficiaries of economic development.
This early ambiguity may well have been hard to avoid, given the Bank's
founding as an explicitly international and negotiated venture. Still, this

foundation made it more likely that external influences would shape the Bank's practice, its conception of public good, and its understanding of how ideas of sovereign legitimacy might play into debt and reputation.

Ramifications of the Wall Street Connection

If in 1944 US Treasury Secretary Morgenthau hoped that a new Bank would "drive . . . the usurious money lenders from the temple of international finance,"[26] his successors encountered difficulty finding capital anywhere else. As a result of its initial funding structure, the IBRD eventually depended on issuing its own bonds in private financial markets to sustain and expand its operating capital. As a consequence, the Bank's own creditworthiness in the eyes of the New York financial establishment—no longer competing with each other for international lending but now jointly and uniformly hostile—was of paramount concern. Paradoxically, there was little alternative that would have allowed the Bank to fulfill its mission. This indirect power of the purse affected the Bank's internal goals, staffing, and dealings with borrowers. In particular, I argue that this early relationship with Wall Street shaped an understanding of sovereign creditworthiness that pooled all states together regardless of potential differences in internal rule or loan legitimacy. In insisting that all debts be repaid regardless of their provenance as a precondition for funding, the new IBRD effectively instantiated a statist framework of debt and reputation and a norm of sovereign continuity for the post-World War II lending system.

The responsibility for any Bank deference to private finance lies largely with the initial funding structure established by the IBRD's state founders. Although the Bank Articles of Agreement allowed the institution to lend based on unpaid subscriptions by its member governments, these governments, perhaps predictably, aimed to minimize their actual financial commitments and liabilities. Although the sources for the IBRD's initial funds were the Bank shareholders—the original member governments—the United States in practice provided most of the usable capital. But the gloomy postwar financial outlook of the major European countries, as well as the multiple demands on US financing, meant that the Bretton Woods institutions received only a relatively small slice of available American funds. In the United States, the Democratic Party had suffered losses in the 1942 congressional elections, and a conservative coalition of Republicans and Southern Democrats became dominant. Even within the executive branch, the strongest New Deal supporters were losing ground,[27] and the new Truman Treasury was less hostile than its predecessor had been to a greater role for Wall Street in international finance. As such, the Bank faced a situation in which its shareholders were unwilling to provide sufficient funding for their own stated goal of establishing a viable, publicly oriented international bank.

The IBRD's subsequent response to this limited financial support ensured that its interaction with New York financiers became very close. As with many an institution in need of funds, the minimal capital available through equity encouraged the Bank to turn to borrowing, and the only institutions with sufficient capital to lend to the Bank resided on Wall Street. Despite the War Treasury's initial desire to limit the role of private finance, there was little alternative. As such, much of the early activity of the Bank's senior staff involved preparing the US regulatory environment, as well as the private American capital market, for the flotation of Bank bonds.[28]

This explicit turn to debt as a source for Bank funding had deep ramifications for its staffing, epistemic approach, internal goals, and relationship with its clients. In their history of the World Bank, Kapur, Lewis, and Webb note that, given the financing difficulties, "it was . . . essential that the Bank's president be a US national, to help bolster confidence in the institution on Wall Street and thereby establish its credit rating in the only market that mattered."[29] Not only the president but also many of the early bank officials, particularly the most senior of them, were drawn from Wall Street and to a lesser degree from the European banking community. By 1947, the Bank had attracted John McCloy, counsel to Chase National Bank, as president, and the vice president of the Bank and the second US executive director also had deep ties with the US financial community. When the Roosevelt-appointed first US executive director of the IBRD departed, the institutional hostility of the Bank toward New York capital markets effectively disappeared.[30]

Two central consequences resulted from this close working relationship. First, the shared community of the Bank and the largely American finance houses resulted in a particular epistemic viewpoint. The Bank's strong links to financiers shaped its views on the proper role of a development institution, and on what constituted productive and wise sovereign lending. This is not to say that the Bank became merely the pawn of Wall Street, as has been contended by some critics. Rather, the early IBRD's staffing and technical expertise eventually shaped the Bank's good-faith interpretation of its mission and its preferred modes of operation. A pamphlet written by Bank Treasurer and Vice President Eugene Rotberg and distributed under Robert McNamara's tenure as Bank president is illustrative:

> We are not a social welfare agency committed to making transfer payments to solve the problems of misery or poverty. We are a development bank using the most sophisticated techniques available to facilitate development, while providing unmatched protection and strength for creditors and shareholders.[31]

We can imagine that if the Bank had been staffed with New Deal economists suspicious of private capital, and if circumstances and political will had allowed an initial funding structure less dependent on New York financial markets, then a different ideological and epistemic framework might have developed around the same Bank Articles of Agreement.

An additional and perhaps more immediately apparent consequence of the IBRD's turn to private borrowing for its funding was that the Bank became increasingly concerned with its own creditworthiness, and thus with the creditworthiness of the borrowers that would make up its loan portfolio. Facing the Bank's first development loan application, Vice President Garner explained to Chilean negotiators that

> the most difficult policy problem facing the Bank is where borrowers are in default on previous debt. . . . The present management does not see how the Bank can make loans in the face of widespread dissatisfaction in financial and investment circles to whom the Bank must sell its own bonds. This principle applies, of course, not only to Chile but equally to all potential borrowers.[32]

Garner's explanation reveals a much more hands-off approach than that envisioned by earlier proposals for a Bank-led sovereign debt restructuring committee, designed to provide a "broader point of view" that could explicitly diverge from the perspective of private investment circles. The Bank's concern with its own financing made it especially sensitive to the hesitation of creditors to engage in post-default lending—particularly now that they acted as a single unified group rather than in competition with each other for international clients. The massive foreign bond defaults during the 1930s had made private finance shrink away from anything foreign in the intervening decade. Eugene Black, the Bank's president between 1949 and 1963, commented that the major credit rating agencies' unwillingness to warm to Bank bonds resulted from "a disposition to be ultra-conservative on anything labeled 'international'."[33] Thus, the Bank was internally committed to achieving the highest ratings for its bonds on the US market, and devoted itself to fastidious payment of its own obligations and the persuasion of bankers and the major credit rating agencies of its own institutional strength and the solidity and sophistication of its portfolio. By 1959, the major credit rating agencies finally upgraded the Bank's rating to AAA.[34]

The Establishment of Strict Continuity
in Sovereign Creditworthiness

Although the IBRD's primary mission was as a development agency designed to assist reconstructing and emerging economies, its early capitalization and lending practices meant that bold choices would be difficult to make. Given that no later Bank lending would be possible without repayment by its initial borrowers, article 3, section 4(v) of the Bank's Articles of Agreement required that the Bank review a country's creditworthiness before extending a loan. And although the Bank was willing to accept lower rates of return than private actors, its basic requirements for creditworthiness were adopted in light of the anticipated concerns of major financial markets and important creditor governments. In summarizing its creditworthiness concerns in an internal memorandum, Bank officials assessed that

> the limit of risk-taking in the Bank's lending operations should be set in such a way as to facilitate the Bank's role as a borrower in the capital markets of developed countries. More important, however, is that the Bank's lending decisions be considered prudent by the member governments which, if necessary, would have to defend a call upon their unpaid subscriptions.[35]

The Bank's awareness that it was being monitored by external funders shaped its own decisions in fundamental ways. In particular, in formulating its basic lending rules, the World Bank relied on what a potential and *abstract* private financial institution or member government might hope for in its borrowers. The creditor competition present during the 1920s had dissipated, and the IBRD, to render its own bonds desirable, needed to appeal to banks, investment analysts, and credit rating agencies treated as a unified whole. The issues of relative market position and geopolitical strategy that might have been relevant to a *particular* creditor or government did not factor into the Bank's guess as to the preferences of a creditor or member government considered abstractly. In certain situations in Bank history the wishes of particular member governments have held sway for a given loan decision. However, in establishing its baseline norms, a more general analysis was important. Therefore, although internal Bank documents noted that it should "assume greater risks than the conventional private capital-exporting institutions,"[36] the early IBRD developed a fairly conservative framework for understanding sovereignty and debt continuity.

This left more fine-grained questions of arguably illegitimate debt at the margins. The Bank's paramount concern was for the blanket repayment of any debt owed by each potential borrower to all potential funders, and the Bank insisted that outstanding debts be satisfactorily dealt with before it would accept loan applications from a new borrower. It made no distinction among these debts, expecting the settlement of debts as old as 1829 and of those contracted by previous colonial rulers. Recognizing that bondholders' conditions might be unreasonable, especially given this additional pressure and power, the Bank's leadership did not necessarily require full repayment but only insisted that a reasonable settlement offer be made by the defaulting country.[37] However, it offered little guidance on the nature of "reasonableness" and even this rule implicitly depended upon a statist analytical framework, deepening the assumptions that any sovereign debt should be presumptively continuous. Questions of whether the previous debts had been consented to by the population, benefited the population, or conformed to underlying constitutional requirements did not feature in the Bank's uniform approach.[38]

This policy was not appreciated by early borrowers, particularly by those who did not also have access to postwar American largesse. In 1946, Chile was the first developing country to request a loan. Among its requirements for accepting a loan application, the Bank stated, "Substantively, Chile had to show that it had adopted an orderly process for disposing of the arrears on its prewar international debts."[39] One observer, accompanying IBRD President Eugene Black to the UN's twelfth session of the Economic and Social Council in Chile in 1951, noted in a later interview that "[the Latin American states] initially got pretty mad at us because we talked about defaulted debt. They regarded this as past, the sins of their fathers. . . . The world did throw a depression at them, and why should they have to be bothering about that now?"[40] This insistence that Chile first deal with any prewar debts, without discussion of their provenance or substance, eventually became the norm for all borrowers.

Two of the most adamant potential borrowers had in fact suffered under arguably illegitimate regimes, and at least part of their debt may well have been considered invalid had the Bank accepted non-statist understandings of sovereign legitimacy. However, the Bank did not make allowances on this basis. Guatemala, which had lived under the juntas of Manuel José Estrada Cabrera and then of Jorge Ubico, and whose debts dated back to 1829 (before full independence), remained unwilling to settle until 1966.[41] Although the Bank made one loan to Guatemala in 1955, suspiciously soon after the US overthrow of the democratically elected but left-leaning Jacobo Arbenz, this refusal to settle was unacceptable to the Bank as a general rule for the next ten years.[42] Indonesia constituted another early problem borrower for the Bank due to its refusal to compensate its former Dutch colonial rulers for asset expropriations following a four-year independence war that ended in 1949.[43] Even in these more clear-cut cases, the Bank refused to veer from its commitment to a strictly statist conception of sovereignty in understanding debt obligations and creditworthiness.

Certainly, the financial constraints of the postwar economy left Bank leaders in a bind. The defaulted interwar debts were held by many of the Bank's own actual and potential funders, who would hardly have welcomed a request for capital to be channeled to states in default on previous loans. But not all of the relevant debt was necessarily held by Bank funders, and Edward Mason and Robert Asher suggest that the commitment to repayment also ran more deeply, based on something like a shared epistemic outlook. Even in relatively technical discussions of how to calculate a borrower's debt servicing capacity over time, the IBRD eventually took the most conservative approach. According to Mason and Asher, "as far as the Bank's management was concerned, debts were debts, and a conception of international lending that was based on anything other than their full repayment seemed immoral."[44] Certainly, the broader economic context for early IBRD development did not force its leadership to consider alternative, non-statist approaches or to risk limiting its client base. Indeed, external pressures worked in the opposite direction. This conservative across-the-board approach, which endeared the Bank to the financial press, narrowed the space for independent assessments of whether all debt repayment is necessarily equivalent in analyzing country creditworthiness.

Creditor Consolidation and Conceptual Monopoly

The ramifications of these early IBRD financing exigencies reached beyond the Bank approach to debt continuity alone. Even after it had established itself, the IBRD remained noncompetitive in its approach to private finance, as might be expected of a public creditor. Furthermore, the Bank not only limited its own flexibility in lending approaches but, I argue, actually helped to consolidate private creditors into something like an oligopolistic market structure with regard to the post-World War

II sovereign debt market. This effective oligopoly closed off the potential forums in which borrower claims based on concerns of sovereign legitimacy might have been heard. Such narrowing reinforced the conceptual monopoly of a strictly statist approach to sovereign continuity in debt and reputation, further normalizing this framework for the late twentieth century.

The postwar relationship of private finance with the IBRD shaped not only the Bank's approach but also how private investors themselves understood sovereign lending, consolidating the voice of private banks in the immediate postwar era. Thinking through the counterfactual, the interests of private investors in a competitive and disaggregated market environment would not have been fully aligned. It is true that sovereign borrowers would still have been unlikely to obtain loans for some time as a result of interwar defaults. However, as international lending resumed, banks would have reconsidered entering the risky foreign market and sovereign states would have approached banks anew.[45] Some states would have come to an agreeable settlement and continued the relationship with their previous bankers. Others might have rejected the validity of their previous debts on the basis of political principle, reintroducing alternative ideas of sovereign legitimacy into understandings of debt and reputation. As part of this, they may have turned to an entirely different set of creditors, as with the Soviet example after World War I. While the holder of the original rejected debt would no doubt have been hostile to such activity, perhaps a different bank, interested in the prospect of a long-term and otherwise viable sovereign client, might have listened with more interest. In short, the long-run attitudes and actions of investors in this kind of a disaggregated context would have been difficult to predict.

However, none of this came to pass in the post–World War II era. The banking centers of Europe were crippled under the weight of the war, and the public importance of international lending was considered too crucial to wait for New York's private financiers to return of their own accord.[46] Although the major banks did return indirectly to sovereign lending in the immediate postwar period, it was not through a competitive market in which different lenders would have had different and sometimes opposing interpretations of risk. Rather, banks tended toward the same two interests with regard to sovereign lending, especially in riskier and developing countries. First and foremost, they sought to encourage the repayment of their own prewar loans. And second, they monitored the practices of public actors actually involved in direct sovereign lending, particularly the IBRD, which had become a private market borrower and through that an intermediary of sorts. Therefore, instead of developing into competing forums in which sovereign state claims might be heard, private investors were effectively consolidated into an indirect cartel position with regard to Bank borrowers. They would not have interpreted risk as coming from other banks seeking to expand their share of the international portfolio. Rather, most risk in this non-competitive creditor structure would have been interpreted to come from debtors. As such, there would have been little financial interest in providing any consideration for sovereign borrowers hoping to argue for distinctions between the repayment of more or less legitimate debt.[47] Effectively, the IBRD provided an authoritative channel and a public imprimatur for a more consolidated and oligopolistic idea of sovereign legitimacy in debt continuity and creditworthiness.

Furthermore, the IBRD's particular position as a *public* creditor only enhanced the noncompetitive character of this sovereign lending. I discussed in chapter 2 how public creditors can be important norm entrepreneurs and gatekeepers, especially given their explicitly public orientation and their coordinating roles. And in addition to being sensitive to the concerns of their founding members and their funders, they are less likely to be oriented to the competitive pressures of market share. This is very true for the IBRD, which was explicit about its close relationship with private finance. Unlike the disaggregated creditors of the early twentieth century, who saw significant risk in the form of competition from other banks, the post-World War II IBRD was *anti*competitive with market lenders, even soliciting their views on the treatment of its own borrower clients.[48] The Bank did not compete with these financiers but rather encouraged its borrowers to "graduate" into private lending.[49] In fact, the Bank's loan terms explicitly incorporated its own understanding of market standards in order to, in the words of Kapur, Lewis, and Webb, "protect its lenders from 'unfair' competition from the Bank."[50]

Thus, the necessarily close working relationship between the IBRD and New York banks was reflected, although not consciously (or conspiratorially), in the Bank's approach to lending and its conception of sovereign creditworthiness and proper borrower action. While the relationship drew the Bank deeper into capital market logic, this was not the logic of a competitive market, which may have been more open to considering how different claims of political legitimacy might differentially affect a sovereign's willingness to repay future debt. Rather, the structure of post-World War II international finance, in which multiple sources of private capital were funneled through a single public channel of sovereign lending, led to a more oligopolistic approach. This structural oligopoly helped to cement what might be understood as a conceptual monopoly regarding sovereignty and debt continuity that continued into the following decades.

The Statist Meaning of Political Neutrality

As part of its lending policy, the early Bank interpreted its mandate to remain politically neutral in ways that reinforced a statist approach to sovereign lending. This understanding did not run counter to the dominant ideologies of mid-twentieth-century international relations, including those espoused by developing and postcolonial countries. Such states hardly welcomed external scrutiny of their own governments, and this shared reluctance to address internal state characteristics further entrenched statism as a seemingly apolitical framework in debt going forward.

In its founding charter and its subsequent actions, the IBRD very explicitly attempted to reject "politics" and chart a neutral financial approach to lending. Indeed, article 4, section 10 of the Bank's founding Articles of Agreement, entitled "Political Activity Prohibited," reads as follows:

> The Bank and its officers shall not interfere in the political affairs of any member; nor shall they be influenced in their decisions by the political character of the member or members concerned. Only economic considerations shall be relevant to their decisions, and these considerations shall be weighed impartially in order to achieve the purposes stated in Article I.[51]

The Bank management interpreted this provision in a statist manner, lending to regimes that managed to control a state's population and territory regardless of any oppression or internal legal violations involved in enforcing that control. This was so even when the United Nations General Assembly formally requested that the IBRD refrain from lending. While the early Bank would no doubt have denied that this practice adopted any particular political theory, it necessarily rested on some understanding of sovereignty itself. As I argued more fully in chapter 2, any sovereign contract—or any attempt to enforce a sovereign contract—inevitably carries with it an implicit theory of sovereignty. The Bank's lending decisions thus reinforced the statist interpretation of sovereignty as legitimate for mid-twentieth-century international relations, including by financially buttressing governments claiming power and legitimacy on the basis of physical force alone. As such, the Bank's refusal to consider *any* question that touched upon explicitly political issues paradoxically took on a political cast.

This came most clearly to a head when the United Nations requested that the Bank stop lending to Portugal and South Africa in the mid-1960s and the Bank refused.[52] In December 1960, the General Assembly passed a "Declaration on the Granting of Independence to Colonial Countries and Peoples," and in November of the following year it passed a follow-up resolution that established a special committee to aid in implementing the resolution.[53] As a specialized agency of the United Nations—at least technically—the IBRD received a copy of the resolution and in mid-1964 was asked by the secretariat about its loans to Portugal. The following year, the General Assembly special committee passed a resolution, which

> *appealed* to all the specialized agencies of the United Nations, and in particular the International Bank for Reconstruction and Development and the International Monetary Fund, and requests them to refrain from granting Portugal any financial, economic or technical assistance so long as the Portuguese Government fails to renounce its colonial policy, which constitutes a flagrant violation of the provisions of the Charter of the United Nations.[54]

A similar reference to specialized agencies was made in a December 1965 resolution condemning apartheid in South Africa;[55] like Portugal, South Africa had recently applied for new Bank loans. Addressing the "political activity prohibited" aspect of the Articles of Agreement, the UN Secretariat argued that

> the primary intention of this section [10] of Article IV is to prohibit actions by the Bank or its officers which involve participation or interference in the internal political life of a member country and also to insure that the type or nature of the government within a member country is of no consequence to the Bank or its officers.[56]

The secretariat further emphasized that the Security Council had concluded that the actions of Portugal and South Africa constituted a threat to world peace and security, and that the Bank had agreed to "have due regard" for Security Council conclusions in its own decision making.[57]

In its response, the IBRD rejected the centrality of general community decisions and the UN Secretariat's interpretation of the political activity clause, instead insisting that its own lending decisions were nonpolitical. The Bank management interpreted its charter as not only allowing the Bank to extend loans to Portugal and South Africa, but also preventing the Bank from taking into account the political oppressions or potentially destabilizing effects of its potential borrowers. In responding to the secretariat, Bank President George Woods stated,

> [T]he Bank's Articles provide that the Bank and its officers shall not interfere in the political affairs of any member and that they shall not be influenced in their decisions by the political character of the member or members concerned. Only economic considerations are to be relevant to their decisions. Therefore, I propose to continue to treat requests for loans from these countries in the same manner as applications from other members.[58]

These World Bank loan obligations were certainly intended and expected to outlast major regime changes and pass to any successor government. In 1966, having completed its review of the loan applications on economic and technical grounds, the IBRD extended additional loan financing to Portugal and South Africa.

Thus, the immediate post-World War II policy to uniformly require repayment as a condition for submitting loan applications was matched by a general decision that countries would be allowed to borrow even if the government failed to meet basic legitimacy standards established by the UN. The financial need to appease a hypothetical group of postwar private creditor banks was reinforced by a particular interpretation of what it means to be politically neutral. The Bank ultimately and implicitly interpreted neutrality to strengthen a statist approach to sovereignty in debt and reputation. Certainly, the Bank itself developed lending criteria that limited loans to productive intended uses—in other words, World Bank contracts were self-consciously *outcome-oriented*, in keeping with the Bank Group's function as a development agency. However, these lending criteria were very clearly embedded in the Bank's own mission; they did not derive from a general concept of valid sovereign statehood as something outcome-oriented in and of itself. As such they would not be—and were not taken to be—a lending limitation for future private creditors unencumbered by such institutional priorities.

This statist "nonassessment" policy of the IBRD was supported by broader norms of sovereignty in the international arena. The legal argument that the Bank's Articles of Agreement actually *prevented* a consideration of Security Council and UN concerns perhaps went too far. However, it was certainly plausible to contend that political neutrality—at least according to mid-twentieth-century understandings—would indeed allow lending to an apartheid regime, an imperial dictatorship, or any other regime that had control of people and territory. Whereas early twentieth-century actors raised the possibility of entrenching alternative approaches to sovereignty more fully in the international arena, this project never reached its full potential. The founding international political and legal document of the midcentury, the United Nations Charter, effectively adopted a statist idea of sovereignty in the international arena. Most importantly, article 2 affirmed the importance of "equal sovereignty" regardless of internal differences or internal coercion, and also emphasized the related principle of nonintervention in state affairs.[59] This was joined by a commitment to self-determination articulated in a range of UN resolutions, including a 1960 declaration that "all peoples have an inalienable right to complete freedom," and a statement of "the necessity of bringing to a speedy and unconditional end colonialism in all its forms and manifestations."[60] A 1970 resolution similarly reaffirmed "self-determination as the universal right of all peoples" and the duty of all states to respect and promote this right.[61] However, these affirmations remained underspecified. Indeed, the "self" to be determined through statehood is still unclear, as demonstrated by outstanding controversy in the Western Sahara (under Moroccan control) and West Papua (under Indonesian control), among others.

Perhaps in part as a consequence, the process and principles of decolonization as it progressed reinforced a statist vision of sovereignty. The international legal doctrine of *uti possidetis*—the principle that a previously colonized polity should maintain the same borders upon reaching independence—arguably smoothed the transition to independence, and was therefore a reasonable choice.[62] However, the often geographically and ethnopolitically irrational construction of earlier colonial boundaries (and governing institutions) left little else beyond the possession of territory and population as an initial basis for statehood. In addition, these postcolonial grants of sovereignty did not come anywhere close to guaranteeing the full array or "bundle" of rights and powers that has been associated with the term.[63]

Unsurprisingly, then, the governments of newly independent states were among the most committed adherents to a strongly statist principle of sovereignty. Already faced with external material constraints on their freedom of action, these governments were generally loathe to allow potentially restrictive political-ideational assessments of their internal freedom of action. Major groupings of developing countries—whether in the Non-Aligned Movement or in associations such as the Organization for African Unity—insisted on noninterference in internal affairs as a cardinal rule.[64] Attention to the relations of rulership between a government and its people—whether in terms of popular sovereignty, beneficial government action, rule of law, or human rights—was not especially welcome and was (and sometimes still is) viewed as a form of neo-imperial control. And such internal scrutiny did indeed have legitimate risks for newly independent and developing countries, which were already subject to unwanted external involvement in the Cold War context. The preferences of these countries thus helped to entrench a statist idea of sovereignty in the international arena. They also would have undermined the resonance of debt cancellation arguments made on the basis of internal political illegitimacy. Along similar lines, A. Bolaji Akinyemi pointed out that "the O.A.U. cannot successfully appeal to the conscience of the international community when Member-States of the Organization are trampling on human rights and human life without a murmur from the Organization."[65]

As a consequence, in the historical context of mid-twentieth-century international norms, a statist approach could plausibly be presented as neutral.[66] This reinforced the IBRD's own interpretation of political impartiality, which in conjunction with its relationship to noncompetitive private creditors strengthened a statist framework for debt continuity and sovereign reputation. If the ideational and material features of the post-World War I arena created an open moment in the debt regime, the characteristics of post-World War II lending and international affairs played a role in closing it. As a key creditor, the IBRD propagated an idea of debt continuity as the neutral or default position, and helped to mark off alternatives as unacceptable challenges to the system of international lending. By normalizing and strengthening statist understandings of appropriate sovereign borrower behavior, this approach had an effect even after the return of private finance to international markets in the 1970s and beyond.

American Lending as a Countervailing Force?

Although IBRD lending was important in the post-World War II world, it is perhaps somewhat surprising that the Bank's view would prevail, given its status as a relative newcomer and the strong presence of other public creditors. Indeed, the main source of post-World War II development aid was the US government, whose capital outflows overtook those of the IBRD for over two decades. The power of the United States to shape norms and understandings of sovereign legitimacy in debt and reputation was, arguably, considerably greater than that of the IBRD. Given the professed American commitment to democracy, it would have been reasonable to expect that the United States might oppose statist international economic practices that disregarded internal governmental characteristics. However, US financial assistance during this period was driven largely by Cold War concerns, and despite the democratic ideology of the Cold War, this rhetoric did not ultimately counter the ideas of sovereign creditworthiness espoused by the Bank. Instead, the American influence further normalized a statist midcentury approach.

The Stated US Commitment to Democracy

Given its significant capacity as a public actor, the United States could have played a major role in promoting alternative ideas of sovereignty in debt and reputation. In particular, its importance as a funder of the IBRD and as a backer of additional financial and development institutions such as the Inter-American Development Bank (IDB) put the US government in an ideal position to challenge the orthodoxy advanced by the Bank and its private investors. This would have translated the explicit American commitment to principles of democracy into global economic practices. However, the US government ultimately interpreted its ideological mandate in line with balance of power Cold War politics, and did not present a countervailing framework for thinking through sovereignty and debt continuity in international economic relations.

Post-World War II American discourse and rhetoric took up the non-statist ideas of sovereignty promoted internationally by Woodrow Wilson in 1917. Even though Truman administration officials initially disagreed about whether to adopt a universalist or a more regionally focused sphere-of-influence policy,[67] they all agreed on the centrality of democratic principles to the postwar American world. In announcing the US commitment to supporting the West-leaning Greek and Turkish governments, the Truman Doctrine of 1947 took up precisely this language:

> At the present moment in world history nearly every nation must choose between alternative ways of life. . . . One way of life is based upon the will of the majority, and is distinguished by free institutions, representative government, free elections, guarantees of individual liberty, freedom of speech and religion, and freedom from political oppression. . . . I believe it must be the policy of the United States to support free peoples who are resisting attempted subjugations by armed minorities or by outside pressure.[68]

We can imagine how the American dedication to helping "free peoples to work out their own destinies in their own way" might have extended to supporting an odious debt-type principle. Such a principle could have been implemented either in dealing with the United States' own aid recipients, or in pressuring the new IBRD to take account of internal political rule in its own practice. Truman had in fact highlighted the role of international economic relations in promoting his vision, stating, "I believe that our help should be primarily through economic and financial aid which is essential to economic stability and orderly political processes."[69] However, American Cold War policy ultimately headed in a fairly traditional sphere–of–influence direction, in which the United States was willing to support—and establish—authoritarian regimes in its alliance.[70] As part of this approach, the American government viewed suspiciously any country that adopted left-leaning policies, even when such policies met with popular support and fell far short of Soviet-style totalitarianism.[71]

Even had the United States *not* espoused a sphere-of-influence policy with statist ramifications, its position as a well-funded public creditor paradoxically may have limited the longevity of any American impact on broader expectations of debt continuity. As I discussed in chapter 2, certain public creditors, such as the World Bank, may not view profit as an end in itself but do still depend on recouping expenses for their own continuance. Another category, which includes the Cold War American government, is even less concerned with recouping expenses, instead extending credit as a more explicit form of aid and as part of a much larger ideological vision and geopolitical strategy.[72] Although much US Cold War political, military, and economic funding technically came in the form of loans, the American government would frequently have been less concerned with the strict repayment of such loans than the IBRD.[73] Given this diminished focus on complete repayment, questions of how sovereign legitimacy might factor into general creditworthiness requirements would not arise in the same way. As such, the impact of US lending was less likely to include the broader reframing of sovereign continuity, illegitimate debt, and appropriate borrower action that might shape the understandings of future creditors.

Soft Competition between the IBRD and the US Government

To the extent that the United States had a deeper effect on the construction of debt continuity and reputational norms in the mid-twentieth century, this influence emerged more through its relationship with international financial institutions than through independent lending. Indeed, the IBRD and the United States were very much in agreement on many ideological points. Although technically the Bank was (and is) a UN agency, its weighted voting structure has made it especially attentive to the concerns of its shareholders. The United States supported the Bank's efforts as a development agency as part of its broader postwar strategy, and the Bank in turn paid heed to the concerns of its most important capital contributor.[74]

This largely collaborative rapport between the United States and the Bank only underscored a basically noncompetitive relationship between the two creditors. The type of market competition that might have forced these public creditors to pay greater attention to independently formulated borrower arguments—including those about legitimate sovereignty—never arose. This more consolidated approach was enhanced by the bifurcation of US and IBRD lending into the two separate logics I mentioned earlier in this chapter, which led to a degree of complementarity. The minimal competition that did result from differences of opinion on lending never developed into a strong enough rift to question basic statist assessments in creditworthiness and debt practices. Thus, neither the American government's role as a propagator of norms nor its position as a potentially competitive public creditor induced it to formulate an alternative long-term approach in international economic relations.

This dynamic resulted in part from US aid decisions after World War II. While preferred Cold War allies received the most direct support, primarily through the significant bilateral grants provided by the Marshall fund, the United States hoped to achieve its goal of general development assistance with fewer and less extensive American organizational and financial obligations.[75] After the 1947 Marshall Plan took over much of the European reconstruction work that was part of the Bank's original mission, the Bank shifted more attention to developing countries, first in Latin America and then elsewhere.[76] Despite the early Bank's meager funds for low-income sovereign lending, the United States left general, non-Cold-War-driven development lending to the Bank for at least the first decade after World War II. Only beginning in the 1950s, as US development aid expanded in light of greater Soviet presence in developing countries, did the Bank receive more US financing for development assistance.[77]

Still, it is worth noting that although their interests and ideology tended to move in concert, the United States and the IBRD did not completely work in tandem. There were several situations in which the Bank came into more direct conflict with American government agencies, actually attempting to limit their foreign lending. For example, in 1953, foreign exchange and inflation problems led the Brazilian government to block foreign earnings remittances and capital repatriation. The IBRD, which was considering a loan to Brazil at that time, decided to put the financing on hold until the policy was reversed. However, any uniform disciplinary pressure that might have resulted from this action was undermined by the extension of a three-year US government loan for $300 million.[78] At a broader structural level, Bank President Eugene Black even lobbied for the liquidation of the US Export-Import Bank, which loaned at cheaper rates than the IBRD.[79] Frustrated with the Bank's hold on sovereign lending, Latin American countries eventually persuaded the United States, then concerned with the recent Cuban Revolution, to support the creation of the Inter-American Development Bank. These countries hoped that the IDB would provide a more welcoming forum for their loan applications and proposed terms than the World Bank.[80]

While these initially may look like the actions of a competitive lender or a protective monopolist, closer consideration further reveals the bifurcated logic of Bank and US government lending at the time. The Bank did not wish to ensure a profitable monopoly by cutting off all US financial flows to these countries. In fact, it had no problem with politically motivated aid as such, but wished it to be in the form of grants rather than "illusory loans." It was committed in its first decade and a half to the view that international development loans should be fairly limited, and that any lending should follow sound economic principles. Bank management believed that its own loans met these guidelines, but remained suspicious of the US government's soft lending. It was particularly concerned about the possibility that such assistance would undermine the discipline and market rationality that it sought to cultivate in the Bank's borrowers.[81] In short, the IBRD's anticompetitive actions did not derive from an effort to exclude other creditors per se. Rather, the Bank hoped to limit altogether what it considered to be corrupting influences within the field of sovereign lending. In fact, the Bank intended that its own *temporary* monopoly over sovereign borrowers would eventually allow them to leave the Bank behind and graduate to the private credit market. Similarly, the US government did not seek to lure sovereign borrowers, and in many cases it would have affirmatively preferred the Bank to act as the major creditor. In the 1953 Brazilian case, for example, the US agency was forced into making the loan itself because of the Bank's refusal.

This interaction between the United States and the IBRD can hardly be understood as a disagreement about the relevance of valid statehood or illegitimate debt in sovereign lending, with the potential to shift global debt norms going forward. Rather, US lending to these countries resulted from broader geostrategic exigencies, and progressed in spite of any creditworthiness concerns. While the American government's politically motivated lending eventually dropped off—in line with diminishing perceptions of a grave Soviet threat—the IBRD's creditworthiness framework and its rejection of alternative approaches became more relevant as its lending increased in volume. Thus the ultimately congruent nature of US and Bank lending helped to entrench statist expectations of debt continuity for the sovereign credit market as the twentieth century unfolded.

The Midcentury Closure of Possibilities: China and Cuba

In the aftermath of the First World War and through the 1920s, private lenders were eager to return to international capital markets and sovereign lending, which had run relatively smoothly until the outbreak of hostilities in 1914. In contrast, the years following World War II involved a very different dynamic. While the war revitalized economic production and cross-border lending to some degree, it had also followed the general collapse of international capital markets and a wave of sovereign debt defaults. Private money, largely American, shifted away from the international arena and was primarily invested in economic growth at home and then in more direct ventures abroad. This left longer-term sovereign lending to public actors such as the US government and the International Bank for Reconstruction and Development, whose early decision-making frameworks laid the foundation for the norms of the evolving sovereign debt regime.

In the case of the IBRD, the close relationship of Bank management to noncompetitive private investors shaped and narrowed its interpretation of acceptable sovereign debtor action. The Bank's early reliance on private bond markets rendered it especially concerned with its own creditworthiness, and thus more insistent on uniform debt repayment by its potential sovereign borrowers. This commitment to debt continuity was reinforced by the Bank's interpretation of political neutrality as ultimately statist, establishing a conceptual template for the postwar sovereign debt regime that was unconcerned with internal forms of rule in either initial lending decisions or expectations of repayment. The US government, driven in part by antipathy to anti-Western and leftist revolutionary activity, adopted a geopolitically driven lending policy that ignored or supported statist approaches to debt instead of reshaping them. Given the centrality of these public actors in resuscitating postwar international capital flows, their early decisions had long-term consequences.

This larger mid-twentieth-century material and ideational structure limited the latent transformative meaning of major regime changes during this period. In particular, the emergence of the People's Republic of China (PRC) and socialist Cuba did not display the same potential as the earlier Soviet and Costa Rican defaults. Their repudiations of the respective previous regimes' external economic relations resulted in an effective ostracization from international capital flows, without the creditor disunity of the earlier cases. They suggest not the inevitability of a statist insistence on debt continuity, but rather the centrality of broader economic structures and dominant political actors and ideologies in enabling or disabling particular outcomes.

Having defeated the Chinese Nationalist Party (or Kuomintang) in a long civil war, the Chinese Communist Party faced the opposition of the United States and the array of international organizations in which the United States was dominant. Particularly given the minimal interest of private capital in international lending at the time, this hostility had serious ramifications for its foreign economic relations. In 1949, the new People's Republic of China issued a "Common Program" that explicitly denied sovereign continuity with the previous regime, at least as a default position. It abolished "all the prerogatives of imperialist countries in China," and enabled the confiscation of "bureaucratic capital [to be put] into the possession of the people's state." In order to further this goal, the new regime indicated that it would "examine the treaties and agreements concluded between the Kuomintang and foreign governments, and shall recognize, abrogate, revise, or re-negotiate them according to their respective contents."[82] As a practical matter, this involved the expropriation of privately held capital, including foreign capital, and the nonpayment of external debt issued by predecessor regimes.[83] These external debts included the Huguang Railway bonds, issued in 1911 in the last days of the imperial Qing government under considerable foreign pressure, and the 5 percent Reorganization Gold Loan Bearer Bonds issued by the new Chinese Republic in 1913.[84]

Cut off from the UN, the newly operative IBRD, and most sources of public credit, the PRC effectively remained outside mainstream international relations and international capital markets during its first thirty years. In the early 1950s it financed the First Five-Year Plan, a major economic development initiative, by issuing two series of national bonds. For the most part, these bonds were sold domestically—in certain cases so forcibly as to constitute expropriation—although there is some evidence of them having been marketed in overseas Chinatowns.[85] During this time the government also engaged in limited external borrowing in the form of modest loans and industrial credits from the Soviet Union, which sought to parallel the United States by engaging (albeit to a lesser extent) in Cold War financial activity. This lasted only until the Sino-Soviet split of the late 1950s, however, and was insufficient to make up for a considerable trade deficit.[86] In 1979, on the eve of China's reengagement with international markets, its external debt amounted to only $2.2 billion[87]—a relatively small amount, particularly in comparison with its absorptive capacity and with other large developing countries flush with external finance through the 1970s.

A similar narrative emerges from the Cuban Revolution of 1959, another defining social and economic revolution of this period. Cuba before the fall of Fulgencio Batista had not been a major international borrower from either public or private sources, including international bond markets.[88] Most foreign funds entered through foreign direct investment, and US citizens and in some cases the American government were centrally involved in the ownership, regulation, and trading relationships of key economic sectors. This US presence was supported by a claimed American right to intervention into Cuban affairs, and a 1956 Department of Commerce survey went so far as to assess that "the only foreign investments of importance are those of the United States."[89] Around 75 percent of the country's land was dominated by elite Cuban families and large Cuban- and foreign-owned sugar and cattle companies. The seasonal nature of the sugar crop meant that much land lay fallow and many remained unemployed for large stretches of the year.[90] The initially popular Cuban Revolution was in large measure a response to this skewed economic system and the increasingly oppressive and corrupt politics with which it was associated.[91]

Given this external financing structure, the repudiation of previous economic contracts after the revolution primarily took the form of expropriations or nationalizations. The Agrarian Reform Law of May 1959 targeted Cuba's crucially important agricultural land, including cattle ranches and tobacco, coffee, and sugar plantations. Particularly due to the poor state of Cuban finances after the revolution, the new regime initially offered long-term nonconvertible bonds for the agricultural enterprises. The previous owners considered this inadequate, and ultimately no bonds were printed.[92] Partially in response to the subsequent US elimination of its sugar purchase quotas and emboldened by Soviet agreement to take over the American sugar quota, the new government soon nationalized other enterprises. These included American oil refineries, banks, chemical plants, and industrial processing facilities.[93] While these policies were not initially presented as antiforeign or anti-American, heightening tensions on both sides led the new regime to take an even stronger stance by 1960. In February of that year, key Castro advisor Ernesto (Che) Guevara stated, "We maintain the point of view that foreign investments in Cuba, as in all countries of Latin America, under the condition on which they are made, constitute a great business for the investor, but a bad business for the country."[94] A month later, he reiterated, "Our economic war will be with the powerful North American nation. . . . Our hardest fight is against the North American monopolies. . . . Private foreign capital comes here only for profit and does nothing for the people of Cuba."[95] Escalation on both sides deepened the hostility between the United States and the new regime, and Cuba further distanced itself from economic arenas dominated by the United States and the IBRD. It formally withdrew from the IBRD in late 1960, giving as its reason that "the economic policy of that institution is far from being effective in regard to the development and expansion of the Cuban economy, which the Government is carrying out according to a definite plan."[96] Cuba defaulted on its largest ($85 million) external dollar bond issue in January 1961, with $44 million in payments outstanding, when the new regime failed to pay a semiannual payment of almost $1 million.[97] Ultimately, US businesses and individuals claimed losses in Cuba of over $1 billion.[98]

The American government and major American economic concerns retaliated by marginalizing Cuba in international economic relations for decades to come. After the elimination of sugar quotas in July 1960 and the subsequent nationalizations, the United States embargoed nonfood and nonmedical trade, and then instituted a complete embargo in February 1962.[99] Soon after, the Cuban Assets Control Regulations of July 1963 froze $33 million of Cuban funds in US banks.[100] Individual banks took further steps, with National City Bank selling collateral that secured outstanding Cuban loans and retaining the excess amounts as unilateral compensation for the expropriation of its Cuban branches. In large part due to the preferences of the State Department, the US Supreme Court declined to apply the Act of State doctrine in the case, which if applied would have prevented US judgment of Cuba's acts taken within its own territory.[101] Unsurprisingly, subsequent Cuban external economic links were not with the United States, which forbade American financial and economic concerns from engaging with Cuba. Indicating the importance of variation in business interests even in the post-World War II era, some European and, eventually, Japanese enterprises, which had not been as heavily involved in prerevolutionary Cuba or as affected by its transformation, remained connected through trading relationships.[102] And although the Castro regime repudiated a number of contracts entered into by the previous regime, certain prerevolution relationships, such as for the public bus system, were retained and renegotiated.[103] However, sustained US pressure on its allies, the narrow approach acceptable to the IBRD, and the general morbidity of international capital markets in the post–World War II era undermined the possibility of discontinuous approaches to sovereign debt and dramatically limited the options available to Cuba. As early as 1961 over 90 percent of Cuban exports went to communist bloc countries, and the young government eventually slipped into financial dependence on the Soviet Union.[104] Later regimes in similar situations—such as Nicaragua under the Sandinistas at the turn of the 1980s—drew lessons from Cuba's relegation to a marginal position. As such, the Cuban example had a narrowing effect on the norms of debt continuity well beyond its time.

The pressures toward maintaining a default position of statism in international lending, inattentive to questions of internal regime legitimacy and sovereign discontinuity, strengthened in post–World War II international economic relations. These pressures may make the material and ideational openings of the post–World War I era, along with the cases of the Soviet and Costa Rican repudiations, seem like isolated anomalies. However, the reconsolidation of debt continuity in the mid-twentieth century depended on historical circumstances that involved an active though not necessarily deliberate normalization process. The IBRD helped to establish a template for what would constitute responsible and acceptable sovereign debt practices going forward, insisting on a uniform repayment rule and espousing a definition of political neutrality that was ultimately statist. The United States, as the other primary actor in international sovereign lending, did not challenge either this underlying political theory or the subsequent reinforcement of debt continuity. In fact, its antileftist political ideology—which strengthened in the twenties, weakened in the 1930s and early 1940s, and returned again in the late 1940s and 1950s—only reiterated this default position, given that major regime changes at this time leaned leftward. These larger structures and processes limited the potential meaning of the Chinese and Cuban revolutions for sovereign debt during this period. Ultimately, the underlying economic structure and broader ideological context of mid-twentieth-century international relations proved to be inhospitable ground for the further development of non-statist approaches incorporating ideas of illegitimate debt. This laid the foundation for a solidification of the expectations, practices, and reputational mechanisms of debt continuity that became dominant in subsequent decades.

6

Continuity and Consolidation
in the Return of Private Finance

We're not dealing with politics. . . . We're dealing with the
continuing institution of the Nicaraguan government.
—DEBT ADVISOR TO SANDINISTAS, paraphrasing bank negotiators

WHILE PUBLIC ACTORS such as the World Bank laid the foundations for the contemporary debt regime after World War II, key private players returned in force during the 1970s. Although they were initially wary of international sovereign lending, developments over two decades had made the sovereign credit markets more attractive. The advanced industrialized countries had fallen into economic difficulties, and the easing of capital controls associated with the Bretton Woods system meant that private capital could flow more freely across borders. Beginning in the late 1960s, private creditors began to look overseas for productive investments. This engagement deepened in the early 1970s, when major banks received an infusion of deposits from member states of the Organization of Petroleum Exporting Countries (OPEC), flush with funds or "petrodollars" resulting from recent oil price hikes.[1] The banks needed to "recycle" this capital, lending the funds in a way that would generate a return, in order to eventually repay the OPEC deposits with interest. With the sovereign defaults of the 1930s more or less dealt with—thanks in part to the IBRD's pioneering efforts—sovereign borrowers, including those in developing regions, looked relatively appealing.

To what degree did this infusion of new players shift the expectations surrounding debt continuity and sovereign legitimacy in the 1970s and into the 1980s? The greater number of potential creditors could well have generated the competition and variation helpful for more flexibility in dealing with odious debt-type arguments. But numerosity in and of itself is not sufficient to generate multiple perspectives. Although heavy competition marked the 1970s' return of private finance to sovereign debt, this dynamic differed significantly from that of the 1920s. The emergence of Eurodollar markets in the 1960s, the spike in multinational branching, and the rise of syndicated lending resulted in considerable integration of global banking structures. These developments encouraged greater consolidation and a shared interpretation of risk among private creditors. Thus, although banks competed with each other, I argue that they did so with a common outlook that undermined the space for heterodox approaches in sovereign debt. With little inclination or pressure to engage with sovereign borrower arguments, private creditors easily adopted the statist approach to politically neutral lending taken by the World Bank. This general framework also resonated with borrowing country elites eager to maintain maximum access to international capital.

The debt restructuring processes of the late 1970s and 1980s incorporated both the integrated structure and the statist framework of the original 1960s' and 1970s' loans. The interaction of private banks with public institutional actors such as the IMF resulted in a joint approach to sovereign debtors that limited the receptivity to non-statist claims. And the general debtor response focused on broader inequities in the economic system, which applied equally to borrowers regardless of their domestic regimes and discounted arguments based on internal political differences. As I highlight in discussions of Nicaragua, Iran, and the Philippines, this narrowed the space for making odious debt-type claims even after major and self-avowedly revolutionary regime changes. Even in cases where debtors internally debated the merits of principled debt repudiation, no open and principled claim actually challenged and tested the statist approach. As such, the creditor interactions and broader sovereignty norms embedded in the lending and restructuring practices of the 1970s and 1980s continued and further deepened the mid-twentieth normalization of statist debt continuity.

Integration and Competitive Consolidation in Sovereign Lending

The material and social structures of sovereign credit markets in the 1970s undermined the degree to which the competitive market of the era might have enabled more flexible debt continuity norms. The

development of the Eurodollar market, the rise of multinational banking, loan syndication, and new contractual provisions in sovereign
loans led to an unprecedented degree of connection between banking
centers. The community of loan officers—implicating virtually every
bank with any interest in sovereign lending—acted not only as competitors but also as cooperative fellow travelers in a globalized credit system
that very deliberately pooled lending risk. Their shared financial and
ideational frameworks helped to unify their interpretations of acceptable action in sovereign debt, limiting the possibilities for alternative
approaches. Thus, although sovereign lending through the 1970s was
highly competitive, this only resulted in a joint embrace of the same
fundamentally statist vision.

The Integrated Structure Underlying
the Return of Private Lending

The shared approach to debtors that emerged through the 1970s and into
the 1980s depended to an important degree on the material integration
of private sovereign lending. One key ingredient in this integration was
the development of the Eurodollar market through the 1960s. The market initially emerged in 1950s' London, where banks held not only their
own capital reserves but also large deposits of dollars that had moved
across the Atlantic with the Marshall Plan and the first wave of foreign
direct investment. Given the difficulty of using European national currencies to finance trade and other credits—initially due to capital controls and then to restrictions imposed as a result of balance of payments
problems—British banks in particular began to finance such credits with
their US dollar deposits. Because such European-based dollar deposits
were not subject to either British capital regulations or to American regulations applicable to dollars on US soil, this largely unregulated market
emerged as a central financing mechanism.[2]

US banks, and then banks in other countries, looked with interest to
this new overseas development. Many New York banks were expanding
into Europe in the post-World War II era, in large part to follow and
finance their American corporate customers engaging in foreign direct
investment. The Euromarkets provided only more reason to accelerate
this expansion in the 1960s, particularly given that American financial
regulations placed constraints on US-based international lending.[3] In
fact, in order to take advantage of the less regulated environment in the
Euromarkets, American banks would sometimes service their American customers through their European-based branches.[4] This transfer

of formerly New York-based business expanded the Eurodollar trade credit system into a serious capital market, and also deepened the links between major financial capitals, particularly London and New York.[5]

To participate more fully in the new developments in London, foreign banks began to establish branches there in large numbers, further co-alescing major money-center banks into a more interconnected system. Whereas American banks had a total of ten London branches in 1958, this number had jumped to fifty-five by 1974.[6] The eight top US banks opened 113 European branches and twenty-nine representative offices, with forty-two new London branches opening between 1967 and the mid-1970s. American banks were not the only ones arriving in London—foreign banks had established 243 branches by the mid-1970s and controlled more than half the total assets (including sterling and foreign currency) in British banks.[7] Attesting to the global reach of this trend, by the late 1960s, Japanese banks made up the second-largest group of foreign banks in London.[8] These developments constituted a major departure from the 1920s, during which time non-European bank branches in European financial centers remained few, despite concerted American efforts to win a larger share of international lending and to expand aggressively in Latin America and the Far East.[9] These earlier European branches had initially opened to finance trade credit and service existing customers, as with the 1970s' branches. However, they were few and far between and never fully took root.[10]

Other structural elements provided additional impetus for integration. A 1966 regulatory change permitted American banks to invest in the stock of foreign banks, launching a series of mergers and encouraging the US bank purchase of minority stakes in nine British banks.[11] Four major British banks deepened this effect by buying into American financial institutions in turn.[12] European banks also made an effort to internationalize significantly, not only by engaging in bank branching but also through participation in banking groups or clubs, particularly during the 1960s. In part as a result of the American entrance into the Eurodollar market, European banks—usually those of different nationalities—entered as shareholders into joint ventures or consortia, which drew in thirty-five of the fifty largest global banks by 1971.[13] A significant number of banks also entered into European-American consortia to broaden their reach.[14] Between 1964 and 1971, 110 financial institutions from fourteen nations had created seventeen consortium banks.[15] In addition, looser banking clubs or coalitions attempted to extend member banks' services more broadly, particularly throughout Western Europe, through less formal integrating mechanisms.[16]

Catherine Schenk points out that, as a result of these changing dynamics of international capital markets, the relationship between the major banking cities was not competitive in the traditional sense: "The starting premise for any assessment of competition among financial centres in the 1960s is to recognize that they were not all performing the same functions. In this sense they were not competitors but rather parts of an increasingly integrated global financial market."[17] She argues that London served as the true linchpin of the system, which allowed head offices of American banks in New York—the top money-center—to take advantage of the Eurodollar regulatory environment. The deep integration among financial centers beginning in that period undermines an assessment of New York and London in particular as conventional competitors. In Schenk's words, "viewed in terms of multinational expansion rather than rivalry, banks were becoming vertically integrated, locating in foreign centres to capture resources for their head office."[18]

Loan Syndication, Social Connections, and a Shared Path in Lending

Cooperative bank lending and the social networks that accompanied this collaboration deepened the cross-border integration of major banks. The more intensive use of syndicated loans, in which multiple creditors from various corners of the globe lent a portion of the full borrowed amount, allowed banks to diversify their portfolios and limit their exposure in any given loan. These syndicates, along with contractual provisions such as cross-default clauses, paralleled and strengthened at the microlevel the consolidation of international banking taking place at the macrolevel. The geographic proximity and social interaction of many banks' loan officers also furthered a shared approach.

Syndicates had already been a feature of private market lending in the nineteenth and early twentieth centuries, particularly in sovereign debt. However, the syndicated loans that emerged from the Eurodollar markets in the 1970s differed to an important degree. First, they were primarily made up of bank credits, which stayed on bank books; earlier sovereign lending had worked largely through bonds sold to individual investors (the final purchasers), with banking houses serving primarily as underwriters.[19] But the more important change in the 1970s involved the immense range of banks participating in these syndicates. The London office of Manufacturers Hanover organized the first syndicated Eurocredit sovereign loan, a relatively minor $80 million loan to Iran that involved multiple transnational banks and included a variable interest rate.[20]

However, over the course of the next dozen years, even economically more marginal countries were able to borrow from hundreds of banks through such syndicates. As the *Wall Street Journal* highlighted in 1983, the rescheduling of Ecuador's comparatively modest $1.2 billion in overdue foreign debt required the participation of 400 commercial banks.[21] A conservative estimate counted 350 creditors for the Philippines' mid-1980s' debt rescheduling.[22] A major debtor like Mexico had so many creditors through syndicated bank loans that its own finance minister was uncertain as to how many might be involved—estimates ranged from 500 to more than a thousand, and 800 banks were invited to an initial meeting to reschedule Mexican debt in 1982.[23] Commentators even after the rescheduling provided different metrics for assessing the final number of Mexico's creditors. Charles Lipson suggests the higher end of "some fourteen hundred commercial banks worldwide,"[24] whereas Vinod Aggarwal estimates about 600 banks involved in the 1983 Mexican rescheduling and 560 in the subsequent Brazilian agreement.[25] While these figures diverge widely—and in any case are at the upper end of numbers involved in sovereign lending—they provide some indication of the degree to which banks were jointly implicated in particular projects. Even small local and regional banks ended up being drawn into far-flung sovereign lending in regions with which they were unfamiliar.

Just as importantly, these syndicates were very international in their participation. Scholars writing in the mid-1980s pointed out, "The largest part of bank credits is now the product of syndicates of mixed nationality. The ease and intimacy with which financiers from different countries work together would have seemed unthinkable, if not treasonous, three-quarters of a century ago."[26] Of the 800 banks invited to the Mexican rescheduling meeting, the 150 that attended came from all corners of the globe, including Argentina, Canada, Japan, European states, and of course the United States, among others.[27] This is not to deny the existence of differential exposure to sovereign lending, regional preferences, or governmental influences. British and American banks were most heavily exposed,[28] and American banks accounted for 35.7 percent of total international lending to Mexico, Brazil, and Argentina—countries that in turn accounted for a large portion of sovereign debt.[29] European and particularly German banks led the way in Eastern Europe, in part as a result of government incentives.[30] Japanese banks participated enthusiastically in international lending, including to sovereigns, when freed by the Ministry of Finance to do so.[31] But even outside their traditional areas of involvement banks were significantly exposed to sovereign lending through these syndicated loans. After American prohibitions on Soviet bloc lending were lifted, US banks lent in these areas in excess of $7 billion by 1982, and the total exposure of all Western and Japanese banks exceeded $60 billion.[32]

Thus, despite these private banks' different regional tendencies and governmental relations, they became "increasingly interlocked" as they returned to sovereign lending.[33] The geographic concentration of the Eurodollar markets and the joint outlook encouraged by syndicated lending resulted in a significantly integrated framework in sovereign lending. As Youssef Cassis points out, "One of the causes of [the] infatuation with loans to the third world was undeniably the herd instinct, or the fear of missing the boat—a fear reinforced by lenders gathering in a few large-scale financial centres."[34] This social geographic element emerges in the words of one banker involved in 1970s' syndicated lending: "Syndication depends on only about a hundred people in London, and you soon get to know them all. Everyone feels that they're in it together. They hate to be left out."[35] Even allowing some space for exaggeration, the sentiment appears to have been widely shared. Anthony Sampson notes that international lending at the time "attracted a special coterie of cosmopolitan younger bankers, constantly talking on the international telephones. They enjoyed a social world of their own: finance ministers treated them as old friends; they entertained each other lavishly; the final signing of a loan was celebrated with a huge banquet at the Ritz or the Berkeley."[36]

To some extent, the banks making up the informal "London Club" of private creditors to sovereign states did exhibit certain features of a social club, at least at the level of loan officers.[37] This aspect of shared outlook, undergirded by proximate geography and the connection of risk through loan syndications, deepened the consolidation taking place with the rise of Eurodollar markets and multinational banking. Given the banks' joint engagement with sovereign lending, there was little challenge to conventional practices, and indeed there was greater pressure to conform to these practices. To the extent that 1970s' and 1980s' debt practices generally adopted the statist midcentury approach, the integration of private creditors as they returned to sovereign lending only furthered its normalization.

Affirming the Statist Approach in Lending and Borrowing

The resurgence of private sovereign lending through this multinational, syndicated framework took place during the heyday of twentieth-century authoritarian rule. Even without any explicit wish to lend to authoritarian regimes,[38] inattentiveness or indifference to questions of sovereign legitimacy implicitly defaulted to a statist standard in sovereign debt contracts. This default was strengthened by its resonance with World Bank and US government practices in the immediate post-World War II period, which were adopted by private lenders upon their return to the sovereign credit market. However, private lenders were perhaps even more indifferent; unlike public international financial institutions with particular development or geostrategic lending goals, they made little real effort to inquire into intended loan purposes. Reinforcing this approach further, sovereign borrowers themselves tended to shun external inquiry and interference into their domestic affairs. As such, although challenges to the international economic system were made, they failed to undermine the statist ideas and presumptions of debt continuity grounding the sovereign debt regime.

The Private Creditors' Implicit Political Theory

Part of the allure of the Eurodollar markets for potential sovereign borrowers involved the willingness of private banks to lend without asking very many questions. The variable rates associated with these loans meant they were hardly risk-free, but the funds were disbursed without lengthy negotiations and burdensome conditions. In the words of one banker involved in 1970s' lending, "When I first started I was amazed at how casual it all seemed. When I first signed a loan agreement for twenty million dollars for a country I hardly knew anything about, I thought 'we must be crazy'."[39] This was particularly the case in countries such as Mexico, where the heavy competition between banks tended to encourage lending without intensive analysis.[40] As a Mexican financial official involved in the 1980s' debt rescheduling said of the initial lending, "The banks were hot to get in. All the banks in the US and Europe and Japan stepped forward. They showed no foresight. They didn't do any credit analysis. It was wild."[41] However, even in far less traditionally secure areas, few questions were asked. Speaking of lending to Zaire, one banker noted, "When you're lending to a corporation at home, one of the first questions is: how can it pay the money back? But in Zaire nobody asked that question."[42] As Anthony Sampson puts it, "The World Bank might take three years after the first application before they finally gave out the money for a dam or a road. . . . But these commercial bankers, once they had decided a country was credit-worthy, were prepared to lend money for no specific project, with no political strings and with far less delay."[43]

This aspect of "no political strings attached" was sometimes stated explicitly and presented as a virtue. As expressed by the head of Citibank's international division in 1977, "I believe we have worked in the whole post-war period to try to live down the accusations of Wall Street imperialism around the world . . . I think our whole basis for survival in the less-developed countries has been that we do not intervene politically in those countries."[44] And as with the IBRD in the immediate post-World War II period, political neutrality was not interpreted to mean simply indifference as to left-leaning or right-leaning economic and political development. It was taken to preclude an assessment of the relations of rulership between the government signing the contract and the underlying population and territory—both in the initial lending process and in the expectation that the funds would be recovered.

This was particularly the case when justifying lending to regimes, such as South Africa, considered illegitimate by large numbers of countries. These banks did not intend to demonstrate political *approval* of such regimes. They presented their lending as basically apolitical, again following the example of international economic institutions such as the World Bank. In the words of one Citicorp vice chairman, "Who knows which political system works? The only test we care about is: Can they pay their bills?"[45] Along the same lines, a Midland Bank official argued, "If we were to allow ourselves to be influenced in our business dealings by political views of this kind . . . our international business would rapidly become impossible."[46] George Vojta, Citibank's executive vice president, offered an explanation of sorts after the 1976 Soweto uprising in South Africa, which was instigated by a deadly police response to high school students protesting requirements that they be taught in Afrikaans. Vojta explained to the US Senate that it would be improper for Citibank to act on the basis of a political judgment of South Africa, stating, "Citibank regards its corporate mission as bringing the provision of a full range of financial services everywhere in the world where it can legally operate at a profit."[47] Individual bank officials occasionally demurred, as did David Rockefeller at a 1967 Chase annual meeting in response to a stockholder divestment petition: "None of us holds any brief for apartheid. . . . In fact, we regard it as a dangerous and shocking policy."[48] Nonetheless, these private creditors maintained lending practices that instantiated a statist vision of sovereign legitimacy. As with the IBRD before them, this ostensibly apolitical approach involved an implicit political choice—one that rendered loans made even to "dangerous and shocking" policy makers binding on subsequent regimes.

Sovereign Borrowers and a Rejection of Limitations

Perhaps unsurprisingly, the elites of most regimes borrowing at the time were eager to maintain a noninterventionist conceptual framework in both the economic and political arena. This was the case notwithstanding certain political disagreements, such as those surrounding apartheid South Africa, and even despite international financial institutions' and creditor country bank regulators' unhappiness about overly loose private lending. A statist framework in sovereign debt and its implicit denial of odious debt ideas allowed borrowing elites to access international bank capital through multiple state organs, for vague purposes, and in some cases in contravention of clear domestic guidelines.

The increasingly easy lending to sovereign borrowers alarmed the IMF and some central bankers, who watched as sovereign loan maturities fell and expressed concern about both the sustainability of such capital flows and also the ways in which they might undermine market discipline. The IMF's managing director, Johannes Witteveen, suggested in 1976 that "competitive enlargement of this role of private banks might well foster a climate of all-too-easy borrowing by deficit countries, thus facilitating inflationary financing and delaying the adoption of needed adjustment policies. . . . In general, therefore, a very careful and balanced policy by the international banks is needed."[49] He emphasized again later in the year that such flows would undermine adjustment efforts, saying that "commercial bank lending should not be so easily available that it made the need for adjustment less clear, and hence caused the authorities to accumulate larger debts than were desirable."[50]

However, countries themselves were loath to accept limitations on or internal assessments of either their economic or political policies. In response to Witteveen's comments, the finance minister of Brazil, Mario Enrique Simonsen, rejected internal assessments in 1977:

> While they would certainly welcome the technical assistance of the Fund and other institutions, in helping them to improve their own statistical and informational systems, the developing countries continued to feel that the Fund could play no useful role as a purveyor to the private sector of judgments, analyses, and forecasts.[51]

Most of the discussion about tightening lending standards focused on the need for macroeconomic adjustment, given that concerns about governmental legitimacy or the use of funds were rarely raised by the international financial institutions. Still, the concomitant absence of any political considerations in lending would not have disturbed most borrowing countries at the time either.

Sovereign borrowing during this period involved, in addition to a rejection of external assessments of country validity, a lack of specificity as to which bureaucratic organs were entitled to borrow under the country's name. As Joseph Kraft points out, in the Mexican rescheduling, "There was the government itself, technically the United Mexican States . . . there was the national oil company, Pemex. Then the Development Bank, Nafinsa. Then the Telephone Company, and the nationalized steel plant, and the fisheries, and sugar mills and so forth."[52] He points out that although these different agencies technically had independent financial bases, thus allowing banks to list the funds as lent to separate entities, in practice the lines between Mexican financial bases were not carefully demarcated.[53] Similar problems emerged in other countries, even when central governments made efforts to bring profligate agency borrowing to heel. State officials and agency heads were frequently eager to build their own fiefdoms on the national balance sheet, and international banks allowed and even encouraged this behavior. The Indonesian national oil company, Pertamina, was run by President (and General) Suharto's military associate, who eventually became very popular with international bankers. He was highly adept at securing international funds, although both the American embassy and the IMF were concerned about excessive lending to Pertamina. More importantly, the Indonesian Central Bank was uncertain about the extent of the oil company's borrowing, new pieces of which would occasionally come to light, and even attempted to bring the state agency under control. This effort was undermined by the willingness of banks to lend in contravention of the central government's concerns, and the governor of the Central Bank complained about his "disappointment" at the banks' behavior.[54]

While these situations highlight the potential problems in lending indiscriminately to multiple state agencies, there existed even more egregious cases in which banks and borrowing government elites blatantly ignored very clearly delineated guidelines. For example, according to the Iranian constitution under the shah (article no. 25), certain types of debt contract required the approval of parliament. However, a multinational bank syndicate led by Chase and involving American, Swiss, Canadian, and British banks decided to make a $500 million loan to the imperial government with the authorization of the shah's executive branch alone and without parliamentary approval. Their Iranian legal advisor warned—at personal risk to himself—that such a loan might not be enforceable. However, the Iranian Ministry of Justice and other (non-Iranian) counsel assured Chase that this constitutional provision should not be a hindrance and that the shah's government was creditworthy.[55]

The syndicate presumably intended to—and in fact did—insist that any subsequent regimes repay this shah-era debt. In doing so, it implicitly assumed a statist political framework in debt and reputational assessment, which treated the shah's control of the underlying territory and population as sufficient for enforceable international loans, notwithstanding any legal irregularities. Other loans to Iran also underlined the willingness of banks and the shah's government to equate the imperial regime and its ruling family with the underlying state. For example, Citibank made a loan through the shah's twin sister ostensibly intended for a housing project but ultimately used for a palace.[56]

In short, private banks and sovereign borrowers in the 1970s followed the midcentury approach of public actors by effectively grounding their lending practices in a statist political theory. However, banks differed from these previous actors in divorcing this implicit framework from any larger economic or geostrategic goal. While these private creditors may have been secondarily interested in helping to develop other countries' productive assets or in promoting their home country's foreign policy, the banks' primary concern remained putting their deposits to profitable use. This accorded with the interests of borrowing country elites—many of whom were in charge of authoritarian regimes—in maintaining unimpeded access to international capital. Thus a statist approach was reinforced from both the lender and the borrower side in the 1970s' return of private capital, further regularizing the theoretical underpinnings of debt continuity going forward.

Maintaining Continuity in Debt Restructuring

The framework for private lending in the sovereign debt regime that emerged in the 1960s and 1970s had a crucial effect on the debt crises and negotiations that ensued. The statist theory of sovereignty implicitly undergirding the 1970s' lending boom remained dominant. And virtually every bank with any interest in international lending was already implicated in this conceptual framework, leaving little flexibility for alternatives to take root. Such narrowness was only enhanced by the processes and the outcomes of the 1980s' debt negotiations, which brought together private banks, governments, and international actors such as the IMF in an unprecedented manner.

The potential countervailing effect of any concerted debtor response was undermined by the tendency of sovereign borrowers to focus on the economic or systemic underpinnings of the debt crisis, which affected all of them more or less equally. Such a holistic approach, which ultimately failed to aid many countries, necessarily brought together a range of countries with very different internal politics. So long as this more systemic economic perspective remained dominant, any conceptual framework that distinguished between the divergent political contexts of debtor countries—such as an odious debt idea—stayed at the margins. As such, the integrative pressures on both the creditor and the borrower side of debt adjustment negotiations further normalized fundamentally statist ideas in the sovereign debt regime through the 1980s. This limited the space for competing practices to fully emerge despite a range of regime changes during this time.

The Unified Framework of Creditor Action

The debt defaults and reschedulings of the 1980s were for many years collectively, and accurately, referred to simply as "the debt crisis." It was a major crisis not only for international sovereign lending but also, due to the large sums involved, for the financial institutions of major industrialized countries. The cooperative lending of large global banks to Latin American countries, for example, became very problematic for the US banking system. The exposure of the twelve largest US banks to Latin America's five biggest borrowers (Argentina, Brazil, Chile, Mexico, and Venezuela) ranged from a low of 82.5 percent of bank capital to a high of 262.8 percent of capital. Any real default or repudiation—and particularly any chain reaction—threatened the viability of the banking system.[57] This inspired the concerted involvement not only of the major banks but also of governmental and international financial actors, who played a pivotal role in organizing and integrating a response. Thus, the creditor consolidation that had developed in the post-World War II era and then in the 1970s only solidified and became more formalized with the emergence of a joint mechanism for handling debt across multiple countries. The statist approach embedded in this global mechanism made it more difficult to make or to accept opposing arguments about debt discontinuity in the international economic arena.

While the loan officers committing their banks to loan syndications may have acted like a social club of sorts, the senior management in global head offices were initially far less familiar with each other. To an important degree, the actions taken in the 1980s' debt restructurings, particularly beginning with the Mexican restructuring of 1982, were novel in the international arena. Although 80 debt restructurings and relief agreements had been signed since 1957, most had dealt with bilateral public debt and only thirteen had involved commercial banks.[58] US Federal Reserve Bank Chairman Paul Volcker called the negotiations "unprecedented," IMF managing director Jacques de Larosière named them "historic," and Citibank head negotiator Bill Rhodes referred to the negotiators as "pioneers."[59] Still, less than a year after the Mexican default of late summer 1982, fifteen countries were renegotiating on about $90 billion of external debt to private financial actors.[60] Although the banks' senior management teams may not have been fully aware of the degree to which their destinies had been joined, the underlying impetus for a unified approach was already present. The syndicated system of lending, through which banks had purposefully pooled (and thus theoretically minimized) their risk, now effectively tied them together. As Aggarwal points out, "the oligopolistic nature of the banking community and the acute overexposure of large banks facilitated cooperation."[61]

The mechanism by which international banks collaborated and dealt with sovereign borrowers ultimately left very little space for debtors to maneuver or present alternative claims. The general operational mode of these debt restructurings took connections that had been made through syndicated lending and converted them into an oligopolistic and fairly top-down approach for dealing with debtors. The precedent-setting Mexican case is aptly described by journalist Joseph Kraft:

> A communications network had been created through a series of regional subcommittees. Each American member of the advisory committee took responsibility for ten different regional banks. Each regional bank took responsibility for ten smaller banks in its area, and so on down the line. . . . The foreign banks on the advisory committee were also given regional assignments—the Bank of Tokyo for Asia; Bank of Montreal for Canada; Deutsche Bank for Germany, Holland and Scandinavia; Lloyds for Britain, Ireland, India, Australia, Greece, Turkey and the Middle East; Société Générale for Belgium, France, Luxembourg, Portugal and Spain; the Swiss Bank Corporation for Austria, Hungary, Italy, Switzerland and Yugoslavia. Latin America was made the responsibility of Citibank.[62]

Although there was some resistance to rescheduling (and eventual re-lending) on the part of private regional banks and occasionally private international banks, they tended to fall in line in due course. This sometimes required pressure from larger banks, as Charles Lipson and others emphasize. Even a small bank tempted to take a different route "[was] threatened . . . with ostracism in a world where financial institutions are highly interdependent and depend for their continued profitability on their links with one another."[63] This hierarchical oligopoly of the 1980s' restructurings only deepened the consolidated approach to sovereign debt that had developed in the 1970s' flood of private finance.

The integration and shared outlook of the private banks was undergirded by the participation of international and governmental actors. The major creditor countries' central banks became involved in the debt crises because of the potential exposure of their own banks. They also became interested in areas outside of their traditional spheres of concern due to the interconnected nature of the banking system, developing a shared community of interest to some degree. As presented by Kraft:

> Just as the Fed was nervous about the vulnerability of the American banks on Mexican debts, the central banks of Europe and Japan were worried about their private banking systems. The US had the primary exposure in Mexico and turned to the others for help. Britain was particularly concerned because London, as an international financial center, had a huge stake in the system as a whole. But the others also had problems—notably in loans to Eastern Europe on which they wanted American support.[64]

This basic concern for the underlying stability of an internationalized banking and financial system had been undergirded by unified conceptual approaches developed through such organizations as the Bank for International Settlements, which helped to arrange short-term or bridge financing during the debt crisis. The Basel Committee of G-10 central bank governors, which had met four times a year since the 1974 banking and currency crisis, provided a more intimate forum for addressing the risk of transnational crises but also deepened a joint sense of purpose and a shared outlook on appropriate remedies.

Perhaps more importantly than any other international institution, the IMF became a key actor in the debt crisis. It had played a far less important role in international finance than had been imagined at its 1944 founding, and the *Economist* described the IMF's role through the 1970s as "helpful, steadying—and very marginal."[65] This was in part due to the fresh availability of private bank finance for countries that had previously been unable to borrow significantly in the international capital markets.[66] However, the IMF gained a far more prominent role as private financing dried up in the 1980s. As part of the Mexican financial package in 1982, it contributed funds and—building on a very minor precedent in the 1970s—made its own contribution contingent on further lending by the private banks. The Fund repeated this pattern multiple times and, perhaps more importantly, private banks eventually only agreed to reschedulings with an IMF-approved economic adjustment package in place. This made the IMF not only an important facilitator of funds, but also an arbiter of acceptable sovereign borrower action on a larger scale.

In its actions, the IMF adopted an explicitly "neutral" approach to questions of internal regime politics. And like the IBRD, it interpreted this decision through a statist lens in both its initial lending decisions and its expectations for country repayment. The IMF's Articles of Agreement did not include as specific an injunction on political assessments as those of the IBRD, referring more generally to the economic grounds on which decisions should be based.[67] However, the Fund's actions effectively overlooked any potential political irregularities to a similar extent. In its lending to Chile, the Fund worked with leftist President Salvador Allende when he was democratically elected in 1970 and then worked just as easily with General Pinochet when he came to power in a military coup in 1973. Internal IMF memoranda effectively acknowledged the compromises that might be involved in financially supporting and thus potentially strengthening the Pinochet regime. A confidential report by the IMF noted,

> [The Junta] seems to be in full control of the country. However, its rather efficient approach in the handling of the military side has led to difficulties in the political sphere. Because of fears of subversion and retaliation, it continues to relentlessly pursue the leaders of the Left who are in hiding, and to keep the principal leaders of the Allende regime on Dawson's Island (near Antarctica).[68]

Notwithstanding these concerns, the report continued that the new regime was "a welcome change from the chaotic conditions prevailing during the last part of the Allende government."[69] The IMF followed similar principles in working with regimes even more broadly acknowledged to be unsavory, such as South Africa. In a practice supported by such major external actors as the US Treasury, the Fund also avoided assessments of what happened to its loans once they had been disbursed. When asked by a US congressman to consider recommending that the IMF audit the books of the Nicaraguan Central Bank upon the discovery that only $3.5 million in reserves remained after the fall of the Somoza regime, the Treasury declined. Writing of the situation, the *Wall Street Journal* pointed out, "Diplomatic sources say it isn't a normal IMF practice to investigate what happens to money a country is lent. To do so would be an intrusion into the country's internal affairs. . . . [T]he IMF's main concern is whether it will be repaid . . . it doesn't know whether the funds were stolen."[70] Although it developed ever stricter programs of economic surveillance through the 1980s, the Fund continued to demur on any retroactive "political" investigations that might have questioned the validity and continuity of earlier debt.

The World Bank maintained its own interest in medium- to long-term sovereign lending as well, and to some degree the approaches of these two major international financial institutions converged in the 1980s' crises. Whereas the Bank had previously focused on project-based lending, in the 1980s it began to extend funding through structural adjustment loans with a more general macroeconomic perspective. And while the IMF had traditionally focused on shorter loans to overcome balance-of-payments problems, this too eventually involved attention to broader economic management. Both institutions roughly agreed on a set of policy prescriptions that came to be known as the "Washington Consensus," generally involving economic liberalization, macroeconomic stabilization, and the limitation of public expenditures and government economic involvement. Each also maintained an ultimately statist conception of political neutrality, both in lending and in a strict and uniform insistence on the principle of debt repayment regardless of any political changes. Perhaps most importantly, these major institutions' interactions with each other and with private banks effectively limited the range of possible arguments and actions for sovereign borrowers. As Charles Lipson has pointed out, by the late 1980s, the two institutions were "closely linked . . . [and had] carefully harmonized their roles to prevent borrowers from shopping around for better conditions."[71]

Through these structures and processes, major private creditors, creditor governments, and international financial institutions jointly settled on a basic framework for dealing with sovereign debtors.[72] This involved an insistence on the principle of uniform repayment, regardless of major regime changes or potential political difficulties, and the implementation of strict economic adjustment programs as a precursor to continued financial engagement. The interconnected nature and shared risk interpretation of international banking also meant that any given bank or creditor country joined the unified approach, regardless of whether it was actually significantly implicated in the loans at issue.

Perhaps as a result of this integrated framework, there seemed to be little concern about the threat of unapologetic default for most countries—never mind the possibility of a full repudiation. In a G-30 study of bankers and supervisors involved with the debt negotiations, most participants did not think that borrowing countries would risk undermining their access to short-term trade credits by engaging in such action.[73] After banks extended $300 million in trade credits to Peru, one New York banker highlighted the potential power of these shorter-term funds: "If they get too confrontational, we'll cut off all that. Then they won't be able to import food or spare parts, and there'll be an immediate political cost."[74] Countries themselves seemed aware of this threat. In the G-30 study, a senior official of a large and advanced developing country suggested that "if his country ever defaulted, its ships and aircraft everywhere would instantly be seized by creditors, as would any goods that his country tried to export."[75] Although some officials in the Mexican government supported a major default—though not an odious debt-type repudiation given the continuity of the regime—the administration ultimately decided against it. As Mexican Finance Minister Jesus Silva de Herzog pointed out, "[A default] didn't make any sense. We're part of the world. We import 30 per cent of our food. We just can't say 'Go to Hell.'"[76] Sovereign states were well aware that they faced a unified group of interlocutors, and thus had fewer forums in which to make the heterodox arguments about repayment and creditworthiness that might have shifted sovereign debt away from strictly statist analyses.

The Economic Focus of Any General Debtor Response

If the consolidated creditors of the 1970s and 1980s developed statist practices that presupposed and reinforced sovereign debt continuity, debtor countries as a group offered little countervailing pressure. The borrower approach to the crisis tended not to distinguish between different types of debt according to underlying popular consent or popular benefit. Even those regimes that had come to power after major political transitions, which might have been more likely to make odious debt-type claims, shied away from this type of open argument in the international arena. Although borrowers were hardly complimentary of international finance, in general the 1980s' debt crisis revolved around not principled repudiations but rather a series of threatened economic defaults. In responding to the crisis as a group, the debtor approach blurred the lines between different borrower regimes, closing off the discursive space for serious consideration of how debt discontinuity might connect to internal political rule. For any given debtor country, this decision likely resulted from reputational concerns in the face of the unified creditor framework at the time. These discrete decisions, when summed across multiple countries, further normalized the idea that reputational assessments and responsible credit practices necessarily involve a statist norm of debt continuity that excludes serious discussion of arguably illegitimate debt.

Certainly, a joint debtor response did make sense to some degree, given the many shared features of the debtor experience. Part of the trigger for the sovereign debt crisis involved US Federal Reserve Chairman Paul Volcker's decision to counter inflation in the United States by sharply raising interest rates. This led to an exponential increase in the debt payment costs of developing countries beginning in 1979. These states had signed debt contracts in the 1970s with interest rates that were low—sometimes below one percent—but were also, alas, variable. And just as these countries' interest payment costs increased dramatically, their debt-servicing ability dropped, as commodity prices (and thus potential export earnings) collapsed in the wake of a recession in the advanced industrial countries.

Perhaps in part as a response, most criticism was targeted at the iniquities of the crisis and adjustment *process,* rather than at the potential substantive illegitimacy of particular debts themselves. Indeed, many of the regimes unable to service foreign debt in the early 1980s were the very same regimes that had contracted debt in the first place—making odious debt ideas less tenable in these cases. Furthermore all debtor countries felt that the pain of adjusting to the shared international predicament had fallen unevenly on their shoulders, with relatively little burden shared by creditors and creditor countries. Mexican President José López Portillo, just weeks after the breaking of the crisis, alarmed Northern financial markets with the following statement:

> The financing plague is wreaking greater and greater havoc throughout the world. As in Medieval times, it is scourging country after country. It is transmitted by rats and its consequences are unemployment and poverty, industrial bankruptcy and speculative enrichment. The remedy of the witch doctors is to deprive the patient of food and subject him to compulsory rest. Those who protest must be purged, and those who survive bear witness to their virtue before the doctors of obsolete and prepotent dogma and of blind hegemoniacal egoism.[77]

The advanced industrialized countries proved unwilling to take steps that could have softened the blow, for example by loosening trade restrictions that might have allowed for greater export receipts and foreign exchange for the debtor countries. And the banks themselves wrote down very little of the debt, at least in the initial restructurings, even despite their less than careful lending.

Debtor country efforts at cooperation—which were largely unsuccessful—also focused on the economic aspects of the crisis. The presidents of Latin America's four largest debtors, including a newly democratic Argentina, issued a statement after a May 1984 meeting in Buenos Aires that drew primary attention to the economic and financial components of the problem. In particular, they emphasized that "successive interest rate increases, prospects of new hikes and the proliferation and intensity of protectionist measures" would likely harm the prospects for economic development and stable democracy. They continued, "We do not accept seeing ourselves forced into a situation of insolvency and continuous economic crisis. . . . Our nations cannot indefinitely accept these hazards."[78] But Argentine officials, bankers and Western analysts all agreed that the position would not lead to a general default.[79] As Miles Kahler points out, "From the South . . . the debt crisis was a crisis of development, one element of the deepest economic downturn since the Great Depression, which had begun for some developing countries after the first oil shock."[80] To an important extent, then, developing countries themselves focused on the global economic sources and aspects of the crisis. Any criticism of international economic relations rarely extended to distinctions between more or less acceptable lending and possible sovereign debt discontinuity.

This attention to the unsustainability of the broader system—along with the effort at a unified approach for the global south—followed the trend of earlier developing country discussions about a possible 'New International Economic Order.' After the first oil price hike of the early 1970s, calls for this new order involved a focus on the possibility of commodity cartels as well as the necessity of allocating global capital flows to developing country industrialization. Such initiatives, it was hoped, would help to free these countries from neocolonial control. These efforts involved the joint self-identification of countries with very different political systems, and the implicit minimization of arguments based on internal political rule. Muchkund Dubey points out the degree to which a holistic approach was central to this strategy:

> The global approach to negotiating North-South issues can be defined as one covering all major North-South issues, designed to bring about a restructuring of international economic relations based on the principle of equality and mutual benefit, involving the participation of all the member states of the United Nations, and conducted in the global forum of the UN General Assembly in a simultaneous manner in order to ensure a coherent and integrated approach to the issues under negotiation.[81]

As part of this program, the G-77 group of developing countries had in 1979 proposed a more institutionalized sovereign debt restructuring commission, intended to be more attentive to debtor concerns and development goals.[82] These efforts at a strong "Southern" strategy ultimately fell through, in part because of the wavering commitment of developing countries themselves. Later attempts at a 1980s' debtor cartel—something that private banks, international financial institutions, and advanced industrial governments were concerned about—similarly amounted to very little. And the economically focused framework that undergirded these endeavors minimized rather than emphasized the different political foundations for arguably illegitimate debt.

This meant that even the renewed interest in odious debt ideas that reemerged partially during this period failed to take root in the international arena. Resuscitating Alexander Sack's 1927 doctrine, several legal articles in the early 1980s highlighted the potential risk of lending to arguably illegitimate regimes.[83] And the International Law Commission draft articles on state succession, which were ultimately never ratified, included an analysis of odious debt.[84] But while these ideas were brought up internally in several countries, they remained outside the purview of international sovereign debt discussions. Borrower arguments tended to focus on the economic-systemic aspects of the debt crisis, undermining the countervailing effect that odious debt-based assessments might have on generally statist norms of debt continuity. In conjunction with the consolidated framework of creditor action, this helped to normalize a statist approach in sovereign debt throughout the period. Despite a range of regime changes, some of them explicitly revolutionary, the basic principle of sovereign debt continuity remained intact and even deepened.

Limiting Alternatives: Nicaragua, Iran, and the Philippines

Given the large number of countries implicated and the aggressive rhetoric occasionally employed during the 1980s' debt crisis, it is perhaps surprising that the period witnessed no real effort at principled repudiation. This was so despite a series of major regime changes, including those in which authoritarian dictatorships were replaced by more representative civilian regimes and those involving major sociopolitical revolutions. These new regimes' decisions emphasize the degree to which a statist expectation of debt continuity had already become dominant and normalized, even in a postcolonial era of massive political upheavals and serious charges against the international economic system. Compliance, if not complete concurrence, with the basic principle of predecessor debt acknowledgment was the default practice even when we might expect to have seen odious debt-type arguments.

The 1970s' and 1980s' consolidation of private creditors, and their interaction with public international financial institutions, helped to regulate this practice. The fact that virtually every bank interested in international lending was already embroiled in sovereign debt issues meant that there was very little space for alternative approaches to take hold. Either banks were retrenching and uninterested in further involvement in sovereign lending or they were concerned that any deviation from standard practice might have systemic effects. Even when internal debates about debt repudiation occurred in some cases, with intimations of a more open challenge, no principled repudiation materialized. And when states did secure deviations from preferred bank terms, these quieter departures failed to shift the broader discourse and related practice possibilities away from a norm of debt continuity.

This background shaped and stiffened the approach taken to key cases in the 1980s, including post-regime-change Nicaragua and the Philippines and the geostrategically complicated case of the Iranian debt negotiations. In discussing them here, I do not intend to undertake a comparative study of why certain regimes in a given period repudiate debt while others do not. Rather, I present them to understand the contours of the historical era itself, and how its dominant norms press very different countries in dissimilar circumstances to act similarly. Thus, these cases are suggestive of both the ways in which larger normative structures shape the possibilities of state action, and also how that action, in turn, solidifies and strengthens the norms faced by subsequent debtor countries.

Technical Debt Acknowledgment in Nicaragua

Among the most interesting and unusual debt reschedulings of the period was that of Nicaragua after the overthrow of the Somoza establishment in 1979. The Somoza family had ruled Nicaragua for a total of forty-three years in the presidency, with their influence extending even beyond this time through the family's control of the powerful National Guard. Anastasio Somoza Debayle in particular engaged in significant oppression of the country's population and actively fought a civil war against the Sandinista guerillas through the 1970s. By the time of the Sandinista victory in 1979, the Somozas had burdened the small country with over $1 billion in public and publicly guaranteed external debt.[85] Faced with this history, the new Sandinista government had reason to raise odious debt ideas, and at least privately attempted to distinguish between their own and the previous regime. However, the banks that had lent to the Somoza regime were extremely concerned about allowing Nicaragua to stand as a precedent, insisting that the final agreement be "commercial" in nature and focusing instead on Nicaragua's unusually poor economic situation. The ultimate outcome, which waived the standard IMF program requirement and included fairly lenient terms, raises questions about whether a non-statist framework may have been incorporated quietly into the analysis. But given the eventual acknowledgment of the debt in principle, the Nicaraguan case remained something of an anomaly that did not fundamentally challenge the norm of debt continuity.

Western interlocutors were aware that, particularly in the last years and even months of its rule, the Somoza family likely had stripped the country of its already modest earning potential. A piece in the *Wall Street Journal* pointed out that

> before they left, the Somozas followed a virtual 'scorched earth' policy. Besides sacking opponents' businesses, they borrowed heavily from outside using the convenient apparatus of a government that was synonymous with the family financial empire, looted the treasury and left behind a staggering short-term foreign debt. . . . What the Somozas leave behind is a bankrupted society, its infant-mortality rate higher than that of India.[86]

After the Somozas fled in July of 1979, the incoming leadership did not repudiate outright the previous regime's debt, as some had feared. Rather, they embarked on a long debt negotiation process with 115 banks from twelve countries, which finally culminated in an agreement in December 1980.[87] There was some discussion of repudiation or at least a deliberate default, and indeed it seemed initially to be a real possibility. Daniel Ortega, a central figure in the new revolutionary government, stated in a September 1979 address to the United Nations General Assembly that repaying the short-term, high-interest loans made in the last years of the Somoza regime would be unsustainable. He emphasized in part the financial difficulty of any repayment, saying that "the people of Nicaragua within these months would have to carry approximately a $600 million debt. And Nicaragua cannot pay that debt. Nor will it indebt itself anew to pay that debt." He continued, however, with a more pointed suggestion that the previous Somoza regime had ruled, particularly in its last years, more in its own interest than for the benefit of the state. He highlighted that Somoza held stolen funds outside of the country and contended that

> It is Somoza and his accomplices who must be sued by the international creditors of Nicaragua . . . It is our opinion that the external debt which Somozaism left in Nicaragua must be taken over internationally, particularly by the developed countries . . . in the first case by those countries which routinely fed Somozaism with financing.[88]

Notwithstanding this opinion, the government eventually chose to honor the debt contracts of the previous regime, at least in principle. By mid-1982, the Sandinista government had emphasized its basic acknowledgment of Somoza-era debts. Finance Minister Joaquin Cuadra noted that the country was determined to pay "the last cent of this debt, despite the economic difficulties aggravated by the recent floods," and emphasized, "Many hoped with glee that Nicaragua wouldn't pay, but we have paid, even though it means a serious sacrifice for our country and our foreign exchange situation."[89]

The new leadership was keenly aware of the weakness and poverty of the country, and therefore of the untenability of rejecting any external engagement. In fact, it followed a strategy not of militant anti-imperialism but rather of "diversified dependency." The incoming regime aimed to shift away from the exclusive dependence on the United States that had marked the country under Somoza, and instead move toward a more balanced engagement with the United States, Western Europe, Japan, the Socialist countries, and the Third World.[90] Interestingly, the decision not to repudiate debt was encouraged and supported by Fidel Castro.[91] As Gary Prevost points out, "From the beginning, Fidel Castro and the Cuban Communist Party counseled the Sandinistas to adopt a mixed economy and to maintain, if at all possible, good relations with Western Europe and particularly the United States."[92] Speaking directly to the difficulty of Cuba's own experience, the Cuban deputy foreign minister in 1984 noted that "we suffered extreme hardship in the early years of our revolution because of isolation, and we did not wish for Nicaragua to suffer through the same problem."[93]

This is not to say that the new Sandinista regime did not request some degree of flexibility for its debt or highlight the fragility and uniqueness of its political situation. Indeed, it argued that the repayment terms would have to be consistent with the goals of resuscitating the destroyed Nicaraguan economy, which meant that a smaller portion of foreign exchange would be used for external debt payments. The new regime also noted that debts had been contracted by the *Somoza* government, which had fallen from grace with substantial private wealth but only a little over $3 million in central bank reserves. Private creditors were unhappy with any attempt to discuss the "Somoza regime," and a Nicaraguan debt advisor noted that "anytime Somoza's name was brought up, the banks started climbing the walls."[94] Attempts to conceptually or discursively distinguish between the Somoza family, the Sandinistas, and the Nicaraguan state met with hostility and with reiterations of a statist definition of sovereignty and political neutrality. According to Nicaraguan advisors, private banks in the debt negotiations would employ this approach fairly explicitly, saying in effect, "We're not dealing with politics. . . . We're dealing with the continuing institution of the Nicaraguan government."[95]

To shore up the validity of their Nicaraguan portfolio, these banks depended upon and furthered the idea—developed initially by late medieval political theorists—that sovereignty exists in a presumptively eternal
realm divorced from political changes on the ground.

The evidence suggests that the creditor consolidation of the 1970s
may have stiffened this statist approach. The banks did not look at the
Nicaraguan case—or indeed any country debt negotiation—as separate
from debt reschedulings more generally. As in the post-Marcos Philippines negotiations discussed below, the banks were especially concerned
that the principles of any debt agreement might serve as a model for future discussions elsewhere. According to Richard Weinert, Nicaragua's
financial advisor at the time,

> The banks' obsession was with precedent. . . . [A]t stake was more than
> the sums involved, which, while substantial in the aggregate, were gener-
> ally less than a month's earnings for any of the individual banks involved.
> However, the concurrent negotiations with Jamaica, Sudan, Zaire, and
> Turkey and untold future negotiations were a constant undercurrent at the
> negotiating table.[96]

This general dynamic is repeated in the G-30 survey of banks involved
in rescheduling. Speaking in 1983 of "a small developing country whose
debt, including some principal arrears and some interest arrears, has
been restructured regularly during the past three years"—likely Nicaragua—the survey author highlighted that the debt was negligible for
the banks and the system more generally, and that "some of the larger
creditor banks would willingly write off their claims on the country excepting for the fear of the dangerous precedent that this might create."[97]

As a result, the banks were insistent that Nicaragua acknowledge the
debt and repay according to what could be understood as commercial
terms or market conditions—those terms that might be determined by
supply and demand on the Eurocredit market. Overall, however, the final
agreement was considered favorable to the new regime, involving a range
of provisions that had not previously existed in any rescheduling. The
private bank rescheduling of government debt included a twelve-year repayment period, five years of deferral on any interest payments (rather
than the usual requirement that interest payments be brought up to date),
the capitalization of interest at lower rates than the initial contract, and
a cap on interest rates for a time.[98] Nicaragua under the new Sandinista
regime was also unlike other countries in that it rescheduled its private
bank debt without first agreeing to an IMF-approved economic program.
Indeed, the government refused to negotiate with private banks on the

basis of an IMF standby program, and ultimately was not required to first enter into a Paris Club agreement.[99] Nonetheless, the private financial community considered the overall result to be a success—the full Somoza-era debt had been officially acknowledged, and the final terms were arguably acceptable at a commercial level—at least in that they included an interest rate high enough for banks to make a profit.[100]

Thus, the final meaning of the Nicaraguan debt negotiations is difficult to assess. On the one hand, the principle of sovereign debt continuity remained intact. After the Sandinista victory, there was fairly widespread acknowledgment of the degree to which Somoza-era debts—particularly for the large volume of short-term, high-interest loans contracted toward the end of the regime—were neither authorized by nor ultimately a benefit for the underlying population or territory. Despite this, the incoming regime in the end decided to acknowledge the debts in full, accepting in principle a statist vision of sovereignty and debt continuity that disavows any break between the contracting and rescheduling regimes.[101] In acknowledging the debt, the new regime also acceded to a definition of political neutrality professed by banks, adopted by the international financial community more generally, and undergirded by broader mid-twentieth-century international norms.

That said, the new regime did insist on taking into account the country's larger context, refusing to route private bank negotiations through the IMF and Paris Club, and fighting for other contractual irregularities. And bank acceptance of those terms marked an important departure from previous practice and raises the question of whether Nicaragua was a special case. Although the banks themselves emphasized the basically commercial parameters of the final agreement, they explicitly asserted that Nicaragua was unique and were adamant that subsequent debtors not expect similar terms.[102] The G-30 study of debt negotiations noted that multiple debt reschedulings on lenient terms might eventually come to represent "default by attrition"—a default in all but name.[103] To the extent that the potential illegitimacy of some Somoza-era debt factored into the special treatment, the Nicaraguan case might be understood as a quiet "repudiation by attrition" that left intact the basic statist norm of debt continuity as the international standard.[104]

The Statist Underpinnings of the Iranian Case

The overthrow of the imperial regime in Iran constituted one of the late twentieth century's most significant social revolutions. Given that the revolution explicitly rejected the political, social, and even the economic foundations of the previous order, it might well have involved a more thorough repudiation of the previous regime's economic undertakings. While this did occur to an important degree in the area of direct domestic investments, events took a very different turn in the realm of external financing. Notwithstanding the incoming regime's threat to withdraw deposits from certain Western banks—a decision entirely within governmental rights under any theory of sovereignty—the new Iranian regime apparently intended to continue payments on its external bank debt. The technical Iranian default of 1980 was precipitated by US bank actions in relation to an American government freeze of Iranian deposits. As such, the Iranian case ultimately represented a minimal challenge to statist sovereign lending frameworks and the norm of debt continuity.

In 1925, following a series of events grounded in the Russian Civil War, military officer Reza Khan overthrew the previous Qajar dynasty to found Iran's Pahlavi dynasty. After the 1941 Anglo-Soviet invasion of Iran during World War II, however, the Allied powers forced him to abdicate in favor of his more compliant 22-year-old son, Mohammad Reza Shah Pahlavi. Following the withdrawal of British and Soviet forces in 1946, the Iranian parliament gained increasing independence, reflecting rising resentment of Western presence in the region and leading eventually to the 1951 decision by secular nationalist Prime Minister Mohammad Mossadegh to nationalize the British-dominated Iranian oil industry. In response, the British and US governments sponsored the 1953 coup that overthrew Mossadegh and cemented the Pahlavis' military control over Iran and the imperial regime's links to the West. The shah's subsequent modernization program followed a largely Western model and made significant space for Western corporations, marginalizing and aggravating both the more radical left and the traditional Islamic clergy. Although pluralist political features were maintained through the first decades of the shah's rule, by the mid-1970s he had abolished the multiparty parliamentary regime in favor of a more explicitly autocratic system. Particularly in the last decade of the shah's rule, the government engaged in oppression and human rights violations on a scale that troubled outside observers.

The shah was overthrown in a popular movement that began in January 1978 and, after several phases and against the wishes of some of its initial supporters, culminated in a new theocratic constitution in December 1979. Although the revolution explicitly condemned the previous regime's links with Western finance, the Central Bank continued regular interest payments on the shah's external bank loans even after the declaration of the Islamic Republic in April 1979. However, the signals coming out of Iran on the issue of debt repayment eventually became somewhat contradictory and confusing.[105] This is in large part because regular financial relations were severely complicated in early November 1979 when radicalized students stormed the American embassy, taking Americans hostage in a diplomatic outrage with significant geostrategic ramifications.[106] The United States responded in part by instituting a boycott on Iranian exports, particularly oil, and acting foreign and financial minister Abolhassan Bani-Sadr in turn threatened to withdraw the considerable Iranian deposits held in American banks (though largely in non-American branches) and place them instead with banks headquartered in countries that had not joined the American boycott.[107] Within hours of this statement, the Carter administration took an unprecedented step by instituting a freeze on all Iranian deposits in US banks, with the jurisdictionally questionable intention that this also apply to overseas branches.[108] Although this asset freeze ultimately proved important in negotiations over the hostage release, the administration emphasized that the two issues were separate and that the freeze was designed only to protect financial claims on Iran by the United States and its citizens.[109]

Despite the heightened tensions, Iranian government actions suggest that it too had intended to separate the hostage crisis from any financial claims. In particular, the new regime continued to make arrangements for interest payments on its external debt. The day after students stormed the embassy, the Central Bank of Iran instructed Chase Manhattan's New York headquarters—which held a significant portion of Iran's US deposits—to make an approximately $4 million interest payment to Chase's own London branch, which had organized a syndicated Eurocredit loan for Iran under the shah. In fact, this was the very loan mentioned earlier in this chapter, which was contracted without the parliamentary approval mandated by the shah's own constitution. Although the request had been made ten days before the asset freeze, the New York headquarters decided to delay the interbranch transfer. After the freeze, however, Chase took the unusual step of declaring the loan in default because—as a result of its own delay—the payment never reached its London branch.[110] With the vote of a majority of its syndicate partners, Chase accelerated the full balance of the loan and proceeded to offset this amount against its Iranian government deposits. Other American financial institutions, including Citibank and J. P. Morgan, acted likewise and thus encouraged still other banks to follow suit lest insufficient funds remain to cover their own claims. This effective run on Iranian deposits, without financial provocation from Iran itself, shocked many European banks in particular, who made known their unhappiness with the precipitous departure from standard banking practice.[111]

Unsurprisingly, the Iranian government balked at the declaration of default, the subsequent loan acceleration, and the decision to offset the loan balances against frozen deposits. Different governmental offices made contradictory statements, with the foreign and finance ministries under Bani-Sadr suggesting that the shah's loans might be repudiated and the Central Bank insisting instead that Iran would repay external bank debt and that financial relations should be regularized.[112] Iran brought suit in British courts to recoup $320 million frozen in Chase's London branch. And once it had clarified its position, the Iranian Central Bank placed ads in early December 1979 to declare that it would "honor all of its legitimate foreign debts"—with legitimacy presumably negotiable within British (or possibly American) courts.[113] Given its attempt to make an interest payment on even the questionably authorized $500 million syndicated credit, this recognized debt would presumably have included the significant and in some cases arguably odious loans made by foreign banks to the shahs' government.

Ultimately, none of the potential lawsuits arising from these events went forward. The release of Iranian deposits and the payment of the shah-era loans became part and parcel of the broader hostage crisis negotiations.[114] The January 1981 Algiers Accords included Iran's affirmation of "its intention to pay all its debts and those of its controlled institutions," along with a provision that the Iranian Central Bank would

> transfer $3.667 billion to the Federal Reserve Bank of New York to pay the unpaid principal of and interest through December 31, 1980 on (1) all loans and credits made by a syndicate of banking institutions, of which a U.S. banking institution is a member . . . and (2) all loans and credits made by such a syndicate which are guaranteed by the Government of Iran or any of its agencies.[115]

In addition, the Islamic Republic placed approximately $1.4 billion in an escrow account for payment of other claims to US banks, such as nonsyndicated loans and excess interest.[116] Although the Algiers Accords allowed for the arbitration of claims not explicitly covered by its provisions, in practice the banks were wary of arbitration. According to a lawyer involved in the bank negotiations, arbitration of significant claims was a process with which they were unfamiliar and which they did not feel was necessary. This was particularly true because

> [the bank claims] were principally loan contracts. Arbitration provisions are not placed in such agreements because banks feel that if someone owes

them money, he ought to pay it and therefore nothing is left to arbitrate. If payment is not made . . . the bank goes to court, receives a default judgment, and seizes the borrowers' assets.[117]

Although the arbitration option was considered, and preliminary steps were taken that might have led to arbitration, the significant issues were dealt with outside any such process.[118]

Thus, the outcome of the Iranian negotiations effectively incorporated a statist approach and assumptions of debt continuity, in which the new Islamic Republic acknowledged the basic validity of the shah-era bank loans. While the new regime conducted internal investigations as to the extent of improper financial dealings by the shah's family,[119] odious debt ideas ended up being a negligible component of the regime's dealings with outside banks. Indeed, as John Crook points out, "Because of the Algiers Accords' extraordinary financial arrangements, the [Iran-U.S. Claims] Tribunal has not dealt in any significant way with interpretation and enforcement of international lending agreements. There has been little analysis of the question of what constitutes a debt."[120] The tribunal proceedings did involve several discussions of agency—that is, of how to attribute to the state any actions taken by government bodies, pseudogovernment bodies, or others acting or purporting to act in an official capacity. However, it focused on decisions made by the Iranian government and other Iranian actors during and following the revolution.[121] These considerations did not extend back to an assessment of whether the private bank debt contracted by the *shah's* government was valid, perhaps in part because this debt had already been dealt with.[122]

In the end, Iran ended up taking an unusual path in dealing with the previous regime's debts. While it is difficult to know exactly what might have happened in the absence of the hostage crisis, Iran's initial actions seem to suggest that—despite a range of internal expropriations—it had every intention of continuing payment on external bank debt, including that debt which might have been considered questionable. In the ten years following the foundation of the Islamic Republic, Iran largely withdrew from relations with Western finance. It did not engage in any official contact with international financial institutions such as the World Bank and the IMF; nor did it seek additional long-term loans from Western banks. This was apparently due to concerns about maintaining the nation's independence, which subsided after the death of founder Ayatollah Ruhollah Khomeini in 1989. Only after this did the Islamic Republic reach out, applying for and receiving a World Bank loan to cover postearthquake reconstruction.[123] This was interpreted as a symbolic reengagement with the Western financial world, and commentators at the time highlighted the relative creditworthiness of Iran. An official at the Institute of International Finance, an organization established by internationally involved banks following the 1980s' debt crisis, pointed out, "Iran has a good history of making payments on its debt, even during the Iran-Iraq war."[124] Nonetheless, considerable ambivalence remained in Tehran about the wisdom of borrowing abroad,[125] and Iran borrowed very little from the World Bank through the turn of the century.[126] Despite the rise of private international lending in the 1990s, now through bond issues, Iran did not join the fray until 2002, when it issued $472 million worth of bonds in an offering organized by Germany's Commerzbank and France's BNP Paribas.[127] Its subsequent efforts have been severely hampered by international sanctions, but the country continues to issue bonds domestically, particularly to develop natural gas reserves, and evidence suggests that international investors would likely be interested in the absence of these exogenous factors.[128] In short, after the 1979 Revolution and through the decades that followed, Iran's external financial practice was that of a wary and geostrategically complicated but otherwise unremarkable sovereign borrower, following and reinforcing statist norms of debt continuity in its own actions.

Minimization of Political Particularity in the 1980s' Debt Crisis

Given its magnitude and its interconnection with significant political upheavals, the 1980s' debt crisis might well have become more of a testing ground for heterodox norms in sovereign lending. However, private creditors, creditor country governments, and international financial institutions tended to interpret the 1980s' debt crisis in an integrated manner, resulting in part from the oligopolistic underpinnings of earlier credit extensions. Sovereign borrowers as a whole also jointly focused on external economic rather than internal political reasons for particular debt burdens, falling in line with broader midcentury sovereignty norms and minimizing the centrality of political distinctions and potential odious debt questions in any given situation. This integrated approach gave rise to a fairly standard and formalized mechanism for dealing with debt problems, and tended to frame particular country contexts as instantiations and potential instigators of a larger systemic threat. In cases including the Philippines and various South American countries, this broader framework undermined the flexibility for raising non-statist arguments about debt discontinuity after regime changes. It also covered over the ways in which alternative courses of action could have developed into potential models for others going forward.

People Power and the Philippines

Even after overthrowing the Marcos regime in a "People's Power Revolution" that surprised the world, the Philippines ultimately acknowledged its predecessor's external obligations and was treated like any other major debtor. Although there was explicit discussion within Philippine civil society and in the incoming cabinet about the possibility of selective repudiation, this never became the official policy. In debt negotiations, the bank advisory committee was unwilling to diverge from conventional restructuring practice lest a new precedent be set. And the fact that the debts of 483 creditors were jointly negotiated rendered it virtually impossible for the Philippines to challenge any particular contract. Against the background of a basic debt acknowledgment, this unified creditor interaction and risk interpretation effectively solidified the dominance of a statist approach in the Philippine case.

Ferdinand Marcos began his first term as president in 1965 and his second in 1969. Although he was initially popular enough, this popularity increasingly became a governmentally enforced façade. Facing rural and urban opposition, including from peasants, workers, and students—and also facing the end of his two-term limit on presidential power—Marcos declared martial law in 1972 and used it to institute a number of major political changes to ground the establishment of a "New Society" more firmly under his control.[129] Over the course of the fourteen years of dictatorship that followed, Marcos became increasingly more committed to maintaining his own political and economic power and those of his close associates. Government funds, including those procured by external financing, went toward covering the failing private ventures of friends and family. A 1983 friendly external audit of the Marcos regime's central bank found that $5 billion in debited funds had gone missing.[130] And no-bid debt contracts were signed that served little ultimate benefit to the public. Among the most controversial of these was that for the Bataan nuclear power station, built by Westinghouse (a US firm) with outdated technology in an area prone to earthquakes. This contract, initially for $2.1 billion but ultimately costing almost ten times that—and resulting in no energy output for the Philippines—had allegedly been secured by a bribe of $80 million and was controversial even under Marcos's own tenure.[131]

An active peasant- and worker-based domestic opposition to the Marcos regime had been developing since at least 1968. However, the full extent of the regime's problems became most clearly apparent to international observers with the August 1983 assassination of former senator Benigno Aquino, and with the acknowledgment two months later that the Philippines was unable to meet its debt-service obligations. In the two and a half years that followed, however, Marcos attempted to entrench himself even more firmly into the country's political and financial structure. He became more blatant about funneling Philippine money into projects that accorded with his own private ends. One Western diplomat working in the Philippines during the last years of the Marcos regime estimated that 30 percent of Philippine public financing was lost to corruption and capital flight to private bank accounts.[132] Members of the international diplomatic and financial community had themselves become aware of the untenability of Marcos's continued rule. In 1984, the World Bank, IMF, and creditor banks effectively shifted their support to the middle- and upper-class opposition led by business leaders like Jaime Ongpin, head of the major Benguet Mining Corporation.[133] Ongpin called on the United States to freeze economic aid until the regime implemented reforms that would allow for a smooth succession.[134]

As Marcos lost the support of his former allies, in late 1985 he called for a "snap election" to be held within several months, in which opposition support coalesced around Corazon Aquino, Benigno's widow. In the February 1986 elections, Marcos's parliament declared Marcos the winner among charges of massive election fraud from many fronts, including the powerful Catholic Church. Corazon Aquino's calls for civil disobedience led to a series of massive rallies and popular protests, centered in the urban areas, making it increasingly clear that Marcos had lost significant popular support, including among the middle and upper classes as well as much of the clergy and military. His family fled the Philippines while Aquino allies abolished the Marcos constitution and prepared a new constitutional referendum. The new constitutional order was formally instituted in 1987 and Aquino was subsequently elected to a full presidential term.

When the Aquino government first took office in 1986, it faced the major problem of its staggering external debt, amounting to over $27 billion. There was some pressure from within the state and the cabinet for a selective repudiation of foreign debts. This was led by Solita Monsod, the secretary for socioeconomic planning under Aquino until 1989.[135] She was supported by key elements within civil society, and discussions were convened to consider the possible bases for dealing with debt. For example, the law school at the University of the Philippines convened a conference on the "debt trap," bringing together academics and Philippine senators to discuss the topic of "selective disengagement" on the basis of "principles or approaches that would legally excuse . . . a debtor-state from all or part of its foreign debts."[136]

Initially, these efforts seemed to garner the sympathy of Jaime Ongpin, the new finance minister. Soon after his appointment, Ongpin suggested, "At the moment our first priority is to feed the population. That concerns me considerably more than the question of how we pay our debts. We did not create them, and the creditors are at least as responsible for them as we are."[137] Ultimately, however, he joined the Central Bank governor to argue against Monsod and her allies in the cabinet, urging recognition of the debt and an effort to negotiate with bankers for more favorable terms. In May 1986, Aquino ultimately decided to acknowledge the Marcos regime debt.[138] Although by March 1987 the Philippines reached agreement with private creditors, the new Philippine legislature balked when elements of the deal came out—such as creditors' insistence that the new regime assume not just government debt but also Marcos-era *private* debt as a condition for further lending.[139] In perhaps the most explicit bank threat to effectuate debtor compliance, Citibank chairman John Reed warned during an address to the American Chamber of Commerce in the Philippines, "If you repudiate your debts, it will cause you immense suffering."[140]

While discussions of potential repudiation continued, ultimately the Marcos-era debts were acknowledged and rescheduled in much the same way as the debt of countries that would not have had recourse to an odious debt idea. The IMF approved a $500 million credit by October 1986, and the March 1987 agreement involved almost five hundred private bank creditors.[141] While the terms were generally good commercial terms, the creditors resisted any attempts at innovation—either in financial instruments or in claims that certain less-legitimate portions of the debt should be excluded from the rescheduling. The Philippine negotiating team sought to introduce Philippine Investment Notes as one possible mechanism for repayment, which would have built on existing debt conversion programs to offer promissory notes with a higher effective yield as part of the debt repayment. This was resisted by the Bank Advisory Committee and, according to finance minister Ongpin, the banks refused primarily because the scheme "departed from conventional practice" and "would set an undesirable precedent." He continued, in a paper presented to the Philippine Council on Foreign Relations, that

resistance to innovation has, indeed, been the hallmark of debt restructuring negotiations. The unwieldiness and the rigidity of negotiations with advisory committees are the result in part of the diversity of interests among the committee members themselves (about 12 large banks holding 30–50 percent of total loans of each debtor country) as well as among the other 400–500 banks ostensibly represented by the committee. Negotiations in this context have more often than not led to Committee positions based on what seems to be "the least concessional common denominator."[142]

Indeed, the banks themselves acknowledged their caution in the Philippine case, aware that it could provide a new baseline for other governments. A senior New York banker, speaking of the Philippine negotiations, indicated that the bank committee would rather have no agreement than risk any potential precedent that might be set by granting the Philippines its desired terms.[143] And even if a particular bank's insistence on the repayment of a questionable loan seemed especially brazen, the integrated advisory committee approach left little room for Philippine arguments along these lines. For example, Philippine officials argued that a loan made by Credit Suisse-First Boston (CSFB) should be excluded due to the bank's "unclean hands" in the loan's origin. The argument never received a full hearing—nor could it easily be separated out for independent treatment—because the advisory committee fully supported CSFB's insistence that all debt was owed by "the Philippines" and should simply be negotiated in bulk. According to Manufacturers Hanover Trust's David Pflug, this particular loan actually substantially held up the commercial negotiations, and Philippine debt negotiators eventually gave in due to the country's need for trade credits.[144]

The new government also established a commission to track down funds that had gone missing from the public coffers and which were presumed to be in the private bank accounts of the Marcos family and its associates. However, very little came of this effort even as the Philippines continued its service of the renegotiated debt. The final result of the People's Power Revolution, in terms of external finance, was hardly revolutionary, leaving the basic repayment framework of the previous regime intact. Against the backdrop of the precedent-sensitive 1980s' debt crisis, the new government acknowledged its predecessor's external obligations and even assumed private Marcos-era debts. In so doing, it helped to normalize the dominance of a statist approach in the last decade of the Cold War, further marking as radical and implausible any resistance to debt payment on the basis of claims about illegitimacy. Thus the data point of debt acknowledgment and sovereign continuity in repayment remained, while the particular context and historical pressures of the Philippine case have faded from collective memory.

CONVENTION IN THE SOUTH AMERICAN CASES

A similar dynamic to that of the Philippine story occurred in other countries that experienced major regime changes in the 1970s and 1980s, particularly those in South America. A range of countries could be taken as examples, but Brazil and Argentina are among the better-known major debtors. Despite significant upheaval resulting from the debt crisis, giving rise to discussions of possible unilateral debt actions, neither country ultimately made an international claim that challenged statist norms. Rather, they focused on the economic problems of repayment, framing their own situations as of a piece with the broader issues facing developing countries.

Upon succeeding two decades of military rule in 1985, the new Brazilian regime continued the debt negotiations begun by its predecessor.[145] Despite embarking upon a range of economic plans and financial negotiations in an effort to deal with both the crippled economy and the external debt—amounting to $105 billion by 1985—Brazil had failed to grow significantly and struggled under the weight of external payments.[146] Following further failed negotiations, finance minister Dilson Funaro suggested in December 1986 the possibility of a full moratorium on debt payments, telling a US congressional summit on debt and trade,

> After strenuous, prolonged attempts at convincing our partners through reasoning, we have now reached a point where all parties involved have to assume their responsibilities. . . . Debtor developing countries can no longer continue to be net capital exporters in these staggering amounts. If the debt is to be paid, it will have to be serviced at a much lower cost in the years to come. We shall be prepared to negotiate what is negotiable, and this does not include the growth of our economy.[147]

In February 1987, as reserves were very low, Funaro instituted a unilateral suspension of foreign debt payments.[148] Despite this major action, he made no principled claims about debt discontinuity or political illegitimacy, instead focusing on the broader economic concerns shared by most developing countries. Indeed, Funaro seemingly anticipated that other borrowers might take a similar route, allowing for potentially greater debtor state bargaining power. However, more concerted debtor coordination ultimately failed to materialize. Trade sanctions were imposed by the United States in late 1987, and the moratorium lasted until January 1988, when Brazil resumed interest payments.[149]

Among the South American borrowers of the 1980s, Argentina was perhaps the most bitter. Aside from a three-year interlude in the mid-1970s, it had been under military rule since 1966. The second return of military authoritarianism in 1976 involved the establishment of a repressive and economically disastrous regime, which targeted domestic opposition and launched a war in large part to drown out criticism at home.[150] The democratic government that took power under Raúl Alfonsín in 1983 clashed with the IMF and private banks over austerity measures required for additional credits. The new regime hinted that it might withdraw from the Western-led international markets altogether in a diplomat's suggestion that "we can go to East Germany, Bulgaria, Hungary. If we are pushed to buy more imports from the Soviet Union, we will and it won't be our fault."[151] And as the *Financial Times* pointed out, "Unlike most other Latin American countries . . . [Argentina] is one of the few countries that could survive for any length of time a repudiation of foreign debt."[152] In the end, however, Alfonsín opted against a principled challenge to the debt, even when slowing payments to a crawl or asking for a write-down.[153] Even the more critical (Peronist) Justicialist Party, which took power in 1989, demurred. An important Peronist economic adviser said, "A repudiation of the foreign debt doesn't interest us. Rather, we want to put a break on the unilateral transfers of funds to creditors."[154] Thus Argentina as well shied away from a challenge to the underlying norm of sovereign continuity.[155]

The South American countries ultimately joined fellow debtor regimes such as the Philippines, Nicaragua, and Iran in furthering the normalization of statist practices and assumptions of debt continuity. Through the 1970s' and 1980s' major social revolutions and postdictatorial democratic transitions, and despite some dissenting internal discussions, there were no principled repudiations along the lines of odious debt. To some degree this unexpected uniformity reflected the tendencies of international relations at the time, which minimized the importance of internal political regime differences in favor of a more universal "Southern" discourse of systemic economic problems. The space for an alternative vision was further closed off by the integrated approach and consolidated interpretations of creditors and international actors in debt restructurings. The outcomes of this historical context, in terms of state decisions and international debt practices, further granted the norm of debt continuity an air of inevitability.

Conclusion: The Resilience of Statism

Western commentators were well aware of some of the new regimes' discontent with both the 1980s' debt negotiations and the larger structures of international relations. Nicholas Kristof, writing then as an economic correspondent for the *New York Times,* noted,

> Countries that have become more democratic, such as the Philippines and Peru, have in recent years often proved themselves more nettlesome to American governments than more authoritarian governments, such as in

Chile or Rumania. The more democratic countries often assert greater legitimacy, allowing them to take a tougher stance against the banks, and they also seem to reflect more of the debt repudiation sentiment that appears to be widespread in many developing countries. While finance experts generally believe that repudiation would do more harm than good, by cutting off a flow of new capital, the public is less bothered by such prospects.[156]

Even if a repudiation sentiment was widespread, there was little way in which this manifested itself in the ultimate norms and practices of sovereign debt. And there was no suggestion and seemingly little possibility that repudiation might *not* result in an end to capital flows, at least in that historical context. Despite a range of major regime changes over the course of the 1970s and 1980s, no country rejected the international economic order outright along the lines of the People's Republic of China. Nor did any new regime attempt to follow the path of the post-World War I cases by combining principled claims with near-simultaneous efforts to obtain new financing. In the intervening decades, creditor interactions and sovereignty norms had shifted to narrow the possibilities for non-statist sovereign debt practices. The post-World War II emergence of public creditors, including the IBRD and the US government, with their noncompetitive orientations and more oligopolistic private market interactions, gave rise to a consolidated interpretation of the risks of sovereign lending. And the normative principles enshrined in the charter and practice of the United Nations, along with the ideological context of the Cold War, deemphasized any non-statist attentiveness to internal political differences. Although the underlying institutional structures changed with the rise of private creditors in the 1970s and 1980s, the pressures toward a statist framework remained. The integrated approach of private banks and public actors, along with the tendency by sovereign borrowers to focus on larger problems of the economic system, meant that there was very little space to make alternative claims.

The recognition of apartheid-era debt by the newly elected South African regime in 1994 is a fitting coda. By the end of apartheid, the fundamental illegitimacy of the regime was near-universally acknowledged. Most of the foreign banks that previously provided the regime with capital had withdrawn, under pressure from a successful international civil society movement through the 1980s and early 1990s.[157] Nonetheless, during the discussions leading up to the establishment of South Africa's Transitional Electoral Council in late 1993 and the first democratic elections in 1994, the elites of the African National Congress decided to assume the apartheid debt. They also chose to embark on a program of fiscal austerity that delighted the IMF and external markets.[158]

The South African debt acknowledgment shows how far things had moved away from the openness of the early twentieth century. The new South African regime would likely have had more goodwill than any other for a principled debt repudiation. Its explicit embrace of pluralist democracy, market principles, and Washington-approved macroeconomic measures, along with its decision not to engage in large-scale expropriations of white-owned land, should have mitigated any lingering anticommunist concern. Even if its previous lenders had complained, new ones may well have come to the fore with credits appropriately priced for an untested but economically viable borrower. Under these favorable circumstances, the conceptual claim that the new South Africa was a distinct and discontinuous sovereign—albeit one involving the same territory and much of the same (formerly disenfranchised) population—should not have been overly complex for potential investors, credit rating agencies, and other international actors to register.

But, by this time, the norm of sovereign debt continuity was deeply embedded and had become central to the definition of a responsible member of the international community, which South Africa wished to be. In acknowledging the debt, it very explicitly embraced the statist expectations of the international capital markets.[159] Any discussion of repudiation, or even a shift away from standard restructuring practices, had already been discursively marked as a radical and unacceptable departure from the ostensibly apolitical and neutral framework of statist lending and borrowing. In the span of time since the Soviet and Costa Rican repudiations, and despite a reemerging allegiance to emancipatory global principles, the possibilities suggested in the 1920s had been rendered both historically remote and seemingly irrelevant to the practices of the sovereign debt regime.

Legitimacy and Debt at the Turn of the Century

The contours of a new social contract are emerging. . . . Individuals are demanding the rights and responsibilities of citizenship, and this includes a sense of fairness in the distribution of material gains, as well as a say in how they are governed.

—WORLD BANK GROUP, *Strengthening Governance: Tackling Corruption* (2012)

DESPITE THE SHOCK of the 1980s' debt crisis, private actors returned to sovereign lending enthusiastically in the last decade of the millennium. This was not without significant adjustment in the international economic system, of course. In particular, sovereign borrowers struggled through serial reschedulings, which extended the time frames for repayment without providing more significant relief. As the 1990s approached, major international players began to acknowledge that debtor countries faced something more intractable than a temporary liquidity problem. The successive measures put in place to encourage growth had fallen short, and countries remained mired in deep economic problems and an incapacity to service debts. Meanwhile, the structural tendencies and systemic concerns that had hardened and consolidated creditor approaches in the early 1980s shifted, and banks in the intervening years moved away from their overinvolvement in sovereign lending. The plan proposed by US Treasury Secretary Nicholas Brady to significantly restructure the lingering debt, centered on an exchange of bank debt for tradable bonds, helped to revitalize sovereign credit markets.

These first Brady restructurings, in March of 1989, were matched later that year by an even more important milestone in the international arena—the fall of the Berlin Wall in November of 1989. Just as the international economic system moved into a new era—including renewed sovereign lending but also a broader shift toward more market-based policies—global political relations experienced a major transformation. The end of the material and ideational competition between the United States and the Soviet Union created more flexibility in international relations than had existed for nearly half a century. This flexibility opened space for a range of global arguments and movements associated with ideas of popular sovereignty, including expanded claims to self-determination and human rights and insistence on more governmental accountability.

To what degree have these twin developments altered the expectations surrounding debt continuity and sovereign legitimacy at the turn of the twenty-first century? The norm of debt continuity—so well incorporated into international economic orthodoxy in the decades following World War II—seemed unassailable heading into the final years of the millennium. Its basic statist structures remained intact, acceded to even after the widely hailed end of apartheid in South Africa. However, there is evidence that a new opening has emerged for thinking through political legitimacy in sovereign debt. In this last historical chapter, I look more closely at recent trends in norms of governance, human rights, and sovereign lending, as well as new modes of creditor interaction and sources of international capital. I tentatively argue that these trends have started to mainstream long-dormant ideas about illegitimate or odious debt, which may yet prove indicative of a longer-term shift. This is not to claim the existence of anything like a full embrace of odious debt principles, for either credit decisions or in the treatment of debt already incurred. Nor is it to say that the reputational judgments associated with any such shift have been worked out or even tested. However, recent cases implicating questions about legitimate debt, including Iraq and Ecuador, raise the possibility of more flexibility in future sovereign debt markets. They also highlight the ways in which the norm of debt continuity, far from being a neutral and unchangeable market principle, is historically variable and politically conditioned—and therefore alterable in the future.

Trends Going into the New Millennium

The Cold War was fought, at least rhetorically, between two countries and two alliances representing different but ultimately humanist visions of the political good. Among its saddest paradoxes remains the way in which, in the ostensible battle between communism and free market liberalism, respect for actual self-determination, human rights, and internal governance fell by the wayside. The 1990s and the early years of the new century marked a major global change, in which these ideals became discursively more central to broader arguments about appropriateness in international policy and global economic governance. Part of this shift has involved a weakening of the core theoretical construct of the debt continuity norm: the statist idea of sovereignty itself, involving nonintervention in (and even nonassessment of) internal forms of rule. In this section, I consider how these ideas have been at least partially adopted by major international actors, including international economic organizations, public and private creditor groups, and international tribunals. I also briefly highlight several key changes in the realm of creditor interaction and structure, such as the increased prominence of bond issues, the rise of alternative funding sources, and the greater importance of credit rating agencies for sovereign borrowers. While alterations in international sovereignty principles should enable greater plasticity in debt practices, the effect of emerging forms of creditor interaction is more difficult to predict. Still, if broader political ideas and shifting creditor structures help to shape the debt continuity norm, then the turn of the twenty-first century may offer more flexibility than has been seen for quite some time.

Economic Actors and the Language of Governance

Among the most remarked upon suggestions in post-Cold War public international law has been that "Democracy . . . is on the way to becoming a global entitlement."[1] Thomas Franck contended in 1992 that the central proposition of the US Declaration of Independence—that governments "derive their just powers from the consent of the governed"—was, over two hundred years later, "rapidly becoming . . . a normative rule of the international system."[2] In saying this, Franck effectively argued that sovereignty, as the source of legitimate authority in a given territory, no longer rested with the de facto government but rather with the underlying population. Michael Reisman, two years earlier, had made a similar point, noting that the meaning of the term "sovereignty" in modern international law had changed and that "international law still protects sovereignty, but—not surprisingly—it is the people's sovereignty rather than the sovereign's sovereignty."[3] More recently, Ruti Teitel has argued that the post-Cold War era has witnessed the emergence of a "new discourse of politics" that places humanity and human security, rather than state security, at the center of discussions and decisions about international criminal justice, human rights, and the laws of war.[4] While I want to avoid triumphalism in this narrative—and will lay aside for now the ways in which such language can mask practices that are hardly emancipatory—it is clear that both the scholarly and the international political conversation about sovereignty has changed in the last thirty years.

More so than at any other period, major international economic actors have taken up variations on these themes. In particular, a discourse of good governance, anticorruption, human rights, and even democratic rule has made its way into the international financial arena. This type of rhetoric is not a clearly articulated alternative approach to the sovereign debt regime, nor is it a statement of support for odious debt ideas, particularly if they involve unilateral borrower state action. But the prevalence of such discourse, and the occasionally open willingness of major actors to act in line with it, does mark a change from previous modes of lending. In particular, such a discursive shift undermines the most stringently statist approaches to sovereign debt, in which assessments of the nature and efficacy of internal rule are considered irrelevant. While it remains unclear whether and how this shift will develop further—my suggestions here are to a large degree still provisional—it does indicate that the greater attention paid to human rights and internal rule in the post-Cold War era may have spillover effects in the sovereign debt arena.

DEVELOPMENT BANKS AND INTERNATIONAL ECONOMIC ORGANIZATIONS

The principles adopted by regional and international development banks through the 1990s indicate a shift from the strictly statist approach of the decades prior. The founding principles of Europe's post-Cold War development bank, while admittedly grounded in a unique geopolitical milieu, led the way. The European Bank for Reconstruction and Development (EBRD) was launched as the world's newest major development bank in 1991. Although it has gone through a series of troubles and retrenchments,[5] its founding goal was to integrate Eastern European transition countries into open markets, particularly those of Western Europe. The EBRD is unique in explicitly adopting both a political and an economic ideology—namely, multiparty democracy and liberal economics along the North Atlantic model, taking almost the opposite rhetorical standpoint to that adopted by the IBRD and IMF when they were first launched.[6] The EBRD's Articles of Agreement specifically dictate that the Bank should promote enterprise in countries "committed to and applying the principles of multiparty democracy, pluralism and market economics."[7] As Lilian Barria and Steven Roper point out, "The EBRD not only sought to promote a specific form of economic policy-making but also a specific form of governance."[8]

Even the World Bank has shifted away from a strictly statist stance, particularly after 1996, indicating that it might take into account concerns that had previously been considered "political" and thus out of its purview. The World Bank had long come under criticism for its involvement in environmental degradation and for ignoring possible human rights violations, including those violations that might have facilitated controversial development projects. As Jessica Einhorn, a former managing director, pointed out, "Critics charged that the bank's . . . willingness to deal with almost any government was wholly insensitive to human rights and other democratic values. . . . Of course, the bank had answers for these charges. But the governments of its largest shareholders increasingly responded to the critics with calls for reform."[9] Over the course of the 1990s, the World Bank became more attentive to these criticisms, and in 1997 its World Development Report focused on the importance of an effective and responsive state for successful economic development.[10] This was hardly an open embrace of popular rule or human rights—indeed, Galit Sarfaty has studied the ways in which such explicit value orientations have been "economized" to fit into the Bank's self-professedly depoliticized organizational goals and processes.[11] Still, the Bank itself acknowledged the shift from its historically dominant approach, noting, "The world is changing, and with it our ideas about the state's role in economic and social development."[12]

This new attentiveness intensified around the turn of the century, with the expansion of World Bank interests in anticorruption, governance, and even more tangentially developmental objectives such as "cultural heritage."[13] In line with this new approach, the Bank made increasing efforts to look into the governing mechanisms of its clients, particularly to curb the corruption that had previously siphoned off development funds. Beginning in the late 1990s, Bank officials made a series of high-profile speeches in support of this policy, with Paul Wolfowitz saying, "Today, one of the biggest threats to development in many countries . . . is corruption. . . . It not only undermines the ability of governments to function properly, it also stifles the growth of the private sector."[14] The Bank board's veto of a Philippine road-building plan in 2007 on the basis of an insufficient corruption investigation is one example, and indeed as part of its efforts the World Bank barred 340 firms and individuals from doing business with the Bank between 1999 and late 2007.[15] The World Bank's 2007 Governance and Anti-Corruption Strategy received a further update in 2012, in acknowledgment of a "changed landscape" resulting not only from the financial and economic crisis but also from increased attentiveness to essentially non-statist political ideas. In particular, the 2012 strategy notes:

> The contours of a new social contract are emerging. Citizens are seeking a relationship with their government based on transparency, accountability, and participation . . . . Individuals are demanding the rights and responsibilities of citizenship, and this includes a sense of fairness in the distribution of material gains, as well as a say in how they are governed.

The Bank presented this increased desire for "openness, transparency, and citizen engagement" not just as an observation of facts on the ground, but also, in an explicitly normative turn of phrase, "legitimate aspirations."[16] Despite the seeming incongruence of such language with a presumption of debt continuity, this broader shift in bank discourse has not led to any adoption of the doctrine of odious debt, either as formulated by Alexander Sack in 1927 or as revised by contemporary debt cancellation advocates. A 2008 Bank discussion paper on the topic found that the doctrine lacked a clear basis in conventional or customary international law and expressed apprehension that its adoption might undermine capital flows to developing countries.[17] Still, while focusing largely on these reservations and conveying unease about the idea's lack of specificity, the Bank acknowledged the "valid concerns that underpin the debate on odious debts."[18] In its open sensitivity to odious debt ideas, along with its assertion that an emerging social contract grants citizens a say in how they are governed, the Bank has shifted decisively away from its earlier insistence on a strictly statist definition of political neutrality.

The United Nations Conference for Trade and Development (UNCTAD) has recently taken more explicit steps toward a non-statist understanding of sovereignty in debt, though it too has shied away from any endorsement of unilateral state action. In a discussion paper on odious debt commissioned by UNCTAD and published in 2007, Robert Howse notes that any international legal obligation to repay debt "has frequently been limited or qualified by a range of equitable considerations, which may be regrouped under the concept of 'odiousness.'"[19] While acknowledging the view that the technical odious debt doctrine lacks sufficient basis to stand as customary international law, he highlights that the concept helps to unify well-established domestic law doctrines in ways that align with "the contemporary demands of transitional justice as well as global justice in the broadest sense."[20] Further discussions led UNCTAD to codify what it considers to be central principles for contemporary sovereign debt, finalized in the January 2012 Principles on Promoting Responsible Sovereign Lending and Borrowing. These principles do not address the idea of odious debt directly, and indeed explicitly note: "Sovereign debts that are contracted by governments bind the continuing legal entity of the State, including its future administrations and future generations of its citizens."[21] However, it adopted an overtly non-statist approach to understanding sovereign governments in its assertion that "Governments are agents of the State and, as such, when they contract debt obligations, they have a responsibility to protect the interests of their citizens."[22] This agency relationship is emphasized further in the section on "Responsibilities of Lenders," which states at the outset:

> Lenders should recognize that government officials involved in sovereign lending and borrowing transactions are responsible for protecting public interest (to the State and its citizens for which they are acting as agents) . . . . Lenders to sovereign borrowers are dealing with agents . . . . Any attempt by a lender to suborn a government official to breach that duty is wrongful.[23]

The Principles further assert that internal legal rules are central to defining the agency relationship, noting that lenders have an independent duty to ensure, to the extent possible, that government officials are actually authorized to enter into applicable transactions.[24] Perhaps wisely, the Principles' drafters identified appropriate and wrongful actions but did not address or recommend remedies for nonconforming behavior. If "governments," as agents of the state and its citizens, can bind future generations, what results when governments and creditors enter into debt contracts that fail to align with an agency concept of rulership? The Principles seem to leave an opening for the noncontinuity of debt in some instances, in line with the odious debt presentation outlined in the 2007 UNCTAD discussion paper. However, the extent and nature of that opening remains, perhaps deliberately, ambiguous.

The IMF has been somewhat more reticent than the World Bank or UNCTAD in its embrace of a non-statist language of sovereignty and governmentality that might link more clearly to debt discontinuity. In 1997, the IMF issued a "Guidance Note" on governance issues, highlighting that "the IMF's role in these issues had been evolving pragmatically as more was learned about the contribution that greater attention to governance issues could make to macroeconomic stability and sustainable growth in member countries."[25] In an address the same year to the United Nations Economic and Social Council, IMF Managing

Director Michel Camdessus noted that the IMF approach focused "on those aspects of good governance that are most closely related to our surveillance over macroeconomic policies—namely, the transparency of government accounts, the effectiveness of public resource management, and the stability and transparency of the economic and regulatory environment for private sector activity."[26] As part of this, the IMF did begin to consider more explicitly the ways in which poor governance and corruption might be undermining loan purposes, taking the step in 1997 of cutting a $220 million loan to Kenya due to concerns about bribery and self-enrichment in the government of Daniel arap Moi.[27]

INDEPENDENT CREDITOR ACTIONS AND PRIVATE CREDITOR GROUPS

Although statements by multilateral public actors tend to receive the most attention, actions by individual creditor governments can also reveal a shift in approach. Norway in particular, motivated by ethical commitments and enabled by its relative wealth, has been at the forefront of new thinking about sovereign debt. In 2006–2007, the Norwegian government unilaterally canceled a range of debts owed by Ecuador, Egypt, Jamaica, Peru, and Sierra Leone to the Norwegian Institute for Export Credits, which had been incurred to purchase ships between 1976 and 1980. This was a significant step, as 2.9 billion of the 4.4 billion Norwegian kroner owed to the government by developing countries were related to the ship export campaign.[28] While the government did not state that the debts were illegitimate per se, it did explicitly take the view that creditors and borrowers were jointly accountable for certain debt obligations. In a series of releases from the Ministry of Finance, the government declared that: "It is now generally agreed that the Ship Export Campaign was a development policy failure. As creditor, Norway shares part of the responsibility for the resulting debts."[29] In particular, the government acknowledged criticism for inadequate needs analyses and risk assessments—that there had been insufficient due diligence before granting the credit.[30] This is a significant departure from the conventional creditor practice, including that historically followed by major international financial institutions, in which due diligence is emphasized prospectively but the sovereign borrower still bears the *ex post* risk of any failure.[31] More recently, the Norwegian Minister of International Development announced in August 2012 that the government would review all debts owed by poor countries to Norway in light of the UN Principles on Responsible Lending and Borrowing. A press release noted that "Norway will continue to be a responsible lender. We hope this work will inspire other lenders to initiate similar reviews."[32]

The Norwegian example of unilateral debt cancellation has certainly not been followed by all official lenders, although public creditors have generally paid increasing attention to the "moral dimensions" of debt, and the poorest countries have obtained a degree of debt cancellation through the 1996 Heavily Indebted Poor Countries Initiative and the 2005 Multilateral Debt Relief Initiative.[33] The UK recently took a step toward limiting the capacity of creditors to use British courts "exploitatively," partially in response to a lawsuit brought against Zambia to collect on debt originally owed to Romania. Romania in 1999 faced a decision similar to Norway's in dealing with a $15 million debt remaining from Zambia's 1979 purchase of agricultural and automotive machinery with Romanian credits, extended in part to subsidize domestic manufacturers. After a series of negotiations with Zambia, and no doubt in the context of significant economic difficulties at home, Romania chose instead to assign the debt to Donegal International Ltd., a British Virgin Isles special purpose vehicle established by US businessman Michael Sheehan. Romania sold its collection rights to Donegal for $3.28 million—an amount slightly less than that offered by Zambia but without the attendant risk of nonpayment—and Donegal ultimately secured a settlement with Zambia for the higher amount of $15 million. Zambia proved unable to complete the settlement payments, however, and Donegal sued in a UK court for $55 million, an amount representing the reinstated principal plus interest. Perhaps in light of criticism it faced for bringing a $55 million suit based on debt for which it paid much less, Donegal asserted to the court that its "proper purpose is to make a profit."[34] The High Court noted disapprovingly that Mr. Sheehan seemed to "mis-state matters which were in his own knowledge" and was "cavalier in presenting his evidence," but did not determine that he had deliberately presented untruthful evidence.[35] Ultimately, the court acknowledged that its primary concern was with "legal questions . . . and not with questions of morality and humanity"[36] and held in Donegal's favor, but did find that the $55 million amount included an impermissible penalty.[37] The parties subsequently agreed to a $15 million settlement payment, plausible (though difficult) for Zambia in part because of other multilateral debt relief it had received. Upset by this outcome and by a subsequent suit by FG Hemisphere to recover Mobutu-era debt from the Democratic Republic of the Congo, the United Kingdom passed legislation in 2010, made permanent in 2011, to "make sure that Vulture Funds will never again be able to exploit the poorest countries in the world within the UK's courts."[38] The Paris Club has also increased its efforts to prevent these funds from undermining debt relief programs, and Paris Club and EU countries have agreed not to sell their loans to such investors.[39] The UNCTAD Principles on responsible lending and borrowing also seek to limit such activity, contending that "a creditor that acquires a debt instrument of a sovereign in financial distress with the intent of forcing a preferential settlement of the claim outside of a consensual process is acting abusively."[40]

Even leaving aside so-called "vulture funds," private lending institutions have tended to be the most resistant to shifting the tenor of their lending. Still, at least for risk management purposes, financial institutions have begun to accede to language that explicitly acknowledges an intended social purpose for debt and a possible social limitation on the measures permitted in international finance. In 2003, nine major banks from seven countries authored guidelines on socially responsible project finance lending, which have been adopted by seventy-nine financial institutions as of mid-2013. These "Equator Principles," formulated with the International Finance Corporation of the World Bank Group, include guidelines on environmental assessments, child labor, and the treatment of indigenous peoples, among other issues.[41] While the guidelines are to be monitored and enforced primarily by the banks themselves, it is nonetheless telling that these private actors are inviting assessment of their activities according to a public benefit and human rights standard. Subsequent redrafting of these principles has tended to incorporate this public outlook even more explicitly. The most recent version, adopted in June 2013, replaces a general comment that participants will "consider reviewing these Principles from time to time . . . in order to reflect ongoing learning and emerging good practice" with a much stronger recognition that participants' collective "role as financiers" provides an opportunity to practice environmental stewardship and socially responsible development, "including fulfilling our responsibility to respect human rights by undertaking due diligence in accordance with the Equator Principles."[42] This language certainly steps away from the 1976 response by Citibank to the US Senate inquiry on corporate relations with apartheid South Africa, highlighted in chapter 6: "Citibank regards its corporate mission as bringing the provision of a full range of financial services everywhere in the world where it can legally operate at a profit."[43] Citigroup itself adopted the Equator Principles in 2011.[44]

It is hard to know the extent to which this shift in the language of major international economic actors will translate into action over the coming years and decades. As I note in the introductory chapters of this book, a discursive shift in and of itself is hardly sufficient to generate movement in practice. Indeed, it may simply constitute a cynical effort to undermine external criticism. Setting aside the actions of a self-professed outlier creditor like Norway, it is still hard to imagine one of the major public or private financial institutions making open assessments of their loan legitimacy retroactively. Even if corruption or other irregularities invalidate a loan in *advance* of its approval, it is a more difficult (if logically consistent) step for these institutions to accept that previous obligations exhibiting the same pathologies should be subject to cancellation. However, the mainstreaming of this language is, I would argue, helpful to further development of non-statist approaches to debt continuity related to ideas of odious debt. In particular, it enables discussions about debt cancellation on the basis of illegitimacy by highlighting that such actions are hardly heterodox and are in fact logically consistent with broader and increasingly uncontroversial norms.

International Tribunals and Corruption: A Look at World Duty Free

This willingness to assess and condemn practices previously considered relatively unremarkable is not limited to international economic institutions and other creditors. The adoption of principles related to and supportive of non-statist concepts of sovereignty has emerged in international tribunals as well, in particular through more frequent discussions of corruption. A general injunction against corruption, defined by Transparency International as "the abuse of entrusted power for private gain,"[45] has been present as an inchoate element of transnational public policy—as well as an overt aspect of most national legal systems—for many years. However, corruption has arisen more frequently as a direct or indirect issue in investor-state arbitrations since the turn of the millennium, and arguably even has developed into a host state defense in such forums.[46] Although these awards tend to deal with concessions and other investment contracts rather than debt assumed through bonds or bank loans, they raise concepts relevant to finance more generally; indeed, the ICSID case of *Abaclat v. Argentina* suggests that the conceptual line between sovereign debt and other sovereign-related investments may be blurring.[47]

Rarely is an instance of corruption so clearly and transparently presented as in the 2006 ICSID arbitral award of *World Duty Free v. The Republic of Kenya.*[48] In particular, the core statements and principles laid out by the *World Duty Free* tribunal resonate with the broader post-Cold War political, economic, and legal discourse, indicating an increased willingness to adopt non-statist ideas about appropriate sovereign behavior.

World Duty Free Company Ltd., an Isle of Man corporation, brought proceedings before the World Bank's International Center for Settlement of Investment Disputes in protest of Kenya's abrogation of a concessions contract for its international airports in Nairobi and Mombasa. The contract had been signed by the government of the previous president, Daniel arap Moi, who relinquished power in 2002 after twenty-four years of authoritarian rule. World Duty Free's owner and CEO, as part of his presentation in support of the claim, stated that he had made a "personal donation" to President Moi of US$2 million in cash. This transfer had been arranged by an intermediary but was delivered directly to President Moi, and was understood by the CEO to be part of the requirement or consideration for obtaining the contract. The Republic of Kenya as respondent, acting after President Moi relinquished power, requested that the tribunal dismiss World Duty Free's claims with prejudice on the basis that the initial agreement was tainted by bribery, contrary to Kenyan and English law and public policy, and therefore unenforceable.[49]

What is most interesting about the statements by World Duty Free is that they seemed to render explicit a range of assumptions and practices that had been implicitly present in international business transactions for several decades. Most notable for the purposes of this chapter, World Duty Free argued that the fact of giving this gift to the head of state effectively obviated any bribery problems, because Moi was "one of the remaining 'Big Men' of Africa, who, under the one-party State Constitution was entitled to say, like Louis XIV, he *was* the State."[50] World Duty Free made this allegation even despite the existence of anticorruption laws in force at the time of signing the contract, which it presumably considered irrelevant or at least secondary given the effective rule by Moi's government outside the boundaries of law and electoral validation.[51] According to a member of Kenya's legal team, World Duty Free not only contended that the cash transfer was a culturally sanctioned gift in line with Kenyan custom, but also that the practice accorded with the "messy realities of international business in the 1970s and 1980s in the developing world."[52]

Faced with an unusually clear and uncontested instance of bribery, the tribunal in a much remarked upon decision decided for the Republic of Kenya. It first rejected the cultural relativism argument, and also denied any elision of Moi with the underlying sovereign state of Kenya. It explicitly stated that "the Tribunal does not identify the Kenyan President with Kenya"[53] and insisted that "the President held elected office under the Kenyan Constitution, subject to the rule of law."[54] In doing so, it rejected a statist approach, determining that effective control of territory is not itself sufficient to authorize a contract. It made explicit that to be enforced against future iterations of "The Republic of Kenya," a contract entered into even under Moi's regime would have to comply with the laws ostensibly in force under the Moi-era constitution.

In support of its decision, and in advance of discussing English and Kenyan law, the tribunal found that "bribery is contrary to the international public policy of most, if not all, States or, to use another formula, to transnational public policy."[55] It therefore found World Duty Free's claim to be based on a contract that violated international public policy as well as English and Kenyan Law from the outset.[56] Although it cited a range of earlier cases and awards as support for the international policy determination, the tribunal also noted that, when arguing for the existence of a universal conception of public policy, "Tribunals must be very cautious in this respect and must carefully check the objective existence of a particular transnational public policy rule in identifying it through international conventions, comparative law and arbitral awards."[57] To demonstrate the codification of international norms against bribery over the course of the 1990s and the early years of the new millennium, it pointed to a number of international and regional conventions dealing with bribery beginning in 1996, ten years prior to the award.[58] Although the general principle against bribery has existed for decades, the tribunal found telling this proliferation of antibribery conventions, which in turn align with the general post-Cold War shift away from a statist indifference to internal mechanisms of sovereign rule. *World Duty Free* has since been cited for the principle that "corruption is contrary to an international public policy common to the community of nations."[59] Of particular note, subsequent tribunals have accepted the existence of this principle apart from underlying national law—and therefore arguably apart from a contract's choice of law provisions: "Violation of international public policy was held to be a *self-standing* ground for refusing to accept jurisdiction over a claim."[60]

World Duty Free is more important as representing emerging thought on governance than as a harbinger of arbitral awards to come. To begin with, no system of precedent exists at the international level, though the tribunal's finding is likely in practice to be persuasive. Furthermore, the open admission of corruption is unique, and claimants (and their counsel) are unlikely to make the same mistake in the future.[61] As such, the award offers a helpful crystallization of the background context for future decisions and negotiations on sovereign economic relations. One wonders whether tribunals could have made as strong a statement of transnational public policy twenty or thirty years ago. As a claimant,

World Duty Free was correct in its contention that the realities of international business in the 1970s and 1980s (and indeed beyond) included widespread corruption that remained largely unremarked upon. This lack of concern accorded with a more general indifference to the ways in which ruling regimes interacted with their populations. As I described in earlier chapters, banks and other lenders were hardly shy about their disinterest in the potentially unrepresentative or oppressive nature of their borrowers, or the degree to which these regimes failed to comply with legal rules they themselves had promulgated. The emergence of an international legal and political discourse privileging human rights, rule of law, and democratic governance in the post-Cold War era—espoused by civil society actors, public institutions, and in some cases by private creditors—marks a notable change.

Trends in Creditor Interaction

While a discussion of sovereign debt could focus exclusively on these larger normative shifts, important changes have taken place in the realm of creditor interaction and structure as well. These include disintermediation in lending, the partial rise of alternative funding sources, and the increased importance of credit rating agencies. The ultimate effect that such trends may have on debt continuity norms is uncertain, however, as there are pressures toward both more flexibility and greater stringency in the treatment of borrowers.

One major change through the 1990s and into the new millennium has been the return to disintermediated borrowing by sovereigns—that is, borrowing through securities offered directly to investors rather than intermediated through banks or other institutions. As I highlighted in chapter 6, the relatively close interaction of large numbers of banks through the 1970s and 1980s resulted in a more unified approach to sovereign debtors, and subsequently to a lower likelihood of flexible interactions related to sovereign legitimacy and debt continuity. With the revival of international capital markets and the renewed interest in sovereign lending, the 1990s saw a return to bonds, partly catalyzed by the use of Brady Bonds after 1989 to restructure, securitize, and make marketable the bank-held sovereign debt. This shift to disintermediation has meant that larger numbers of small creditors can participate in lending, which could in theory disaggregate lenders, increase the possibility of divergent and potentially non-statist reputational assessments, and provide a greater number of forums in which sovereign borrowers might make their argument.

This disaggregation does pose risks, however. In particular, debtors who aim to restructure debt—regardless of whether an odious debt idea lies in the background or not—may have greater trouble securing agreement from far-flung creditors. Building on the erosion of sovereign immunity through, in the US context, the 1976 Foreign Sovereign Immunity Act and a series of subsequent cases interpreting the Act of State doctrine as it pertains to sovereign debt, creditors have proved increasingly willing to sue for payment on sovereign bonds.[62] The possibility that holdout creditors will disrupt restructurings, connected to the "vulture fund" phenomenon mentioned above, has been discussed with concern by official actors.[63] It has also instigated calls for a sovereign debt restructuring mechanism, with proposals ranging from a full international bankruptcy court to more modest modifications of loan contracts to include provisions such as collective action clauses, aggregation clauses, and exit consents.[64] Still, although disintermediation may prove a problem for debtors seeking a restructuring agreement *ex post,* its *ex ante* effect could be more benign. If a sovereign borrower were to seek funding after a principled default, based in part on appeals to non-statist reputational assessments, a larger number of disconnected creditors with divergent risk interpretations might prove helpful.

The recent emergence of alternative potential funding sources might also strengthen any trend toward flexibility in debt discontinuity for similar reasons. Beginning with the rising availability of oil money in the 1970s, there has been an increase in capital flows between countries in the global South. Although initially much of this moved through deposit accounts in advanced-country banks, recent years have witnessed the appearance of a direct and growing South to South capital market. As globalization further deepens, a shift away from routing these financial relations through the North has also occurred. According to a 2006 World Bank assessment, banks based in developing countries had increased their syndicated lending to $6.2 billion by 2005, up from $700 million in 1985.[65] In the same year, 27 percent of all foreign banks in developing countries were owned by a bank from another developing country. Although the assets involved remain small (at 5 percent of the foreign total), this engagement is new and notable, and especially important in lower income countries where more established foreign banks are wary of entering.[66] Foreign aid by developing countries has also seen some movement, although it has not yet reached the high proportions disbursed by Arab countries in the 1970s. Traditional donors have been joined not only by OPEC countries but also by newly wealthier donors such as India, China, and South Korea.[67]

Perhaps even more noteworthy than this official development aid is the increased number of sovereign wealth funds operating today, which constitute an important and growing source of financing that might be deployed in sovereign lending. The largest thirty-six of these public and semipublic actors invest funds worth nearly $5 trillion, with both the Abu Dhabi Investment Authority and Norway's Government Pension Fund (Global) controlling assets of over $600 billion.[68] The transnational reach of these funds raised concerns in Europe and the United States in particular—two regions recently unaccustomed to watching government officials and titans of industry rely on potentially powerful foreign investors—although the European stance has softened considerably.[69] The world's major sovereign wealth funds have propagated voluntary guidelines, the 2008 Santiago Principles, that aim to reassure potential host countries that the investment vehicles are not secretive and political.[70] Principle 19 is most directly on point, stating, "The SWF's investment decisions should aim to maximize risk-adjusted financial returns . . . based on economic and financial grounds. If investment decisions are subject to other than economic and financial considerations, these should be clearly set out in the investment policy and be publicly disclosed."[71] The emphasis is similar to that of the international financial institutions in the post-World War II era, which sought to reassure both clients and their owner-investors that they would remain separate from any political conflicts. It will be interesting to see how this guideline is interpreted by an increasingly important set of creditors.

One of the key factors that could limit future flexibility in the debt regime is the heightened importance of credit rating agencies in sovereign debt in the latter part of the twentieth century. Although Standard & Poor's and Moody's began rating sovereign bond issues in the 1920s, the absence of direct private lending to sovereigns through the 1960s meant that sovereign ratings too virtually disappeared for some time. While the agencies rated other securities through this period, their business received a significant boost in the mid-1970s. In 1975, the US Securities and Exchange Commission developed the category of "nationally recognized statistical rating organization" (NRSRO), and ratings from designated organizations (Moody's, Standard & Poor's, and Fitch at the time) were incorporated into a range of financial regulations, initially those dealing with bank and broker-dealer capital requirements.[72] With the increase in sovereign bond issues in the 1990s, the agencies became crucial to these new entrants into the securities markets, who faced a relatively unified front in terms of preferred policy. Although the agencies are technically in competition with each other, in practice their appraisals tend not to differ drastically—including when their assessments have proven patently wrong. The US Department of Justice expressed concern about this dynamic in the late 1990s, suggesting that the NRSRO designation in particular is anticompetitive.[73] Describing this concentrated, semiprivate authority in the context of sovereign ratings in particular, Christopher Bruner and Rawi Abdelal note that "the post-war years have witnessed the remarkable rise of a kind of market-based authority that is almost as centralized as the state itself."[74] They highlight that the ratings agencies function as "gatekeepers" to the US investing public and thus act as arbiters of appropriate policy, tending to privilege a neoliberal ideology for both private and sovereign issuers.[75] This context gives the credit rating agencies considerable power to shape what constitutes acceptable and neutral sovereign behavior, though of course it does not guarantee their wisdom in exercising this authority. Thus, even if larger market structures become disaggregated, to the extent that sovereign lending assessments continue to be outsourced to these credit rating organizations, they may have a significant and likely a unifying effect. This unifying consequence would extend, presumably, to determinations related to sovereign legitimacy and debt continuity. The increasing skepticism directed at credit rating agencies, deepened by their failure to warn of the risks involved in the complex financial instruments that exacerbated the 2008 financial meltdown, may moderate this effect somewhat. However, the understandable reaction to this failure—increased monitoring and regulation of the agencies—could also have the opposite result of further fusing (and making more conservative) the agencies' approach.

Indeed, the general response to the financial crisis has involved intensified transnational efforts to supervise both bank and sovereign state activities. As with the 1980s' debt crisis, the sense of systemic weakness has led, at least for the last several years, to more extensive cooperation and to a consolidated approach among creditors. This cooperation has been fueled by fears about bank overexposure across multiple countries, mirroring earlier debt problems, but also by credit-default swaps that implicate a potentially expansive range of financial actors in the outcome of particular debt negotiations.[76] These efforts taken together, particularly if they result in long-lasting movements toward more unified creditor interactions and risk interpretations, may provide less rather than more flexibility for sovereign debtor action going forward.

In short, trends in creditor interaction since the end of the Cold War seem to lead in multiple directions. Along with the larger changes wrought by the lowering of trade and investment barriers, more specific shifts occurred that may well affect the cooperation and risk interpretations of creditors. Thus, alterations in the international economic structure matched the developments in the broader global political discourse, with major actors attending more explicitly to values such as human rights, internal self-determination, and the rule of law. These non-statist ideas gained center stage in discussions of appropriate foreign policy and economic governance, and made their way into creditors' presentations of their own social goals and positions. If the sovereign debt regime is contingent on historical context, and two key elements are broader sovereignty norms and underlying economic structures, then the turn of the twenty-first century may offer a more open moment than has existed for quite some time.

Iraq and an Opening at the Turn of the Century?

To what degree has this apparent openness translated into actual activity on the sovereign debt front? At some level the poor country debt cancellation initiatives of the 1990s and 2000s seem to derive motivation not only from charity but also from a vague sense of injustice at the circumstances under which certain debts were incurred. However, any such motivation is hard to determine and does not apply across all situations. The case of post-Saddam Iraq, however, is interesting if atypical for thinking through the contemporary relationship of debt continuity and sovereign legitimacy. In particular, the US administration couched its virtually unilateral decision to overthrow the Hussein government in the language of democracy and human rights. In line with the excoriation of Saddam Hussein's regime, key members of the US leadership also condemned Saddam-era debt. Such an approach paired strange bedfellows in the world of sovereign debt cancellation, bringing Richard Perle, Paul Wolfowitz, and Treasury Secretary John Snow together with actors more commonly associated with the global (and anti-imperial) left. Although the new Iraqi government ultimately decided against a unilateral repudiation on an odious debt basis, the arguments and atmospherics surrounding the Iraqi negotiations may have helped in the final debt write-down. They undoubtedly brought ideas of sovereign legitimacy, debt discontinuity, and odious debt into the mainstream, putting them front and center in policy discussions, legal analyses, and the popular press.[77] While the Iraq story—and perhaps the Iraq debt story—is far from over, it has already linked powerful actors with claims previously associated with those at the margins of international economic authority.

It thus highlights how establishment figures can adopt very comfortably non-statist positions that were previously framed as radical, in part by connecting these arguments to more broadly legitimized discourses of sovereignty.

The years following the invasion witnessed significant dialogue about Saddam-era debt, particularly the portion of the $130–140 billion that could arguably fit into an odious debt framework.[78] Much of the Iraqi debt principal had been borrowed prior to the regime's invasion of Kuwait, with the interest accumulating throughout its virtual exile from international economic relations during the 1990s. Some of the debt went to military acquisitions and operations necessitated by the Iran-Iraq war, which was instigated by Hussein partly to preempt the destabilizing effects of revolutionary Iran on Hussein's own power base. But this military hardware, most infamously chemical weapons, was sufficiently fungible to be used against Iraq's own population. Still another portion of the debt, however, was contracted for infrastructure upgrades and basic goods—a portion that would presumably be left out of any odious debt cancellation.

There was considerable discussion within Iraq of repudiating the debt, with this possibility receiving significant support in various segments of civil society.[79] And there were high-placed Iraqi officials that might have been expected to press more strongly for a full debt repudiation. According to Ali Allawi,

> The CPA [Coalition Provisional Authority] adopted a particular path for debt restructuring that might not have been freely chosen by a sovereign Iraqi government. The governor of the Central Bank, for example, had been a leading member of the Jubilee Fund initiative which called for the repudiation of "odious debt," that is, debt incurred by dictatorships and tyrannies for wars and internal repression. His views were not sought when the debt-restructuring plan was being developed.[80]

Allawi suggests that the subsequent governor of the Central Bank of Iraq, Sinan al-Shabibi, was also initially committed to the cancellation of odious debt, particularly given that "nearly all Iraq's debts were incurred during the 1980s, as Iraq engaged in fighting the Iran-Iraq War and Saddam Hussein was extending his tyrannical authority."[81]

However, the transitional government, which took power in mid-2004, ultimately decided against such a path in its negotiations. Iraq's Ministry of Finance and its Central Bank presented the request for debt cancellation as primarily economically motivated. This did not mean that they rejected odious debt ideas as inapplicable; indeed, repudiation might have remained a background option. However, in public settings, the post-Saddam (and post-CPA) Iraqi government denied that this was the basis of their request. Iraq's minister of finance stated in a September 2004 interview with *Euromoney* that

> Iraq's need for very substantial debt relief derives from the economic real-
> ities facing a post-conflict country that has endured decades of financial
> corruption and mismanagement under the Saddam regime. Principles of
> public international law such as the odious debt doctrine, whatever their
> legal vitality, are not the reason why Iraq is seeking this relief.[82]

According to Lee Buchheit, the primary legal advisor to both the Minis-try of Finance and the Central Bank, this decision was ultimately taken for several reasons. For one, as negotiations began, there appeared to be a considerable amount of trade finance which would have been difficult to write down under an odious debt theory. As Buchheit says, "The flip side of seeking a write-off of the odious debt would be an acceptance and repayment of the non-odious debt." And the process of any such sepa-ration and assessment would have been time consuming and difficult:

> Who would decide the illegitimacy? How would we set up the arbitrations?
> We had twelve to thirteen thousand separate commercial contracts to deal
> with. Would each one have to be arbitrated? Remember that this was 2004,
> when economic rebuilding was considered central. . . . The imperative was
> to get rid of the debt stock and do it fast.[83]

Given that there already seemed to be a fair amount of willingness to write down debt, at least among Paris Club creditors, there was also a desire not to be antagonistic in Iraq's opening salvo. Against this back-ground, making claims on the basis of odious debt may have prompted unnecessary creditor antipathy. As Buchheit continues, "[creditors] would have said no. It is so amorphous, they couldn't accept it. It ef-fectively would have forced a unilateral repudiation."[84] Jeremy Pam, another member of the Iraqi legal team and later US Treasury attaché to Iraq, concurs: "[The odious debt issue] was there and periodically raised, but it was basically off the table for practical reasons—in partic-ular because this was a negotiation, where the goal was an agreed-upon compromise." He emphasizes that, to the extent that Iraq was interested in a negotiation, the alternative would have been difficult. "There was no scenario in which an odious debt approach could have produced a consensus. . . . [I]t was very clear to all of us looking at it strategically that it would shut down negotiations."[85]

Notwithstanding the earlier comments of Secretary Snow, the US Treasury was ultimately far less comfortable with openly basing any cancellation on broader principles, though it favored a substantial write-down for Iraqi debt. Given the US position as a major creditor country that would be significantly affected by a widely applicable principle, internal disagreement would hardly be surprising. The Treasury helped to pave the way for a more conventional debt restructuring, arranging for an initial assessment of Iraqi indebtedness and enlisting former secretary of state James Baker to engage in shuttle diplomacy on bilateral debt reductions. In the spring of 2004, the CPA invited law firms to submit proposals for representation, and these were available for the transitional government with the transfer of formal sovereignty in mid-2004.[86] The close working relationship (to put it mildly) between the Iraqi government and the US Treasury no doubt affected the subsequent path as well. In his retrospective, Allawi assessed that "the odious debt argument was not acceptable inside the US Treasury. . . . An early decision was therefore made by the CPA that Iraq should try to recognize, reconcile, quantify and then settle the debt on terms that allowed for a large, though not complete, write-off."[87]

And indeed the Iraqi transitional government ultimately asked for an across-the board write-down in the Paris Club, its first negotiating forum, maintaining silence on the odious debt principles animating domestic discussions. The Paris Club of creditor countries reached a key agreement in late November 2004 in which 80 percent of Iraq's debt to Paris Club creditors would be cancelled.[88] And given that the remaining 20 percent would be stretched over six years, the net present value of the 2004 write-down amounted to 89.75 percent of the $40 billion Paris Club total. Using the Paris Club principle of comparable treatment, this formed the basis for a 10.25 percent offer to commercial and other creditors.[89] Despite the Paris Club requirement of an IMF program, the Iraqi government was very satisfied with the results, and Allawi claimed that "the resolution of Iraq's debt was one of the unalloyed successes of the entire post-war period."[90]

This leaves open the question of whether the ongoing discussions of odious debt and the arguments about debt illegitimacy had any effect on the negotiations. The creditors were fully aware of this background, and indeed the Jubilee debt cancellation and odious debt movements are very active in creditor countries. But Paris Club negotiations are private and the creditors themselves have tended to maintain this privacy. According to Buchheit, however, this background did make a difference, even if it did not result in unilateral Iraqi action:

> [An odious debt idea] was definitely present—the atmospherics are unavoid-able. The creditors all dealt with Saddam, and now half castigated him as

Beelzebub. But repudiation or full payment was not a binary choice in the negotiating context. . . . If we have reached a point where we could legitimately make a claim on odious debt, then they're already softened up.[91]

Still, Buchheit is cautious about saying whether any other countries might be able to follow an Iraqi precedent, emphasizing the unique geopolitical circumstances and timing of the case. But this does not mean that the background norms of legitimacy or illegitimacy will be irrelevant going forward: "[T]he circumstances are obvious. They weigh on creditors, who at the very least have a public relations problem." Speaking of restructurings in which an odious debt idea might be relevant, he notes, "A degree of background noise doesn't hurt negotiators."[92] That said, Pam emphasizes that any background noise should not get too loud, lest it spook interlocutors.[93]

Thus, even without a unilateral repudiation, the Iraq case may have somewhat shifted the "neutral" standard of legitimate sovereignty in sovereign debt. Even in advising *against* the use of the odious debt doctrine to repudiate Iraqi debt, Ted Truman, the former head of the Federal Reserve's international division and the former assistant secretary for international affairs at the US Treasury, acknowledged that there might be a portion of the Saddam-era debt that should *not* be considered continuous. In a *Financial Times* editorial, he stated, "It would be economically, politically and morally misguided to expect Iraq to pay all of its accumulated external obligations."[94] However, he presented several reasons that the United States as a creditor nation might not want to recommend a unilateral course of action. Among these, he pointed out that Iraq owed the United States relatively little compared to other creditors, and argued that it would be unfair to "spend other people's money" in calling for a repudiation. Some of those other creditors, such as Russia, had themselves assumed the debts of arguably odious previous regimes—in this case the Soviet Union, come full circle. Furthermore, he highlighted that other countries—specifying Indonesia, Nigeria, and South Africa—would be only too eager to use an Iraqi odious debt precedent to repudiate their own inherited obligations.[95]

Truman's approach, a fairly popular one, attempts to reconcile two potentially competing views. It combines a generally statist belief that creditors are "owed" (and of course a US Treasury concern for precedent) with a non-statist acknowledgment that it would be wrong—as a point of principle as well as of political expediency and economic efficiency—for all of Iraq's debts to be uniformly continuous. This view tends to coincide with a preference for negotiation rather than unilateral action, but favors compromise on both sides. While arguably internally inconsistent, this approach is nonetheless a much more flexible starting point for mainstream thinking than the dominant framework through most of the twentieth century.

The Ambiguous Lessons of Ecuador

While the Iraqi case certainly brought arguments about debt illegitimacy to the fore, it is difficult to extrapolate from such an atypical series of events. The 2008 Ecuadorean default, however, offers another layer of insight into how the discourse and creditor structures surrounding sovereign debt may enable more flexibility in the future. Indeed, the language of illegitimacy played a more explicit role in Ecuador's default than it did in Iraq's restructuring, even though the argument did not garner the same widespread sympathy. Nonetheless, the reaction to Ecuador's decision has been telling and in some cases surprising. Debt cancellation advocates tended to approve of the action, certain commentators criticized Ecuador's default as unwise and its invocation of odious debt as inappropriate or counterproductive, and yet other unaffected official creditors appear to have expressed indifference or even mild support. This array of responses demonstrates both how ideas of odious debt have entered the mainstream—even if they do not apply as easily in the Ecuadorean case—and also how changes in creditor structure can enable greater flexibility in sovereign debt more broadly.

The Ecuadorean default of December 2008 elicited little shock among external markets or observers.[96] Rafael Correa, a leftist former finance minister, had openly expressed his opinions as to the illegitimacy of much of Ecuador's external debt before being elected president in November 2006. As early as March 2005, while still a government economic advisor, Correa presented a paper asserting the invalidity of Ecuador's 2000 debt restructuring. He insisted that it granted insufficient relief while establishing payment structures that benefited external creditors over the local population.[97] When appointed finance minister later in 2005, Correa began to dismantle policies associated with the restructuring, such as successfully encouraging the legislature to abolish a debt buyback fund established as part of the restructuring program and distancing his ministry from multilateral development institutions and eventually even from President Palacio. Correa's subsequent 2005 resignation was followed by a presidential campaign that included additional challenges to the legitimacy and efficacy of external debt payment, and Correa was finally sworn into the presidency in January 2007. His inauguration speech again included significant references to Ecuador's external debt, part of which he stated was illegitimate, entered into under dubious circumstances, and already "repaid several times."[98]

In July 2007, President Correa established the Integral Auditing Commission for the Public Credit (CAIC) in order to assess the "legitimacy, legality, transparency, quality, capacity and efficiency" of all debt contracted in the thirty years prior to 2006.[99] The one-year time frame for this significant task was ambitious, to say the least, with the CAIC ultimately publishing its formal findings in November of 2008. The commission's report expressed dissatisfaction with its own inability to access what should have been public documents, stating that it received requested information from only four of eighteen government agencies, with eleven agencies providing materials that did not correspond to the CAIC's requests and three departments offering no response whatsoever.[100] The military, which had played a sometimes problematic part in Ecuadorean politics during the thirty years covered by the audit—though nothing approaching the role of Saddam Hussein's armed forces in Iraq—stated that it "had not found any documentation that details any loans received from foreign commercial banks during the period 1976–2006."[101] The report acknowledged that, in light of such fragmentary answers from these public agencies, "it was not possible to confirm the origin of registered debt" for these departments, and recommended that a supplementary examination be undertaken to determine the responsibility for such loans and the degree to which they achieved their stated objectives.[102]

Despite the significant—and perhaps unavoidable—gaps in its audit, the CAIC's 2008 report adopted strong and sometimes hyperbolic language in its characterization of Ecuador's external debt. It contended that much of the debt owed to international commercial and multilateral banks failed to meet the CAIC's requirements of legitimacy, legality, transparency, quality, and efficiency. The report did not attribute the debt to a fallen dictatorial regime (perhaps the paradigmatic odious debt case), but rather in effect challenged the legitimacy of the international lending regime as a whole. It denounced, for example, the US Federal Reserve's far-reaching decision to raise interest rates in 1979, which constituted an effort to deal with domestic inflation and economic stagnation but also raised Ecuador's (and many other countries') debt servicing costs, in line with the terms of floating-rate loans.[103] The report condemns this US decision as a "unilateral action" constituting an "important infraction" of international law, and lists it as part of the evidence for the "illegalities and illegitimacies" detected in Ecuador's international bank loans.[104] Practices such as the specification in bond contracts of New York governing law and the inclusion of sovereign immunity waivers—standard clauses intended to attract and lower the cost of external capital—are also offered as legally problematic elements of the external commercial debt.[105] The loan conditionalities of multilateral development organizations, including the IMF, World Bank, and the Inter-American Development Bank (IDB), are characterized as "a violation of the jus cogens standards," including those incorporated into international human rights instruments.[106] Noting, among other things, the environmental degradation, public sector job and service cuts, and popular displacement resulting from certain projects or loan conditions, the CAIC states, "Violating human rights due to the impositions of multilateral banks is reason enough to consider the debts contracted for under these conditions to be odious, illegitimate, and illicit."[107] Although the term "odious" does occur several times in the document, there is no clear reference to the doctrine of odious debt itself, or to its modest ascendance in the last decade.[108] The ideas of odiousness, illegality, and illegitimacy presented in the CAIC report are broader than either the original doctrine or most of its variations in the academic literature. Indeed, Ecuador is unique in openly challenging almost all of the dominant international private and public capital market practice on sovereign debt.[109]

The commission finally recommended that Ecuador default on almost 40 percent of its $10 billion of external debt.[110] The Ecuadorean government announced a formal default on December 12, 2008, calling at least part of the external debt "obviously immoral and illegitimate" and Ecuador's external creditors "monsters."[111] By then, Correa had already decided not to pay an upcoming $30.6 million coupon payment on its 2012 bonds, which had been part of the 2000 restructuring.[112] Ecuador ultimately defaulted on its 2012 and 2030 Global bond issues, both of which had been part of the 2000 restructuring Correa criticized earlier. It continued payments, however, on bonds prepared for the external market and issued in 2005, which overlapped with Correa's time as finance minister. It also continued payment on all its multilateral bank debt, despite the report's accusation that certain of the conditions associated with those loans had resulted in human rights violations. Although the price of oil (accounting for 60 percent of Ecuador's exports) dropped significantly prior to the default, Correa insisted that the decision to default was on the basis of principle rather than economic necessity. Homeland security minister Fernando Bustamante similarly stated, "I want to dispel the notion that this has any connection with any potential troubles related to our finances."[113] And, indeed, Ecuador's debt service as of 2008 was comparatively modest, at less than 1 percent of GDP, in part as a result of the excoriated 2000 restructuring.[114] Notwithstanding the accusatory language of the default, Correa suggested that Ecuador did not actually intend to repudiate the payment entirely, instead suggesting that it would seek a "very big discount" in restructuring. He acknowledged that "there is a legitimate part to the debt.... We want to present a proposal where some of the value of the debt is recognized but at a much lower price than what they say we owe."[115] In the end, Ecuador did not present a bond exchange proposal, instead restructuring the debt through a buyback for thirty-five cents on the dollar (and possibly additional purchases on the secondary market) offered through 2009 and with an eventual 95 percent participation rate.[116]

The response to Ecuador's action has been varied, as one might expect. Among debt cancellation activists, the Ecuadorean audit and its call for principled default received significant support. Following a September 2008 meeting in Ecuador of the First North-South Study and Strategy Meeting of the International Campaign on Illegitimate Debt, the representatives of fifty networks and organizations from thirty-six countries, including multiple national Jubilee organizations, signed a statement to express support for the audit. The statement also noted its support for the potential default "on all credits which the audit has established and demonstrated to be irregular, illegal, illicit and therefore illegitimate."[117] It further expressed the commitment of the participating organizations to disseminate information on the audit process and results, with the partial aim of realizing "comprehensive audits in all those countries that have suffered the same illegitimate processes of indebtedness."[118] Writing about the Ecuadorean default, Wade Mansell and Karen Openshaw also seem to accept the basic claim of debt illegitimacy, noting, "it can be asserted that the percentage of the Ecuadorian population that benefited from the incurring of sovereign debt was miniscule."[119] They present Correa's combination of principled default with a more pragmatic acceptance of partial payment obligations as a success and potential example, stating, "while Ecuador's successful bond buyback appears to strengthen the adoption of a legal or quasi-legal approach to debt resolution . . . it is necessary to maintain a long-term working relationship with the other party."[120]

The wisdom of Ecuador's decision was called into question in other venues, however, particularly by writing in the financial press. For example, Felix Salmon, a financial journalist and frequent commentator on sovereign debt issues, offered a column on "Ecuador's Idiotic Default." He noted Ecuador's already-low debt service burden at the time of the default, and wondered whether Ecuador would be able to defend itself against suits brought by distressed debt or vulture funds, or deal with the likely acceleration of debt payments.[121] However, the discussion in the months following the default shifted to a degree, with some private-sector investors even acknowledging begrudging admiration of the Ecuadorean strategy, at least in the short term. Salmon's coverage of an Emerging Markets Trade Association (EMTA) panel on the default in May 2009 notes that the exclusively private-sector participants felt that, in Ecuador's exchange offer, "the country has won, and the private sector has lost." He quotes Hans Humes of Greylock Capital as calling Ecuador's strategy "one of the most elegant restructurings that I've ever seen," and highlights both the planned and the serendipitous factors that supported this seeming success.[122] He notes that the unilateral restructuring further lowered the country's debt-to-GDP ratio, which could be viewed favorably by future creditors, and also that the continued payment of Ecuador's 2015 global bonds (issued in 2005) offers creditors an example of the country's willingness to pay *certain* debt: "Look, [Correa's] saying: we pay back the money that *we* borrow. We just don't pay back debt which was originally borrowed decades ago and which was restructured *twice* in a manner designed to be as friendly as possible to private-sector creditors."[123] Indeed, Ecuador has reiterated that it will continue to repay these particular securities, with Central Bank President Pedro Delgado noting, "It's been very clearly established that with the 2015 bonds there was no presumption of wrongfulness . . . . These are being paid and they are being paid on time."[124]

As of yet, Ecuador has not tested the private financial markets following its 2008 default. It entered into talks with Bermuda-based Lazard Ltd. and law firm Clifford Chance LLP about the possibility of issuing bonds in 2012.[125] However, it ultimately returned to borrowing from public creditors, which it had continued paying after its default and which have offered Ecuador financing since 2008. Indeed, Ecuador had reached out to alternative sources of funding in apparent anticipation of the default. For 2009, Correa secured a $40 million line of credit from Iran and up to $1 billion from the Andean Development Corporation (CAF).[126] Luis Palau-Rivas, representing the CAF in Quito, noted of Ecuador's unusual restructuring, "We see the process positively because it's a voluntary process . . . . It's helping to solve a difficult situation . . . and will benefit everyone."[127] Even more notably, the IDB stated, "The good results obtained (in the restructuring) will benefit all Ecuadoreans during difficult times . . . . The IDB reiterates is predisposition to work alongside Ecuadoreans to promote economic development."[128] An IMF representative responded to a reporter's question with, "We understand that Ecuador's decision to default on these bonds is based on a dispute about [their] legal validity rather than [on] debt sustainability [grounds], and of course we don't take sides on the merits."[129] Ecuador did not ultimately apply to the international banks, but regional multi-lateral funds backed up their verbal support with additional financing, with the IDB approving $515 million in new loans for 2009, the CAF ultimately approving $873 million, and the Latin American Reserve Fund lending $480 million in July 2009.[130] At least as important has been the emergence of alternative bilateral creditors, including China, Russia, and Iran. China in particular has become the major source of bilateral funding, lending about $7.3 billion as of 2012—approximately 16 percent of the country's outstanding debt—in exchange for future oil exports.[131] According to finance minister Patricio Rivera, Ecuador expected in 2012 alone to receive $4.38 billion in loans from lenders including the IDB and nations such as China and Russia.[132] It is unclear when Ecuador will attempt a return to private markets, and what the emerging market bond purchaser response will be. However, the credit ratings agencies have shown some movement in their assessment of Ecuador's prospects, with Fitch Ratings affirming Ecuador's long-term foreign currency debt rating at B- but revising its outlook to "positive" in October 2012, and Standard & Poor's upgrading Ecuador's rating to B/B with a stable outlook in July 2012 on the basis of a "perceived improvement in the government's willingness, as well as capacity, to service its debt."[133] Moody's upgraded Ecuador's long-term government bond rating to Caa1 in September 2012, highlighting Ecuador's favorable government debt ratios and low interest payments compared to B-rated peers, along with its ability to secure significant external financing from China and the fact that it "has also continued to service all of its debt since the last default.[134]

This relatively mild response is especially interesting given that the Ecuadorean case is less sympathetic than that of other more obvious candidates for a principled default on the basis of odious debt or broader ideas of sovereign discontinuity. Still, by basing its default on principled arguments, Ecuador pushed the discourse of debt and legitimacy further into the public arena—even if a number of commentators consider that discourse ultimately inapposite for its own case. In his discussion of Ecuador, Arturo Porzecanski notes:

> The case of Ecuador does not fit the odious-debt doctrine or related grounds for repudiation. To begin with, the country has been under continuous civilian, constitutional rule since mid-1979. Though it has been mismanaged, it was not plundered by an egomaniacal dictator. The greatest

build-up in foreign public indebtedness took place from 1980–1994. . . . During this extended period, duly elected civilians were in charge, none of whom has been found guilty of any illegal conduct. Issues of state succession, war-related debts, widespread corruption, the absence of informed consent, or collusion on the part of creditors to divert funds for contrary purposes—none of these criteria seem applicable here.[135]

Adam Feibelman, writing of a "pyrrhic victory" for odious debt, expresses similar doubt about the Ecuadorean action:

While the obligations Ecuador effectively restructured may have been the product of mismanagement and inequitable policies of prior Ecuadorean administrations, they can only be understood as odious or illegitimate under a very broad definition of these terms. It is hardly clear, for example, that the citizens of Ecuador did not benefit—directly or indirectly—from the resources that their government initially obtained in exchange for these obligations or from their government's ability to restructure earlier obligations. Furthermore, at least some of the terms and circumstances that Ecuador cited as odious or illegitimate are predictable and conventionally acceptable aspects of sovereign borrowing, default, and forbearance.[136]

Feibelman expresses concern that Ecuador's use of the language of odious and illegitimate debt will effectively tarnish these ideas, even for "sympathetic skeptics."[137] Part of the potential difficulty with these concepts is their lack of a clear limiting principle:

Ecuador's episode may end up heightening concerns that a mechanism for addressing odious or illegitimate debt would inevitably implicate transactions that are potentially beneficial to sovereigns and their citizens, making it harder for sovereigns to borrow for productive purposes. Heightening such concerns only serves to undermine efforts to convince legal actors and policymakers to adopt such a mechanism.[138]

Feibelman acknowledges the possibility of another outcome as well—that Ecuador's actions could strengthen the support for a more institutionalized determination of debt illegitimacy, as "the official sector and financial markets might find it strategically preferable to admit that some debt should be discharged if it is odious or illegitimate, but only if it is unambiguously so."[139] Indeed, there is at least a hint that Ecuador's actions could weaken the hostility of financial market participants to more centralized (and thus potentially more predictable or even controllable) mechanisms for sovereign debt restructuring. Speaking on the 2009 EMTA panel on Ecuador, Humes of Greylock Capital remarked, "The world has changed . . . . Maybe [the solution is to] go back to Anne Krueger's model"[140]—IMF deputy managing director Anne Krueger's

2001 proposal for a sovereign debt restructuring mechanism, which met with near-universal hostility from private market participants at the time. While it is unclear what the final market and institutional response will be to the default, particularly given the many other variables that necessarily factor into Ecuador's economic and political future, the Ecuadorean case does hint at a potential shift in the possibilities of the sovereign debt regime.

Although it does not speak directly to issues of debt continuity, especially given the absence of any real regime change, the Ecuador case raises important questions about sovereignty, reputation, and legitimacy in the contemporary debt arena. Ecuador is the first country in many decades to forthrightly challenge the legitimacy of its external debt, and default not on the basis of economic difficulties but rather as a point of principle. Thus, although the Ecuadorean episode has not rallied many actors around its expansive understanding of illegitimacy, like the Iraq restructuring it brought such arguments out of the shadows and into the mainstream discussion. Even Porzecanski's insistence that Ecuador's case fails to correspond with the requirements of odious debt ideas is telling in its own right. Porzecanski is hardly a debt cancellation activist, as befits his background as former chief or senior economist for emerging markets at ABN AMRO, ING Bank, Kidder, Peabody & Co., and J. P. Morgan. Yet, in contending that odious debt arguments do not properly apply in the Ecuadorean case, he implicitly suggests that they might apply elsewhere. Furthermore, the response from external creditors has been far from uniform, with some regional institutions expressing mild support for Ecuador and new players such as China making the reputational judgment to deepen their financial ties even despite the default. In short, shifts in both the broader normative discussion and in creditor structures have shaped the Ecuador case, and may well enable more flexibility in sovereign debt going forward.

Europe and the Boundaries of Odious Debt

Where does all of this leave us in the second decade of the new millennium? Sovereign debt issues have taken center stage across a range of countries and in multiple contexts. In many of these situations, attentiveness to the relationship between external financing and popular control and benefit has emerged as central. The nature of this discussion varies significantly—ranging from the classic odious debt arguments about post-Saddam Iraq, to Ecuador's much broader rebuff of international financial practices, and even to the distress of European populations repaying debt for which they do not feel entirely responsible. Indeed, calls of "odious debt" and "illegitimate debt" occasionally have arisen in corners of the European crisis as well, suggesting the purchase of such language even in relatively stable Western democracies. While the applicability of the originally formulated doctrine is even less obvious in Europe than in Ecuador, these arguments highlight that claims about popular sovereignty, implicating as they do control over external financing and its effects, resonate regardless of a state's internal political and economic forms. And they again point to the way in which this terminology has entered into the broader discourse, suggesting that—even as its applicability in Europe is contested—its relevance elsewhere may become more difficult to question.

Although it is not widespread, the language of odious and illegitimate debt has certainly filtered into some of the public anger about the European debt crisis and the austerity measures that it has entailed. As one example, Jason Manolopoulos alleges in *Greece's 'Odious' Debt* a public economic culture that is "a modern day hydra" made up of cronyism, nepotism, corruption, and waste. He lays the primary blame with Greek political elites but notes that private banks and EU leaders had "no excuse" for ignoring the lax accounting, corruption, and public sector waste, especially given that much of the information was on public record.[141] While he acknowledges that "it is a stretch to define all or most of Greece's debt as 'odious' given that there were elections during the period the debt accrued," he effectively argues in favor of burden sharing and significant restructuring, "given the corrupt nature of the Greek political class and the complicity of the European Union and German and French banks."[142] A crowd-funded political film released in April 2011, *Debtocracy*, more aggressively places the primary blame on a small number of politicians and business people who allegedly enriched themselves at public expense. It calls for a public audit of the Greek debt along Ecuadorean lines, to be followed by a default on "odious" or "immoral" debt.[143] Even without any recourse to this language, the anger at austerity measures required for bailout funds, the feeling that such measures have harmed rather than helped Greece's recovery, and the sense that creditors (including public creditors) should bear a larger share of the restructuring burden is widespread.[144]

This language has made its way into Ireland as well, in support of writing down debt incurred not to finance public spending but rather as part of a rescue plan for private banks, especially Anglo Irish Bank, whose lending helped to fuel the Irish property bubble (and bust) of the

2000s. According to Peter Mathews, Fine Gael TD (member of Parliament) for Dublin South,

> Approximately €75bn of this was lent to the Irish banks by the European Central Bank [ECB] to enable the banks to repay bondholders in full. Clearly, this was inappropriate and therefore we can say with justification that half the money owed by the banks to the European Central Bank and Irish Central Bank is odious debt. Through a political chain of events, it has ended up on the backs of Irish citizens. This is patently unfair.

Again, while the odious debt language here is not widespread, the public outcry against continued austerity measures to repay nationalized private bank debt persists, fueled by the liquidation of Anglo Irish and the rough equivalence in value between annual debt payments and the austerity measures themselves.[145] The activist group Anglo Not Our Debt makes an even more explicit link to the global debt discussion, estimating payments for the (now defunct) Anglo Irish Bank at over €47 billion by 2031 and noting that "People in Ireland have joined millions of people worldwide repaying unjust and illegitimate 'debts.'"[146]

The anger at government nationalizations of private debt is hardly new—indeed, it percolates on both sides of the Atlantic and featured in Ecuador's arguments for its default.[147] Governments generally make this decision to avert disruptive banking and economic crises, and ideally the choice is followed by careful efforts to scrutinize (and perhaps limit) the systemic position of such private institutions in the nation's financial system. While leaders often shield their decisions from broader scrutiny, the Icelandic administration took the unusual step of calling for public referenda on its financial negotiations. Following the late 2008 Lehman Brothers bankruptcy and the subsequent freezing of international financial markets, Iceland's largest bank proved unable to make good on the deposits of its online subsidiary (Icesave), which had lured domestic and overseas clients with high interest rates. As Iceland's financial system spiraled downward and the magnitude of the crisis became clear, Central Bank governor David Oddson indicated that Iceland would not pay the foreign deposits owed by private banks, stating, "We have decided that we are not going to pay the foreign debts of reckless people . . . . Placing such a burden on our children and grandchildren would be slavery for other people's fault."[148]

Concerned about the possibility of broader bank runs, the United Kingdom and the Netherlands decided to pay in full the Icesave deposits of their own residents. They then attempted to compel complete reimbursement from Iceland—with a £4.3 billion claim in the UK case alone—under a European directive requiring deposit insurance for foreign branch depositors, went so far as to invoke antiterror legislation in their efforts.[149] Iceland's president, Olafur Grimsson, called for a referendum to confirm the resulting negotiated settlement, stating, "It is ridiculous to heap this debt burden on a nation so small."[150] The public refused to accept and repay the deposits in the two referenda ultimately held, and subsequently a specialized European court found in favor of Iceland on the requirements of the deposit insurance scheme.[151] While the regulations were extensively rewritten following the Icesave fiasco, the decision remains interesting in emphasizing the special nature of a "systemic crisis," which the Court seems to distinguish from the more quotidian individual bank failures originally envisaged by the regulations.[152] Thus, the Iceland case is remarkable in responding to a public outcry over arguably "sovereign" debt by placing external financial decisions directly in popular hands at the moment of crisis.

These European discussions, grounded in claims about democracy and good governance, connect to arguments that have intensified in the broader international arena in the post-Cold War decades. This discourse has not been limited to public international law or international "political" relations, but has shaped the language and self-described goals of major international economic actors as well. All this raises the question of whether a new opening has emerged for thinking about issues of sovereign legitimacy in debt and reputation. The European debt crisis, while central to financial discussions generally, is only at the outer boundaries of questions about debt continuity and odious debt. Still, it points to the depth of feeling surrounding the desire for popular voice and popular benefit in sovereign debt, and emphasizes that these concerns exist on a broad continuum. It also implies that, even if charges of debt illegitimacy are more complicated to make in democratic Europe, perhaps they are harder to dismiss in other settings. In particular, a strict insistence on debt continuity counters key elements of the contemporary international political discussion, and more flexible approaches also appear to be enabled by new developments and entrants in contemporary capital markets. If, as I argue, the norm of debt continuity is indeed politically conditioned and historically variable, then the turn of the twenty-first century may provide a more open moment than we have seen in quite some time.

8

Politics and Prospects

WE HAVE reached a strange place in world history. On the one hand, global law and politics have increasingly emphasized the accountability of leaders, expecting them to represent the interests and respect the rights of state populations. Discussions of corruption and good governance insist on distancing legitimate sovereign rule from self-serving prerogative, and separating the public purse from that of private citizens. Institutions such as the International Criminal Court hold leaders accountable for crimes committed against their own populations, drawing the brightest line possible between rule by brute force and emerging ideas of public benefit and rule of law. Yet the debt payment expectations of international finance, along with the bargaining positions they enable, continue to rest on a political and legal theory that blurs each of these distinctions. This statist theory effectively assumes that, regardless of any potential illegitimacy or internal change, the sovereign state exists as an opaque, undifferentiated entity—one that stretches indefinitely through time. Although these expectations are softening somewhat, as demonstrated by the shifts I discuss in chapter 7, the background norm remains relevant across the majority of debt interactions. Indeed, we can now imagine prosecuting the leaders of a fallen regime for crimes against a state's population while simultaneously asking that population to acknowledge and repay the fallen regime's debts.

What allows us to maintain this legal and conceptual rupture in international relations, and to what degree is it stable? There is a tendency, in both practical work and in academic study, to become expert in specialized fields. While there is much to be said for the depth of knowledge that results from this trend, it also risks closing off inquiries and approaches that are inherently interdisciplinary. In the area of sovereign debt, it has left important questions unasked and connections unmade. Public international lawyers and political theorists carefully consider how sovereign statehood relates to broader norms or higher ideas of the public good, while scholars of international economic and financial issues elucidate the mechanisms by which states and other actors interact to generate particular market outcomes. Too rarely, however, do these groups speak to each other. Unsurprisingly, therefore, when thinking about "sovereign debt," it is easy to forget that both the practices and the discussion in this area depend upon an implicit but politically controversial theory of sovereign legitimacy.

This rupture is further enabled by the fact that global financial relations seem particularly mysterious to many, with practices grounded in market principles that appear basically uniform and unchangeable. This air of inevitability offers a buffer against the questions of political and legal principle that tend to fuel discontent and action. In the sovereign debt arena, the norm of debt continuity—the basic rule that debtors must repay even after a major regime change or suffer reputational consequences—counters emerging political commitments and widespread ideas of moral decency. But these expectations are buttressed by the sense that debt continuity is a fundamentally apolitical and largely inevitable market principle, and the background belief that its reputational supports are equally neutral if admittedly unfortunate. Although the stark repayment standard is most visible in transitional political situations, the norm shapes expectations and bargaining positions across *all* sovereign debt negotiations. If repayment is the default rule even in the extreme circumstance of regime change, then every other financial obligation is rendered comparatively safer from challenge, regardless of any potential illegitimacy.

In writing this book, I have sought to demonstrate that this market narrative overlooks key elements of the story, and to show how the repayment norm is far from an apolitical, consistent, and inevitable financial principle. Rather, debt continuity is inherently political and, especially given the conceptual trends in international politics over the last century, its seeming inevitability only deepens the question of why it continues to hold sway. The puzzle here is not that creditors make reputational judgments that shape the acceptable boundaries of sovereign state action. Instead, the key question is why we think such judgments foreclose claims about odious or illegitimate debt and assume that there is only one rational creditor response to principled debt default.

I suggest that an important piece of the explanation lies in the twentieth-century interaction among political actors, broader ideological shifts, and changing dynamics of creditor competition and consolidation. My historical argument begins in the post–World War I era, during which a statist insistence on debt continuity weakened somewhat and ideas of odious debt might have made headway. This openness was enabled in part by a significant change in the major organizing principles of international law and international relations, including the emergence of new ways of thinking about legitimate sovereignty. This period also saw a shift in the underlying structure of capital markets, in particular with the rise of new American banks willing to lend even when more established financiers held back. These changes resonated in the world of debt, as highlighted by my reinterpretations in chapters 3 and 4 of the 1918 Soviet repudiation of tsarist debt and the 1923 Costa Rican repudiation of obligations incurred by the Tinoco regime. These very different states both made principled claims that explicitly challenged the legitimacy of debt continuity, and—counter to the presentations in previous studies—there remained interest in lending to both of these governments even after their principled repudiations. The reason the Soviet regime ultimately failed to issue bonds in US capital markets had more to do with the political antipathy of an anticommunist US government than a uniform creditor reputational response.

But any openness in the post-World War I era disappeared when international capital markets broke down during the 1930s, as I note in chapter 5. When sovereign lending returned after World War II, it did not develop the same possibilities as the previous decades. Public creditors such as the new World Bank played an important role in this closure, propagating sovereign debt practices that comported with their own financial and operational needs but that also undermined non-statist approaches more broadly. This helped to regularize debt continuity as the only seemingly responsible practice going forward—a conceptual monopoly supported by the basically noncompetitive nature of public and private creditor interaction at the time. This approach was further strengthened by a reconsolidation of more statist understandings of sovereignty, in part in line with the interests of newly independent states.

When private creditors returned to competitive lending in the early 1970s, their interaction was very different from the competitive dynamic of the 1920s, as detailed in chapter 6. In particular, the rise of multinational branching and syndicated lending deepened the integration of global banking structures and encouraged more congruent risk interpretations. Thus, although banks competed with each other, they did so with a common outlook that undermined the space for heterodox approaches in sovereign debt. This supported the tendency of private creditors to adopt the statist approach to lending maintained by the World Bank. Such a statist framework also resonated with borrowing country elites, who were then (as now) eager to borrow as much money with as little oversight as possible. This background affected the subsequent loan restructurings of the late 1970s and 1980s. In particular, the systemic risk posed by the private banks' interconnected loans—and the banks' interaction with public actors such as the IMF and the US Treasury—resulted in a joint approach to sovereign debtors that limited the space for non-statist claims about debt discontinuity. The general debtor response in turn reinforced this narrowing tendency, as it focused on broader inequities in the economic system and discounted arguments based on internal political difference. All of these tendencies served to further strengthen the norm of debt continuity into the 1990s, and meant that even clearly revolutionary governments in Nicaragua, Iran, the Philippines, and South Africa ultimately acknowledged the debts of their predecessors.

Although my arguments in chapter 7 about the post-Cold War era and the turn of the twenty-first century are still tentative, the divide between strict repayment expectations and the emerging values espoused by the international community is perhaps greater now than at any previous time. The shift in international political and legal discourse toward a non-statist language of governance, democracy, and human rights has intensified. Even major economic organizations and private creditor groups have adopted this language to some degree, despite continuing to insist on the principle of debt continuity. These trends have helped bring ideas of odious debt into the light, as evidenced by discussions in Iraq, Ecuador, and even Europe. Although expectations of uniform repayment still dominate, new modes of creditor interaction and sources of international capital have enabled flexibility in some cases, and might alter the future balance of competition and consolidation. Thus, we can imagine that the distance between conceptions of legitimate sovereign action in the political and financial realms may shrink in future years.

All of this goes to demonstrate the theoretical and historical variability of the debt continuity norm, and undermines any assumption of a uniform, apolitical, and basically unalterable creditor interpretation of debtor actions. Challenging that assumption, in part by understanding where it comes from, is a first step to rethinking sovereign debt in future years. In the remaining pages of this concluding chapter, I consider two concerns about noncontinuous approaches that emerge not from assumptions about market principles and reputational judgment but rather from policy questions about political choice and moral hazard. I then think through the conditions for implementing alternatives to strict debt continuity, highlighting the importance of attending not just to specific doctrinal developments but also to the broader contexts that might enable or block their success. I also suggest that, even without intervention by the international community, market actors have the requisite political intelligence to make reputational judgments that could countenance debt cancellation in some situations. While I do not intend these policy reflections to be anything close to comprehensive, they further emphasize the theoretical openness and potential variability of debt continuity ideas, and call for a more balanced discussion about the politics and prospects of sovereign debt in the future.

The Risk of Non-Statist Politics

Part of this book's argument is that politics is inescapably at the center of sovereign lending and borrowing. For one, the practices and reputational judgments of the debt regime necessarily depend on an implicit theory of sovereignty. In addition, both broader political ideas and deliberate political actions have shaped sovereign debt norms through the twentieth century. Reconceptualizing the relationship between debt and ideas of legitimate sovereignty can thus help to clarify policy goals and political commitments across different issue areas.

Given this linkage, one objection to moving away from sovereign continuity in debt could arise from concerns about the application of non-statist political principles to other issue areas. Would we want to extend the implications of a debt analysis to international relations more generally? Although we might expect debt activists to challenge the negative ramifications of a framework that ignores internal legitimacy, it is worth asking whether a headlong rush in the opposite direction is entirely preferable. It may seem that ever-greater attention to the population as the core of sovereign legitimacy in international relations and international law would be ideal. However, there may be good reasons to maintain some attentiveness to statist accounts of sovereignty in the global arena. On the one hand, sympathy for internal rule, popular benefit, and democratic control could strengthen the position of debtor countries in certain cases. On the other hand, the strong version of a project of popular sovereignty risks an updated, more legalized, and perhaps more coercive reinscription of the civilized/uncivilized paradigm that existed prior to the twentieth century.[1] Weakening the statist framework of sovereignty could justify greater monitoring (or meddling) by other states and by international political and economic institutions with regard to debtor countries' internal affairs—an outcome that may not be desired by all constituencies calling for debt cancellation.

One response might be to attempt a more explicit separation between the concepts of sovereignty at work in international finance and in global politics or human rights. This is a possibility, and to some degree it characterizes the current situation. However, although there may be a disconnect or a time lag between these arenas, efforts to keep them entirely separate are likely to prove futile. The sovereign debt regime necessarily depends upon an implicit conception of sovereignty to remain comprehensible. There is no way to distinguish between a "political" or "legal" approach and a "pragmatic financial" approach, because the political-legal concept stands at the core of the financial system. A statist norm of sovereignty in the international political arena is likely to support a similar approach in debt, whereas the rise of a discourse of human rights, governance, and corruption—more associated with non-statist approaches—should allow odious debt claims to be more resonant. Furthermore, the position taken in the international financial arena bears upon the actual sovereign capabilities of any given state. A regime considered minimally legitimate by its own population can nonetheless strengthen its rule—and therefore become more "state-like" in the eyes of the international community—by virtue of accessing international capital markets under a statist approach. Thus the implicit rule dominant in international economics already has clear public law ramifications and vice versa.

Given this complex relationship between international norms, state autonomy, and political and economic relations in any discussion of sovereignty, a degree of care is warranted going forward. But this care should not foreclose serious consideration of non-statist ideas. This is especially true as the international community does not face a purely binary choice between strictly statist and purely popular accounts of sovereign legitimacy. As I discuss in chapter 2, multiple theories of sovereignty have emerged in political and legal thought, including accounts focusing on rule of law and public benefit. Justice Taft's decision in the *Tinoco* arbitration, analyzed in chapter 4, combines the two elements of rule of law and public outcome in a way that might be widely acceptable. And the UNCTAD Principles on Promoting Responsible Sovereign Lending and Borrowing, which I mention in chapter 7, also combine ideas of governmental agency and popular benefit while remaining agnostic about particular political institutions.[2] These and other intermediate approaches could ground frameworks that adopt noncontinuity in debt while remaining sensitive to concerns about an absolutist (and arguably neo-imperial) non-statist global politics.

Moral Hazard and Moral Equivalence

Even were we to identify a non-statist political vision as clearly superior, would this actually result in preferable sovereign debt outcomes? One theme that emerges from the historical narrative, and indeed recurs regularly in international finance, is that sovereign debt markets can easily become a forum for both debtors and creditors behaving badly. One concern along these lines is that shifting away from a strict repayment norm might actually aggravate irresponsible behavior on the debtor side. In particular, allowing debt discontinuity in some cases could result in a moral hazard problem for states, leading them to act in riskier and even less productive ways than they would in the absence of any flexibility. But a closer consideration emphasizes that moral hazard problems cut in multiple directions, suggesting that here too greater balance is warranted.

The International Monetary Fund defines moral hazard as existing "when the provision of insurance against a risk encourages behavior that makes that risk more likely."[3] Part of the concern with accepting odious debt ideas may be that successor regimes would fail to accurately distinguish between legitimate and illegitimate debt, and would attempt to repudiate all debt under the guise of odiousness.[4] It is possible that a poorly defined odious debt-type framework could legitimize this kind of reckless repudiation, which might aggravate the preexisting problems of uncertainty associated with sovereign lending. In practice, however, such recklessness seems unlikely to develop, at least in the absence of an already-reckless disposition on the part of a debtor country's leaders. As Seema Jayachandran and Michael Kremer point out, "[c]urrently, countries repay debt even if it is odious because if they failed to do so, their assets might be seized and their reputations would be tarnished, making it more difficult for them to borrow again or attract foreign investment."[5] While part of my argument is that reputational judgment is actually fairly flexible, I agree that the already-existing compliance mechanisms need only be altered, rather than eliminated, by the introduction of odious debt or similar ideas. The significant alteration would be in the catalyst for the compliance mechanism: instead of being triggered by repudiation or major default alone, it would be triggered by the repudiation of debt not considered sufficiently "odious" by the relevant audience—be it private creditors making a reputational judgment or a tribunal or court adjudicating an asset seizure. The repudiation of only that portion of debt found to be illegitimate should not result in retaliation against either overseas assets or a country's general creditworthiness. This leaves unanswered, of course, the question of how to define properly illegitimate debt, and also highlights the desirability of clear rules to the extent possible. That said, even the ostensibly bright line rule of full repayment is rarely followed in a debt restructuring; the default standard is most useful—and most frequently used—as a starting point for negotiations, in part by affecting the leverage of the parties.

In fact, under the current framework of strict continuity, two opposite moral hazard problems seem to have prevailed. First, the norm of universal repayment, by failing to distinguish between different types of debt, has created a moral hazard problem with regard to creditors. The debt continuity rule helps to insure against the risk of lending to sovereign states (even arguably illegitimate states) in times of crisis and uncertainty. Ideally, this should allow for the productive use of capital even in the face of political volatility. The effect of a purely statist conception, however, seems to have gone beyond this to encourage greater (and perhaps unthinking) lending for questionable ends. It minimizes the risks associated with wasteful lending and shifts additional risk onto borrowing state populations by effectively absolving creditors of a due diligence requirement. Folding in and forcing the repayment of arguably objectionable debt with all other sovereign debt effectively minimizes any risk of lending to regimes that violate their own laws or use funds for non-beneficial purposes. This risk is further diminished by the historical willingness of institutions such as the IMF to extend emergency loans to its borrower members, including those with notoriously problematic governments, rather than allow major defaults and a potential bank and financial crisis.[6] The moral hazard problem for commercial banks may be even more significant in situations where the debt burden originally held by commercial banks is assumed by multilateral institutions, which arguably have even greater power to encourage debt servicing.[7] Thus, a more flexible approach, incorporating ideas of illegitimate debt, might help to direct the international capital stock back to more productive and transparent uses.

A second moral hazard problem resulting from debt continuity arises in the borrowing country domestic arena. Currently, sovereign states have relatively easy access to capital through international markets, which, as I discuss in chapter 6, have historically been willing to lend for insufficiently considered purposes and even occasionally through processes that violate internal legal rules. This effectively creates a corresponding borrower-side moral hazard problem. Just as a strictly statist approach encourages creditors to lend in uncertain political times, it encourages sovereign states to borrow in the knowledge that future generations will repay the debt.[8] Ideally, this would allow all states (again including those of arguably unsavory origin) to make timely and well-priced investments in infrastructure, healthcare, and other productive assets and services. However, strict debt continuity may also have the perverse effect of encouraging profligate borrowing for non-state purposes and in contravention of the transparency associated with internal legal rule. This means that government leaders with access to international capital have less need to draw on public resources and are therefore even less accountable to their publics.[9] By contrast, a framework allowing selective debt cancellation, by limiting the pool of external funds available illegally or for non-beneficial purposes, might eventually encourage state actors to confront more squarely the political and economic risks of corruption and repression. Future regimes would not have the same (often externally derived) resources at hand as regimes past. This should limit the rents extractable from being a member of the ruling elite and may increase domestic leverage for internal reform. In short, compelling reasons related to economic efficiency exist for a shift away from strict debt continuity. At the very least, this suggests the importance of balance in the moral hazard analysis, and of a more honest discussion of the benefits, detriments, and perverse incentives that exist on both sides of the debtor-creditor relationship.

Agency, Structure, and Legal Development

Assuming that an alternative to strict debt continuity might in fact be preferable, what are some of the conditions that could aid in the development of a competing approach? Certainly, the variable and historically contingent nature of the repayment norm should be encouraging to anyone hoping to change the current framework. After all, to the extent that a norm has been constructed, it presumably can be reconstructed. But this does not at all suggest that determined action alone is sufficient to change the trajectory of sovereign debt. In fact, my historical narrative implies quite the opposite. While I counter any seeming inevitability in debt practices, I also contend that the choices and efforts of particular actors may be enabled, strengthened, or undercut by larger structural features in international relations.

What does this interdependence mean for both the explicit development of legal doctrine and the less directed progress of customary international law in the area? The rule of debt continuity has come under considerable scrutiny over the last decade in particular—in legal and economic scholarship, debt activist networks, and wider public policy circles. A significant portion of this energy has been directed toward revivifying a doctrine of odious debt, considering institutions that might render the doctrine clearer and more workable, or formulating alternative contractual or common law approaches that approximate odious debt ideas. However, if the historical record offers any guidance, the degree to which such formal proposals resonate may relate to broader material and ideational structures in the global arena. To the extent that such proposals coincide with and explicitly connect to generally agreed-upon norms, they should receive a warmer reception. If, however, they contradict widespread ideas of legitimacy, or even if they contravene more traditional sovereignty claims otherwise espoused by advocates of selective debt cancellation, this disconnect could undermine their acceptance. Similarly, a competitive market in which creditors are more amenable to debtor claims should be more flexible than one in which they are consolidated into a unified (and potentially hostile) voice. Of course, it is possible that global norms could undergo such an ideological revolution that a purely statist idea of sovereignty becomes entirely unacceptable in *any* realm of international relations, in which case variations in creditor structure would become less relevant. But, given that we are still far from such a shift, paying attention to these material and ideational contexts remains important for strategic thinking about particular projects.

This attentiveness to the role of broader structures in sovereign debt applies not just to the development of entirely new proposals, but also to the potential for a more organic emergence of customary international law on the subject. Customary law, accepted in key international documents as one potential source of law along with treaties and general legal principles, is identifiable through "evidence of a general practice accepted as law."[10] While I mentioned in chapter 1 that there is no treaty in force on the issue of debt continuity, there have been recent discussions on whether odious debt ideas or principles of sovereign lending that allow for selective cancellation are developing as customary law.[11] While there is compelling evidence to suggest that basic principles of responsible lending are now sufficiently widespread to be emerging as custom, the specific issue of arguably illegitimate debt after regime change is more difficult to categorize. Indeed, there is something of a disconnect in the two elements of state practice and acceptance of a legal obligation (or *opinio juris*, in the technical Latin terminology) that together might demonstrate a customary international legal principle. If anything, the ideational trends of the last two decades suggest that an incipient sense of legal obligation may attach to practices that comport with non-statist ideas of internal rule and human rights. But although there is certainly some state practice in support of selective debt cancellation, the book's historical chapters demonstrate that the record is far from uniform. Debt continuity, on the other hand, while commanding more consistent state practice, does not appear to follow from any sense of legal obligation. Instead, it tends to result from more quotidian concerns about capital access and the likely reputational assessments of creditors. These judgments are in turn shaped, I argue, by dynamics of creditor competition and broader political norms at any given moment. Individual states, faced with these larger structures, may decline to make the decisions that, over time, could accrue into a sufficiently general state practice to support a shift in customary international law.

Thus both the likely success of particular proposals and the possible development of legal custom depend on broader structural features of international politics and finance. As such, lawyers and activists concerned with strictly statist approaches in sovereign debt should ideally expand their efforts beyond the most immediate tasks of advocacy and doctrinal development. They should give greater consideration to the larger features of international relations that enable or undermine both state decisions and their own activities in indirect but important ways. For example, they would do well to pay closer attention to national and transnational financial regulations that not only directly affect sovereign debt but also shape the ways that private investors and official creditors interact and interpret risk, including regulations that may encourage or diminish creditor competition or consolidation in the global arena. And particularly when creditors *are* acting in a consolidated or even collusive fashion, it makes sense to pay closer attention to the mechanisms that increase their power as a single entity, both in the national politics of key countries and in the international realm. These broader regulations could, in the long run, have second-order effects on both the acceptance of particular reform proposals and the emergence of new customary international law.

The Political Intelligence of Market Actors

One risk of any transition in finance is that uncertainty will freeze essential capital flows and ultimately the change will do more harm than good. Indeed, some may suggest that the whole discussion of altering sovereign debt frameworks is too risky to engage in altogether. International capital markets are notoriously jumpy even in good times, especially with regard to sovereign borrowers. Particularly in light of the vagaries of the global arena, certainty and predictability in the basic norms of lending are essential to maintaining creditor engagement. Given the prominence of a statist approach for much of the modern sovereign debt regime—and its associated default rule that *all* debt should be repaid, at least in principle—any shift away from this framework could permanently wreak havoc on sovereign lending. Indeed, this concern for capital market reactions motivates one central policy recommendation for dealing with odious debt—the proposal by Seema Jayachandran and Michael Kremer to establish an institution that could make an *ex ante* determination of regime odiousness, which would then heighten a creditor's obligations (and known risks) in dealing with such a regime.[12] Such an institution—under the aegis of the United Nations Security Council, one of the international financial institutions, an independent commission of jurists, or even a nongovernmental organization—would offer the certainty required to incorporate non-statist ideas into international lending.

This book casts doubt on such alarmism about capital market reactions. Incorporating odious debt ideas into contemporary lending does not necessarily require the adoption of a new international organization. This would be a difficult task even without the need to agree on an institutional mandate to pass controversial judgments on behalf of the international community. It may admittedly behoove some market actors to deny their ability to distinguish between a cancellation of arguably odious as opposed to non-odious debt (in reputational assessments, for example). However, the early case studies of this book suggest that creditors are more politically savvy than they let on or even acknowledge to themselves. They are certainly capable of understanding the argument that a new regime's unwillingness to repay debt incurred by a predecessor may have little bearing on future debt payments. And they could choose to act on this understanding if prompted by a sufficiently competitive market to go against the grain. Indeed, the historical record suggests that a debtor country's actions surrounding any default—including fastidious repayment of any admittedly *legitimate* debt and otherwise careful attendance to financial market sensibilities—might also over time reassure potential new lenders.

A creditor may still disagree with a particular debtor state that the debt in question is illegitimate—as always, the possibility of divergent political views about legitimate sovereign action remains. And the absence of a clear dividing line between acceptable and unacceptable lending behavior could raise borrowing costs. But, assuming an informal understanding did emerge, market actors should be able to differentiate between the more and less onerous debt entered into by previous regimes in their assessments of a successor's actions. The absence of creditors willing to defect from the group and make these judgments independently has little to do with the inherently narrow nature of creditworthiness analyses. This lacuna has much more to do with the intervention of public actors at key historical moments and with larger economic structures that have shaped competitive risk assessments and helped to normalize practices of debt continuity. However, in a competitive setting and ideally with a relatively stable understanding of legitimate sovereign action, capital markets should be able to absorb a norm of selective debt discontinuity even in the absence of an institutionalized coordinating mechanism.

This is not at all to diminish the importance of predictability as an ideal. Any shift in dominant practices will inevitably be accompanied by a period of uncertainty and possibly higher debt pricing. Once the new framework is better understood, however, there is little reason not to expect markets to stabilize and settle into a new normal. This is not to say that debt instruments for all potential borrowers would be priced equally. Rather, we might expect that debt pricing would vary along a gradation of perceived legitimacy. This would be another and more explicit element of the political risk assessments that already constitute part of country creditworthiness analyses. And perhaps—given the historically close relationship of a ruling regime's capacity to access external financing and its capacity to exert internal and sometimes oppressive control—higher debt pricing, shorter maturities, and the background possibility of debt cancellation are indeed desirable for certain states.

Still, given the centrality of predictability for continued capital market flows, efforts to develop standards for responsible sovereign debt practices should receive greater support. As a matter of *positive* international law, a strict insistence on democratic governance for lending is unlikely to solidify—nor, as I have mentioned, would it necessarily be desirable, particularly given that nondemocratic regimes are similarly capable of beneficial government investment. Indeed, representative government is hardly a guarantee of the productive use of borrowing on external capital markets. However, it appears that rule-of-law and outcome-oriented approaches to sovereignty, which still broadly conceive of governments as agents for the underlying population, are becoming more accepted already. Indeed, the UNCTAD Principles mentioned above provide a middle ground between the extremes of indifference and excessive intervention that should be acceptable to creditors and borrowers alike. Furthermore, scholars have highlighted broadly acknowledged domestic law principles—including doctrines of unclean hands, unconscionability, fraudulent transfer, debt recharacterization, and equitable subordination—that could be more forcefully applied in line with post-Cold War norms of internal rule and governance.[13] In this way, even an ad hoc approach including recourse to domestic courts or special tribunals could incorporate emerging ideas of legitimate sovereignty while attending to capital market concerns of creditworthiness.

Our current moment is perhaps a better time than any to engage in this kind of experimentation. The system of international economic governance has come under fire from multiple directions, including for failing to account adequately for the complex issues of political control and economic distribution implicated in international finance. And while we may assume that sovereign debt practices are produced by inexorable market logics, in fact these logics are theoretically unstable and historically underdetermined. They have been shaped by political actors, broader ideologies, and creditor interactions that have varied across the last century and are certain to vary into the future. Although a recognition of this contingency is hardly sufficient in and of itself to effect change, it does remind us that the practices and political meaning of sovereign debt and reputation are not set in stone.

Notes

Chapter 1. Open Questions in Sovereign Debt

1. Robert Howse, "The Concept of Odious Debt in Public International Law," UNCTAD Discussion Paper No. 185 (July 2007), 20. Howse notes that, regardless of whether or not this is empirically true, "it does appear to influence decision-making of transitional regimes (e.g. South Africa)." Ibid.

2. This most common formulation was first offered by Alexander Sack in 1927. Alexander N. Sack, *Les Effets des Transformations des États sur leurs Dettes Publiques et Autres Obligations Financières* (Paris: Recueil Sirey, 1927), 157.

3. "Iraq's Debt," *The Financial Times,* June 16, 2003.

4. This understanding that sovereign debt involves implicitly accepted contingencies that might excuse nonpayment is modeled in Herschel I. Grossman and John B. Van Huyck, "Sovereign Debt as a Contingent Claim: Excusable Default, Repudiation, and Reputation," *American Economic Review* 78, no. 5 (December 1988): 1088–1097. There is some empirical support for this idea, in particular in findings that countries return to capital markets faster than the expected baseline if a default is precipitated by unexpected and uncontrollable factors such as a natural disaster. Daniel A. Dias, Christine Richmond, and Taeree Wang, "Duration of Capital Market Exclusion: An Empirical Investigation," UIUC Working Paper (2012).

5. As I discuss more fully in chapter 2, this is a mainstay of discussions of creditworthiness in political science and economics, which tend (with exceptions, of course) to aggregate all creditors into a single body.

6. See, for example, Michael Tomz, *Reputation and International Cooperation: Sovereign Debt across Three Centuries* (Princeton: Princeton University Press, 2007), 80, 87. In support of this argument, Tomz looks at the data on bond issues from the 1920s and beyond and surveys the investment advice literature of the time.

7. In their important work resuscitating odious debt ideas, Seema Jayachandran and Michael Kremer highlight the possibility of multiple reputational equilibria in sovereign debt and model the equilibrium that might develop with an *ex ante* determination of government odiousness. Seema Jayachandran and Michael Kremer, "Odious Debt," *American Economic Review* 96, no. 1 (2006): 82–92.

8. Sack, *Les Effets,* 157. For contemporary discussions of issues surrounding odious debt, see among others Lee C. Buchheit, G. Mitu Gulati, and Robert B.

Thompson, "The Dilemma of Odious Debts," *Duke Law Journal* 56 (2007); Seema Jayachandran and Michael Kremer, "Odious Debt," in *Sovereign Debt at the Crossroads: Challenges and Proposals for Resolving the Third World Debt Crisis,* ed. Chris Jochnick and Fraser A. Preston (Oxford and New York: Oxford University Press, 2006), 215–225; Howse, "Odious Debt"; Ashfaq Khalfan, Jeff King, and Bryan Thomas, "Advancing the Odious Debt Doctrine," McGill University Centre for International Sustainable Development Law Working Paper (2003), http://www.odiousdebts.org/odiousdebts/publications/Advancing_the_Odious _Debt_Doctrine.pdf; Patricia Adams, *Odious Debts: Loose Lending, Corruption and the Third World's Environmental Legacy* (Toronto: Earthscan, 1991). For definitions of "illegitimate debt" more broadly, see Joseph Hanlon, "Defining 'Illegitimate Debt': When Creditors Should Be Liable for Improper Loans," in Jochnick and Preston, *Sovereign Debt at the Crossroads,* 109–132. For contemporary legal analyses of the doctrine, including potential modifications, extensions, and ramifications, see Yvonne Wong, *Sovereign Finance and the Poverty of Nations: Odious Debt in International Law* (Cheltenham, UK, and Northampton, MA: Elgar, 2012) and the double issue on odious debt of Duke's *Journal of Law and Contemporary Problems* 70, nos. 3&4 (2007).

9. As the connector "and" between the doctrine's two parts makes clear, if a debt was in fact incurred to benefit the people, then it should not be considered odious even if it lacked popular consent (i.e., for an infrastructure project entered into by a dictator). And similarly, a popularly incurred debt that ultimately failed to benefit the people would still be valid (i.e., for an unwise war supported by a democratic public). The doctrine thus draws from both a procedural conception of sovereignty as a legitimate representative relationship, and an outcome-oriented conception of valid sovereign action as serving the public benefit or national interest.

10. Furthermore, the remedy of repudiation may not be available under international law unless the lender knew about the illegitimate nature of the debt—that is, that the end uses would be contrary to the interests of the people. Thus, if a lender makes a loan in good faith, it should be able to collect on that loan despite its ultimate ill use. This requirement is highlighted in Sack's 1927 formulation and is reiterated by most definitions. However, US Supreme Court Justice William H. Taft noted in the 1923 *Tinoco* arbitration, which I discuss in chapter 4, that the claimant failed to present a case for its own good faith, stating "It must make out its case of actual furnishing of money to the government for its legitimate use," Great Britain v. Costa Rica (*Tinoco Case,* October 18, 1923), *Record of International Arbitral Awards,* vol. 1 (1923): 399, reprinted in *American Journal of International Law* 18, no. 1 (1924): 174. Although Justice Taft suggests that the creditor in fact knew that the funds were to be used by Tinoco for his personal support, the general requirement for good faith suggests that a creditor could fail to recover if it knew *or should have known* that the money would be ill used. This formulation has been deployed in other contexts to close a loophole that could exist by excusing willful ignorance and a lack of due diligence. See also Odette

Lienau, "Who is the 'Sovereign' in Sovereign Debt? Reinterpreting a Rule-of-Law Framework from the Early Twentieth Century," *Yale Journal of International Law* 33, no. 1 (Winter 2008): 63–111. For a discussion of the mythology surrounding Alexander Sack, see Sarah Ludington and Mitu Gulati, "A Convenient Untruth: Fact and Fantasy in the Doctrine of Odious Debts," *Virginia Journal of International Law* 48, no. 3 (2008): 595–639.

11. The case study of Costa Rica in chapter 4 presents US Supreme Court Justice William H. Taft's alternative formulation from 1923, in which what I call a rule-of-law conception of sovereign action is combined with a minimal requirement of public benefit.

12. See, for example, Jayachandran and Kremer, "Odious Debt"; Khalfan, King, and Thomas, "Advancing the Odious Debt Doctrine"; Wong, *Sovereign Finance*.

13. Sack, *Les Effets,* 157, as translated in Adams, *Odious Debts,* 165.

14. For these formulations, see Peter Malanczuk's presentation of the *Restatement of the Law (Third), Foreign Relations Laws of the United States,* vol. 1 (Philadelphia: American Law Institute, 1965), paras. 208–210, in Peter Malanczuk, *Akehurst's Modern Introduction to International Law* (New York: Routledge, 1997), 161–168. In fact, the international law of state succession falls into different classes and encompasses varied obligations. Forms of state succession include state unification, dismemberment, and enlargement, in addition to the establishment of a new state through decolonization. Ibid. For the purposes of this preliminary definition, however, these distinctions remain of secondary importance. Changes of government leadership or administration are the least problematic under international law. A state's private and public contracts remain valid, and no problem of recognition arises with regard to other states. See ibid., 86.

15. The difference between state succession and what I call regime change (or government succession) may well be disappearing in modern international law and practice. Indeed, Tai-Heng Cheng has argued that the traditional international legal division between the two should be rejected in light of the recent international practice of states, creditors, and other key global actors, which does not reflect the technical distinction. *State Succession and Commercial Obligation* (Ardsley, NY: Transnational Publishers, 2006), 37–38. I mention the two separately here largely to limit the universe of data for analysis. However, the arguments I make could well be extended from regime change as I define it to sovereign succession more broadly understood, and the analytical framework presented here may be applicable to a broader range of cases.

16. According to John Basset Moore's 1906 description, the American commissioners argued that "the loans were hostile to the people required to pay them . . . [and] Cuba had not consented to the debts." John Bassett Moore, *Digest of International Law,* vol. 1 (Washington, DC: GPO, 1906), 359. For a brief overview of the subsequent interpretation of this case, see Howse, "Odious Debt," 10–11. This US action followed upon the repudiation of all Confederate debt in

the Fourteenth Amendment to the American Constitution: "any debt or obligation incurred in aid of insurrection or rebellion against the United States, or any claim for the loss or emancipation of any slave . . . shall be held illegal and void." U.S. Const. amend. XIV, § 4 (1868). In subsequently interpreting the amendment, the Supreme Court distinguished between voided debts undertaken to support rebellion and permissible debts entered into for more quotidian civil functions. See Sarah Ludington, G. Mitu Gulati, and Alfred L. Brophy, "Applied Legal History: Demystifying the Doctrine of Odious Debts," Duke Law School Public Law & Legal Theory Paper No. 236 (2009), 27–30.

17. I discuss in chapter 7 the rise of non-statist ideas of sovereignty in the contemporary moment, and the degree to which they may enable challenges to the norm of debt continuity going forward.

18. Reply of the Allied and Associated powers to the observations of the German delegation on the conditions of peace, part 4, section 3 (b), 16 June 1919 (London: Her Majesty's Printing Office, 1919), 20.

19. Indeed, important recent work has highlighted the ways in which key features of the international political economy cannot be understood in terms of stable economic models free from political and historical construction. For example, see the studies in Rawi Abdelal, Mark Blyth, and Craig Parsons, eds., *Constructing the International Economy* (Ithaca, NY: Cornell University Press, 2010); Rawi Abdelal, *Capital Rules: The Construction of Global Finance* (Cambridge, MA: Harvard University Press, 2007); Jacqueline Best, *The Limits of Transparency: Ambiguity and the History of International Finance* (Ithaca, NY: Cornell University Press, 2005); Jonathan Kirshner, ed., *Monetary Orders: Ambiguous Economics, Ubiquitous Politics* (Ithaca, NY: Cornell University Press, 2003).

20. For an excellent discussion of a similar dynamic of individual action and the rise of powerful global standards, see David Singh Grewal, *Network Power: The Social Dynamics of Globalization* (New Haven, CT: Yale University Press, 2009).

21. This classic formulation, particularly with its focus on material capacity, is often related to traditional balance of power ideas of politics. For an overview of ideas of power in international relations theory, see among others Michael Barnett and Raymond Duvall, "Power in International Politics," *International Organization* 59, no. 1 (2005): 39–75; David A. Baldwin, "Power and International Relations," in *Handbook of International Relations,* ed. Walter Carlsnaes, Thomas Risse, and Beth A. Simmons (Los Angeles and London: Sage, 2013), 275–297.

22. This anecdote is frequently cited as an example of the use of military power by Western states to enforce sovereign debt claims specifically, a practice presented by some scholars as a common occurrence in the nineteenth century. See, for example, Martha Finnemore, *The Purposes of Intervention: Changing Beliefs about the Use of Force* (Ithaca, NY: Cornell University Press, 2003), 24; Alexander Wendt, "Driving with the Rearview Mirror: On the Rational Science of Institutional Design," *International Organization* 55, no. 4 (2001): 1019–1049, 1026. Michael Tomz casts doubt on whether such "gunboat diplomacy" on

behalf of bondholders (as distinct from tort claimants and investor claimants seeking to recover civil war losses) was in fact dominant at all. He considers the historical evidence to demonstrate that, in most of these instances, bondholder debt enforcement was a secondary concern if it featured at all. Tomz, *Reputation and International Cooperation*, 114–153.

23. In referring to debt continuity as soft law, I use "law" in its broadest sense, not as a binding set of rules promulgated by state actors but rather as interrelated standards, practices, and norms that are treated as legitimate and that compel or deter specified action. As Chris Brummer points out, the formulation and enforcement of international financial law generally has moved forward through "soft law" practices that nonetheless command significant adherence. Chris Brummer, *Soft Law and the Global Financial System: Rule Making in the 21ˢᵗ Century* (Cambridge and New York: Cambridge University Press, 2012), 2–16, 115–176.

24. In adopting this analytical framework, I draw in part from recent work in constructivist international political economy and related legal scholarship that seeks to understand how key elements of the international economy are constructed as natural or normal over time. For a recent overview of work in constructivist international political economy, see Abdelal, Blyth, and Parsons, *Constructing the International Economy*.

Chapter 2. Theoretical Underpinnings of Modern Finance

1. "Iraq's Debt," *The Financial Times*, June 16, 2003.

2. In fact, there may be two interconnected principal-agent relationships here. The first is that linking the underlying population to the government or organs of the state, with the former being the principal (bearing the ultimate consequences of incurred debt through increased benefits but also, at the time of repayment, through increased taxation or reduced benefits related to austerity measures) and the latter the agent in this scenario. The second is the relationship between the government and its officials, now with the government acting as principal and its officials acting as agent. Both relationships must exist, but my primary interest is in the first principal-agent relationship—between the underlying population and the governmental state writ large. In this, I differ from the approach that Deborah DeMott takes in discussing common law agency principles with respect to the odious debt doctrine. See Deborah DeMott, "Agency by Analogy: A Comment on Odious Debt," *Law and Contemporary Problems* 70 (2007): 157–160. DeMott relies on common law principles of agency, which already assume the centrality of consent to the agency relationship. Ibid., 158 (quoting the Restatement (Third) of Agency, § 1.01 (2006), "Agency is the fiduciary relationship that arises when one person (a 'principal') manifests assent to another person (an 'agent') that the agent shall act on the principal's behalf and subject to the principal's control, and the agent manifests assent or otherwise consents so to act)." As DeMott notes, the presumption of consent and popular control is far from valid in all sovereign states, limiting the applicability of analogies from common law formulations of

agency on this front. Ibid., 165–166. Nonetheless, in sovereign debt situations, the governmental regime (along with its officers) is *assumed* to act as an agent for the underlying population, such that—even should the contracting regime fall and the population select a new and diametrically opposed government—the contracts of the ousted regime can still be enforced against the underlying population. My question is precisely *how* different theories of sovereignty construct and support that agency assumption in the international context.

3. For example, Andrew Guzman highlights how a state's reputation is particularly important for compliance with international law, particularly given the absence of direct sanctions in this arena. Andrew Guzman, *How International Law Works: A Rational Choice Theory* (Oxford and New York: Oxford University Press, 2008), 33–48. Oona Hathaway also highlights the "collateral" importance of reputation, particularly in the absence of domestic or international enforcement mechanisms for international agreements. "Between Power and Principle: An Integrated Theory of International Law," *University of Chicago Law Review* 71 (2005): 506–507.

4. As examples of those who emphasize the risk of direct retaliation, see Charles Lipson, "The International Organization of Third World Debt," *International Organization* 35 (Autumn 1981): 603–631; Jeremy Bulow and Kenneth Rogoff, "Sovereign Debt: Is to Forgive to Forget?," *American Economic Review* 79, no. 1 (1989): 43–50; Kenneth Schultz and Barry Weingast, "Limited Governments, Powerful States," in *Strategic Politicians, Institutions and Foreign Policy*, ed. R. M. Siverson (Ann Arbor: University of Michigan Press, 1998). Indeed, some scholars have argued that investors have paid little heed to past actions. See for example Peter H. Lindert and Peter J. Morton, "How Sovereign Debt has Worked," in *Developing Country Debt and Economic Performance: The World Financial System,* ed. Jeffrey Sachs (Chicago: University of Chicago Press for the National Bureau of Economic Research, 1989), 39–106; Erika Jorgensen and Jeffrey Sachs, "Default and Renegotiation in Latin American Foreign Debts in the Interwar Period," in *The International Debt Crisis in Historical Perspective,* ed. Barry Eichengreen and Peter H. Lindert (Cambridge, MA: MIT Press, 1989). As examples of those who emphasize the centrality of reputation, see Michael Tomz, *Reputation and International Cooperation: Sovereign Debt across Three Centuries* (Princeton, NJ: Princeton University Press, 2007); Sule Ozler, "Have Commercial Banks Ignored History?," *American Economic Review* 83 (1993): 608–620. See also Bulow and Rogoff, "Is to Forgive to Forget?," *American Economic Review* 79 (1989): 43–50; William B. English, "Understanding the Costs of Sovereign Default: American State Debt in the 1840s," *American Economic Review* 86 (March 1996): 259–275.

5. Tomz, *Reputation and International Cooperation,* 17, 23.

6. Ibid., 20–22.

7. Ashok Vir Bhatia, "Sovereign Credit Risk Ratings Methodology: An Evaluation," IMF Working Paper No. 02/170 (2002), 12. Bhatia himself used to work for Standard & Poor's.

8. Robert H. Frank, *Passions within Reason: The Strategic Role of the Emotions* (New York: W. W. Norton, 1988).

9. James Forder, "'Credibility' in Context: Do Central Bankers and Economists Interpret the Term Differently?," *Econ Journal Watch* 1, no. 3 (2004): 413–426.

10. Jonathan Mercer, *Reputation and International Politics* (Ithaca, NY: Cornell University Press, 1996). Tomz finds little evidence for this approach in his analysis of creditor assessments of sovereign borrowers. Tomz, *Reputation and International Cooperation,* 29, 230. Other literature suggests that social communication and established relationships condition perceptions of credibility. Kathleen Valley, Joseph Moag, and Max H. Bazerman, "'A Matter of Trust': Effects of Communication on the Efficiency and Distribution of Outcomes," *Journal of Economic Behavior and Organization* 34 (1998): 211–238; see also Jennifer Halpern, "Elements of a Script for Friendship in Transactions," *Journal of Conflict Resolution* 41, no. 6 (1997): 835–868. While I am convinced by Tomz's argument, countering Mercer, that positive reputations can develop, my assessment of the Soviet case suggests that a creditor's interpretation of an outcome as less desirable (which may differ across creditors) may be more likely to result in a character-based conclusion, rather than one based in the situational explanation offered.

11. Rachel Brewster, "Unpacking the State's Reputation," *Harvard International Law Journal* 50, no. 2 (2009): 231–269.

12. The two standard components of risk or creditworthiness analysis are the "ability" and "willingness" of a country to meet its obligations.

13. In Tomz's assessment, such countries would be interpreted as the worst lemons and thus the most likely to be subject to strict credit rationing.

14. Tomz, *Reputation and International Cooperation,* 26. Tomz continues, "These parties have no incentive to extend new credit, because each independently knows that lending to a lemon would be a money-losing proposition. Thus, my theory provides a convenient solution to the problems of credibility and collective action that were discussed in chapter 1." Ibid., 26.

15. This vision primarily applies to bank lending, but the form of competition for bond issues may be somewhat different. In this book, I discuss the distinction between bonds and bank loans in the historical contexts in which they are relevant.

16. Such creditors may include private financial houses, bank groups, international financial institutions, and major creditor governments. Credit rating agencies, organizations such as the Paris and London Clubs, and other institutions involved in the sovereign lending regime could also conceivably play a role in this dynamic of competition and consolidation.

17. Although this presentation is set forth in rationalist terms, it is unlikely that creditor institutions self-consciously go through these steps of rationalization. In situations of consolidation, it is more likely that a statist view has been naturalized and assumed necessary.

18. Repudiation on the ground of odious debt is not *necessarily* a large-scale repudiation of all the sovereign state's debt. It is possible that the "odious" label

would apply to only some of the public debt. In chapter 7, I discuss Ecuador's 2008 default on a portion of its external private debt, which offers a selective effort along these lines, albeit one that does not comport with most understandings of odious debt. For a discussion that suggests the desirability of burden sharing for incentivizing optimal precautionary measures on both the debtor and creditor side, see Omri Ben-Shahar and Mitu Gulati, "Partially Odious Debts," *Law & Contemporary Problems* 70, no. 4 (2007): 47–82.

19. For the argument that much of the debt owed to public creditors (particularly bilateral government debt) should not be considered as "debt" in the conventional sense, see Anna Gelpern, "Odious, Not Debt," *Law and Contemporary Problems* 70, no. 3 (2007): 81–114.

20. There are situations in which a public or publicly owned actor engages in commercial activity (including lending) purely for profit, but these can be set aside for the purposes of this analysis.

21. This presentation of public creditors as largely noncompetitive, or at least competitive in a different way, is oversimplified to some degree. In particular, the possibility of "soft competition" will be highlighted in the discussion of the mid-twentieth century in chapter 5. Additionally, mission creep and institutional self-aggrandizement may shift creditor concerns away from their original public purpose.

22. Of course, this presentation is a stripped down ideal type. To some degree, public actors can also shape the viewpoints of those who ostensibly control them, and shape the direction of future interests and policy.

23. Although this formulation makes most sense in the case of private bank lenders, private institutions that facilitate securities issues are subject to similar balancing pressures between borrowers and investors.

24. This is, I argue in chapter 5, part of what accounts for the World Bank's requirement of uniform repayment in the mid-twentieth century. This tension is not new or limited to the international arena, or to public "creditors" as opposed to public actors more broadly. One example drawn from everyday life is the existence of public television stations that receive limited public funding and as such must turn to commercial sponsorship (with the risks and pressures that involves) to promote its larger goals.

25. Noted in Jack Weatherford, *Genghis Khan and the Making of the Modern World* (New York: Crown Publishers, 2004), 175.

26. Ata-Malik Juvaini, *Genghis Khan: The History of the World Conqueror*, trans. J.A. Boyle (Seattle: University of Washington Press, 1997), 602–604.

27. *Moody's Analyses of Investment and Security Rating Books: Government and Municipal Securities* (New York: Moody's Investors Service, 1922), 998. The *New York Times* published an op-ed in May of 1867 offering support for Mexico's repudiation, and comparing it to the US repudiation of confederate debt. "The Mexican Debts," *New York Times*, May 19, 1867, 4.

28. The relevant text reads: "any debt or obligation incurred in aid of insurrection or rebellion against the United States, or any claim for the loss or

emancipation of any slave . . . shall be held illegal and void." U.S. Const. amend. XIV, § 4 (1868).

29. For example, in the *Financial Times* editorial, "Iraq's Debt."

30. Perhaps most famously, Carl Schmitt claimed that "all significant concepts of the modern theory of the state are secularized theological concepts." He asserts that this is the case, "not only because of their historical development . . . but also because of their systematic structure." Carl Schmitt, *Political Theology: Four Chapters on the Concept of Sovereignty* (Boston, MA: MIT Press, 1985), 36.

31. John Ruggie has argued that this traditionalist conception of the state drew from theories of sovereignty built on a paradigm of the rights associated with an absolutist version of private property. John G. Ruggie, "Continuity and Transformation in the World Polity: Toward a Neorealist Synthesis," *Neorealism and its Critics,* ed. Robert O. Keohane (New York: Columbia University Press, 1986), 144–145.

32. Jean Bodin, *On Sovereignty: Four Chapters from the Six Books of the Commonwealth,* trans. Julian H. Franklin (Cambridge: Cambridge University Press, 1992), 1.

33. See, e.g., Thomas Hobbes, *Leviathan,* ed. Edwin Curley (Indianapolis, IN: Hackett, 1994), 109. Spinoza similarly identified the sovereign as having "the sovereign right of imposing any commands he pleases." Benedict de Spinoza, *A Theologico-Political Treatise,* trans. R. H. M. Elwes (New York: Dover, 1951), 207. For Spinoza, as for Machiavelli, right effectively followed might or power.

34. Bodin, *On Sovereignty,* 6.

35. Hobbes, *Leviathan,* 127.

36. This is a common shorthand for Austin's conception of the law; another frequently used formulation is "the command of the sovereign backed by a sanction." In laying out the essential elements of "law properly so called," Austin highlights three key features: (1) a command from a determinate body, (2) a sanction or "eventual evil annexed to a command," and (3) the source of the command from a political superior. John Austin, *The Province of Jurisprudence Determined,* ed. David Campbell and Philip Thomas (Aldershot: Dartmouth, 1998), 101–102. Austin also makes clear that "the sovereign power is incapable of legal limitation . . . without exception." Ibid., 183

37. Lassa Oppenheim, *International Law,* 2nd ed. (New York: Longmans, Green, 1912), 19–22. Although Oppenheim effectively allows for the internal conception of sovereignty suggested by this traditionalist school in political theory, it is important to distinguish him from Austin in the arena of international law. In particular, Austin felt that the absence of a sovereign in the international arena obviated the possibility for international law. Oppenheim, however, aimed to construct a unique vision of law for the international realm based on the principle of sovereign equality and state consent.

38. Such a view is presented most clearly in neorealist works of international relations theory, which conceive of state institutions and preferences as subservient to larger structural factors in explaining international conflict. See, for the

classic example, Kenneth Waltz, *Man, the State, and War: A Theoretical Analysis* (New York: Columbia University Press, 1959).

39. John Bassett Moore, *Digest of International Law,* vol. 1 (Washington, DC: GPO, 1906), 249, as cited by Justice Taft in *Tinoco Case,* 146 et seq., esp. 150–151. This principle applied only to those states already recognized as members of the international community and therefore within the modernist sovereign equality paradigm. For states outside the "family of nations" (most non-European states), considerations of internal civilization and barbarism were still permitted.

40. "Failed states" in this model are only those which lack a constitutional structure or ruling group able to impose a unified governing framework on the entire territory.

41. Benedict Kingsbury cites the 1986 ICJ case of *Nicaragua v. USA* as evidence of the traction of Oppenheim's basic model well into the twentieth century. A world of "functionally and juridically similar territorial units implied that, provided the entity was treated internationally as a state, its domestic structure and type of regime did not matter." Benedict Kingsbury, "Sovereignty and Inequality," in *Inequality, Globalization, and World Politics,* ed. Andrew Hurrell and Ngaire Woods (New York: Oxford University Press, 1999), 74.

42. Austin, *Province of Jurisprudence,* 94. Hobbes similarly distinguished between sovereign and subject. Hobbes, *Leviathan,* 109.

43. Quoted in Jens Bartelson, *A Genealogy of Sovereignty* (Cambridge: Cambridge University Press, 1995), 99.

44. Bodin, *On Sovereignty,* 1. Bartelson suggests more broadly that Bodin's conception of sovereignty displays "disturbing traces of a different age." He argues that, despite Bodin's insistence on the indivisibility of sovereignty, his effort to connect the theory of sovereignty to a divinely led harmonious order displays only a "superficial modernity." Bartelson, *Genealogy of Sovereignty,* 141–142.

45. Bartelson, *Genealogy of Sovereignty,* 97.

46. Ibid., 99, citing with approval Ernst Kantorowicz's turn of phrase in *The King's Two Bodies: A Study in Mediaeval Political Theology* (Princeton, NJ: Princeton University Press, 1957), 299. Bartelson points out that, in addition to sovereign states, the inhabitants of the intermediate realm between the eternal divine and the temporal profane included angels and their earthly counterparts. Bartelson, *Genealogy of Sovereignty,* 97.

47. Moore, *Digest of International Law,* 249, as cited by Justice Taft in *Tinoco Case,* 150–151.

48. Hobbes, *Leviathan,* 459.

49. Ibid., 124–125.

50. Ibid., 135.

51. "But if the sovereign demand or take anything by pretence of his power, there lieth in that case no action of law, for all that is done by him in virtue of his power, is done by the authority of every subject, and consequently, he that brings an action against the sovereign brings it against himself." Ibid., 144.

52. Jean-Jacques Rousseau, *On the Social Contract, or the Principles of Political Right,* reprinted in *The Basic Political Writings,* ed. Peter Gray, trans. Donald A. Cress (Indianapolis, IN: Hackett, 1987), bk. 1, ch. 6, p. 148.

53. Emmanuel Joseph Sieyès, *What is the Third Estate?,* reprinted in *Political Writings, Including the Debate between Sieyès and Tom Paine in 1791,* ed. Michael Sonenscher (Indianapolis, IN: Hackett, 2003), 98.

54. Thomas Paine, "The Rights of Man," reprinted in *Complete Writings,* ed. Philip S. Foner (New York: Citadel, 1944), 342.

55. See, for example, Immanuel Kant, "What is Enlightenment?," reprinted in *Perpetual Peace and Other Essays on Politics, History, and Morals,* trans. Ted Humphrey (Indianapolis, IN: Hackett, 1983), 41–48. Kant's eventual political goal was also more universalist and cosmopolitan, and he hoped that political organization would reach beyond the bounds of a territorial state. This is not to say that Kant exhibited no preference as to state form. Although he considered constitutional monarchy consonant with human freedom, he did argue that international peace is most likely to come about from a world of democratic republics. See Immanuel Kant, "To Perpetual Peace: A Philosophical Sketch," reprinted in *Perpetual Peace,* 107–144.

56. For a review of these different approaches, see Andrew Moravcsik, "Taking Preferences Seriously: A Liberal Theory of International Politics," *International Organization* 51, no. 4 (1997): 513–553. Immanuel Kant provides the most famous of these theories in his essay, "Perpetual Peace," which argues that world peace is most likely to come about from a federation of democratic states.

57. One example of Wilson's nonrecognition policy is his refusal to recognize these "illegally constituted" governments in Central America. See, for example, George W. Baker Jr., "Woodrow Wilson's Use of the Non-Recognition Policy in Costa Rica," *The Americas* 22, no. 1 (July 1965): 3–21. This project of linking particular requirements for internal sovereignty to the acceptance of sovereign states externally into the "family of nations" was part of the central impetus toward the mandate system and regime reform after World War I. See Antony Anghie, *Imperialism, Sovereignty, and the Making of International Law* (New York: Cambridge University Press, 2004), 115–195. This type of liberal constitutionalism links to what might be understood as a particularly American approach to international law. See, for example, Harlan Grant Cohen, "The American Challenge to International Law: A Tentative Framework for Debate," *Yale Journal of International Law* 28 (2003): 554–567.

58. Ruti Teitel, *Humanity's Law* (New York: Oxford University Press, 2011).

59. See, e.g., W. Michael Reisman, "Sovereignty and Human Rights in Contemporary International Law," *American Journal of International Law* 84 (1990): 866.

60. Thomas Franck, "Democracy as a Human Right," in *Human Rights: An Agenda for the Next Century,* ed. Louis Henkin and John Lawrence Hargrove (Washington, DC: American Society of International Law, 1994), 73–101.

61. Rousseau, *Social Contract,* bk. 1, ch. 7, p. 149. It is important to point out that the sovereign, properly constituted, may still bind itself vis-à-vis other, external parties. "This does not mean that the whole body cannot perfectly well commit itself to another body with respect to things that do not infringe on this contract. For in regard to the foreigner, it becomes a simple being, an individual." Ibid., 149.

62. Sieyès, *Third Estate,* 137.

63. Max Weber, *Politics as a Vocation* (1918, 1921), reprinted in *From Max Weber: Essays in Sociology,* ed. H. H. Gerth and C. Wright Mills (New York: Oxford University Press, 1946), 78. Note that Weber identified legality as only one among different potential sources of legitimacy.

64. In Weber's model, legitimacy or inner justification can derive from traditional forms (as in a monarchy), from charismatic authority, or from "legality." Ibid., 78–79. Although Weber viewed all three of these as equally possible legitimations or inner justifications for state power, he considered that increased rationalization and bureaucratization—in part through greater reliance on "legality" or the rule of law—would be a likely (and potentially problematic) corollary of modernity.

65. Kelsen is considered the best example in legal philosophy of "high positivism." See especially Hans Kelsen, *The Pure Theory of Law* (Berkeley: University of California Press, 1967), originally published in Europe in 1929.

66. Kelsen, *Pure Theory,* 195.

67. "What else did Sieyès do but simply put the sovereignty of the nation into the place which had been vacated by a sovereign king? What could have been more natural to him than to put the nation above the law, as the French king's sovereignty had long since . . . meant the true absoluteness of legal power, a *potestas legibus soluta,* power absolved from the laws? And since the person of the king had not only been the source of all earthly power, but his will the origin of all earthly law, the nation's will, obviously, from now on had to be the law itself." Hannah Arendt, *On Revolution* (New York: Penguin, 1963), 156. Arendt's admiration for the American constitutional system drew from her view that the checks and balances of the US Constitution effectively divided the power of an unfettered popular sovereign, which constituted the danger of the French system. "In this respect, the great and, in the long run, perhaps the greatest American innovation in politics as such was the consistent abolition of sovereignty within the realm of the body politic of the republic, the insight that in the realm of human affairs sovereignty and tyranny are the same." Ibid., 153.

68. David Patterson highlights that the founders of this more conservative legalist element initially came from "lawyers who wanted the United States to lead in the quest for pacific alternatives to international violence but were reluctant to have their nation join in boldly innovative schemes of world order." David S. Patterson, "The United States and the Origins of the World Court," *Political Science Quarterly* 91 (1976): 294.

69. Kelsen, *Pure Theory,* 194.

70. See generally Ruggie, "Continuity and Transformation."

71. Emmanuel Sieyès, "Views of the Executive Means Available to the Representatives of France in 1789," reprinted in *Political Writings,* 58.

72. Ibid., 57.

73. See Emmanuel Sieyès, "Further Developments on the Subject of a Bankruptcy," appendix to "Views of the Executive Means," *Political Writings,* 60–67.

74. David Hume, "Of Public Credit" as quoted in Istvan Hont, *Jealousy of Trade: International Competition and the Nation-State in Historical Perspective* (Cambridge, MA: Harvard University Press, 2005), 325.

75. Hont, *Jealousy of Trade,* 332.

76. This insistence on legitimate purpose has a corollary in domestic business transactions. Although the officers and directors of a company or corporation may have considerable leeway in making decisions on the company's behalf, these decisions must at least ostensibly be in the best interests of the company itself. This constitutes the core of the "business judgment rule," which (rebuttably) presumes that corporate contracts would not serve illegitimate or poorly considered ends. Perhaps the major legal case grounding this rule is *Sinclair Oil Corporation v. Levien,* 280 A.2d 717 (Supreme Court of Delaware, 1971). For an overview, see Kenneth B. Davis Jr., "Once More, the Business Judgment Rule," *Wisconsin Law Review* 2000, no. 3 (2000), which discusses explanations for the business judgment rule and how it relates to the legal duty of care.

77. In addition to the writing focused on odious debt that I mentioned in chapter 1, an excellent and more general discussion of the normative issues surrounding sovereign debt and repayment can be found in Sanjay Reddy, "International Debt: The Constructive Implications of Some Moral Mathematics," *Ethics and International Affairs* 21, no. s1 (2007): 81–98.

78. Robert H. Jackson, "Sovereignty and World Politics: A Glance at the Historical and Conceptual Landscape," in *Sovereignty at the Millennium,* ed. Robert H. Jackson (Oxford: Blackwell, 1999), 11.

79. Ibid., 11.

80. Such regimes would include Russia (1917), China (1949), Cuba (1959), Nicaragua (1979), and Iran (1979). Other regimes may be considered partial social revolutions, i.e., South Africa (1994), which sought to overturn to the social and political basis of the state but only partially undid the economic foundations of the previous regime. Other social revolutions are combined with or are prolongations of earlier independence movements and have characteristics of both forms (i.e., Angola, Mozambique, and Vietnam). There is also a subset of states that emerged from social revolutions without a substantial debt burden and as such may be less relevant for this study (i.e., many of the post-Soviet states did not have heavy debt burdens as they were assumed by the USSR in exchange for the majority of Soviet assets.)

81. These regimes might include Costa Rica (1919), the Philippines (1986), Argentina (1982), and Brazil (1985), among many others. Within this set of states,

it would make most sense to exclude those which have emerged from dictatorial regimes but which remain in transition, i.e., have not yet established an entirely stable new regime (e.g., Democratic Republic of the Congo).

82. For a review of the law of state succession in matters of commercial obligation, see generally Tai-Heng Cheng, *State Succession and Commercial Obligation* (Ardsley, NY: Transnational Publishers, 2006). Cheng argues that, particularly in light of recent international practice, the technical distinction between state succession and regime change should in fact be rejected. Ibid., 37-38.

83. Such regimes would include Turkey (1923), Austria (1920), Hungary (1920), Sweden (1917), and potentially Japan (1950) and Russia (1990).

84. Martha Finnemore, *The Purposes of Intervention: Changing Beliefs about the Use of Force* (Ithaca, NY: Cornell University Press, 2003), 15. For further discussions of this distinction, see also Alexander Wendt, "On Constitution and Causation in International Relations," *Review of International Studies* 24, no. 5 (1997): 101–117; Alexander Wendt, *Social Theory of International Politics* (Cambridge: Cambridge University Press, 1997).

Chapter 3. Costly Talk?

1. Herbert Feis, *Europe: The World's Banker, 1870–1913* (New Haven, CT: Yale University Press, 1930), 210. Moody's puts the number at £920 million, as cited in L. Moore and J. Kaluzny, "Regime Change and Debt Default: The Case of Russia, Austro-Hungary, and the Ottoman Empire Following World War One," *Explorations in Economic History* 42 (2005): 247. Other studies of pre-World War I and interwar finances present similar numbers.

2. *Moody's Analyses of Investment and Security Rating Books: Government and Municipal Securities* (New York: Moody's Investors Service, 1922), as cited in Moore and Kaluzny, "Regime Change and Debt Default," 247.

3. Arno Mayer, *Wilson vs. Lenin: Political Origins of the New Diplomacy, 1917–1918* (New York: World Publishing, 1964), 35.

4. Antonio Cassese, *Self-Determination: A Legal Reappraisal* (Cambridge: Cambridge University Press, 1995), 5.

5. Ibid., 5.

6. While the emergence of external self-determination as a political ideal had profound effects on international politics, scholars have emphasized a degree of continuity between this conception of sovereignty and older colonial forms. Although communities should no longer be subject to the whim of foreign powers, they may remain subject to *local* forms of absolutism. Robert Jackson argues that the twentieth-century commitment to independent statehood is "a mixed blessing" and that "independence in itself is neither good nor bad." Robert H. Jackson, *Quasi-States: Sovereignty, International Relations and the Third World* (Cambridge: Cambridge University Press, 1990), 11–12. From this controversial perspective, the post-World War I conceptual shift was emancipatory only to the extent that the strict statist approach moved down one level. As

I discuss in chapters 5 and 6, this tension was evident in the commitment of postcolonial regimes to internally statist forms of sovereignty in the post-World War II era.

7. Ibid., 17–18.

8. Mayer, *Wilson vs. Lenin,* 35.

9. Quoted in ibid., 276.

10. Quoted in Cassese, *Self-Determination,* 22.

11. *Le Temps,* 26 December 1918, and 9 January 1919, cited in Mayer, *Wilson vs. Lenin,* 382. Critics of Lenin certainly recognized the potential of national self-determination to undermine the goals of socialism. Rosa Luxembourg, for example, "warned Lenin that by sponsoring the self-determination cause, and thereby making the proletariat a supporter of nationalism, the Bolsheviks were helping the bourgeois leaders to pervert the self-determination campaign into a counter-revolutionary instrument." Ibid., 301.

12. See Antony Anghie, *Imperialism, Sovereignty, and the Making of International Law* (Cambridge: Cambridge University Press, 2004), 139.

13. Quoted in Cassese, *Self-Determination,* 20.

14. Woodrow Wilson, "The Fourteen Points (1918)," in *Woodrow Wilson: Essential Writings and Speeches of the Scholar-President,* ed. Mario R. DiNunzio (New York and London: New York University Press, 2006).

15. Mayer, *Wilson vs. Lenin,* 344.

16. Woodrow Wilson, "Address to Congress, Analyzing German and Austrian Peace Utterances (1918)," quoted in Cassese, *Self-Determination,* 20.

17. While this new discursive mode forced a different framing of international action, continuities did exist between nineteenth-century and early twentieth-century European (and American) practices. Liberal colonialists such as John Stuart Mill had long conceived of imperial projects as a way to enlighten and modernize foreign populations. For an extensive discussion of the ostensibly civilizing possibility of English imperial rule, see John Stuart Mill, *Considerations on Representative Government* (New York: Harper, 1862), 336–365.

18. Anghie, *Imperialism,* 156. In particular, he contends that metropole-oriented interpretations of "development" took precedence over other forms of "well-being" and certainly over the expansion of self-rule. Anghie argues that this resulted in what might be called the "economization of government" or the "economization of sovereignty." Ibid. 156–157. For example, promoting this larger vision of progress involved borrowing capital against future resource extraction, thus necessitating the sometimes coercive conversion of local populations into labor power on a larger scale. Ibid. 172–177.

19. Particularly in discussions of American approaches to international law in the early twentieth century, the two are frequently combined and confused. Francis Anthony Boyle highlights that a modern legalist approach, grounded in rules and custom established by states, "was purposefully designed and established to function in a manner diametrically opposed to a moralist or moralistic attitude toward foreign affairs." Francis Anthony Boyle, *Foundations of World Order:*

The Legalist Approach to International Relations, 1898–1922 (Durham, NC: Duke University Press, 1999), 11.

20. John Norton Pomeroy, *Lectures on International Law in Time of Peace* (Boston: Houghton-Mifflin, 1886), 75, cited in Ashfaq Khalfan, Jeff King, and Bryan Thomas, "Advancing the Odious Debt Doctrine," McGill University Centre for International Sustainable Development Law Working Paper (2003), 24. Khalfan et al. point out that Alexander Sack cites the Mexican repudiation as the first precedent for his formalized doctrine. Ibid.

21. M. H. Hoeflich quotes the US arguments to this effect. M. H. Hoeflich, "Through a Glass Darkly: Reflections upon the History of the International Law of Public Debt in Connection with State Succession," *University of Illinois Law Review* (1982), 53.

22. Ernst H. Feilchenfeld, *Public Debts and State Succession* (New York: Macmillan, 1931), 450–453. Khalfan, King, and Thomas suggest that this repudiation, along with the US repudiation of Cuban debts in 1898, is a direct application of the odious debt doctrine as conceived by Sack in 1927. Khalfan et al., "Advancing the Odious Debt Doctrine," 26–27.

23. The exemption of Poland from the apportionment of debt entered into for the German colonization of Poland is provided for in Article 254 of the Treaty of Versailles. See D. P. O'Connell, *State Succession in Municipal Law and International Law,* vol. 1 (Cambridge: Cambridge University Press, 1967), 189.

24. See Mitu Gulati and Sarah Ludington, "A Convenient Untruth: Fact and Fantasy in the Doctrine of Odious Debts," *Virginia Journal of International Law* 48 (2008): 595–639.

25. In fact, he considered the wholesale debt repudiation of the new Soviet regime an affront to the practice of international law and the basic norms of respect for international obligations. Alexander N. Sack, "Diplomatic Claims against the Soviets (1918–1938)," *New York University Review of Law* 15 (1938): 507–535.

26. The post-Hussein Iraq debt negotiations, which I discuss in chapter 7, are a case in point.

27. "Decree of January 1918," in *Documents of Soviet-American Relations,* vol. 2, ed. Harold J. Goldberg (Gulf Breeze, FL: Academic International Press, 1995).

28. "Full Text of the Russian Reply to the Memorandum of the Powers," *New York Times,* May 12, 1922, 1.

29. Letter from the Russian Ambassador (B. Bakhmeteff) to the Secretary of State (Hughes), April 28, 1922, reprinted in Goldberg, *Documents,* 346–347.

30. "The Declaration of Hughes," Soviet Response to U.S. Secretary of State Charles Hughes in *Moscow Pravda,* No. 68, 28 March 1923, reprinted and translated in Goldberg, *Documents,* 251–252.

31. "Russian Reply," 1-2.

32. "Russian Reply," 1.

33. *Pravda,* October 29, 1921, cited in Stephen White, *Britain and the Bolshevik Revolution: A Study in the Politics of Diplomacy, 1920–1924* (London and Basingstoke: MacMillan, 1979), 59.

34. The antiwar movement in the United States was based in part on unwillingness to become embroiled in the squabbles of imperial tyrants, in particular Russia under the Tsar and Germany under the Kaiser. While not causal, it is worth pointing out that the United States entered the war around the same time as Russia's February Revolution of 1917, which brought a provisional (and weak) parliamentary government into power before its overthrow by the Bolshevik Revolution of October 1917.

35. Quoted in Margaret MacMillan, *Peacemakers: The Paris Conference of 1919 and Its Attempt to End War* (London: John Murray, 2001), 76. This is not to say that the Allies were anything close to *supportive* of the Bolshevik regime, which they regarded with considerable distaste and apprehension.

36. "Russian Reply," 1.

37. Citing the 1872 Court of Arbitration in Geneva ordering Great Britain to pay the United States $15,500,000 for losses caused by a privateer in the American Civil War, the Russian delegation argued that "practice and theory agree in imposing responsibility for losses caused by intervention and blockade on Governments which institute them." Ibid., 1. It pointed out that the Western powers intervened heavily in the Russian Civil War, supporting factions willing to continue fighting on the eastern front and fearing the rise of socialism in Europe. Churchill himself noted that over 180,000 foreign troops were stationed on Russian soil by the end of 1918. See MacMillan, *Peacemakers*, 76.

38. Letter from the Russian Ambassador (B. Bakhmeteff) to the Secretary of State (Hughes), April 28, 1922, reprinted in Goldberg, *Documents*, 346–347.

39. These amounts from Moody's are tabulated by Moore and Kaluzny, "Regime Change and Debt Default," 247, summing to a total debt of £3385 million.

40. As Curtis Keeble points out, "As the war in the West dragged on . . . the prospect of ultimate victory depended to a significant extent upon the maintenance of an Eastern front which would continue to tie down substantial enemy forces . . . Had it been open to the Germans to deploy even half these forces in the West at an early stage in the war, it is questionable whether the Allied front in France would have held." Curtis Keeble, *Britain and the Soviet Union, 1917–1989* (London and Basingstoke: MacMillan, 1990), 8.

41. It is important to point out, however, that without the western front, German armies would have marched even more deeply into Russia, having little need of (or perhaps in spite of) any pact with the new regime.

42. Keeble notes that, in addition to over a million and a half dead and wounded, it is estimated that Russia lost two million prisoners. Keeble, *Britain and the Soviet Union*, 8.

43. "Russian Reply," 1.

44. Kim Oosterlinck and John S. Landon-Lane, "Hope Springs Eternal—French Bondholders and the Soviet Repudiation (1915–1919)," *Review of Finance* 10, no. 4 (2006): 507–535, 513. Though vague, the Versailles Treaty did include clauses suggesting that Russia might claim war reparations as well, as pointed out in MacMillan, *Peacemakers*, 90.

45. Citing an October 23, 1919, article in *The Times,* Oosterlinck and Landon-Lane note, "Notwithstanding [the Omsk government position on Tsarist War debt], on October 22, 1919, a British-American consortium issued a short-term loan to the Omsk government worth $40,000,000, backed by gold deposited in Hong-Kong." Oosterlinck and Landon-Lane, "Hope Springs Eternal," 513.

46. *Pravda,* 29 October 1921, cited in White, *Britain and the Bolshevik Revolution,* 59.

47. "Russian Reply," 2. The October note first indicated that the Russian government would be willing to acknowledge the claims of small bondholders for whom debt recognition was "of vital importance." *Pravda,* 29 October 1921, cited in White, *Britain and the Bolshevik Revolution,* 59.

48. "Russian Reply," 1.

49. Ibid., 2.

50. The reprinted memorandum continues, "On the contrary, the fact that the Russian delegation in the question of the settlement of debts takes into most serious account the interests of the Russian people and the economic possibilities of Russia proves it desires only to assume engagements which it is sure Russia can carry out." "Russian Reply," 1.

51. Michael Tomz, *Reputation and International Cooperation: Sovereign Debt across Three Centuries* (Princeton: Princeton University Press, 2007), 17, 23. For more on this terminology and a brief overview of Tomz's argument, see the discussion on reputation in chapter 2.

52. "Trotsky Comments on Trade with U.S.," Interview, 30 September 1923. Reprinted in Goldberg, *Documents,* 254–256. The quotation is on ibid., 256.

53. In what may come as a surprise now, the new Soviet regime genuinely seemed to believe that its arguments would be taken seriously by its interlocutors.

54. "Debt Repudiation Rouses All Nations: Joint Protest Made by 19 Envoys in Petrograd—Bonds Used as Currency," *New York Times,* February 20, 1918.

55. Tomz, *Reputation and International Cooperation,* 80.

56. Ibid., 80.

57. Ibid., 80. Contemporary economists similarly emphasize the difference between repudiation and default. See, for example, Herschel Grossman and John B. Van Huyck, "Sovereign Debt as a Contingent Claim: Excusable Default, Repudiation, and Reputation," *The American Economic Review* 78, no. 5 (December 1988): 1088–1097.

58. Genoa Conference Memorandum of the Allied Powers, clause 2, para. 1, reprinted in Leo Pasvolsky and Harold G. Moulton, *Russian Debts and Russian Reconstruction* (New York: McGraw-Hill, 1924), 203.

59. Quoted in White, *Britain and the Bolshevik Revolution,* 76. The subcommission explicitly claimed that these principles of civilization were apolitical, noting its own makeup of "experts, men of business, who consider real facts, not devoting their attention to any political questions." Ibid., 76.

60. White, *Britain and the Bolshevik Revolution,* 67, citing Memorandum of a Conversation at 10 Downing Street, February 10, 1922, Cabinet Papers S-39,

Cab 23/35. In outlining the government policy to the House of Commons in April 1922, Lloyd George similarly insisted that the Soviet Union must "recognize all the conditions imposed and accepted by civilized communities, as the test of fitness for entering into the comity of nations." This would include the acknowledgment, if not the immediate settlement, of debts. H. C. Debs, Cols 1900–1902, April 3, 1922, as cited in White, *Britain and the Bolshevik Revolution,* 66.

61. Statement of the Position Taken by the Department of State, Letter addressed on July 19, 1923, to the President of the American Federation of Labor by the Secretary of State of the United States. Reprinted in Pasvolsky and Moulton, *Russian Debts,* 237–239.

62. President Coolidge on Russia, Message to Congress, December 9, 1923. Reprinted in Pasvolsky and Moulton, *Russian Debts,* 241.

63. Tomz quotes Dwight Morrow, senior partner at J. P. Morgan, saying that "it must never be forgotten that there are rules of conduct accepted by the silent approval of civilized men." Morrow, April 1926 public address, as quoted in Tomz, *Reputation and International Cooperation,* 75. And, linking civilized repayment to Anglo-American values, at least one investor condemned countries that failed to "regard obligations in the same light as the average Britisher or American does." Tomz, *Reputation and International Cooperation,* 88.

64. Edwin L. James, "Russia Agrees to Take Over Old Debts and Settle Private Foreign Claims, But Demands Recognition and Loan," *New York Times,* April 21, 1922, 2. The same article summarized the Russian reply as "give us some cash and recognize us and we will sign on your dotted line." Ibid., 1.

65. Leo Pasvolsky and Harold G. Moulton, *World War Debt Settlements* (New York: MacMillan, 1926), 69.

66. Pasvolsky and Moulton, *Debt Settlements,* 68; emphasis added.

67. Pasvolsky and Moulton, *Russian Debts,* 163.

68. White, *Britain and the Bolshevik Revolution,* 67, citing Memorandum of a Conversation at 10 Downing Street, 10 February 1922, Cabinet Papers S-39, Cab 23/35. Similarly, in early British discussions of Soviet recognition and the conclusion of a trade agreement, the two factors of greatest importance were "issues of propaganda and the question of Russian debts and obligations, the acknowledgement of which, if not their repayment in full, was regarded as a matter which much be satisfactorily resolved before an agreement could be contemplated." White, *Britain and the Bolshevik Revolution,* 6.

69. A range of largely American organizations, including the American Relief Administration and the Red Cross, offered significant assistance on a voluntary basis. British aid was less forthcoming. While Lloyd George openly admitted that the famine was "so appalling a disaster that it ought to sweep every prejudice out of one's mind [but] pity and human sympathy," he continued that "the Soviet government should be required, as a condition of that assistance, to recognize all its financial obligations towards foreign governments and their nationals." White, *Britain and the Bolshevik Revolution,* 57. See also Keeble, *Britain and the Soviet Union,* 84.

70. Pasvolsky and Moulton, *Debt Settlements,* 69. Harold Moulton served as the director of the Institute of International Economics.

71. Pasvolsky and Moulton, *Russian Debts,* 5.

72. Ibid., 10.

73. Address by Edward A. Harriman, "The Recognition of Soviet Russia," *American Society of International Law Proceedings,* No. 84 (April 24–26, 1924): 94.

74. Genoa Memorandum, clause 2, para. 1., reprinted in Pasvolsky and Moulton, *Russian Debts,* 203.

75. James, "Russia Agrees," 2.

76. Ibid., 2.

77. Genoa Memorandum, clause 2, para. 3, reprinted in Pasvolsky and Moulton, *Russian Debts,* 203.

78. Pasvolsky and Moulton, *Russian Debts,* 6. Italics in original.

79. Ibid., 165–166.

80. Ibid., 166.

81. Katherine A. S. Siegel, *Loans and Legitimacy: The Evolution of Soviet-American Relations, 1919–1933* (Lexington, KY: The University Press of Kentucky, 1996), 68. The Soviet regime, however, considered this form of powerful internationally run syndicate too imperial in flavor, and in any case was unwilling to budge on the principle of repudiation.

82. Indeed, Admiral Kolchak, who the Western Allies supported and whose government they considered recognizing during the Russian Civil War, issued a proclamation shortly after coming to power in November 1918 that accepted the obligations of the former Russian governments and promised repayment as soon as his government had reunified Russia. Richard H. Ullman, *Britain and the Russian Civil War* (Princeton, NJ: Princeton University Press, 1968), 169. Ullman notes that the text of the proclamation is printed in the minutes of the Council of Four, 24 May 1919, 4m.; *Foreign Relations, Paris Peace Conference,* vol. 6, 16–17. He lists the conditions for Allied support on pages 168–169.

83. Quoted in Tomz, *Reputation and International Cooperation,* 81. Indeed, Tomz points out that "though no country went to the Russian extreme of repudiating its debts, a few probably paid less than investors expected, even given the difficult economic circumstances." Ibid., 96.

84. This theme of equality and reciprocity runs throughout the memorandum. For example, "the idea of reciprocity . . . is not yet sufficiently recognized by all the powers." "Russia has accepted the principles . . . on condition that it be made reciprocal." "Russia is still ready . . . to consent to important concessions . . . but upon the absolute condition that concessions equivalent to and corresponding to these concessions are made in favor of the Russian people . . . . The great mass of the people of Russia could not accept an agreement in which these concessions were not balanced by real and corresponding advantages." "Russian Reply," 2. Indeed, the new Soviet regime was extremely sensitive to potential slights in all arenas. When the United States proposed that an American trade commission be

admitted to Moscow, some were surprised by Moscow's insistence that a parallel Soviet commission be admitted to the United States, to avoid any perception of inferiority and thus protect national honor. See Siegel, *Loans and Legitimacy*, 72.

85. White, *Britain and the Bolshevik Revolution*, 73.

86. L. S. O'Malley, memorandum of 8 May 1922, DBFP, vol. 19, 702–703. Cited in White, *Britain and the Bolshevik Revolution*, 73. The remaining conferences of 1922 resulted in similar outcomes with regard to the Russian question.

87. Tabulated in B. V. Anan'ich and V. I. Bovykin, "Foreign Banks and Foreign Investment in Russia," in *International Banking, 1870–1914*, ed., Rondo Cameron and V. I. Bovykin (New York and Oxford: Oxford University Press, 1991), 256.

88. For a discussion, see Barry Eichengreen, *Elusive Stability: Essays in the History of International Finance, 1919–1939* (Cambridge: Cambridge University Press, 1993), 125.

89. Ibid., 127, citing the Archives of the French Ministry of Foreign Affairs (Min. Aff. Etr.) B82/112, "Réunion Interministérielle au sujet de L'Equitable Traitement du Commerce," January 28, 1922. In contrast to Britain in particular, France objected to the idea of a trade policy conference and opposed the universal application of the Most Favored Nation principle.

90. Feis, *World's Banker*, 211. Fourteen percent was held in Great Britain. The French were also dominant in investing in Russian private enterprise, owing about one-third of the investment, excluding investment in railways. British ownership amounted to slightly less than one-quarter and German ownership about one-fifth. Ibid., 211. For an overview of the institutions involved in international (including) Russian securities issues in Paris, see Samir Saul, "Banking Alliances and International Issues on the Paris Capital Market, 1890–1914," in *London and Paris as International Financial Centres in the Twentieth Century*, ed. Youssef Cassis and Éric Bussière (Oxford: Oxford University Press, 2005).

91. Feis argues that French diplomatic endeavors constituted the central reason for lending to Russia. "Since the Alliance was the foundation on which French diplomatic effort was built, this demand (for credit) had to be met—favor was given for favor." Feis, *World's Banker*, 52. While Feis's broader argument that political and military issues drove European lending is controversial, the claim with regard to France is somewhat better accepted. Certainly in the 1920s commentators believed that France, more than any other nation, considered capital flows to be a central diplomatic tool. See, for example, George W. Edwards, "Government Control of Foreign Investments," *American Economic Review* 18, no. 4 (December 1928): 684–701, especially 687–689. Edwards particularly emphasizes that this was the case for capital flows to Russia. Ibid., 690.

Somewhat modifying this view, Marc Flandreau suggests that banking houses such as the Crédit Lyonnais, which specialized in 'risky' regions such as Russia and the Mediterranean, did consider Russian securities a good credit risk. In particular, because most loans to the Russian government went to industrial investments (rather than consumption finance), French market leaders perceived an economic basis for such lending. Marc Flandreau, "Caveat Emptor: Coping with Sovereign Risk under the International Gold Standard, 1871–1913," *International Financial History in the Twentieth Century,* ed. Marc Flandreau, Carl-Ludwig Holtfrerich, and Harold James (Cambridge: Cambridge University Press, 2003), 48–49.

92. Feis, *World's Banker,* 217–218. The French position as an international financial center was heavily dependent on its role in long-term capital markets, particularly in issuing and trading foreign loans for governments, and was less involved than London in financing international trade. Youssef Cassis, *Capitals of Capital: A History of International Financial Centres, 1780–2005* (Cambridge: Cambridge University Press, 2006), 102. Thus the financial ramifications of a securities default for the banks would have been difficult to offset by even significantly increased trade.

93. Feis, *World's Banker,* 52. Cassis also notes that over 50 percent of French overseas investment stayed in Europe, including 25 percent in Russia. Youssef Cassis, *Capitals of Capital,* 78. See also Alain Plessis, "When Paris Dreamed of Competing with the City," in Cassis and Bussière, *London and Paris,* 45. As such, World War I and the Russian repudiation dealt a more serious financial blow to France than to any other country.

94. Anan'ich and Bovykin, "Foreign Banks," 264.

95. Joël Freymond suggests that pre-World War I Russian securities holdings in France continue to be widespread, presenting a map indicating the current density of Russian security holders throughout France. Joël Freymond, *Les Emprunts Russes: Histoire de la Plus Grande Spoliation du Siècle* (Paris: Journal des Finances, 1995), graphic insert.

96. Ibid., 46. Freymond also notes that French publications and individuals were complicit in the overplacement of Russian securities, presenting a list of those that had accepted gifts from the Tsar's government for their support. Ibid. 22–24. He further argues that the high commissions demanded by banks for the French placements made the banks themselves the primary beneficiaries of such securities offerings. Ibid., 12–13.

97. Antony C. Sutton, *Western Technology and Soviet Economic Development, 1917–1930* (Stanford, CA: Hoover Institution Publications, 1968), 293. Freymond lists an industrial group, individual security holders, banks and credit establishments, and a commercial group as the main French associations concerned with the Russian repudiation and subsequent negotiations. Freymond, *Emprunts Russes,* 44–45.

98. Although not nearly as trade-oriented as the United Kingdom or the United States, France was occasionally concerned with other countries gaining greater access to the Russian market. Keeble notes that this corresponded to a period of British estrangement following Curzon's rise to power. Keeble, *Britain and the Soviet Union,* 89.

99. Sutton lists the names and countries of origin of the operating concessions signed by the Soviet regime between 1917 and 1930. The French proportion is

estimated from a review of that list, although there are several concessions for which the country of origin is unknown. Sutton, *Western Technology,* appendix B, 354–363.

100. Keeble, *Britain and the Soviet Union,* 52. The French also refused an invitation to join commercial talks in 1920. Ibid., 69.

101. David Carlton, *Churchill and the Soviet Union* (Manchester and New York: Manchester University Press, 2000), 30. Lloyd George and Churchill clashed considerably over Soviet policy, and the former had to back down in late 1922 for domestic political reasons.

102. Plessis, "When Paris Dreamed," 47. The situation for French lending improved after the stabilization of the franc in 1926–1928, but issuances of foreign securities (which again received some governmental encouragement for political reasons) never approached the prewar level. Ibid., 48. For a brief overview of the effects of the war on the Paris capital market, see Cassis, *Capitals of Capital,* 167–173.

103. Indeed, Joel Freymond, who has compiled much of the French information, is a prewar Russian bondholder himself and his commentary suggests that feelings around the 1918 repudiation can still run high.

104. See the note of the Secretary of State to the French Ambassador (Claudel), March 10, 1928. US Department of State, *Foreign Relations of the United States: Diplomatic Papers,* vol. 3 (Washington, DC: GPO, 1928), 830–831 (hereafter cited as FRUS). The associated correspondence, including the reiteration of the Russia policy for US mints and assay offices, is in FRUS 1928, 3:827–831.

105. French Ambassador (Claudel) to the Secretary of State p. Frank Kellogg), March 15, 1928, FRUS 1928, 3:826. A favorable response was issued on April 16, 1928, indicating that the State Department had contacted the US financier, Percival Farquhar, to express its disapproval.

106. The British government remained a major public creditor to the Russian government, with war loans amounting to £526 million, including £74 million for US supplies. Keeble, *Britain and the Soviet Union,* 8, citing PQ answered by Chancellor of the Exchequer, 19 April 1921, quoted in FO 371/9363 (N3530/2407/38).

107. This shift was made even more pronounced by the English reselling of Russian securities on other national markets at reduced prices. Anan'ich and Bovykin, "Foreign Banks," 257–258.

108. Whereas French banking houses and investors continued to support and buy Russian bonds after 1900, some British investors expressed concern that new loans were being floated to cover coupon payments on previous bonds. Although this lending into arrears became a common feature of sovereign lending in the mid- to late twentieth century, at least some turn-of-the-century British investors were less enthusiastic. Moore and Kaluzny, "Regime Change," 246.

109. Anan'ich and Bovykin, "Foreign Banks," 263. For example, while English banks did participate in the 1906 and 1909 state loans, the considerable majority in each case was taken by French banks.

110. Feis, *World's Banker,* 23. Feis notes that one of his sources, Paish's table of figures in the *Statist Supplement,* February 14, 1914, gives an even lower figure of £66.7 million for Russian investment. Ibid. 23. Youssef Cassis lists similar figures in *Capitals of Capital,* 78–79. Mira Wilkins notes that at least one estimate of British loans to governments suggested that over 70 percent of such lending stayed within the empire, which more clearly set the rules of the game and thus lowered potential transaction costs. Mira Wilkins, "Long-Term Investments in the Gold Standard Era," in *International Financial History,* Flandreau, Holtfrerich, and James, 58. The French invested far less heavily in its own colonies, which were less productive in trade terms than those of Great Britain. In addition to Europe, French lending focused on the Mediterranean and the Ottoman Empire. Wilkins, "Long-Term Investments," 78.

111. Lloyd George to Churchill, Churchill Papers, in *World in Torment: Winston Churchill, 1917–1922,* vol. 4 (London: William Hienemann, 1975), 538–539. Quoted in Carlton, *Churchill and the Soviet Union,* 12.

112. The British Foreign Office thought the figures for private claims of £300–350 million, including direct investment, were considerably inflated in light of prewar investment figures. Keeble, *Britain and the Soviet Union,* 86.

113. Keeble, *Britain and the Soviet Union,* 86. Keeble argues that French influence was an important factor in Soviet relations. "The Government . . . found difficulty in compromising over private debt, the more so as the French Government, whose citizens had more substantial private investments in Russia, was intransigent. So, no agreement was reached." Ibid., 86.

114. Siegel points out that the subsequent breakdown of the Genoa and Hague conferences also freed and empowered the US government, as there was no agreed upon template for issues such as debt repayment, tariffs, reparations, and immigration. Siegel, *Loans and Legitimacy,* 71.

115. Keeble, *Britain and the Soviet Union,* 89.

116. As such, Lloyd George was held back during the 1922 conferences not only by the French position but also by the prevailing political climate. Keeble, *Britain and the Soviet Union,* 86.

117. F. S. Northedge and Audrey Wells, *Britain and Soviet Communism: The Impact of a Revolution* (London: MacMillan, 1982), 220.

118. *The Manchester Guardian,* October 28, 1932, quoted in Northedge and Wells, *Britain and Soviet Communism,* 218.

119. *The Spectator,* October 22, 1932, quoted in Northedge and Wells, *Britain and Soviet Communism,* 218.

120. Conservative MP Robert Boothby, *The Times,* November 20, 1935, quoted in Northedge and Wells, *Britain and Soviet Communism,* 220–221.

121. Anan'ich and Bovykin, "Foreign Banks," 273.

122. By 1930, British government claims amounted to £902 while private debt claims reached £262 million. Keeble, *Britain and the Soviet Union,* 110.

123. Feis, *World's Banker,* 212–214. As noted above, German capital in the late nineteenth and early twentieth centuries was also absorbed by domestic

industry, and France's political conditions for Russian loans alienated German banking houses. Although German banks did not participate in the major Russian securities issues, they remained in contact with Russian banks and the Tsar's finance ministry and placed railway loans between 1908 and 1913. Anan'ich and Bovykin, "Foreign Banks," 261–263.

124. Feis, *World's Banker*, 74–79. Only about half of this amount was in fixed interest-bearing securities such as government bonds. Ibid., 74–79.

125. Sutton, *Western Technology*, 293. The 1918 Treaty of Brest-Litovsk between the new Soviet regime and the soon-to-be defeated German imperial regime had included a lump sum payment of 6 billion gold rubles to cover prewar German economic claims. However, this amount was handed over to the Allied powers when the postwar German regime repudiated Brest-Litovsk during the Versailles Conference.

126. Sutton cites this as "provided that the Soviet Government does not satisfy similar claims of other States." Sutton, *Western Technology*, 316–317.

127. In this, there was continuity with prewar relations. Germany had been a major prewar trading partner of Russia's, and by 1913 Russia bought 52.6 percent of its imports from and sold 31.8 percent of its exports to Germany (compared with 13.9 percent and 18.8 percent to Britain). Germany overtook Britain as Russia's primary trading partner by 1870. Northedge and Wells, *Britain and Soviet Communism*, 211, citing Jules Gay, "Anglo-Russian Economic Relations," *The Economic Journal*, June 1917.

128. Sutton, *Western Technology*, 278.

129. Sutton notes that the first trade credits were made on a barter basis, and that the first straight short-term financial credit was made in October 1925 for 100 million marks at 8.5 percent. Ibid., 278–279.

130. James, "Russia Agrees," 2.

131. The new Soviet regime tended to prefer the United States to its former European allies, and even hoped toward the end of the civil war and in the early 1920s that the United States might eventually convert the entire Russian debt, partially in exchange for considerable resource concessions. Siegel, *Loans and Legitimacy*, 25–26, 45.

132. Cassis, *Capitals of Capital*, 114. Wilkins similarly notes that "unlike London, Paris, Amsterdam, and other European stock markets, the NYSE in 1914 was basically a domestic market." Wilkins, "Long-Term Investments," 58.

133. Vincent Carosso and Richard Sylla, "U.S. Banks in International Finance," in *International Banking, 1870–1914*, ed. Cameron and Bovykin, 49. Cleona Lewis points out that only 25 percent of these American investments were portfolio investments, and 75 percent were direct. Cleona Lewis, *America's Stake in International Investments* (Washington, DC: Brookings Institution, 1938), 605.

134. Lewis, *America's Stake*, 447. New American lending focused primarily on the previously British-dominated domains of Latin America and Asia (to some degree mirroring US geopolitical interest), but in any case took a decidedly international turn.

135. Roosa reinforces this link, saying, "In part this reflected the newness of international finance (apart from old, established ties with London) in American financial circles, and their fears of risking money in a largely unknown Russian market." Ruth AmEnde Roosa, "Banking and Financial Relations between Russia and the United States," in *International Banking, 1870–1914,* ed. Cameron and Bovykin, 317.

136. Roosa, "Banking and Financial Relations," 293.

137. Cassis, *Capitals of Capital,* 131. This integration existed between creditors and also through long-term creditor-borrower relationships. Mira Wilkins suggests that "in the years 1880–1914 probably there was greater worldwide integration through long-term international investment (with its network of ongoing obligations) than at any subsequent time between 1914 and the late 1980s . . . . The gold standard aided the movement of capital, sharply reducing exchange rate risks for investors in those countries whose currencies were backed by gold." Wilkins, "Long-Term Investments," 53.

138. See Carosso and Sylla, "U.S. Banks in International Finance," citing Folke Hilgert, *Industrialization and Foreign Trade* (Geneva: League of Nations: 1945), 56–58.

139. Roosa, "Banking and Financial Relations," 303.

140. Ibid., 305–308.

141. Siegel, *Loans and Legitimacy,* 83n35. Roosa notes that "as of 1909 National City did the largest bond trading business of any banking institution in New York. However, despite Vanderlip's long interest in Russia and his desire to promote the bank's interest in Europe, its bond investments in January 1914 included virtually none in Russia. Yet its funds in the State Bank were listed as of June 1, 1912 as amounting to $24,799.38 . . . . These small sums seem to reflect only the needs of these banks for the fulfillment of the general financial requirement of American firms in Russia." Roosa, "Banking and Financial Relations," 303–304. Its president, James Stillman, was interested in extending City's presence in Russia primarily to promote business in the Far East. Ibid., 311.

142. These were largely in support of its domestic insurance business, as the Tsar's government had strict capital controls effectively requiring a large portion of funds to be reinvested domestically. Roosa provides an excellent overview of New York Life's prewar involvement in "Banking and Financial Relations," 296–302.

143. Chicherin, the Soviet foreign minister, considered National City to be "one of our leading established enemies in the American capitalist circles." Siegel, *Loans and Legitimacy,* 83. While the United Kingdom had a Corporation of Foreign Bondholders as of 1868 (later incorporated by an act of Parliament), the United States founded the Foreign Bondholders Protective Council when defaults began in the early 1930s. As noted in Tomz, *Reputation and International Cooperation,* 81–82.

144. Sutton, *Western Technology,* 290; Siegel, *Loans and Legitimacy,* 84.

145. Siegel, *Loans and Legitimacy,* 40n12.

146. The economic and regulatory environment changed at the end of 1914 in such a way as to shift the patterns of US bank interaction and capital export. Prior to 1914, a relatively small number of East Coast financial institutions had dominated US international financial activity. The freedom of joint-stock banks was inhibited by a range of state and national regulations, which benefited locally controlled and domestically oriented independent unit banks. Carosso and Sylla, "U.S. Banks in International Finance," 51–55.

147. Siegel, *Loans and Legitimacy*, 84.

148. Siegel, *Loans and Legitimacy*, 83–84. Sutton mentions Chase's extension of credits for cotton in *Western Technology*, 226.

149. The *New York Times* ad ran on January 19, 1928. As noted in Sutton, *Western Technology*, 290.

150. US State Dept. Decimal File, 316–110–250, as cited by Sutton, *Western Technology*, 290.

151. This is among the correspondence between the State Department and those who opposed or supported the railway-bond transaction. US Dept of State, General Records, Record Group 59, File 861.51 State Bank/1–38, cited in Joan Hoff Wilson, *Ideology and Economics: U.S. Relations with the Soviet Union, 1918–1933* (Columbia: University of Missouri Press, 1974), 41. Wilson also notes protests from the National Tin Corporation, the Allied Patriotic Societies, the National Civil Federation, individuals, and anti-Soviet newspapers such as *The Wall Street Journal*. Wilson, *Ideology and Economics*, 41.

152. Sutton, *Western Technology*, 291. Citing Letter from Chase National to US State Dept. (Decimal File, 316–110–341).

153. The Secretary of State to the Law Firm of Davis, Polk, Wardwell, Gardiner & Reed, representatives of W. A. Harriman and Co., April 2, 1926, FRUS 1926, 2:907.

154. Noted in Antony C. Sutton, *Western Technology*, 90. Sutton suggests that part of the reason for the State Department's concern was the use of American capital to support German rather than American manufacturers. Ibid. That said, the State Department was not any more inclined to allow securities flotations to support American purchases, preferring instead for manufacturers to arrange credits in a more direct (and short-term) manner.

155. The department noted that, as in other instances, "in its essence, the proposed transaction would be Russian financing and in effect the employment of American credit for the purpose of making an advance to the Soviet regime." The Secretary of State to the New York Trust Company, July 15, 1926, FRUS 1926, 2:910.

156. The Secretary of State (Kellog) to the French Ambassador (Claudel), April 16, 1928, FRUS 1928, 3:827. See also the initial inquiry from the French Ambassador, FRUS 1928, 3:826.

157. Vice President of the American Locomotive Sales Corporation (Charles M. Muchnic) to the Under Secretary of State (Olds), October 17, 1927, FRUS 1927, 3:652–653.

158. The Under Secretary of State (Olds) to the Vice President of the American Locomotive Sales Corporation (Charles M. Muchnic), November 28, 1927, FRUS 1927, 3:654.

159. For more on this agreement, along with the original concession contract itself, see Stephen D. Fitch, "The Harriman Manganese Concession in the Soviet Union: Lessons for Today," *International Tax and Business Law* 9, no. 1 (Summer 1991): 209–271. Available at: http://scholarship.law.berkeley.edu/bjil/vol9/iss1/5.

160. US State Dept. Decimal File, 316–138–18. Memorandum from US Embassy in London dated October 28, 1924. Quoted in Sutton, *Western Technology,* 89.

161. US State Dept. Decimal File, 316–138–299, cited in Sutton, *Western Technology,* 299. Despite its unconventional form, the Soviet government certainly considered it to be a loan, and boasted as much. The US commercial attaché in Prague noted that the Soviets were bragging about a loan from Harriman at 7 percent. (316–138–332/5). Cited in Sutton, *Western Technology,* 91.

162. Businesses involved in foreign trade complained about the lack of export markets and the difficulty of obtaining payment from postwar Europe. Siegel, *Loans and Legitimacy,* 13. In initially encouraging the government to lift the trade embargo against the new Soviet regime, some business leaders explicitly pointed to the fact that Britain and Canada were already trading with the Soviet Union and expressed concern at losing out to British competition. Siegel, *Loans and Legitimacy,* 28. The government at this time, despite the hard line taken by the State Department, was also concerned that other countries would secure an advantage in trade if the United States moved too slowly. Siegel, *Loans and Legitimacy,* 50–51.

163. W. L. Clayton, quoted in Siegel, *Loans and Legitimacy,* 82n29. Clayton's lobbying efforts were ultimately unsuccessful.

164. Sutton, *Western Technology,* 144. Saul Bron, writing for Amtorg (the Soviet trading agency) in 1930, estimated that over two hundred companies provided credit extensions of one year or more, with others extending financing for at least three years. Saul Bron, *Soviet Economic Development and American Business: Results of the First Year under the Five Year Plan and Further Perspectives* (New York: H. Liveright, 1930), 57. The following broader claim made by Sutton probably goes too far, however: "From a position of 'no credit' the United States moved to one of long-term loans and security issues within a period of eight years, in a graduated erosion of executive interpretation and under constant pressure from the Soviets and American financial and manufacturing houses." Sutton, *Western Technology,* 277.

165. New York State's Martin Act, promulgated in 1921 and amended in 1925, would have been the most relevant state legislation. Prior to 1925, any issuer could sell securities in New York. The 1925 amendments involved significant changes, in particular granting the attorney general expansive investigatory powers to deal with problems of fraud. However, the key change relevant to the Soviet regime involved a perfunctory requirement to register as a dealer before issuing debt in New York, given that it did not meet the Section 359-f registration

exemption for "Any security issued . . . by any foreign government with which the United States is at the time of the sale or offer for sale thereof maintaining diplomatic relations, or by any province or political subdivision thereof." Given the *de minimis* nature of the requirement, it does not appear that more conservative financial institutions took advantage of the Martin Act's revision to insert clauses that would have posed a greater obstacle to Soviet financing. Indeed, the legislative history and press coverage of the 1925 amendment does not provide evidence of any particular concern about the Soviet Union or foreign sovereign issuers generally, with the vast majority of discussion centering on the prevention of fraud and the addition of new securities categories. See, for example, Letter from N.Y. Attorney General Albert Ottinger to Governor Alfred E. Smith, April 1, 1925; Committee on the Amendment of the Law, 1925, Bulletin No. 7, 286–88; "Our Blue Sky Law Hailed as Best Now," *New York Times*, April 12, 1925.

166. "Flotation of Foreign Loans," press release issued by the Department of State, March 3, 1922, FRUS 1922, 1:557–558.

167. Edwards, "Government Control," 695. The statement had followed upon and clarified the informal agreement resulting from a May 1921 meeting between Harding cabinet members and a group of investment bankers, in which the government officials indicated their wish to have information on as well as input into US capital flows. Ibid., 693.

168. Ibid., 695.

169. *Journal of Commerce,* February 2, 1928, as quoted in Edwards, "Government Control," 698.

170. The Secretary of State to the Chairman of the Republican National Committee (Butler), February 23, 1928, FRUS 1928, 3:822–826 (quotation on p. 825).

171. The Secretary of State to Messrs. Davis, Polk, Wardwell, Gardiner & Reed, April 2, 1926, FRUS 1926, 2:907.

172. The Under Secretary of State (Olds) to the Vice President of the American Locomotive Sales Corporation (Charles M. Muchnic), November 28, 1927, FRUS 1927, 3:653–654. The department indicated that it would not object to American manufacturers or banks themselves granting commercial credit.

173. The Assistant Secretary of State (Dearing) to the Assistant Secretary of the Treasury (Gilbert), April 9, 1921, FRUS 1921, 2:774–775, reprinted in Goldberg, *Documents,* 233.

174. Press Release Issued by the Treasury Department, March 6, 1928, reprinted in Goldberg, *Documents,* 269. As noted above, this was partly at the instigation of the French ambassador. Sutton indicates that Chase and Equitable Trust for a time conducted some of their Soviet business on the basis of platinum credits. Sutton, *Western Technology,* 277.

175. The Under Secretary of State (Olds) to the Vice President of the American Locomotive Sales Corporation (Charles M. Muchnic), November 28, 1927, FRUS 1927, 3:654.

176. October–November 1927. US State Dept Decimal File, 316–124–0032, cited in Sutton, *Western Technology,* 298.

177. Siegel, *Loans and Legitimacy,* 16–23. The representative of the first Soviet trading bureau was eventually deported by the Wilson administration. This move was opposed by some in Wilson's administration, including Assistant Secretary of State Roland Morris, who stated, "It saddens me so to see how completely the President—the greatest 'liberal' of his generation—is so completely out of touch with the liberal opinion on this Russia problem." Quoted in Siegel, *Loans and Legitimacy,* 35n77.

178. Siegel, *Loans and Legitimacy,* 39.

179. I discuss Wilson's nonrecognition policy further in the next chapter, focusing on the Latin American context and the Costa Rican repudiation case.

180. Press Release Issued by the Department of State, March 21, 1923, FRUS 1923, 2:755–758. Reprinted in Goldberg, *Documents,* 351–354 (quotation drawn from page 353).

181. Siegel, *Loans and Legitimacy,* 60n127.

182. Siegel, *Loans and Legitimacy,* 60.

183. The ambassador of the provisional Kerensky government, explaining his resignation from official duties in the spring of 1922, cited the successful conclusion of this property liquidation and the repayment of US government loans to the provisional government. Letter from the Russian Ambassador (B. Bakhmeteff) to the Secretary of State (Hughes), April 28, 1922, reprinted in Goldberg, *Documents,* 346–347.

184. Tomz, in his discussion of interwar investment, looks at sovereign debt issue data to suggest that defaulting countries, including the Soviet Union, were unable to obtain financing due to reputational consequences. Such a creditor interpretation of borrower creditworthiness, shared uniformly, would have made any kind of collusion or embargo unnecessary. Tomz, *Reputation and International Cooperation,* 88, 100.

185. This particular term is used in Joan Hoff Wilson, *Ideology and Economics,* 36. Wilson notes that "by 1927 the [Commerce] department was privately admitting that its advice was probably responsible for the harsh credit terms Soviet purchasing agents had to face." Ibid., 37.

Chapter 4. Costa Rica, Public Benefit, and the Rule of Law

1. For an earlier discussion of this decision, which includes a consideration of how it resonates with Justice Taft's broader legal and political commitments, see Odette Lienau, "Who is the 'Sovereign' in Sovereign Debt?: Reinterpreting a Rule-of-Law Framework from the Early Twentieth Century," *Yale Journal of International Law* 33, no. 1 (Winter 2008).

2. See George W. Baker, "Woodrow Wilson's Use of the Non-Recognition Policy in Costa Rica," *The Americas* 22 (July 1965): 3, 5; Dana G. Munro, *Intervention and Dollar Diplomacy in the Caribbean, 1900–1921* (Princeton, NJ: Princeton University Press, 1964), 427.

3. Munro, *Intervention,* 433. Although Costa Rican politics were generally far more orderly and accountable than those of its Central American neighbors, business interests, including the coffee elite and the United Fruit Company, held considerable sway.

4. Ibid., 435.

5. By 1919, the capital had experienced considerable domestic unrest, and a small group of counterrevolutionaries had convened at the border. The United States and the United Kingdom had not recognized the Tinoco regime, but also did not provide any support for the counterrevolutionaries, insisting on a noncoercive restoration of the constitutional government. However, a US Naval Commander's independent decision to land his forces at the coastal city of Limón in June 1919 engendered suspicion of a US policy change. Thomas M. Leonard, "Central America and the United States: Overlooked Foreign Policy Objectives," *The Americas* 50, no. 1 (1993): 12.

6. This relatively orderly approach to governmental transitions was a hallmark of Costa Rican politics throughout the twentieth century. With the exception of the Tinoco coup, Costa Rica has experienced regular elections with direct voting since 1912, and it constitutionally abolished the military in 1949. See Hector Perez-Brignoli, *A Brief History of Central America* (Berkeley, CA: University of California Press, 1989), 113, 115.

7. Telegram from Benjamin Chase, U.S. Consul in Costa Rica, to Alvey A. Adee, Acting U.S. Secretary of State, August 11, 1920, in US Department of State, *Foreign Relations of the United States: Diplomatic Papers,* vol. 1 (Washington, DC: GPO, 1920), 838 (hereafter cited as FRUS).

8. Message of the President of the Republic of Costa Rica to the Constitutional Congress in Regard to the British Claims, July 20, 1921, reprinted in *Costa Rica-Great Britain Arbitration: The Case of Costa Rica in the Matter of Claims Presented by His Britannic Majesty's Government Against the Republic of Costa Rica Before the Chief Justice of the United States of America, Arbitrator, Under Convention Between the Republic of Costa Rica and His Britannic Majesty, Dated January 12, 1922, as Ratified March 7, 1923* (Washington, DC: B. S. Adams, 1923), appendix, 146–148.

9. The Constitutional Congress of the Republic of Costa Rica, Law of Nullities (Law No. 41), as published in *La Gaceta,* August 22, 1920, reprinted in *Costa Rica-Great Britain Arbitration,* Appendix, 381–387. Quote drawn from Decrees, article 1(a) and (b), 383.

10. Law No. 41, Paragraphs 1–2, reprinted in *Costa Rica-Great Britain Arbitration,* Appendix, 381.

11. *Costa Rica-Great Britain Arbitration,* 28.

12. Ibid., 32–41.

13. Ibid., 19. The argument quotes several instances in which the Wilson administration formulated and advanced the policy. This section also does indicate, however, that resistance existed within the United States against the policy,

particularly as the Tinoco regime had declared itself a belligerent against Germany in World War I. Ibid., 19–26.

14. Ibid., 26.

15. Ibid., 80–81.

16. Law No. 41, Paragraphs 5–6, reprinted in *Costa Rica-Great Britain Arbitration*, Appendix, 382.

17. *Costa Rica-Great Britain Arbitration*, 68–72, 85.

18. Ibid., 80.

19. Ibid., 80. The poor deal for Costa Rica in the Amory concession was emphasized again by the Committee on Foreign Relations of the Costa Rican Congress, responding to a presidential effort to conciliate with Great Britain. See Report of the Committee of Foreign Relations of the Constitutional Congress of Costa Rica, August 9, 1921, reprinted in *Costa Rica-Great Britain Arbitration*, Appendix, 149–155, esp. 153–154.

20. *Costa Rica-Great Britain Arbitration*, 99–104.

21. Law No. 41, Paragraph 7, reprinted in *Costa Rica-Great Britain Arbitration*, Appendix, 382. The presentation to the arbitral tribunal also makes this point, emphasizing the difference between an assertion of nullity and a mere failure to ratify a previous regime's acts. See *Costa Rica-Great Britain Arbitration*, 63.

22. Ibid., 41.

23. Ibid., 87.

24. *Moody's Manual of Investments: American and Foreign* (New York: Moody's Investor Service, 1920), 1304.

25. See, for example, *Moody's Manual of Investments*, 1916, 1918, 1920, and 1922.

26. Indeed, the Tinoco regime itself seems to have continued payment on this debt. This falls in line with Tinoco's broader efforts to gain the official recognition and support of the United States and Great Britain.

27. For more on Wilson's commitment to political stability through constitutional reform, see Munro, *Intervention*, 271.

28. Telegram from Secretary of State Lansing to the American Delegation in Guatemala City, February 9, 1917, reprinted in *Costa Rica-Great Britain Arbitration*, Appendix, 561. The US embassy was to publicize this policy to the government to which it was accredited. The same telegram was sent to Tegucigalpa, San Salvador, and Managua.

29. Statement Given to the Press by the Department of State of the United States, February 22, 1917, reprinted in *Costa Rica-Great Britain Arbitration*, Appendix, 562. Wilson considered the Tinoco regime to be an affront not only to his own policy but also to the 1907 Central American treaty system. See Leonard, "Central America," 12. Because one of the British claimants used an American shell concern to sign the initial contract, Costa Rica cited President Wilson's declaration that Americans should not contract with the Tinoco regime as one reason the oil claim should be rejected. Leonard, "Central America," 10.

30. Leonard, "Central America," 12.

31. There is some intimation that key players in the United Fruit Company had been involved in the Tinoco coup. Certainly the interests of the landed gentry, with whom these American investors had intermarried, were initially aided by the coup, and Minor Keith himself was related to Tinoco. In fact, the group that fought the Tinoco regime and eventually came to power believed that Tinoco had been bribed by American-owned concerns to overthrow the previous regime. They indicated as much to the US government and even claimed to have the original correspondence as evidence of this plot. Telegram from Alfredo González and J. Rafael Oreamuno to the President of the United States, November 12, 1918, reprinted in *Costa Rica-Great Britain Arbitration,* Appendix, 563–564. See also Munro, *Intervention,* 430, 439.

32. Munro, *Intervention,* 433–434. There is some suggestion among historians that Gonzalez may in fact have been sympathetic to the Germans, but the seriousness of the German threat is unclear. Leonard notes that a *New York Times* correspondent close to Tinoco planted stories of German plots against Costa Rica in an effort to encourage recognition. Leonard, "Central America," 12.

33. Baker, "Non-Recognition Policy," 11–17.

34. The Consul at San José (Chase) to the Secretary of State, September 4, 1920, FRUS 1920, 1:838. Consul Chase indicates that British, Spanish, Colombian, and Panamanian concessions were most at stake. Ibid., 838.

35. It also appeared that the real challenger to this concession was another American concern—Standard Oil of California, in which case, US officials decided that "the correct procedure would be to have the matter adjudicated by the parties in the Costa Rican courts." The Acting Secretary of State to the Chargé in Costa Rica (John F. Martin), December 13, 1920, FRUS 1920, 1:846.

36. See State Department documents regarding Costa Rica in early 1921, FRUS 1921, 1:646 et seq.

37. Seymour's Minute on Graham to Foreign Office, F.O. 371/4535, PRO (July 1, 1920), quoted in Richard V. Salisbury, "Revolution and Recognition: A British Perspective on Isthmian Affairs During the 1920s," *The Americas* 48, no. 3 (1992): 335.

38. British Consulate (Frank N. Cox) to the Secretary of Foreign Relations of Costa Rica, August 24, 1920 (No. 68/20), reprinted in *Costa Rica-Great Britain Arbitration,* Appendix, 28–31 (quotation on page 30).

39. British Minister (A. Percy Bennett) to the Secretary of Foreign Relations of Costa Rica, December 28, 1920, reprinted in ibid. 42–43 (quotation on page 42). See also British Minister (A. Percy Bennett) to the Secretary of Foreign Relations of Costa Rica, January 9, 1921, in which it is argued that Law No. 41 constitutes a "clear breach of International Law" and "infringed the canons of International law." Reprinted in *Costa Rica-Great Britain Arbitration,* Appendix, 49–55 (quotation on pages 53–54).

40. Telegram from Thurston, Chargé in Costa Rica, to Charles Evan Hughes, U.S. Secretary of State, February 24, 1921, FRUS 1921, 1:646.

41. Costa Rican concern about this is mentioned in US diplomatic correspondence. Telegram from Martin, Chargé in Costa Rica, to the Acting Secretary of State, December 31, 1920, FRUS 1920, 1:839.

42. Telegram from Thurston, Chargé in Costa Rica, to Charles Evan Hughes, U.S. Secretary of State, August 12, 1921, FRUS 1921, 1:665.

43. Great Britain initially recommended a Spanish minister as arbitrator, but Costa Rica rejected this suggestion and counter-offered ex-Costa Rican President Jimenez. Spanish interests had also been repudiated in the Law of Nullities, and it is possible that Costa Rica perceived Spain as having fewer long-run interests in maintaining positive relations. Telegram from Thurston (Chargé in Costa Rica) to Hughes, August 12, 1921, FRUS 1921, 1:665. Indeed even the US chargé acknowledged that the choice of the Spanish minister would likely result in a decision in favor of British interests. Telegram from Thurston to Hughes, February 14, 1921, FRUS 1921, 1:646.

44. Telegram from Thurston to Hughes, August 18, 1921, FRUS 1921, 1:666.

45. Great Britain v. Costa Rica (*Tinoco Case,* October 18, 1923), *Record of International Arbitral Awards,* vol. 1 (1923), 369, 381–382, reprinted in *American Journal of International Law* 18, no. 1 (1924): 153–154.

46. See, among others, Ashfaq Khalfan, Jeff King, and Bryan Thomas, "Advancing the Odious Debt Doctrine," McGill University Centre for International Sustainable Development Law Working Paper (2003), 13–14; Rob Howse, "The Concept of Odious Debt in Public International Law," UNCTAD Discussion Paper No. 185 (July 2007), 11–12.

47. *Tinoco Case,* 150–151, citing John Bassett Moore, *Digest of International Law,* vol. 1 (Washington, DC: GPO, 1906), 249. Justice Taft cites several other authorities to the same effect on pages 150–151.

48. It is also worth pointing out that one reason for the acquiescence of the people to the Tinoco regime even as its popularity plummeted may have been Wilson's own nonrecognition policy. Wilson indicated that he would not recognize a government established in a counterrevolution, and this could have dampened Costa Rican efforts to overthrow Tinoco for a time, extending the period for which Tinoco had effective control of the country.

49. Ibid., 149, 154–155.

50. Ibid., 154.

51. Taft specifically stated, "The merits of the policy of the United States in this non-recognition it is not for the arbitrator to discuss," and noted that he was drawing purely from international law principles. Ibid., 153.

52. Modern-day proponents of a Wilsonian ideal of popular sovereignty criticize this finding in Taft's decision, which may well be used as a shield by oppressive regimes seeking to avoid international censure. Michael Reisman, among others, expresses concern that the *Tinoco* decision "stands in stark contradiction to the new constitutive, human rights-based conception of popular sovereignty." W. Michael Reisman, "Sovereignty and Human Rights in Contemporary International Law," *American Journal of International Law* 84 (1990): 870.

53. *Tinoco Case,* 172.

54. Ibid., 173–174.

55. Ibid., 169. Taft quickly acknowledged that the British assignees of the concession had acted properly under the contract, and dismissed Costa Rica's argument that Great Britain could not bring a claim on behalf of a company incorporated in the United States. Ibid., 171–172.

56. Ibid., 173.

57. According to the facts of the case, the taxing power was one of the ten exclusive congressional powers enumerated under article 26 of the 1917 Costa Rican Constitution. Ibid., 172.

58. Ibid., 173.

59. Ibid. Taft further writes that this exemption was "too vital an element in its value" to be excluded from the contract. Ibid., 174.

60. Ibid., 174.

61. For more on Austin and others, see the discussion of the theoretical bases of sovereignty in chapter 2.

62. This means that, in Taft's framework, a contract can be invalidated on one of two grounds: either a violation of the internal rule of law *or* inconsistency with legitimate government purpose. (Both prongs would be contingent on creditor knowledge, as is discussed later in this section.) This differs somewhat from Alexander Sack's formalized doctrine of odious debt, in which a government contract must meet all three prongs (despotism/lack of consent, nonbeneficial purpose, and creditor knowledge) before being considered odious. In other words, to be valid in the Taftian framework, a contract must be both consistent with internal rule of law and in service of a legitimate government purpose.

63. This is approximately $2,800,000 in 20013 dollars.

64. *Tinoco Case,* 168.

65. Ibid., 168.

66. Ibid., 168.

67. Ibid., 167.

68. Ibid., 168.

69. Considerable case law has developed to explain the standard of care and investigation involved in meeting this requirement. For an extensive discussion of how requirements vary across different types of business transaction, see Gary M. Lawrence, *Due Diligence in Business Transactions* (New York: Law Journal Press, 1994).

70. *Tinoco Case,* 168.

71. Ibid., 168.

72. Alpheus Thomas Mason, *William Howard Taft: Chief Justice* (New York: Simon and Schuster, 1965), 13.

73. Taft considered the judiciary to be, among other things, the institution designed for the protection of property rights. Mason, *Taft,* 291. Henry Pringle notes that, at his 1921 appointment to the Supreme Court, the fact that Justice Taft "was conservative, if not reactionary, in his political and social views is not

open to question. . . . To Taft, clearly, the difference between conservatism and radicalism was the difference between right and wrong, between the known and the unknown, between the sound and the unsound." Henry F. Pringle, *The Life and Times of William Howard Taft* (New York: Farrar and Rinehart, 1939), 967.

74. In fact, Taft's view of major corporate actors was decidedly mixed. He wrote in a letter to his broather, "[a]s you say, Wall Street, as an aggregation, is the biggest ass that I have ever run across." Letter from W.H. Taft to Henry Taft (Feb. 21, 1910), quoted in Henry F. Pringle, *The Life and Times of William Howard Taft: A Biography*, vol. 2 (New York: Farrar and Rinehart, 1939), 655.

75. J. L. Brierly, "Arbitration Between Great Britain and Costa Rica," *British Yearbook of International Law* 6 (1925): 204.

76. "Costa Rica Wins Amory Case," *Wall Street Journal,* October 20, 1923, 4. American newspaper reports tended to focus on the oil concession rather than the bank loan.

77. Costa Rican leaders proposed paying off this French debt in full, while the franc was severely depreciated, but the bondholders demanded payment in dollars, pounds, or gold francs. This resulted in diplomatic tensions and the halting of a refinancing loan in the United States intended to replace the French debt. Thomas Schoonover, *The French in Central America: Culture and Commerce, 1820–1930* (Wilmington, DE: Scholarly Resources, 2000), 166–168.

78. "Costa Rica Shows Big Financial Gain," *New York Times,* May 20, 1928, 33. At the time, Moody's had begun publishing sovereign credit ratings but did not have a rating for Costa Rica.

79. See the discussion above of the internal governmental disagreement in Costa Rica surrounding the repudiation decree.

80. Although companies might enter into agreements with the Tinoco regime in Costa Rica, it would have been more difficult for Western banks to facilitate securities issued on their own soil.

81. Indeed, Soviet leaders themselves ultimately did not seem to consider the repudiation to be incompatible with capitalism, pointing out that the regime would have to play by the rules of repaying *its own* debt in order to maintain (capitalist) international economic relations with foreign creditors. For more, see the discussion in chapter 3.

82. In the Far East, Taft's presidential administration displayed far greater concern than previous administrations with promoting concessions for American banks and corporations. Walter V. Scholes and Marie V. Scholes, *The Foreign Policies of the Taft Administration* (Columbia: University of Missouri Press, 1970), 109.

83. Scholes and Scholes, *Foreign Policies,* 247–248.

84. The British had been historically interested in establishing a Central American foothold in the Spanish Empire, and they founded a logging colony at present day Belize as early as 1622. Leonard, "Central America," 4.

85. Robert Freeman Smith, "Latin America, the United States, and the European Powers, 1830–1930," in *The Cambridge History of Latin America,* vol. 4, ed. Leslie Bethel (New York: Cambridge University Press, 1986), 112.

86. Commentators have remarked upon the unity of the motivating factors behind the Roosevelt, Taft, and Wilson approaches to the Latin American and particularly the Caribbean countries. See, for example, Michael J. Kryzanek, *U.S.-Latin American Relations,* 3rd ed. (Westport, CT: Praeger, 1996), 51.

87. Quoted in ibid., 29.

88. The Central Americans actually had made efforts to involve the United States as a bulwark against foreign intervention earlier, particularly as Britain had laid claim to the Caribbean coast as far south as the San Juan River (on the border of Costa Rica and Nicaragua) by the mid-1840s. Leonard, "Central America," 5. Notwithstanding the efforts of Central American elites to become economically closer to the United States, Central America remained dependent upon British and German merchants and markets as of 1900. Kryzanek, *U.S.-Latin American Relations,* 7.

89. Kryzanek, *U.S.-Latin American Relations,* 48.

90. Ibid., 7.

91. For an excellent overview of "dollar diplomacy" in the early twentieth century, see generally Munro, *Intervention.* Wilson, despite his initial wish to stay out of Central America, also followed the policies of his predecessors. See, for example, ibid., 51.

92. The Clayton-Bulwer Treaty of 1850, negotiated in response to the British taking control of the mouth of the San Juan river, provided that neither the United States nor Britain would attempt to control any part of Central America or any possible canal. See ibid., 4.

93. For a discussion of Taft's work on the Panama Canal, see Ralph Eldin Minger, *William Howard Taft and U.S. Foreign Policy: The Apprenticeship Years, 1900–1908* (Urbana: University of Illinois Press, 1975), 102–117, and David H. Burton, *William Howard Taft: Confident Peacemaker* (New York: Fordham University Press, 2004), 37–40. Taft took a special interest in maintaining stable republics in Central America given American interests, and he believed that stability in the Central American republics was even more desirable than peace in South America, due to their proximity to the Panama Canal. Pringle, *Life and Times,* 697.

94. British Ambassador (A. C. Geddes) to the Secretary of State (Charles Hughes), May 19, 1921, FRUS 1921, 1:662. Indeed, Mexico, which had been a borrowing country for over a century in all the major capital markets, had defaulted on its debt (particularly that of Porfirio Diaz) in 1914.

95. The Secretary of State (Hughes) to the British Ambassador (Geddes), May 24, 1921, FRUS 1921, 1:663.

96. Cable from Moore to Hale, December 2, 1913, FRUS 1919, 1:866, also cited in Munro, *Intervention,* 431.

97. The American Sinclair Oil Company was able to obtain a Costa Rican concession in 1916. Munro provides an excellent narrative of US interests in Costa Rica, paying special attention to oil concerns. Munro, *Intervention,* 426–448.

98. The US chargé in San Jose felt that the interest of President Acosta and the Minister for Foreign Affairs in protecting the Amory concession had a strategic

dimension in that they wished to diversify out of entirely American oil concessions. Chargé in Costa Rica (Thurston) to the Secretary of State, February 24, 1921, FRUS 1921, 1:646–647.

99. Chargé in Costa Rica (Thurston) to the Secretary of State, February 25, 1921, FRUS 1921, 1:647.

100. Secretary of State Hughes to the Chargé in Great Britain (Wright), April 15, 1921, FRUS 1921, 1:651–652. Secretary Hughes instructed Wright to address a note to the British Foreign Office to this effect.

101. The United States had initially supported the Sinclair Oil Company in their defense of an oil concession granted by Gonzalez but then definitively approved by Tinoco, which had also been repudiated by Law No. 41. The determination by 1923 that there was in fact little oil in the Caribbean basin would have lessened Taft's concerns on this front, however. Munro, *Intervention,* 448. In any case, by 1923 there would have been little love for Sinclair in the American government, as the oil company was also implicated in the Teapot Scandal of 1923. Pringle, *Life and Times,* 1020.

Chapter 5. Public and Private Capital in Mid-Century Repayment Norms

1. This change in the major actors involved in international lending has been remarked upon. See, for example, Randall Germain's discussion of the macrohistory of the capital recycling mechanism. Randall Germain, *The International Organization of Credit* (Cambridge: Cambridge University Press, 1997). Of post-World War II capital movements in particular, he writes that they were, "made possible only through the active intervention of public authorities, who took it upon themselves to reverse a decade and a half of inadequate private capital recycling. . . . The story of the Bretton Woods era, therefore, revolves around the ways and means in which public authorities worked to re-establish a global credit system consistent with the domestic aims and ambitions of those states with the strongest and most important postwar economies." Germain, *International Organization of Credit,* 75.

2. Henry Morgenthau, Letter to President Truman, quoted in *The New York Herald-Tribune,* March 31, 1946. In Richard N. Gardner, *Sterling-Dollar Diplomacy: The Origins and the Prospects of Our International Economic Order* (New York: McGraw-Hill, 1969), 76.

3. For a thoughtful discussion of the factors shaping World Bank and IMF policy, including those elements that led them to prescribe more aggressive global liberalization than their founders might have supported, see Ngaire Woods, *The Globalizers: The IMF, the World Bank, and Their Borrowers* (Ithaca, NY: Cornell University Press, 2006).

4. While the new development bank was initially involved in European reconstruction, the scale of that project so clearly overtook its capacity that the US government became more deeply involved with the launching of the Marshall

Plan. A similar plan was established for Japan and for the entrenchment of a US presence in the Pacific.

5. This lending division is highlighted in Devesh Kapur, John P. Lewis, and Richard Webb, *The World Bank: Its First Half Century: Perspectives,* vol. 2 (Washington, DC: Brookings Institution, 1997), 142. They note that the US focus broadened somewhat in the late 1950s and early 1960s, when the Cold War shifted from the "periphery" of the American sphere of influence to more general political competition, but note that, as of 1960, the United States was spending only 2 percent of its economic aid money on Latin America and even less in Africa. Kapur et al., *World Bank,* 142.

6. Kapur, Lewis, and Webb point out, "In such developing regions as Sub-Saharan Africa and parts of South Asia, the scale of private foreign investment available was small relative to the need for external capital." Kapur et al., *World Bank,* 452. Jeff Frieden also notes the change from pre-World War II FDI concentrations in developing country agriculture or mining to a postwar FDI focus on developed country manufacturing. "By the 1960s the typical foreign direct investment was a factory in a developed country. Now American companies had three times as much invested in Europe and Japan than in Latin America, primarily in factories." Jeffry A. Frieden, *Global Capitalism: Its Fall and Rise in the Twentieth Century* (New York: W. W. Norton, 2006), 293.

7. Private banks began as lenders to the Bank and then became more directly involved in sovereign lending, in part through the use of International Finance Corporation (IFC) guarantees. The Bank also raised money from loan sales, that is, selling a portion of its own borrower obligations, which helped to establish the borrower's credit rating and direct relationship with the financial community. For a brief discussion of this dynamic, see Kapur et al., *World Bank,* 924.

8. "Proposal for a United Nations Stabilization Fund and a Bank for Reconstruction and Development of the United and Associated Nations" (April 1942). International Monetary Fund Records Office. Quoted in Edward S. Mason and Robert E. Asher, *The World Bank since Bretton Woods* (Washington, DC: Brookings Institution, 1973), 15.

9. Contrary to what is often assumed, a number of non-Western countries were involved in the initial planning stages of the Bretton Woods institutions. Eric Helleiner argues that early 1940s US-Latin American relations in particular shaped the Bretton Woods discussions, incubating the IBRD's original commitment to economic development and its suspicion of private finance. Eric Helleiner, "The Development Mandate of International Institutions: Where Did it Come From?," *Studies in Comparative International Development* 44 (2009): 189-211; Eric Helleiner, "Reinterpreting Bretton Woods: International Development and the Neglected Origins of Embedded Liberalism," *Development and Change* 37, no. 5 (2006): 943-967. See also Helleiner's discussion in "Active at the Creation: China and the Bretton Woods Negotiations," working paper on file with author (November 2012).

10. Quoted in Mason and Asher, *World Bank,* 18. Morgenthau noted that "with the return of an assured peace, private financial agencies may be expected to supply most of the needed short-term foreign capital." However, he felt that an international agency would be needed to reestablish long-term lending. "The primary aim of such an agency should be to encourage private capital to go abroad for productive investment by sharing the risks of private investors in large ventures." Quoted in ibid., 18.

11. Eugene Black commented that the major credit rating agencies' unwillingness to warm to Bank bonds resulted from "a disposition to be ultra-conservative on anything labeled 'international.'" Letter, Eugene R. Black to Maple T. Harl, chairman FDIC, January 29, 1951, 2, cited in Kapur et al., *World Bank,* 929. See also Frieden, *Global Capitalism,* 293 (noting that, in addition to being burned by the 1930s' defaults, bankers had sufficient domestic opportunities for profit); Karin Lissakers, *Banks, Borrowers, and the Establishment: A Revisionist Account of the International Debt Crisis* (New York: Basic Books, 1991), 15 (highlighting how the "debt debacle" of the 1930s "was followed by a hiatus in private foreign lending of more than twenty years during which few countries had access to commercial financing outside their own borders.")

12. Youssef Cassis, *Capitals of Capital: A History of International Financial Centres, 1780–2005* (Cambridge: Cambridge University Press, 2006), 201.

13. When Hitler's finance minister warned President Roosevelt in 1933 that Germany might not be able to service $2 billion in debt held by American investors, Roosevelt is said to have responded, "Serves the Wall Street bankers right!" Roosevelt's advisors encouraged him the following day to alter his response. Ron Chernow, *The House of Morgan: An American Banking Dynasty and the Rise of Modern Finance* (New York: Atlantic Monthly Press, 1990), 395. The US Senate Committee on Banking and Currency found the flotation of foreign securities by major investment banks "one of the most scandalous chapters in the history of American investment banking. The sale of these foreign issues was characterized by practices and abuses which were violative of the most elementary principles of business ethics." John T. Madden, Marcus Nadler, and Harry C. Sauvain, *America's Experience as a Creditor Nation* (New York: Prentice-Hall, 1937), 205.

14. Gardner, *Sterling-Dollar Diplomacy,* 76.

15. Address of Morgenthau at the final session of the Bretton Woods Conference, July 22, 1944, cited in Gardner, *Sterling- Dollar Diplomacy,* 76.

16. Eugene Staley, *War and the Private Investor* (Garden City, NY: Doubleday, Doran, 1935), as cited in Frieden, *Global Capitalism,* 258.

17. Harry Dexter White, "Preliminary Draft: United Nations Stabilization Fund and A Bank for Reconstruction and Development of the United and Associated Nations," March 1942, HDWP, Box 6, Folder 6, II-59, quoted in Eric Helleiner, *Forgotten Foundations of Bretton Woods* (Ithaca, NY: Cornell University Press, forthcoming 2014), chapter 5; manuscript draft on file with author. For a discussion of these proposals, along with an analysis of three other failed

proposals for sovereign debt restructuring mechanisms since the 1930s, see Eric Helleiner, "The Mystery of the Missing Sovereign Debt Restructuring Mechanism," *Contributions to Political Economy* 97 (2008): 91–113.

18. Harry Dexter White, "Suggested Plan for a United Nations Stabilization Fund and a United Nations Bank," January 1942, BWA, Box 44, 23, quoted in Helleiner, *Forgotten Foundations*, chapter 5.

19. White, "Preliminary Draft," III-12,13, quoted in Helleiner, *Forgotten Foundations*, chapter 5.

20. Ibid., III-13.

21. The exception is listed in White, "Suggested Plan," 23, quoted in Helleiner, *Forgotten Foundations*, chapter 5.

22. Quoted in Helleiner, "Mystery of the Missing Sovereign Debt Restructuring Mechanism," 102.

23. Mason and Asher, *World Bank,* 12.

24. Helleiner argues, based on newly available archival evidence, that White's early proposals for the Bank had more development content than has been understood previously. See Helleiner, *Forgotten Foundations*, chapter 5.

25. Opening Remarks of Lord Keynes at the First Meeting of the Second Commission on the Bank for Reconstruction and Development, cited in Kapur et al., *World Bank,* 60.

26. Address of the Honorable Henry Morgenthau, President of the Conference, at the Closing Plenary Session, July 22, 1944, cited in Kapur et al., *World Bank,* 912. Kapur, Lewis, and Webb highlight the contentious Treasury-Wall Street relationship and note that part of the impetus for locating the Bretton Woods institutions in Washington was to establish a new power center for international finance. This went against the wishes of the New York financial community and the British, who were concerned about the institutions becoming embroiled in US politics. Kapur et al., *World Bank,* 911–915.

27. Gardner, *Sterling-Dollar Diplomacy,* 77. For a discussion of the American debate on approval of the Bretton Woods institutions, see ibid., 129–144. It was seemingly during this debate that the phrase "pouring money down a rat hole" was first used in the context of the international financial institutions. Ibid., 130. An overview on the British debate, which was somewhat less contentious, is available at ibid., 128–129.

28. These early attempts are detailed in Kapur et al., *World Bank,* 915 et seq. Although the US dollar dominated the currency structure of the Bank's debt, the geographical origin of its funding eventually diversified, with the US share falling from almost 90 percent in 1949 to around 40 percent in 1959. Ibid., 925.

29. Ibid., 911.

30. Collado was the last of the New Deal officials in the Bank. His successor as US executive director, Eugene Black (who became the Bank's next president from 1949 to 1962), had been senior vice president at Chase National Bank. IBRD vice president Robert Garner had previously been treasurer of the Guaranty Trust Company. Ibid., 915.

31. Eugene H. Rotberg, *The World Bank: A Financial Appraisal* (Washington, DC: World Bank, January 1981), 12. The longevity of this self-identification as a "bank" is especially striking given the avowed shift in the Bank's focus away from large-scale, "productive" industrial and infrastructure lending to long-term poverty alleviation under McNamara's tenure. In fact, Mason and Asher point out that this shift toward poverty-oriented lending was a result of McNamara being influenced by Kennedy administration officials especially concerned with social welfare.

32. Notes in Bank files on meeting of May 21, 1947, of Garner and Burland (for the Bank) with Pedregal, Vergara, Santa Cruz, and Levine (for Chile), cited in Mason and Asher, *World Bank*, 156–157.

33. Letter, Eugene R. Black to Maple T. Harl, chairman FDIC, January 29, 1951, 2, cited in Kapur et al., *World Bank*, 929.

34. Kapur et al., *World Bank*, 928–929.

35. International Bank for Reconstruction and Development/International Development Association (IBRD/IDA), "Creditworthiness Analysis," confidential draft, December 11, 1968, 2, para. 5. On file with author. I am indebted to Devesh Kapur for access to the internal memoranda referenced in this section, which he collected during research for *The World Bank: Its First Half-Century*.

36. IBRD/IDA, "Creditworthiness Analysis," 2, para. 4.

37. Mason and Asher, *World Bank*, 156n9.

38. As noted in earlier chapters, the first two alternatives constitute the elements of the odious debt doctrine as formulated by Alexander Sack in 1927, which states that sovereign state debt is "odious" and should not be transferable to successors if the debt was incurred (1) without the consent of the people, and (2) not for their benefit.

39. Kapur et al., *World Bank*, 453–454.

40. Harold Larsen, World Bank Oral History Program, 1961, 16, cited in Mason and Asher, *World Bank*, 157–158.

41. Kapur, Lewis, and Webb highlight Guatemala's unwillingness to settle, but the exact grounds for this refusal remain unclear. Kapur et al., *World Bank*, 106.

42. Arbenz was especially concerned with economic reform and development, and in fact the IBRD conducted a General Survey Mission in Guatemala after his 1950 election. Mason and Asher, *World Bank*, 302. Notwithstanding this commitment, Arbenz himself was not able to obtain a loan from the Bank, presumably due to the unsettled debts. Even the US-installed Colonel Armas, flown in on the US ambassador's plane after the coup against Arbenz, was unable to obtain a loan for ten more years.

43. The guerilla war was estimated to kill approximately 150,000 Indonesians and 6,000 Dutch citizens. Kapur, Lewis, and Webb suggest that the Bank leadership's underlying political discomfort with the popular and left-leaning Sukarno may also have been an issue. Kapur et al., *World Bank*, 106. Indonesia finally joined the Bank in 1954, but withdrew in 1965, shortly before the coup that overthrew Sukarno and installed General Suharto. Mason and Asher, *World Bank*, 64. It rejoined in 1967 and eventually became a preferred borrower of the Bank.

44. Mason and Asher, *World Bank,* 181. They emphasize this element of immorality again in discussing how the Bank chose to assess debt repayment capacity: "[According to Bank management] international lending based on any other conception than that "debts are debts" was considered as not only financially irresponsible but immoral." Ibid., 213.

45. The cyclical nature of lending and the occasional myopia of lenders is a favorite topic for economists and international economic historians. See, for example, Carmen M. Reinhart and Kenneth Rogoff, *This Time is Different: Eight Centuries of Financial Folly* (Princeton, NJ: Princeton University Press, 2009). One engaging account of the development of the debt crisis in the 1970s and 1980s, in part as a result of this myopia, is offered in Lissakers's *Banks, Borrowers, and the Establishment.* Lissakers also served as US executive director to the IMF in the 1990s.

46. See, for example, Germain, *International Organization of Credit,* 75.

47. Debtors' actions could undermine the general practice of debt repayment and with it the credit standing of the new IBRD and, more generally, the stability of the post-World War II US-centered economic order.

48. Kapur, Lewis, and Webb point out that debtors had nowhere to turn: "The effectiveness of nonlending as a leverage tool depends on how easy it is for would-be borrowers rebuffed by the Bank to find alternative funding, as well as how firmly the institution has defined and pursued its policy preferences." Kapur et al., *World Bank,* 449.

49. One reason that Bank loan terms conformed to market standards was to get borrowers "accustomed to conventional lending terms so that they adjust their financial practices to conditions they would meet if they were to borrow on their own credit." Ibid., 927.

50. Ibid., 927. The establishment of IDA loan facilities with more concessional terms deviated from this standard somewhat and was initially controversial. In fact, the main Bank group actually fought against the establishment of IDA and only adopted the project when it appeared that a similar lending organization might find an institutional home at the United Nations through UNCTAD.

51. "International Bank for Reconstruction and Development: Articles of Agreement between the United States of America and Other Powers," December 7, 1944, in *U.S. Treaties and Other International Acts Series,* No. 1502 (Department of State Publication 2511) (Washington, DC: GPO, 1946).

52. The legal facets of this interaction are provided in helpful detail in Samuel Bleicher, "UN v. IBRD: A Dilemma of Functionalism," *International Organization* 24, no. 1 (Winter, 1970): 31–47.

53. Resolution 1514 (XV), December 14, 1960, and Resolution 1654 (XVI), November 21, 1961.

54. UN Document A/AC.109/124 and Corr.1 (June 10, 1965), cited in Bleicher, "UN v. IBRD," 32.

55. General Assembly Resolution 2054 (XX), December 15, 1965, para. 10, cited in Bleicher, "UN v. IBRD," 32.

56. This language is in General Assembly Resolutions 2107 (XX), December 21, 1965, and 2184 (XXI), December 12, 1966, and Security Council Resolutions 191 of June 18, 1964, and 218 of November 23, 1965. Also cited in Bleicher, "UN v. IBRD," 38. I agree with Bleicher's assessment that the secretariat's reading of article 4, section 10 as referring only to internal political characteristics is inaccurate: "The section was certainly intended to prevent the bank from discriminating against members who, for example, refuse to recognize, trade with, or ally with other powerful members of the bank." Bleicher, "UN v. IBRD," 40.

57. Bleicher points out that the Security Council, in Resolutions 191 (1964) of June 18, 1964, and 218 (1965) of November 23, 1965, found the Portuguese colonial and South African apartheid policies to be in violation of the principles of the Charter of the United Nations, as had the General Assembly. Resolution 191, pertaining to apartheid policies in South Africa, indicated that apartheid South Africa "is continuing seriously to disturb international peace and security." Resolution 218 also "affirmed" that Portuguese colonial policies "seriously disturb[] international peace and security" and requested all states "to refrain from offering the Portuguese Government any assistance which would enable it to continue its repression of the people of the Territories under its administration." Bleicher, "UN v. IBRD," 41n41.

58. Quoted in General Assembly *Official Records*, Fourth Committee (twenty-first session), 1645th meeting, November 28, 1966, 318. Cited in Bleicher, "UN v. IBRD," 33.

59. Charter of the United Nations, article 2, section 1.

60. UN General Assembly Declaration 1960, 13cf27—UN Review (January 1961), 6 et seq.

61. UN General Assembly Resolution 2625 (XXV), October 24, 1970, Principle 5, para. 1.

62. This principle was affirmed by the International Court of Justice in *Frontier Dispute Case (Burkina Faso v. Mali)* (1986) ICJ 554, in which the Court stated, "[Uti possidetis] is a general principle, which is logically connected with the phenomenon of obtaining independence, wherever it occurs. Its obvious purpose is to prevent the independence and stability of new states being endangered by fratricidal struggles provoked by the changing of frontiers following the withdrawal of the administering power." Ibid., 565.

63. See Stephen D. Krasner, *Sovereignty: Organized Hypocrisy* (Princeton, NJ: Princeton University Press, 1999). While a grant of sovereignty formally warranted a large degree of control over internal and external actions, these capabilities may in fact be very limited.

64. See, for example, article III(2) of the Charter of the Organization for African Unity, reasserting the centrality of "non-interference in the internal affairs of states."

65. A. Bolaji Akinyemi, "The Organization of African Unity and the Concept of Non-Interference in Internal Affairs of Member-States," in *Third World*

Attitudes toward International Law, ed. Frederick Snyder and Surakiart Sathi-rathai (Boston, MA: M. Nijhoff, 1987), 85.

66. This is not at all to deny that there existed significant ideological conflict between newly emerging states and the Western leaders of the postwar global order. There was considerable disagreement on how best to manage the transition from colony to independent state, in the economic no less than in the political arena. However, this divergence is best characterized as a clash *within* the statist approach, in particular between its continuous and discontinuous forms. As I noted in chapter 2, a statist approach to sovereignty would allow any government with control of its territory and people to enter into sovereign contracts, regardless of its internal form of rule. On this substantive point the major Western states and the newly independent and emerging nations, many of which were authoritarian, agreed. They disagreed on how preexisting contracts might be ab-rogated (such as in expropriation), and on the appropriate forum for making and adjudicating such contract cancellations or modifications. Nonetheless, the basic statist framework of sovereignty remained fairly stable.

67. A classic account of this discussion among American policy makers is pre-sented in Arthur M. Schlesinger Jr., *Origins of the Cold War* (1967), excerpted in James V. Compton, ed., *America and the Origins of the Cold War* (Boston: Houghton Mifflin, 1972), 3. The universalists hoped for a system of collective security, modeled on the failed League of Nations but with a stronger commit-ment by the great powers to cooperate in the international arena. Advocates of a spheres-of-influence approach argued that the maintenance of American security and international order would be best served by traditional balance-of-power politics, in which major states would be buffered by security zones and separated by neutral territories, encouraging their secure coexistence. Schlesinger and other orthodox historians put much of the onus for the Cold War on the Soviet Union, characterizing American policy makers as merely responding to Soviet aggression. Revisionist historians such as William Appleman Williams and Gabriel Kolko argue that in fact Cold War policies were of a piece with larger, capitalist-driven American foreign policy trends. See, for example, William Appleman Williams, *The Tragedy of American Diplomacy,* 2nd ed. (New York: Dell, 1972), 202–306.

68. The Truman Doctrine, March 12, 1947, excerpted in John Spanier, "Amer-ican Foreign Policy Since 1945," in Compton, *Origins of the Cold War,* 34.

69. As quoted in Spanier, "American Foreign Policy," 34.

70. Indeed, the Truman Doctrine framed the global commitment to freedom as a support to domestic security: "Totalitarian regimes imposed on free peoples, by direct or indirect aggression, undermine the foundations of international peace and hence the security of the United States." Quoted in ibid., 35.

71. The US overthrow of Guatemala's Jacobo Arbenz, mentioned briefly above, offers only one example. Arbenz was elected in 1950 and was commit-ted to extensive social reform, including land reform. These left-leaning reform tendencies, which included permission for the organization of labor unions and

communist political parties, eventually led him to be branded "communist" himself. He was exiled after a 1954 coup in which Colonel Carlos Castillo Armas was flown into Guatemala City in the plane of the US ambassador and installed as president.

72. Anna Gelpern argues that official debt is "never extended at arm's length or for direct economic gain; the usual goal is policy influence over the borrower." Anna Gelpern, "Odious, Not Debt," *Law and Contemporary Problems* 70, no. 3 (2007): 83. She considers the motivations behind the US domestic law doctrines of equitable subordination and recharacterization for insight into dealing with official (and potentially odious) debt in the international public arena. Ibid., esp. 104–112.

73. This was of course not always the case, but US policy makers were certainly aware of the possibility that foreign aid loans would not be repaid. Gelpern quotes one participant in the 1960s' congressional debates as saying, "I think we are fooling ourselves and the world if we think that these loans are really going to be repaid. Indeed . . . [such] loans . . . tend in the very nature of the case to become disguised grants." Ibid., 95.

74. For a discussion of US influence in the World Bank and IMF, see Woods, *Globalizers*, 15-38. US financial assistance in the early Cold War era tended to be divided into targeted aid for preferred allies and more general support for "underdeveloped countries." In particular, the Point Four Program, named for the fourth point of Truman's 1949 inaugural address, aimed to boost aid and scientific and industrial progress in these areas. See Catherine Gwin, "U.S. Relations with the World Bank, 1945–1992," in Kapur et al., *World Bank*, vol. 2, 205.

75. Once the "reconstruction" aspect of the IBRD was taken over by the Marshall Plan and other similar aid programs, US support for the Bank waned somewhat. Gwin, "U.S. Relations," 204.

76. There were certainly exceptions to this, including World Bank loans to Yugoslavia after its 1948 break with the Soviet Union, in line with George Kennan's suggestion that the West not provide obvious support. Kapur et al., *World Bank*, 103.

77. Gwin points out that, by the late 1950s and early 1960s, the Soviet Union had developed nuclear weapons, launched Sputnik, and extended its diplomatic reach and offers of help to developing countries. In response, the Kennedy administration in particular increased US aid activity, including through the creation of the Peace Corps and the umbrella Agency for International Development (AID). In 1956, the United States dropped its opposition to the World Bank's International Finance Corporation (IFC), which helped to mobilize direct loans to private-sector corporations in developing countries. The Bank's International Development Association, which provided concessional loans to poor countries using government funds, was not established until 1960. See Gwin, "U.S. Relations."

78. This incident is mentioned in Kapur et al., *World Bank*, 455.

79. An overview of the Bank's pronounced hostility to official lending is available at ibid., 929–931.

80. Ibid., 931.

81. Ibid., 931.

82. Common Program of the Chinese People's Political Consultative Conference, articles 3 and 55, reprinted in *The Important Documents of the First Plenary Session of the Chinese People's Political Consultative Conference* (Peking: Foreign Languages Press, 1949), 1–20.

83. Foreign loans negotiated by Chinese regimes from 1861 until the Japanese invasion of 1937 came to $1.25 billion. Robert F. Dernberger, "The Role of the Foreigner in China's Economic Development, 1840–1949," in *China's Modern Economy in Historical Perspective,* ed. Dwight H. Perkins (Stanford, CA: Stanford University Press, 1975), 28–29; also cited in Lu Aiguo, *China and the Global Economy since 1840* (New York: St. Martin's Press, 2000), 43. This was not the amount outstanding at the declaration of the PRC, however. Customs revenues had been used to repay foreign loans and war indemnities during the period of foreign administration over customs collection. Lu, *China and the Global Economy,* 32.

84. The PRC's refusal to pay on both of these resulted in litigation and diplomatic negotiations. On the Huguang Railway bonds, see the discussion in James V. Feinerman, "Odious Debt, Old and New: The Legal Intellectual History of an Idea," *Law and Contemporary Problems* 70, no. 4 (2007): 193–220. Feinerman takes a closer look at the later US litigation surrounding these bonds, Jackson v. People's Republic of China, in which the PRC brought up the odious debt idea among other potential defenses to repayment. He concludes that the ultimate twentieth-century benefit to the PRC of the railway, despite the questionable origin of the bonds, would make them difficult to characterize as odious if Alexander Sack's or a similar doctrine were adopted by international law. Ibid., 201–202. The final outcome of the suit in Jackson was that the 11th Circuit affirmed a district court decision that it did not have subject matter jurisdiction over the case, as the Foreign Sovereign Immunities Act of 1976 did not apply retroactively. 794 F.2d 1490. See also the discussion in Monroe Leigh, "Case Notes, Jackson v. People's Republic of China, 596 F. Supp. 386," *American Journal of International Law* 79, no. 2 (April 1985): 456–458. The latter loan is still the subject of controversy in the United States, although the PRC came to some agreement with British and French bondholders in the late 1980s. "China, Britain Settle Claims," *New York Times,* June 8, 1987; "Historical Debts Accord Clears Way for China to Eurobonds," *Xinhua General Overseas News Service,* June 5, 1987.

85. For the presentations in the *New York Times,* see Tillman Durdin, "Peiping Bond Sale Aimed at Wealthy," *New York Times,* January 12, 1950, 11; Will Lissner, "Communist China Seeks Cash Here in Secret Campaign to Sell Bonds," *New York Times,* February 5, 1950, 1; Tillman Durdin, "Red China to Launch a New Bond Issue to Finance Continuance of 5-Year Plan," *New York Times,* December 9, 1953, 3.

86. Lu, *China and the Global Economy,* 84, 98; see also Erika Platte, "China's Foreign Debt," *Pacific Affairs* 66, no. 4 (Winter, 1993–1994): 481.

87. Platte, "China's Foreign Debt," 485.

88. Ann Helwege, "Three Socialist Experiences in Latin America: Surviving US Economic Pressure," *Bulletin of Latin American Research* 8, no. 2 (1989): 214.

89. The Department of Commerce survey further noted that US interests included "[over] 90 per cent of telephone and electric services, about 50 per cent in public service railways, and roughly 40 per cent in raw sugar production. The Cuban branches of United States banks are entrusted with almost one-fourth of all bank deposits." Quoted in Leland L. Johnson, "U.S. Business Interests in Cuba and the Rise of Castro," *World Politics* 17, no. 3 (April 1965): 443. Foreign (especially North American) interests also owned significant portions of sugar plantations, chemical and rubber processing, cement production, and cattle ranching. By the early 1950s, the cumulative value of American investments in Cuba exceeded that even in Mexico. Helwege, "Three Socialist Experiences," 214–215.

90. As noted in Johnson, "U.S. Business Interests in Cuba," 454.

91. In particular, it focused on overthrowing Batista, who had been an important strongman since 1933 (with an interlude in the forties), but became increasingly problematic after he took power in a 1952 coup. For an overview, see Jorge I. Dominguez, "The Batista Regime in Cuba," in *Sultanistic Regimes,* ed. H. E. Chehabi and Juan J. Linz (Baltimore and London: The Johns Hopkins University Press, 1998), 113–131.

92. "Cuba Land 'Reforms' Become Law; U.S. Sugar Properties Threatened," *Wall Street Journal,* June 8, 1959, 20. While many inside and outside Cuba agreed with the need for land reform, this particular law caused a major split in the new Cuban cabinet, perhaps marking the first shift toward an explicitly socialist republic under Castro's control. R. Hart Phillips, "Land Law Splits Castro's Regime," *New York Times,* June 13, 1959, 1. Cuba cited as precedent the use of similar bonds as payment for Japanese land reform under the American occupation. The United States argued that, while such payment might be acceptable for domestic landowners, it was insufficient for foreign investors. E. W. Kenworthy, "U.S. Seeks Talk with Cuba on Land-Seizure Payments," *New York Times,* January 10, 1960, 1, 33.

93. Archibald R. M. Ritter, "The Compensation Issue in Cuban-US Normalization: Who Compensates Whom, Why and How?," in *Cuba in the International System: Normalization and Integration,* ed. Archibald R. M. Ritter and John M. Kirk (New York: St. Martin's Press, 1995), 269. Other enterprises included Coca-Cola bottling plants and Sears and Woolworth stores. "Reaction to Seizure," *Wall Street Journal,* October 26, 1960, 28. National City Bank, the largest US bank operating in Cuba, estimated its losses in January 1961 at $45 million; it had already written off around $36 million in 1960 when branches were unable to remit earnings from loans, made mostly to US-owned companies working in Cuba. "First National City Bares Cuba Loss," *New York Times,* January 18, 1961, 43; "Big Bank Registers its 'Losses' in Cuba," *New York Times,* January 13, 1961, 46. Chase estimated $14.8 million in actual and potential losses, including capital

investments in branches and the earnings those branches were unable to remit to the United States. "Chase Bank Says Loss of its Cuban Branches Comes to $14.8 million," *Wall Street Journal,* January 24, 1961. As an apparent exception to the lack of compromise on all sides, the government did take over the operations of the Royal Bank of Canada (held through twenty-three branches) in exchange for $8.4 million, perhaps in part due to Cuba's interest in developing closer commercial ties with Canada. See R. Hart Phillips, "Cuba Funds Saved by Canadian Bank," *New York Times,* December 11, 1960, 34; "Cuba Pays 8 Million for Bank Interests," *New York Times,* January 13, 1961, 39.

94. As quoted in Johnson, "U.S. Business Interests in Cuba," 445.

95. R. Hart Phillips, "Cuba's Bank Chief Views U.S. as Foe in Economic Fight," *New York Times,* March 21, 1960, 1. See also Johnson, "U.S. Business Interests in Cuba," 445. Johnson's article provides a good overview of the shift in approach from 1959 to 1960.

96. "Cuba Withdraws from World Bank," *New York Times,* October 19, 1960, 21. Particularly as Cuba under the Batista regime fell squarely into the US sphere of activity, neither the Bank nor the International Finance Corporation had made any investments in Cuba. World Bank, "Cuba Withdraws from IBRD and IFC," World Bank Press Release, November 15, 1960 (Washington, DC: World Bank Group, 1960).

97. "Cuba Defaults on Dollar Bonds for the First Time Since 1935," *New York Times,* January 4, 1961, 6. At the same time, it failed to submit payment for an additional $1.4 million to pay off bonds called for redemption by the Manufacturers Trust Company. However, funds were made available for a November 1 payment on a smaller $8 million issue of 4 percent bonds due in 1983. "Holders of Cuban Bonds Fear Interest Payment Might be Suspended," *Wall Street Journal,* January 4, 1961, 17.

98. Paul Heffernan, "Congress Acting on Expropriation, *New York Times,* May 13, 1962, F1.

99. Helwege, "Three Socialist Experiences," 216. The United States also pushed an embargo through the Organization of American States that lasted until the mid-1970s.

100. This involved a number of banks in freezing Cuban assets. See "Government Freezes Cuban Assets in U.S. Stepped-Up Effort to Isolate Castro," *Wall Street Journal,* July 9, 1963, 6.

101. Banco Nacional de Cuba v. National City Bank, 406 U.S. 759 (1972). The Supreme Court remanded the case to the lower court for further proceedings, and the district court ultimately found in favor of National City Bank but determined that the compensation amounts claimed, which included speculative expected profits, were excessive.

102. The United States and Western Europe disagreed over the risks of Soviet influence in Cuba, and some European countries resisted the US trade embargo even during the Berlin crisis of the early 1960s. Washington Wire, *Wall Street Journal,* September 21, 1962, 1.

103. The Cuban relationship with the British Leyland Motor Company is an interesting example. Leyland first became involved in Cuba in the 1920s and 1930s and continued providing public buses and related parts and services through the early 1970s. George Lambie, "Anglo-Cuban Commercial Relations in the 1960s: A Case Study of the Leyland Motor Company Contracts with Cuba," in *The Fractured Blockade: Western European-Cuban Relations During the Revolution,* ed. Alistair Hennessy and George Lambie (London and Basingstoke: MacMillan, 1993). One key component of the relationship was the willingness of Leyland to grant five-year credit terms backed by the British government, a factor that was particularly galling to the US government. Lambie, "Anglo-Cuban Commercial Relations," 168–170.

104. "Cuba Prohibits Foreign Capital; Holdings by Citizens Outlawed," *New York Times,* May 7, 1961, 4.

Chapter 6. Continuity and Consolidation in the Return of Private Finance

1. It is estimated that the OPEC countries accumulated $383 billion in liquid assets between 1974 and 1980, much of which was deposited in the major American and European banks. Youssef Cassis, *Capitals of Capital: A History of International Financial Centres, 1780–2005* (Cambridge: Cambridge University Press, 2006), 236.

2. Stefano Battilossi, "International Banking and the American Challenge in Historical Perspective," in *European Banks and the American Challenge: Competition and Cooperation in International Banking under Bretton Woods,* ed. Stefano Battilossi and Youssef Cassis (Oxford: Oxford University Press, 2002), 10–11. Eric Helleiner emphasizes that the British and the American governments actually supported the development of this unregulated market. Eric Helleiner, *States and the Reemergence of Global Finance: From Bretton Woods to the 1990s* (Ithaca, NY: Cornell University Press, 1994), 81–91.

3. For example, New York banks moved much of their foreign issuance business to Europe after the introduction of the Interest Equalization Tax in 1963 and the Voluntary Foreign Credit Restraint Program in 1965. Cassis, *Capitals of Capital,* 226.

4. This practice, particularly prevalent during the domestic credit squeezes of 1966 and 1969–1970 and designed to avoid interest rate ceilings, was referred to as "roundtripping" through the Euromarket. Helleiner, *States and the Reemergence of Global Finance,* 88.

5. Ibid., 89.

6. Battilossi, "International Banking," 15.

7. Richard Sylla, "United States Banks and Europe: Strategy and Attitudes," in Battilossi and Cassis, *European Banks and the American Challenge,* 66–67. Sylla puts the number of American branches in London by the mid-1970s at 58, and highlights that nearly half of all foreign-bank assets were American. Ibid., 66–67. See also Catherine R. Schenk, "International Financial Centres, 1958–1971:

Competitiveness and Complementarity," in Battilossi and Cassis, *European Banks and the American Challenge,* 95.

8. Helleiner, *States and the Reemergence of Global Finance,* 153.

9. Even in London, only Bankers Trust Company, Hanover Bank, and the Bank of America (among American banks) established branches in the 1920s. Battilossi, "International Banking," 6. By the time of the crash, direct American presence in Europe remained minimal, with only six banks working in London and even fewer in Paris. Battilossi, "International Banking," 6. Battilossi argues that most US banks remained "marginal competitors at best" in the 1920s, with British banks maintaining their global dominance. Battilossi, "International Banking," 26–27.

10. This is not to say that cooperation did not exist in the 1920s and earlier. As I discuss in chapter 3, a number of major American financial houses, particularly the more venerable New York houses, had important links with European finance and participated in international syndicates that distributed foreign securities. See ibid., 6. However, the integration was far less deep than than the interactions that eventually developed through the 1960s and 1970s.

11. Schenk, "International Financial Centres," 84.

12. Anthony Sampson, *The Money Lenders: Bankers and a World in Turmoil* (New York: Viking, 1982), 207.

13. Duncan M. Ross, "Clubs and Consortia: European Banking Groups as Strategic Alliances," in Battilossi and Cassis, *European Banks and the American Challenge,* 136. See also Cassis, *Capitals of Capital,* 224, 231–232.

14. Battilossi, "International Banking," 20. While consortium banking might have been helpful in the initial internationalization and integration of some banks, Battilossi points out that consortia became minimally important and were even disbanded as shareholder banks embarked on international activities on their own. Battilossi, "International Banking," 20.

15. Schenk, "International Financial Centres," 83–84.

16. Ross, "Clubs and Consortia," 136–139. Banking consortia in and of themselves were not new, as European banks prior to 1914 also had established joint subsidiaries to explore newer arenas of international lending. Cassis, *Capitals of Capital,* 224.

17. Schenk, "International Financial Centres," 78

18. Ibid., 82–83. Schenk also warns against overstating the centrality of New York in American international banking, highlighting that many major banks had head offices outside of New York. Ibid., 81. Sylla points out the example of Citibank, which established its own London-based merchant bank, Citicorp International Bank Limited, from which it earned huge fees for the home office by organizing London-based international syndicates. Sylla, "US Banks and Europe," 67–68.

19. This difference should not be overstated, though—even in the 1970s, the most creditworthy countries were able to issue Eurobonds, with Swiss banks heavily involved in this business. And the major private banks of the earlier

wave of lending, through the 1920s, maintained significant shares of bonds on their own books. Vinod K. Aggarwal, *Debt Games: Strategic Interaction in International Debt Rescheduling* (New York: Cambridge University Press, 1996), 21.

20. Sampson, *Money Lenders,* 114.

21. *Wall Street Journal,* September 8, 1983, 31; also cited in Charles Lipson, "International Debt and International Institutions," in *The Politics of International Debt,* ed. Miles Kahler (Ithaca, NY: Cornell University Press, 1986), 223.

22. Penelope Walker, "The Philippines, 1983–1986: Negotiating Under Uncertainty," in *Dealing with Debt: International Financial Negotiations and Adjustment Bargaining,* ed. Thomas J. Biersteker (Boulder, CO: Westview, 1993), 159.

23. Joseph Kraft, *The Mexican Rescue* (New York: Group of Thirty, 1984), 21.

24. Lipson, "Debt and International Institutions," 228, 240.

25. Aggarwal, *Debt Games,* 16.

26. Benjamin J. Cohen, "International Debt and Linkage Strategies: Some Foreign-Policy Implications for the United States," in Kahler, *Politics of International Debt,* 134.

27. Kraft, *The Mexican Rescue,* 21.

28. Cassis, *Capitals of Capital,* 237. For an overview of the geographic tendencies in international banking, see Donald Fryer, "The Political Geography of International Lending by Private Banks," *Transactions of the Institute of British Geographers, New Series* 12, no. 4 (1987): 413–432, esp. 422–428.

29. Aggarwal, *Debt Games,* 35.

30. Ibid., 35; Sampson, *Money Lenders,* 258.

31. Japanese banks also responded enthusiastically when the Ministry of Finance encouraged them to lend. For example, Japanese bank lending to Mexico increased after the second oil shock of 1979, when the government's concern about oil access led to a series of initiatives designed specifically to encourage such lending.

32. Cohen, "International Debt and Linkage Strategies," 133.

33. Sampson, *Money Lenders,* 211.

34. He continues, "Tellingly, this resurgence of international bank flows [to third world] did not disrupt the organisation and hierarchy of the main centres. It was as if previous developments were being consolidated, especially the transformations caused by the emergence of the Euromarkets ten to fifteen years earlier." Cassis, *Capitals of Capital,* 237. For more references to herd logic, see also Miles Kahler, "Politics and International Debt: Explaining the Crisis," in Kahler, *Politics of International Debt,* 12, 23; Vinod K. Aggarwal, *International Debt Threat: Bargaining Among Creditors and Debtors in the 1980s* (Berkeley, CA: Institute of International Studies Policy Papers, 1987), 19.

35. As related in Sampson, *Money Lenders,* 115.

36. Sampson, *Money Lenders,* 115.

37. Relatedly, Peter Haas has suggested that one source of cooperation in the international arena is the existence of epistemic communities, which share "a

set of principled and causal beliefs" as well as "shared notions of validity and a shared policy enterprise." Peter Haas, "Introduction: Epistemic Communities and International Policy Coordination," *International Organization* 46 (1992): 16. These loan officers, and the advanced industrial country central bankers that began to interact more heavily in the 1970s, can be understood as epistemic communities of sorts.

38. That said, authoritarian governments may be more willing to force through sometimes oppressive internal measures that would allow for higher foreign debt payments.

39. As quoted by Sampson, *Money Lenders,* 115. Whereas many academic studies focus on the 1980s' rescheduling process, Sampson's more journalistic account of 1970s' international finance, including interviews with participants, provides insight into the reasoning and dynamic of the original lending decisions.

40. Kraft points out that one Mexican loan organized by Bank of America, planned for $1 billion, ended up heavily oversubscribed, raising $2.5 billion. Kraft, *Mexican Rescue,* 19.

41. Ibid., 19–20.

42. As quoted by Sampson, *Money Lenders,* 151. Sampson points out that much of this funding ended up in the private bank accounts of Mobutu and his family. Ibid., 153. It is worth pointing out, however, that the prices of Zaire's key export commodities (particularly copper) had been high through the 1960s and 1970s, and thus (assuming a statist approach in which the internal political framework is not a problem), the country's economic capacity should have been sufficient for debt payment through the mid-1970s. See Peter Körner, "Zaire: Indebtedness and Kleptocracy," in *The Poverty of Nations: A Guide to the Debt Crisis from Argentina to Zaire,* ed. Elmar Altvater et al. (London: Zed Books, 1991), 230.

43. Sampson, *Money Lenders,* 144. Kraft also points out that "as a result the IMF share of international financing had dropped from 12 per cent in 1965 to 3 per cent in 1978." Kraft, *Mexican Rescue,* 6.

44. Statement by Costanzo, House Banking Committee, International Banking Operations, 1977, as quoted in Sampson, *Money Lenders,* 146.

45. Quoted in the *Wall Street Journal,* December 21, 1981, cited in Aggarwal, *Debt Threat,* 38.

46. World Council of Churches and Bank Loans to South Africa, WCC, Geneva 1977. Cited in Sampson, *Money Lenders,* 162.

47. Senate Foreign Relations Committee: US Corporate Interests in South Africa, Washington, 1978, cited in Sampson, *Money Lenders,* 168–169.

48. However, he did somewhat undermine the strength of this condemnation by suggesting in the same statement that, despite apartheid's ethical implications, "one must acknowledge that the black people of South Africa are far better off economically than the black people anywhere else on the African continent." As cited in Sampson, *Money Lenders,* 161.

49. Johannes Witteveen, "The IMF and the International Banking Community," Address to the Financial Times Conference, New York, April 29, 1976,

as cited in Harold James, "Central Banks and the Process of Financial Internationalization: A Secular View," in Battilossi and Cassis, *European Banks and the American Challenge,* 210.

50. International Monetary Fund Central Files, G142.42, Interim Committee, October 2, 1976, cited in James, "Financial Internationalization," 210.

51. International Monetary Fund Central Files, G142.42, Interim Committee, September 24, 1977. Cited in James, "Financial Internationalization," 211.

52. Kraft, *Mexican Rescue,* 20.

53. Ibid., 20.

54. One banker described the following dynamic: "The banks forced money on Pertamina, and Pertamina ate it." *The Billion Dollar Bubble,* ed. Seth Lipsky (Hong Kong: Dow Jones Publishing, 1978), quoted in Sampson, *Money Lenders,* 148.

55. Bill Paul, "Caveat Lender: Chase Bank and Others Face Court Challenges on Huge Loans to Iran," *Wall Street Journal,* March 28, 1980; see also Jeff Gerth, "Chase's Lawsuit Against Iran," *New York Times,* November 11, 1980, D13. While the requirements of this constitutional provision were brought up by the subsequent regime as a potential defect in the loan contract, the issue was never fully addressed by a court. The January 1981 Algiers Accords between the United States and Iran, covering finances and the return of American hostages, ended all litigation and specified the repayment of all shah-era debt claimed by syndicates involving US institutions. Algiers Accords, January 19, 1981, Undertakings of the Government of the United States of America and the Government of the Islamic Republic of Iran, para. 2.

56. Perhaps the bank understood the palace to be a subspecies of housing project. Iran's postrevolutionary Central Bank governor, Ali-Reza Nobari, complained as well about a particular bank wholly owned by the shah's family, "All the banks knew that the Bank Omran was the Shah's personal repository for his pocket money . . . . But they went on lending to Bank Omran. Citibank lent, for example, fifty-five million dollars to Princess Ashraf for a housing project. On the site of the housing project she built a palace. And yet Citibank debits our account for it," quoted in Sampson, *Money Lenders,* 236.

57. Cohen, "International Debt and Linkage Strategies," 145, citing William R. Cline, "International Debt and the Stability of the World Economy," Policy Analyses in International Economics, no. 4 (Washington, DC: Institute for International Economics, September 1983), 34.

58. M. S. Mendelsohn, *Commercial Banks and the Restructuring of Cross-Border Debt* (New York: Group of Thirty, 1983), 3. Mendelsohn points out that, in the six years through 1982, only nine countries restructured their debt to private markets, with most of these instances (excepting Turkey in 1979 and Poland in 1982) being easily handled and even negligible. Ibid., 3.

59. Kraft, *Mexican Rescue,* 3. A lead Mexican negotiator felt similarly: "The blueprints for dealing with the situation quite simply did not exist; we had to draw them up." Ibid., 3.

60. Ibid., 3.

61. Aggarwal, *Debt Threat,* 21.

62. Kraft, *Mexican Rescue,* 27.

63. Lipson, "Debt and International Institutions," 226.

64. Kraft, *Mexican Rescue,* 18.

65. *The Economist,* September 26, 1981, 16, cited in Kahler, "Politics and International Debt," 20. The Fund had played a role in approving economic policies as part of the 1970s' debt reschedulings, but this did not come close to its role in the 1980s and beyond.

66. See, for example, Lipson, "Debt and International Institutions," 233.

67. Again, this political independence—or at least the appearance of independence and neutrality—is important to the legitimacy of these organizations. As Antony Anghie argues, "The appearance of independence is crucial to the rational-legal authority that the IFIs claim to wield, and the governing law of the IFIs attempts, however inadequately, to ensure and protect this independence." Antony Anghie, "International Financial Institutions," in *The Politics of International Law,* ed. Christian Reus-Smit (Cambridge: Cambridge University Press, 2004), 224.

68. IMF Confidential Memorandum from Carlos Sanson to Acting Managing Director, December 11, 1973, quoted in Sampson, *Money Lenders,* 302.

69. Sampson, *Money Lenders,* 302. The Pinochet government, despite its willingness to use military or other oppressive means to control popular dissent, eventually also found the IMF's expectations of structural adjustment unduly harsh, and expressed concern as to the political unfeasibility of additional austerity measures. See Sampson, *Money Lenders,* 302–303.

70. Greg Conderacci, "IMF Asked to Investigate Possible Theft of Loan Funds by Ex-Nicaraguan Aides," *Wall Street Journal,* August 6, 1979, 28.

71. Lipson, "Debt and International Institutions," 235. Sampson points out that the two institutions began to overlap more after the 1979 oil crisis, after which there was some acknowledgment that Fund programs might extend beyond a year. Sampson, *Money Lenders,* 305.

72. Kahler notes, "The Northern coalition of the banks, the G-5 governments, and the IMF shared an interest not only in avoiding disruption of the international financial system but also in the rough outlines of a rescheduling and adjustment regime for debtors. . . . Much of Northern policy was directed to deepening the divergent interests among large debtors and between large debtors and those countries that could not on their own threaten the system." Kahler, "Politics and International Debt," 29.

73. Mendelsohn, *Commercial Banks,* 9.

74. *New York Times,* July 30, 1985, cited in Aggarwal, *Debt Threat,* 6.

75. Mendelsohn, *Commercial Banks,* 9.

76. Kraft, *Mexican Rescue,* 4.

77. José López Portillo, September 1, 1982, quoted in Kraft, *Mexican Rescue,* 39. This was after the initial US and Bank for International Settlements central

bank infusion to deal with the immediate liquidity crisis in late August. Notwithstanding this strong language, López Portillo resigned himself to an IMF accord by early November, a course of action cemented when the more market-oriented de la Madrid administration came to power in December.

78. Edward Schumacher, "4 Latin Chiefs Join in Debt Warning," *New York Times,* May 21, 1984, D1. See also Cohen, "International Debt and Linkage Strategies," 147.

79. Schumacher, "4 Latin Chiefs."

80. Kahler, "Politics and International Debt," 11.

81. Muchkund Dubey, "A Third-World Perspective," in *Power, Passions, and Purpose: Prospects for North-South Negotiations,* ed. Jagdish N. Bhagwati and John Gerard Ruggie (Cambridge, MA: MIT Press, 1984), 65. Dubey provides a brief overview of the developing country meetings and efforts from the mid-1970s to the early 1980s to address international economic relations from an integrated perspective. See esp. ibid., 65–75.

82. Eric Helleiner, "The Mystery of the Missing Sovereign Debt Restructuring Mechanism," *Contributions to Political Economy* 27 (2008): 104–105. For a discussion of North-South dialogue on sovereign debt in the 1970s, see Lex Rieffel, *Sovereign Debt Restructuring: The Case for Ad Hoc Machinery* (Washington, DC: Brookings, 2003), 132–148.

83. See, for example, Günter Frankenberg and Rolf Knieper, "Legal Problems of the Overindebtedness of Developing Countries: The Current Relevance of the Doctrine of Odious Debt," *International Journal of the Sociology of Law* 12 (1984): 415–438; James L. Foorman and Michael E. Jehle, "Effects of State and Government Succession on Commercial Bank Loans to Foreign Sovereign Borrowers," *University of Illinois Law Review* (1982); M. H. Hoeflich, "Through a Glass Darkly: Reflections Upon the History of International Law of Public Debt in Connection with Succession," *University of Illinois Law Review* (1982).

84. Mohammed Bedjaoui, Special Rapporteur, "Ninth Report on Succession of States in Matters Other Than Treaties," *Yearbook of the International Law Commission,* vol. 2, no. 1 (New York: United Nations, 1977), 67–74.

85. A significant portion constituted the accumulation of the regime's own interest obligations. Ann Helwege, "Three Socialist Experiences in Latin America: Surviving US Economic Pressure," *Bulletin of Latin American Research* 8, no. 2 (1989): 222. Over and above the graft from borrowed funds, the Somoza family had also embezzled considerable additional international aid money that arrived after an earthquake devastated Managua in 1972. The regime had entered into debt negotiations in mid-1978 and already suspended principal payments as of September 1979. Richard S. Weinert, "Nicaragua's Debt Renegotiation," *Cambridge Journal of Economics* 5 (1981): 188.

86. Roy Prosterman and Jeff Riedinger, "Shore up Nicaragua's Moderates," *Wall Street Journal,* October 2, 1979, 22. See also, Greg Conderacci, "IMF Asked to Investigate Possible Theft of Loan Funds by Ex-Nicaraguan Aides," *Wall Street Journal,* August 6, 1979, 28; "Where Did Somoza's Borrowed Millions

Go?," *Euromoney* (September 1979), 25. Prosterman and Riedinger suggested that the new Sandinista government had been something of a pleasant surprise—more pluralist and less radical than might have been expected. It highlighted that "nationalizations have been limited to Somoza-controlled enterprises, except for domestically owned banks, where reasonable compensation arrangements have been made and a huge burden of debts of doubtful collectibility has been assumed." Prosterman and Riedinger, "Shore up," 22.

87. Weinert, "Nicaragua's Debt Renegotiation," 187. Richard Weinert served as the financial advisor and main negotiator for the new Sandinista regime in its negotiations. The brief discussion of the Nicaraguan case here is indebted to Weinert's own account. Of the approximately $1.26 billion in public sector debt, about $490 million was owed to private foreign banks, and three-quarters of this amount was owed to US banks, including many smaller banks that had been involved in syndicated loans. "Nicaragua Debt Focus of Talks," *New York Times,* December 17, 1979, D4.

88. "Nicaragua Says it Will Repudiate Somoza-Era Debt," *New York Times,* September 29, 1979, 3.

89. These statements were made when authorizing a $36 million payment on the $2.5 billion foreign debt and calling for a rapid reestablishment of private credit lines. "Nicaragua Says it Paid $36 Million of Foreign Debt," *Wall Street Journal,* June 17, 1982, 32.

90. Gary Prevost, "Cuba and Nicaragua: A Special Relationship?," *Latin American Perspectives* 17, no. 3 (Summer 1990), 125, based on an interview with Francisco Campbell, Minister-Counselor, Nicaraguan Embassy, Washington, DC, in Collegeville, MN, October 31, 1984.

91. Interview with a Nicaraguan debt advisor by James Henry, Mexico City, June 24, 1988, in James S. Henry, *Blood Bankers: Tales from the Global Underground Economy* (New York: Four Walls Eight Windows, 2003), 184.

92. Prevost, "Cuba and Nicaragua," 132. Cuba was a main advisor to Nicaragua, placing it as a high priority aid recipient and eventually convincing the Soviet Union to pledge more aid despite its skepticism about the Sandinista regime's pluralism and insufficiently orthodox commitment to socialism. Ibid., 131.

93. Oramas Oliva, Cuban deputy foreign minister, Havana, July 17, 1984, as interviewed by Gary Prevost, ibid., 132.

94. According to a debt advisor to the Nicaraguan government interviewed in Henry, *Blood Bankers,* 187.

95. Henry, *Blood Bankers,* 187.

96. Weinert, "Nicaragua's Debt Renegotiation," 190.

97. Mendelsohn, *Commercial Banks,* 9–10.

98. See, for example, Ann Crittenden, "Nicaragua Renews Debt, Gaining 'Lenient' Terms," *New York Times,* September 9, 1980, D1. See also Weinert, "Nicaragua's Debt Renegotiation," 190–191. Weinert points out that "the terms did exceed, by a noticeable margin, any terms granted in a debt rescheduling in recent decades," and highlighted that the final terms were fashioned in a manner

consistent with the country's ability to pay—an idea borrowed from domestic restructurings for corporate debtors and a principle that banks had long rejected for sovereign states. Ibid., 191–192.

99. See, for example, ibid., 193.

100. Several months after the main restructuring agreement, a *New York Times* article pointed out that, "Nicaragua's revolutionary regime has so established its international credit standing since the overthrow of the late President Anastasio Somoza that even Switzerland is lending it money." Juan de Onis, "Lenders Now Consider Nicaragua a Good Risk," *New York Times,* December 25, 1980, 35.

101. This acceptance of sovereign state immortality supported private creditors' divergent treatment of corporate and sovereign actors. Writing about the debt negotiations, a key advisor to the Nicaraguan government noted, "Bankers . . . tirelessly point out that companies can disappear while countries cannot, and therefore banks cannot treat them similarly." Weinert, "Nicaragua's Debt Renegotiation," 193.

102. Charles Lipson, "International Debt and National Security: Comparing Victorian Britain and Postwar America," in *The International Debt Crisis in Historical Perspective,* ed. Barry Eichengreen and Peter H. Lindert (Cambridge, MA: MIT Press, 1989), 208, citing John Dizard, "Why Bankers Fear the Nicaraguan Solution," *Institutional Investor, International Edition,* November 1980, 53.

103. Mendelsohn, *Commercial Banks,* 10.

104. While the banks were committed to a statist principle, Charles Lipson has suggested that the banks not only "understood the weakness of Nicaragua's economy," but also "recognized the political difficulties of repaying debts that Somoza had personally appropriated." Lipson, "International Debt and National Security," 209.

105. In the midst of the Iranian hostage crisis, the new acting foreign and financial minister suggested that the regime would not honor debt contracts of the shah, while the Central Bank issued statements indicating that debt would be repaid and continued to attempt regular interest payments. Robert D. Hershey Jr., "Banking World Puzzled over Iran's Stand on Debt," *New York Times,* November 24, 1979, 30.

106. This was partially in reaction to the shah's admission into the United States, which was allowed against the strong advice of American embassy staff in Tehran (who rightly feared for their own safety). The Carter administration made this decision under pressure from David Rockefeller (of Chase) and Henry Kissinger, among others. This only cemented the impression within Iran that the United States and certain of its banks facilitated both the shah's rule and his absconding with government funds.

107. Although Iran had been shifting money out of some American banks, this movement had primarily been away from banks (like Chase) that had been closely associated with the shah's regime, and toward institutions—including US institutions like Bank of America—that had been less politically intertwined. See Sampson, *Money Lenders,* 242. Sampson points out that in general private

loans were not in doubt, and that only a few private loans raised any concerns. Ibid., 242.

108. "Risky Maneuvers: Bank-Account Moves by Iran, U.S. are Seen Setting Bad Precedents," *Wall Street Journal,* November 15, 1979, 1.

109. Ibid., 33. In a briefing with reporters, Treasury Secretary Miller insisted that the action was narrowly limited, "and shouldn't cause anyone, private or public, or government, to have any fear about maintaining deposits in American institutions." Iran very deliberately suggested that it had the ability to cripple the US financial system, although subsequently it was determined that this would not have been the case. However, there were certainly several important American banks that would have been vulnerable to a complete Iranian withdrawal.

110. "Iran Defaults to Group of International Banks on a $500 Million Loan," *Wall Street Journal,* November 23, 1979, 3.

111. Sampson, *Money Lenders,* 246, 249. For a narrative of bank involvement in Iran, see ibid., 234–250.

112. Hershey, "Banking World Puzzled over Iran's Stand on Debt," 30.

113. "Iran Schedules Ad to Aid Legal Position, Saying it will Honor 'Legitimate' Debts," *Wall Street Journal,* December 3, 1979, 2.

114. See John R. Crook, "Debt and Contract Claims Before the Tribunal," in *The Iran-United States Claims Tribunal: Its Contribution to the Law of State Responsibility,* ed. Richard B. Lillich and Daniel Barstow Magraw (Irvington-on-Hudson, NY: Transnational Publishers, 1998), 297.

115. Algiers Accords, January 19, 1981, Undertakings of the Government of the United States of America and the Government of the Islamic Republic of Iran, para. 2(A).

116. Ibid., para. 2(B).

117. John E. Hoffman, Jr., "The Iranian Asset Negotiations," *Vanderbilt Journal of Transnational Law* 17 (1984): 47–57.

118. Hoffman provides an overview of the first several years of the bank approach in ibid., 47–57. Although some claims for excess interest and nonsyndicated loans were filed at the Iranian-US Claims Tribunal, ultimately no such claims were arbitrated. Crook, "Debt and Contract Claims," 298.

119. Ray Vicker, "Trying the Shah: Iran Seeks to Prove its Ex-Leader Stole Millions from Nation," *Wall Street Journal,* February 22, 1980, 1.

120. In one rare (and somewhat orthogonal) debt case, the tribunal dealt with the technical question of whether a court judgment on a debt created yet a separate debt that might provide the basis for tribunal jurisdiction. Crook, "Debt and Contract Claims," 299, citing Marks & Unmann and Islamic Republic of Iran, 8 C.T.R. 290, 295 (1985-I).

121. For an analysis of this jurisprudence, see David D. Caron, "The Basis of Responsibility: Attribution and Other Trans-Substantive Rules," in Lillich and Magraw, *Iran-United States Claims Tribunal,* 129–151. But tribunal arbitrators did assert early on that the revolution itself was not a "wrong" for which investors were entitled to compensation, noting that "a revolution as such does

not entitle investors to compensation under international law." Starrett Housing Corp. and Islamic Republic of Iran, 4 C.T.R. 122, 156 (1983-III), as quoted in Crook, "Debt and Contract Claims," 282. In this, they paralleled the view of Bolshevik Russia in 1922 in denying claims made by foreign investors due to damage during the Russian Revolution and subsequent civil war.

122. In general, the tribunal declined to accept jurisdiction over Iranian bank claims filed against US banks or companies, that is, for standby letters of credit. Crook, "Debt and Contract Claims," 298–299. It did, however, decide against Iran in one 1996 case that challenged the enforceability of a specific 1948 supply contract for American arms and equipment purchases. Although it would not decide on the transferability of subjugation or odious debts in international law, and also suggested that any relevant doctrine applied only to state succession, it did contend that the contract would not be odious if such a determination were to be made. 32 Iran-US Claims Trib. Rep. 164 (1996) (Chamber Two Award No. 574-B36-2 of 3 December 1996)), as discussed in Jeff King, "The Doctrine of Odious Debt in International Law: A Restatement," Working Paper (January 2007), 43–44.

123. Philip Shenon, "World Bank May Grant Teheran First Loan Since 1979 Revolution," *New York Times,* October 13, 1990, 1. The loan amounted to $250 million, with a twenty-year maturity. "World Bank Loan to Iran," *New York Times,* March 16, 1991, 35.

124. Shenon, "World Bank May Grant," 4.

125. "Iran to Receive Loan from World Bank for Earthquake Aid," *Wall Street Journal,* March 18, 1991, A11.

126. Iran applied for two IBRD loans for $232 million in 2000, after seven years of receiving no IBRD loans. The US executive director objected to the loans (as required by US law) but it was approved in May 2000. Sean D. Murphy, ed., "Contemporary Practice of the United States Relating to International Law," in *American Journal of International Law* 94, no. 4 (October 2000): 698–699.

127. Nicola Clark, "Iran Bonds: Flashback to the '70s," *International Herald Tribune,* June 11, 2002. The US Treasury opposed the issuance, informing US-based Moody's credit-rating agency that its 1999 B2 rating for Iran violated a 1995 US ban on trade and investment in Iran (Moody's subsequently withdrew its rating). Americans were strictly prohibited from investing in the bonds. Ibid.

128. "Iran Plans to Issue $4.2 Billion Bonds for Gas Projects," *Reuters,* June 25, 2012. Some commentators have suggested that international investors have found ways to circumvent sanctions, granting Iran a degree of access to external capital. See, for example, Avi Jorisch and Lee Prisament, "Iran's Merry-go-bonds," *The Jerusalem Post,* April 5, 2011; Avi Jorisch, "Pay to Play: European Banks and Iranian Sanctions," *UPI,* August 30, 2012.

129. The certainty and stability promised by the new regime was not entirely unwelcome by the major international financial institutions, who suggested that the political developments held out the promise of "considerable progress." See, for example, Robin Broad, *Unequal Alliance: The World Bank, the International*

Monetary Fund, and the Philippines (Berkeley, CA: University of California Press, 1988), 63. Indeed, World Bank lending increased significantly after the institution of martial law, as earlier economic measures encouraged by the Bank had been halted in the legislature. Bank president McNamara expressed this past disappointment to Marcos's Philippine delegation and indicated that, "provided the political environment was stable and the Administration was making an effective attack on the fundamental economic problems, the Bank was fully prepared to more than double its current rate of lending if an adequate number of projects could be prepared in time." Memorandum for the record, "Philippines—Meeting of the Philippine Delegation to the 1972 Annual Meeting with Mr. McNamara on September 29, 1972," October 2, 1972, 1, cited in Devesh Kapur, John P. Lewis, and Richard Webb, *The World Bank: Its First Half Century: Perspectives*, vol. 2 (Washington, DC: Brookings Institution, 1997), 558.

130. This audit was carried out by bankers from MHT and Chemical Bank, and its findings were shared with US and Philippine authorities but not made public. As interpreted by a banker involved in the audit, "[The $5 billion] had been disbursed by us, but it was completely missing from the Central Bank's books! It turned out that most of these loans had been disbursed to account numbers assigned to Philippine OBUs (offshore banking units) or other private companies. Apparently what happened was, the Central Bank gave MHT the account numbers, and we never questioned whether they were Central Bank accounts—we just wired the loans to them. And they disappeared offshore . . . . So the Philippines is still servicing all these Central Bank loans." As interviewed by James S. Henry, January 19, 1989; December 22–23, 1988. Henry, *Blood Bankers*, 73.

131. Niña Boschmann, "The Philippines: The IMF's Intractable Regular," in Altvater, *Poverty of Nations*, 189. In fact, the Philippines attempted (and failed) to stop payment on this debt in particular in US courts, in an action arguably akin to that of Costa Rica's repudiation of certain Tinoco contracts.

132. Broad, *Unequal Alliance*, 217–218, citing Norman Peagam, "The Spectre that Haunts Marcos," *Euromoney* (April 1984): 51. The diplomat suggested that the "normal" percentage of such graft in developing countries was closer to 10 percent. Ibid.

133. Broad, *Unequal Alliance*, 229. Broad quotes a banker expressing disappointment with the seeming loss of control by economic technocrats, particularly in the tendency toward using government funds for crony bailouts and in the falsification of Central Bank data: "I thought 18 months ago that the technocrats were running a first-class operation. I've since learned that they're running a zoo out there." Ibid., 229.

134. Walker, "The Philippines," 163.

135. Nicholas D. Kristof, "Tough Talks on Manila Debt Likely," *The New York Times*, March 2, 1987. See also Hal Hill, "The Philippine Economy under Aquino: New Hopes, Old Problems," *Asian Survey* 28, no. 3 (March 1988): 274; Walker, "The Philippines," 169.

136. Raphael Perpetuo M. Lotilla, "Selective Disengagement of Foreign Sovereign Debts: Some Principles Relevant to the Philippine Dilemma," in *The Debt Trap: How to Get Out of It* (Quezon City: International Studies Institute of the Philippines, August 24, 1987), 1.

137. As quoted in Boschmann, "The Philippines," 188. Ongpin explicitly pointed out that portions of the Philippine external obligations arose from the foreign borrowing of Marcos government banks and agencies that "financed hundreds of ill-advised capital intensive projects that have now become white elephants." Jaime Ongpin, Address delivered for the Debt Negotiation with Advisory Committee, October 31, 1986, reprinted in Alfred A. Yuson and Ricardo B. Ramos, *The Public Conscience of Jaime Ongpin* (Manila: Jaime V. Ongpin Foundation, 1988), 90.

138. As quoted in Boschmann, "The Philippines," 189. Within several months, the Aquino government had also embarked upon a fairly broad program of privatization of state-owned businesses, including the national oil company, the national airline, a steel plant, a hotel, and others. Ibid., 189.

139. Leonor M. Briones, "The Morning After: Approaches to the Debt Crisis," in *The Debt Trap,* 1, 8.

140. *Asia Banking,* September 1986, as quoted in Henry, *Blood Bankers,* 79.

141. Boschmann, "The Philippines," 189. Almost half ($13.2 billion) of the total debt to be repaid by 1992 was rescheduled, spread over seventeen years with a seven-year grace period and a spread of .875 percent over Libor—seemingly one of the lowest spreads allowed since the Mexican and Argentinean reschedulings. Ibid., 189.

142. Jaime Ongpin, "It's Time to Consider Lasting Solutions to the World Debt Problem," Paper Presented to the Philippine Council on Foreign Relations, July 24, 1987, reprinted in Yuson and Ramos, *Public Conscience,* 127.

143. That said, another banker expressed the role of precedent in the other direction—Brazil had suspended payments on loans owed for foreign banks in February 1987, and this move "provided a new definition of what the downside is." Kristof, "Tough Talks on Manila Debt Likely".

144. Henry, *Blood Bankers,* 80, citing his January 24, 1989 interview with David Pflug and the Philippine debt negotiator Cesar Virata's testimony before the Philippine Congress Committee on Ways and Means, August 17, 1987.

145. Under the military regime in Brazil, which had come to power in a 1964 coup, the country had seen considerable if unevenly distributed growth. Foreign borrowing, a key engine for this growth, had shot up precipitously during the 1970s' boom in private lending, with the external debt amounting to $43.5 billion by 1978. By May 1983, when the government effectively halted payments on its foreign debt, the amount had reached almost $90 billion. See Hugo Presgrave de A. Faria, "Brazil, 1985–1987: Pursuing Heterodoxy to a Moratorium," in Biersteker, *Dealing with Debt,* 176.

146. Although the military regime had taken slow steps toward a democratic transition, by 1984 a popular movement (the Diretas Ja campaign) helped to

quicken the government's movements toward civilian rule. The new regime took power in 1985, and although president-elect Tancredo Neves's sudden death meant that the more military-friendly Jose Sarney ultimately took office, the new pluralist democracy began work on the Neves platform. See Presgrave de A. Faria, "Brazil," 171–191.

147. Dilson Funaro, "Statement by Mr. Dilson Funaro, Minister of Finance of Brazil," US congressional summit on debt and trade, Waldorf Astoria, New York City, December 5, 1986, 3–5, Mimeo, quoted in Presgrave de A. Faria, "Brazil," 191.

148. Internally, he was criticized for suspending payments from a position of weakness rather than one of strength (as would have been the case with higher reserves in 1986). Ibid., 192.

149. Ibid., 194.

150. Robert R. Kaufman, "Democratic and Authoritarian Responses to the Debt Issue: Argentina, Brazil, Mexico," in Kahler, *Politics of International Debt,* 201.

151. The diplomat, Argentina's ambassador to the Latin American common market, continued, "Frankly, no one will tell you that the government is making contingency plans, but we are." *Wall Street Journal,* June 26, 1984, as quoted in Aggarwal, *Debt Threat,* 7.

152. "Argentina can demonstrate the ability to pay off a substantial portion of its $39 billion foreign debt. . . . [It] does not need to be active in foreign trade." *Financial Times,* November 4, 1983, as quoted in Aggarwal, *Debt Threat,* 9.

153. In proposing reduced rates on foreign debt, Alfonsín cited Argentina's economic problems as the justification. "Argentina's Alfonsín Asks for Reduced Rates on Debt," *Wall Street Journal* (Eastern edition), June 1, 1988, 1.

154. Quoted in Judith Evans, "Alfonsín Attacks IMF, Outlines Debt Offensive," *Wall Street Journal,* September 11, 1987, 1.

155. A similar pattern was followed in Peru, which returned to civilian government in 1980. The new president, Fernando Belaúnde Terry, stated that a top Peruvian priority was to service international debts, very much in line with statist norms. And even when declaring that debt service would be limited to 10 percent of export revenues, Alan García, his successor, insisted that this was an *economic* measure, that the debt had been acknowledged in principle, and that he wished to continue with bank negotiations. Barbara Stallings, *Banker to the Third World: U.S. Portfolio Investment in Latin America, 1900–1986* (Berkeley, CA: University of California Press, 1987), 288.

156. Kristof, "Tough Talks on Manila Debt Likely".

157. At the end of the apartheid era in late 1993, South Africa's foreign debt obligations amounted to about $17 billion, owed to about two hundred international banks, chief among them Swiss, German, UK, and US banks. Neil Behrmann, "South Africa Hopes to Reschedule Debt as Total Declines," *Wall Street Journal,* June 11, 1993. The South African government had embarked upon a program of paying down this debt, which had been considerably higher when

the apartheid government defaulted in 1985. A significantly larger proportion of the national debt was owed domestically, however, and since 1970—both before and after apartheid—foreign debt has been estimated to rarely exceed 3 percent of the total. Richard Walker and Nicoli Nattrass, "'Don't Owe, Won't Pay!' A Critical Analysis of the Jubilee SA Position on South African Government Debt," in *Development South Africa* 19, no. 4 (October 2002): 467–481, 472. Lawrence Hamilton and Nicola Viegi, "The Nation's Debt and the Birth of the New South Africa," Working Paper (September 2007) (on file with author) 6, 9. During the period of greater international isolation, between 1987 and 1993, the share of foreign to total debt dropped to almost zero. Hamilton and Viegi, "The Nation's Debt," 10.

158. They also chose to embark upon a program of fiscal austerity more rigorous than what might have been recommended by the IMF. Hamilton and Viegi, "The Nation's Debt," 2. Hamilton and Viegi identify three main reasons for the ANC's position: "(1) a desire not to be dependent upon national capita; (2) the perceived need to ensure against dependence upon international financial institutions; and (3) a political and economic compromise between the old and new regime that prioritised the interests of existing and potential creditors." Ibid., 4. They argue, however, that this initial decision may have ultimately undermined the ANC's larger goals of political and economic autonomy.

159. The capital markets responded well, at least initially, with Moody's granting the new South Africa an investment-grade rating of Baa3 in October 1994. Anthony Ramirez, "Confidence in South Africa Debt," *New York Times,* October 4, 1994, D1. S&P's issued a rating of BB, just below investment grade, but with a notation indicating a "positive outlook." Ibid., D5. Two months later, the first bond issue of the new government was oversubscribed. Anthony Ramirez, "South African Bonds Sell Briskly at 9.625%," *New York Times,* December 9, 1994, D2.

Chapter 7. Legitimacy and Debt at the Turn of the Century

1. Thomas M. Franck, "The Emerging Right to Democratic Governance," *American Journal of International Law* 86, no. 1 (1992), 46

2. Ibid., 46.

3. W. Michael Reisman, "Sovereignty and Human Rights in Contemporary International Law," *American Journal of International Law* 84 (1990), 869. The claims presented by Franck and Reisman, among others, have certainly proven controversial in international law scholarship, inspiring a series of further investigations and a range of rebuttals. Two major volumes compiling work in this area include Gregory H. Fox and Brad R. Roth, eds., *Democratic Governance and International Law* (2000) and Richard Burchill, ed., *Democracy and International Law* (2008). For the purposes of this book, I lay aside the question of whether a democratic conception of sovereignty is in fact emerging as a positive international legal entitlement or obligation.

4. Ruti Teitel, *Humanity's Law* (Oxford and New York: Oxford University Press, 2011), 216.

5. In particular, the 1994 ascension of Jacques de Larosière, former managing director of the IMF, to the EBRD presidency weakened the initial vision of founding president Jacques Attali. See Janet Guyon, "European Bank Gets Down to Business: Under Larosière, Lender to East Eschews Politics," *Wall Street Journal*, March 14, 1994, A8. The EBRD subsequently came under fire for its continued engagement with certain countries, particularly Uzbekistan. It did cut aid to Uzbekistan in 2004, however, citing that the government had failed to improve human rights conditions and develop democracy. "EBRD Cuts Aid to Uzbekistan Due to Poor Rights Record," *BBC Monitoring Former Soviet Union*, April 7, 2004, 1.

6. On the launch of the EBRD, see for example, Jacques Attali, "An International Institution of the Third Kind," *Europe* 305 (April 1991): 18–19.

7. Agreement Establishing the European Bank for Reconstruction and Development (1990), article 1.

8. Lilian A. Barria and Steven D. Roper, "Economic Transition in Latin American and Post Communist Countries: A Comparison of Multilateral Development Banks," *International Journal of Politics, Culture, and Society* 17, no. 4 (Summer 2004): 619–638, 625. They also point out the importance of the Cold War for explaining the difference between the IBD and the EBRD: "The international environment in which the discussions took place also provides a picture of how politics play an important role in developing IFIs . . . . The collapse of the Soviet Union leads NBMCs to pay special attention to democratization and citizen's rights. These concerns were not expressed in the 1950s, where the discussions of an IFI for Latin America were not constrained by whether democracy and human rights were being respected in the region. Preventing the spread of communism was perhaps a much more important factor." Ibid., 636.

9. Jessica Einhorn, "The World Bank's Mission Creep," *Foreign Affairs* 80, no. 5 (September/October 2001): 22–35, 27.

10. See generally World Bank, *The State in a Changing World—World Development Report Summary* (Washington, DC: World Bank, 1997).

11. Galit Sarfaty, *Values in Translation: Human Rights and the Culture of the World Bank* (Stanford, CA: Stanford University Press, 2012), 108–132.

12. World Bank, *State in a Changing World*, 1.

13. For one of many critiques of the World Bank's approach to governance, see S. Guhan, "World Bank on Governance: A Critique," *Economic and Political Weekly* 33, no. 4 (January 24, 1998): 185–187, 189–190.

14. Paul D. Wolfowitz, Speech on April 11, 2006, Jakarta, Indonesia, as quoted in Debra K. Rubin, "World Bank Sunshines Anti-Corruption Efforts," *Engineering News-Record* 256, no. 16 (April 24, 2006): 12. One early salvo against corruption was in Bank president James Wolfensohn's opening address to the Board of Governors at the Bank's 1996 Annual Meeting, in which he said, "Let me emphasize that the Bank Group will not tolerate corruption in the programs that we support; and we are taking steps to ensure that our own activities

306 Notes to Pages 197–200

continue to meet the highest standards of probity." James D. Wolfensohn, "Annual Meetings Address," World Bank, Oct. 1, 1996. Also see James P. Wesberry Jr., "International Financial Institutions Face the Corruption Eruption: If the IFIs Put Their Muscle and Money Where Their Mouth Is, the Corruption Eruption May be Capped," *Northwestern Journal of International Law & Business* 18, no. 2 (Winter 1998): 498–523, 498–499.

15. Bob Davis and Glenn R. Simpson, "World Bank Seeks Right Balance; Veto of Philippines Plan Shows Continued Divide Over Corruption Issues," *Wall Street Journal,* November 19, 2007, A4. Part of the problem on the Philippine road-building loan seems to have been that the main contractor, a Chinese firm, may have colluded with other contractors on this and other projects. A second more bureaucratic issue may have been that Bank president Robert Zoellick was not informed of the East Asia Division's decision to go forward with board approval on the loan. Ibid. Soon after, in 2008, the Department of Institutional Integrity, established in 2001 to investigate external and internal corruption, was elevated to a vice presidency. See also, "My Beautiful Laundrette: The World Bank and Corruption," *The Economist,* February 10, 2007, 71.

16. World Bank Group, *Strengthening Governance: Tackling Corruption—The World Bank Group's Updated Strategy and Implementation Plan* (Washington, DC: World Bank Group, 2012), 5.

17. Vikram Nehru and Mark Thomas, "The Concept of Odious Debt: Some Considerations," Economic Policy and Debt Department Discussion Paper (May 22, 2008), 14, 41. This was later published by the Bank as part of a larger volume on debt issues, Carlos A. Primo Braga and Dörte Dömeland, ed., *Debt Relief and Beyond: Lessons Learned and Challenges Ahead* (Washington, DC: World Bank, 2009), 205–228.

18. Nehru and Thomas, "Odious Debt," 41.

19. Robert Howse, "The Concept of Odious Debt in Public International Law," UNCTAD Discussion Paper No. 185 (July 2007), 21.

20. Ibid., 7.

21. United Nations Conference on Trade and Development (UNCTAD), *Principles on Promoting Responsible Sovereign Lending and Borrowing* (January 2012), article 8.

22. Ibid., article 8.

23. Ibid., article 1.

24. Ibid., article 3.

25. International Monetary Fund, *The Role of the IMF in Governance Issues: Guidance Note* (Washington, DC: International Monetary Fund, July 1997), article 1.

26. Michel Camdessus, "Fostering an Enabling Environment for Development," Address at the High-Level Meeting of the United Nations Economic and Social Council (July 2, 1997).

27. Cited in Wesberry, "Corruption Eruption," 517. The IMF had earlier issued guidelines attempting to reconcile this more conventionally "political"

interest with its macroeconomic concerns, stating, "Financial assistance from the IMF . . . could be suspended or delayed on account of poor governance, if there is reason to believe it could have significant macroeconomic implications that threatened the successful implementation of the program, or if it puts in doubt the purpose and use of the IMF resources." Ibid., 515.

28. See, for example, Norwegian Ministry of Foreign Affairs, "Cancellation of Debts Incurred as a Result of the Norwegian Ship Export Campaign," February 10, 2006 (Oslo, Norway: Ministry of Foreign Affairs).

29. Ibid.

30. Ibid.

31. In his assessment for UNCTAD of the current status of the odious debt doctrine in international law, Robert Howse notes that the Norwegian action, while not direct precedent, is important in that "the notion of co-responsibility exemplified by the unilateral and unconditional cancellation of these debts . . . does reflect the idea that repayment may be subject to broader considerations of the equities of the debtor-creditor relationship." Howse, "Odious Debt," 16.

32. Norwegian Ministry of Foreign Affairs, "Norway First in the World to Review Loans to Developing Countries," August 17, 2012 (Oslo, Norway: Ministry of Foreign Affairs). Norway is admittedly unique and has self-consciously adopted the role of a leader in multilateral debt cancellation programs, including by funding World Bank and UNCTAD reports on odious debt. However, it has in the past gone where others have eventually followed, including by being among the first Western countries to condemn apartheid in South Africa and awarding the 1960 Nobel Peace Prize to Albert Luthuli, leader of the banned African National Congress.

33. For an overview of these efforts, including eligible countries as of June 2012, see Martin A. Weiss, "The Multilateral Debt Relief Initiative" (Washington, DC: Congressional Research Service, June 11, 2012).

34. Donegal International Limited v. Republic of Zambia and Anr., Case No: 2005–190, [2007] EWHC 197 (Comm.) (decided July 15, 2007), Para. 2.

35. Ibid., Para. 544.

36. Ibid., Para. 2.

37. Ibid., Paras. 447, 458, 523.

38. Her Majesty's Treasury, "Government acts to halt profiteering on Third World debt in the UK," Press Notice (London, UK: H. M. Treasury, May 16, 2011). Paris Club debt cancellations have also made note of "non cooperative behavior from some litigating creditors," and the Club seems to have admonished official creditors for assigning away responsibility for HIPC-eligible debt. See for example, Paris Club, "Paris Club Agrees on a Reduction of the Debt of the Democratic Republic of the Congo in the Framework of the Enhanced Heavily Indebted Poor Countries Initiative," press release (Paris, France: Paris Club, November 17, 2010). Thomas Laryea notes the Paris Club admonishment in "*Donegal v. Zambia* and the Persistent Debt Problems of Low-Income Countries," *Law and Contemporary Problems* 73, no. 4 (2010), 199. Similar 2008 and 2009 legislative efforts in the US Congress (H.R. 6796 (110th) and H.R. 2932 (111th)),

sponsored by Congresswoman Maxine Waters, have thus far failed. However, in June 2012 New York state civil society groups, including the New York State Bar Association, the New York Bankers Association, the Securities Industry and Financial Markets Association, as well as Jubilee USA Network debt cancellation advocates, blocked recent efforts by hedge fund manager Paul Singer to alter New York law in favor of distressed sovereign debt or "vulture" funds. Jacob Gershman, "In Albany, Obscure Bill Rattles Wall Street and Argentina," *Wall Street Journal,* June 12, 2012.

39. Ben Hall, "Paris Club Steps up Vulture Fund Action," *Financial Times,* June 12, 2008.

40. UNCTAD, *Principles,* article 7.

41. This move was also expected to increase pressure on European export credit agencies to be more careful in their own funding. Along with the IFC, the main drafting banks were ABN Amro, Barclays, Citibank, and West LB. Demetri Sevastopulo, "Banks Commit to Socially Responsible Lending," *Financial Times,* June 3, 2003, 1. See also, "Banks' Social Conscience Takes Shape," *The Banker* 153, no. 929 (July 2003): 18.

42. The Equator Principles, June 2013, 2. Available at http://www.equator-principles.com/resources/equator_principles_III.pdf (accessed 7/18/2013).

43. Statement by George Vojta, executive vice president of Citibank, to the Senate Foreign Relations Committee, "US Corporate Interests in South Africa," Washington, DC (1978), 226, cited in Anthony Sampson, *The Money Lenders: Bankers and a World in Turmoil* (New York: Viking, 1982), 168–169.

44. Equator Principles, "Members & Reporting," www.equator-principles.com/index.php/members-reporting/members-and-reporting (accessed 2/15/13).

45. Transparency International, *The Anti-Corruption Plain Language Guide* (Berlin, Germany: Transparency International, 2009), 14.

46. See Jason Webb Yackee, "Investment Treaties & Investor Corruption: An Emerging Defense for Host States," *Virginia Journal of International Law* 52, no. 3 (2012): 723–745. Cecily Rose, based on a survey of nearly sixty arbitral awards involving allegations of corruption, suggests that tribunals have had to consider these allegations with increasing frequency since the mid-2000s in particular. Cecily Rose, "Questioning the Role of International Arbitration in the Fight against Corruption," Working Paper (2012), on file with author.

47. Abaclat and Others v. The Argentine Republic, ICSID Case No. ARB/07/5, Decision on Jurisdiction and Admissibility (August 4, 2011). The jurisdictional award held that the tribunal has the authority to hear a claim that a sovereign default and restructuring may have breached a bilateral investment treaty, and also that the 60,000 Italian claimants may file a mass claims arbitration under ICSID rules. This decision was controversial, with tribunal member Georges Abi-Saab writing a dissenting opinion and resigning from the tribunal in October 2011. For a consideration of possible ramifications of ICSID arbitrations on sovereign debt, see, among others, Michael Waibel, *Sovereign Defaults before International Courts and Tribunals* (Cambridge: Cambridge University Press, 2011), 316–329;

Jessica Beess und Chrostin, "Sovereign Debt Restructuring and Mass Claims Arbitration before the ICSID, The *Abaclat* Case," *Harvard International Law Journal* 53, no. 2 (Summer 2012): 505–517.

48. Award, *World Duty Free Company Limited and The Republic of Kenya,* ICSID Case No. ARB/00/7 (October 4, 2006).

49. *World Duty Free,* Recitation of Facts.

50. Paragraph 5 of World Duty Free's written submissions, dated 18 January 2006, quoted in *World Duty Free,* para. 185.

51. *World Duty Free,* para. 170.

52. Comments by Constantine Partasides, "World Duty Free v. The Republic of Kenya: A Unique Precedent?," Summary of the Chatham House International Law Discussion Group, March 28, 2007, 4.

53. *World Duty Free,* para. 178.

54. *World Duty Free,* para. 185.

55. *World Duty Free,* para. 157.

56. *World Duty Free,* paras. 188, 190, 192.

57. *World Duty Free,* para. 140–141.

58. *World Duty Free,* para. 143–146.

59. Phoenix Action, Ltd. v. The Czech Republic (ICSID Case Number ARB/06/5) (2009). See also *Plama Consortium Ltd (Claimant) v. Republic of Bulgaria (Respondent)* (ICSID Case Number ARG/03/24) (2008) (noting that World Duty Free held as a matter of international public policy or universal standards that "claims based on contracts of corruption or contracts obtained by corruption cannot be upheld by this Arbitral Tribunal").

60. See, for example, *Rumeli Telekom A.S., Telsim Mobil Telekomikasyon Hizmetleri A.S. (Claimants) v. Republic of Kazakhstan (Respondent)* (ICSID Case Number ARB/05/16) (2008).

61. Rose suggests that arbitral tribunals generally have made only minor contributions to corruption adjudication due to the significant evidentiary problems they usually face. They may avoid rulings through jurisdictional maneuvers, and parties have also abandoned corruption claims given the difficulty of presenting clear corroborating evidence. See generally Rose, "Questioning the Role."

62. Key cases include *Allied Bank International v. Banco Credito Agricola,* 757 F.2d 516 (1985) and *Republic of Argentina v. Weltover, Inc.,* 504 U.S. 607 (1992). The claimant in *Allied Bank* was a bank syndicate member, highlighting the possibility of creditor suits in any market structure. However, the number of potential claimants in the bond-lending era has increased exponentially. In the *Abaclat v. Argentina* ICSID case, for example, the claimants number 60,000.

63. The first case in which these funds were successful was *Elliott Associates, L.P. v. Banco de la Nacion and Republic of Peru,* 194 F.3d (2d Cir. 1999).

64. IMF first deputy managing director Anne Krueger's 2001 speech calling for an international sovereign bankruptcy procedure was important in bringing this discussion to the policy forefront. See Anne Krueger, "International Financial Architecture: A New Approach to Sovereign Debt Restructuring," speech given

at the American Enterprise Institute (Washington, DC: International Monetary Fund, November 26, 2001). For a review of various proposals for a sovereign debt restructuring mechanism (SDRM), see Brad Setser, "The Political Economy of the SDRM," Columbia Initiative for Policy Dialogue (IDP), Task Force on Sovereign Debt (January 3, 2008).

65. World Bank, *Global Development Finance: The Development Potential of Surging Capital Flows* (Washington, DC: World Bank, 2006), 108. Chapter 4 of the 2006 GDF provides an excellent overview of increased financial integration among developing countries. Ibid., 107–136.

66. Neeltje Van Horen, "Foreign Banking in Developing Countries: Origin Matters," *Emerging Markets Review* 8, no. 2 (May 2007).

67. Richard Manning, "Will 'Emerging Donors' Change the Face of International Cooperation?," *Development Policy Review* 24, no. 4 (2006): 371–385, esp. 373–377.

68. For an overview of top funds as of 2012, see the data provided by *Global Finance* magazine, www.gfmag.com/tools/global-database/economic-data/12146-largest-sovereign-wealth-funds.html#axzz2IDUuqOZw (accessed 2/15/13).

69. China's holding of US government debt in particular is considered a vulnerability—a sentiment that could be exacerbated by recent indications that the Chinese government may seek to reallocate some of its $1.6 trillion US Treasury holdings. See, for example, "China Sovereign Wealth Fund May Cut US Debt Holdings," *Agence France-Presse Shanghai,* January 15, 2013; Holly Ellyatt, "China's Sovereign Wealth Fund in Big 2012 Turnaround," *CNBC.com,* Jan. 14, 2012.

70. But, as an article in the *Financial Times* noted, "A core principle will stipulate that funds make their investment decisions on commercial, not political, grounds. While the US government welcomed the principles, it also recognised there was no way to ensure political motives were not involved." Demetri Sevastopulo and Krishna Guha, "Fifth of SWFs 'Unaccountable'," *Financial Times (Asia Edition),* September 15, 2008, 4. For another discussion of political concerns involved, see Peter Mandelson, "The Politics of Sovereign Wealth," *Wall Street Journal,* June 11, 2008, A11. Those concerned about political lending should find some solace in Rolando Avendaño and Javier Santiso's finding that the investment choices and outcomes of sovereign wealth funds and mutual funds have not appeared to be politically motivated. Rolando Avendaño and Javier Santiso, "Are Sovereign Wealth Funds' Investments Politically Biased? A Comparison with Mutual Funds," OECD Development Centre Working Paper No. 283 (December 2009).

71. International Working Group of Sovereign Wealth Funds, *General Principles and Practices (GAPP)—Santiago Principles* (October 2008), Principle 19.

72. The foundational legislation is "Net capital requirements for brokers or dealers," 17 C.F.R. 240.15c3–1, July 16, 1975.

73. Rawi Abdelal, *Capital Rules: The Construction of Global Finance* (Cambridge, MA: Harvard University Press, 2007), 192, noting that the Department

of Justice urged the SEC to increase competition for ratings agencies. For an overview of the importance of credit rating agencies in the construction of ideas of orthodoxy and heterodoxy in the use of capital controls, see ibid., 162–195.

74. Christopher M. Bruner and Rawi Abdelal, "To Judge Leviathan: Sovereign Credit Ratings, National Law, and the World Economy," *Journal of Public Policy* 25, no. 2 (2005), 191–192. Bruner and Abdelal provide an excellent overview of ratings agencies, particularly as they relate to sovereign borrowers.

75. Ibid., 192, 211.

76. The potential systemic risk of credit-default swaps led former FDIC Chairwoman Sheila Bair, among others, to suggest that they should be subject to regulations akin to those regulating insurance markets. See for example, A. M. Best Company, "Default Swaps Post Systemic Risk, Should be Regulated as Insurance," www.insurancenews.net, November 4, 2011.

77. See, for example, Joseph Stiglitz, "Odious Rulers, Odious Debts," *Atlantic Monthly* (November 2003); the studies mentioned earlier for the World Bank and UNCTAD; and the special double issue in *Law & Contemporary Problems* (2007).

78. This discussion is presented in greater detail elsewhere. See, for example, Patricia Adams, "Iraq's Odious Debts," *Cato Policy Analysis No. 526* (September 28, 2004); Anna Gelpern, "What Iraq and Argentina Might Learn from Each Other," *Chicago Journal of International Law* 6, no. 1 (Summer 2005): 391–414; Justin Alexander and Wajeeh Elali, "Iraq and the Odious Debt Doctrine," Working Paper (2009).

79. See, for example, Justin Alexander, "Saddam's Debt: The Emerging Conflict Over How to Deal With Saddam's Devastating Economic Legacy," *Multinational Monitor* 25, no. 3 (March 2004).

80. Ali Allawi, *The Occupation of Iraq: Winning the War, Losing the Peace* (New Haven, CT: Yale University Press, 2007), 201.

81. Ibid., 428.

82. Interview with Adil Abdul Mahdi, minister of finance in the interim government of Iraq, "Restructuring Debt is Top Priority," quoted in Gelpern, "Iraq and Argentina," 406.

83. Author's interview with Lee Buchheit, New York, NY, September 23, 2008.

84. Ibid.

85. Author's telephone interview with Jeremy Pam, October 14, 2008.

86. Ibid.

87. Allawi, *Occupation of Iraq*, 428.

88. Craig S. Smith, "Major Creditors Agree to Cancel 80% of Iraq's Debt," *New York Times,* November, 22, 2004. Although the Paris Club debt constitutes less than half of the overall debt, this agreement has formed the basis of Iraq's offers to other creditors. Author's interview with Buchheit.

89. Author's interview with Buchheit. See also Allawi, *Occupation of Iraq,* 428. The remaining amounts included $20 billion for other sovereign public creditors working bilaterally (including China, Turkey, and some members of the

former Soviet bloc); $20 billion to banks and trade creditors from over fifty countries; and over $50 billion for Saudi Arabia ($39 billion), Kuwait ($8 billion), the UAE, and Qatar. Allawi, *Occupation of Iraq,* 428.

90. Allawi, *Occupation of Iraq,* 428.

91. Author's interview with Buchheit.

92. Ibid.

93. Pam felt that, for the most part, the jubilee movement was not altogether helpful. Author's interview with Pam.

94. Edwin Truman, "The Right Way to Ease Iraq's Debt Burden," *Financial Times,* April 28, 2003, 13.

95. Ibid.

96. As an indicator of external secondary market expectations on the likelihood of payment, prices for Ecuador's 2012 bond fell to 21 cents on the dollar in late November 2008. Of course, throughout 2008 Ecuador's inconsistent signals had certainly confused the markets, with the same bonds trading at full face value in September 2008. Felix Salmon, "Ecuador Approaches Default," www. seekingalpha.com, November 18, 2008.

97. Rafael Correa, "Canje de Deuda: Todo en Función de los Acreedores," *La Insignia,* June 20, 2005, cited in Arturo Porzecanski, "When Bad Things Happen to Good Sovereign Debt Contracts: The Case of Ecuador," *Journal of Law and Contemporary Problems* 73, no. 4 (Fall 2010), 251–271, 259.

98. Porzecanski, "Sovereign Debt Contracts," 260–261, citing Rafael Correa, "Discurso de Rafael Correa Presidente de Ecuador," 4–5 (January 15, 2007) (Porzecanski's translation).

99. Executive Decree 472, reprinted in Internal Auditing Commission for Public Credit of Ecuador, *Final Report of the Integral Auditing Commission of the Ecuadorian Debt* (CAIC Report) (Quito, Ecuador: Ministry of Economy and Finance, 2008), appendix, 156.

100. CAIC Report, 28.

101. CAIC Report, 28, as translated in Porzecanski, "Sovereign Debt Contracts," 263. The official English translation reads, "we have not found documentation about the information that will detail received loans by the Honorable National Defense Junta from the International Private Banking in the indicated period from January 1976 until December 2006." CAIC Report, 28.

102. CAIC Report, 28.

103. This dynamic is discussed in chapter 6.

104. CAIC Report, 31–32. The summary of the CAIC's conclusions on the commercial external debt, listing its principal illegalities and illegitimacies, is available at 48–49.

105. See, for example, CAIC Report, 52–53, 57–58. The CAIC Report lists a range of additional clauses and agreements as "violations of the juridical order," with particular attention to the local constitutions, civil code, and other domestic laws. CAIC Report, 63.

106. CAIC Report, 97.

107. CAIC Report, 97.

108. CAIC Report, 149 (noting that "odious debt" is among the international doctrines ignored in contracting and restructuring debt, but not specifying the way in which it might be applicable). Indeed, the doctrine of odious debt is relatively narrow, requiring a lack of popular consent and a failure to benefit the underlying population for applicability.

109. While it is hardly controversial to suggest that the international financial system leaves much to be desired in terms of equity and transparency, the absolutism of the CAIC's language remains something of a strange choice. Although Ecuador seems to have intended its audit and default to be a possible international role model, the tone of the CAIC report implies that it largely preaches to the converted. And the awkward translation and editing of the official English language version further suggests that the CAIC's target audience may have been domestic rather than external.

110. "Ecuador Defaults on Foreign Debt," *BBC News,* December 13, 2008.

111. Ibid.

112. Naomi Mapstone, "Ecuador Defaults on Sovereign Bonds," *Financial Times,* December 13, 2008.

113. Anthony Faiola, "Calling Foreign Debt 'Immoral,' Leader Allows Ecuador to Default," *Washington Post,* December 13, 2008.

114. Figure noted in Felix Salmon, "Ecuador's Idiotic Default," *Upstart Business Journal,* December 12, 2008. Porzecanski points out that by 2008 Ecuador's public external debt was less burdensome than it had been in three decades, and that the country held more liquid international reserves than ever before, at $6.5 billion. Porzecanski, "Sovereign Debt Contracts," 256.

115. Stephan Kueffner, "Ecuador Wants 'Big' Discount in Debt Restructuring, Correa Says," *Bloomberg News,* December 13, 2008.

116. Lee C. Buchheit and G. Mitu Gulati, "The Coroner's Inquest," *International Financial Law Review* (September 2009): 25; Porzecanski, "Sovereign Debt Contracts," 266–267.

117. International Campaign on Illegitimate Debt (CADTM), *Resolution of Support for Ecuadorian Debt Audit,* September 19, 2008, Resolution 1.

118. CADTM, *Resolution,* Resolution 4.

119. Wade Mansell and Karen Openshaw, "Suturing the Open Veins of Ecuador: Debt, Default and Democracy," *Law and Development Review* 2, no. 1, (2009), 184. In saying this, they call particular attention to Ecuador's ethnic minorities. More broadly, they note that "we have a situation in which legality and morality both seem to suggest that repudiation is entirely justified." Ibid., 184.

120. Ibid., 182.

121. Salmon, "Idiotic Default."

122. Felix Salmon, "Lessons from Ecuador's Bond Default," *Reuters,* May 29, 2009.

123. Felix Salmon, "The Cost of Sovereign Default Turns Negative," *Reuters,* May 26, 2009.

124. Nathan Gill, "China Loans Ecuador $1 Billion as Correa Plans First Bond Sale Since 2005," *Bloomberg News,* January 24, 2012.

125. Ibid.

126. Naomi Mapstone, "Ecuador Defaults on Sovereign Bonds".

127. Alexandria Valecia and Alonso Soto, "Regional Lenders Back Ecuador in Debt Talks," *Reuters,* May 18, 2009. Palau-Rivas indicated at the time that the CAF planned to disburse $700 million in loans to Ecuador in 2009.

128. Ibid.

129. Caroline Atkinson, Director of External Relations, International Monetary Fund, Remarks at the Regular Press Briefing (December 18, 2008), quoted in Porzecanski, "Sovereign Debt Contracts," 269.

130. Porzecanski, "Sovereign Debt Contracts," 268. These multilateral creditors have continued lending, with the Latin American Reserve Fund making an additional $515 million loan in July 2012. Pan Kwan Yuk, "Ecuador: Going from Bad to Worse?," *Financial Times Blog,* July 7, 2012.

131. Nathan Gill, "China Loans Ecuador $1 Billion as Correa Plans First Bond Sale Since 2005," *Bloomberg News,* January 24, 2012; Nathan Gill, "Ecuador Crowding out Bond Issuers as Oil Slumps," *Bloomberg News,* December 5, 2012.

132. Nathan Gill, "Ecuador Scraps Planned Bond Sale on Increased China Lending, *Bloomberg News,* February 17, 2012. More recently, Ecuador revised domestic bank regulations to require local banks to double their holdings of government debt, offering an additional layer of funding but also risking that local private borrowing will drop somewhat. Gill, "Ecuador Crowding."

133. "Fitch Affirms Ecuador's FC IDR at 'B-'; Outlook Revised to Positive," *Businesswire,* October 24, 2012; Standard & Poor's Ratings Services, "Republic of Ecuador Upgraded to 'B/B' from 'B-/C' on Improved Growth Prospects and Willingness to Pay Debt," June 7, 2012.

134. Moody's Investors Service, "Moody's Upgrades Ecuador to Caa1 and Maintains a Stable Outlook," Sept. 13, 2012.

135. Porzecanski, "Sovereign Debt Contracts," 270.

136. Adam Feibelman, "Ecuador's Sovereign Default: A Pyrrhic Victory for Odious Debt?," *Journal of International Banking Law and Regulation* 25, no. 7 (2010), 362.

137. Ibid., 360–361.

138. Ibid., 362.

139. Ibid., 361.

140. Felix Salmon, "Lessons from Ecuador's Bond Default," *Reuters,* May 29, 2009. It is at this point unclear whether this sentiment is widely shared, of course.

141. Jason Manolopoulos, *Greece's 'Odious' Debt: The Looting of the Hellenic Republic by the Euro, the Political Elite and the Investment Community* (London and New York: Anthem, 2011), 81–82.

142. Ibid., 249, 250.

143. The narrators of *Debtocracy* base their argument for partial repudiation on the contention that "it is immoral to repay an immoral debt." *Debtocracy,*

film, directed by Katerina Kitidi and Aris Chatzistefanou (Athens, Greece: 2011), www.debtocracy.gr/indexen.html (accessed 2/15/13). For a review, see Aditya Chakrabortty, "Debtocracy: The Samizdat of Greek Debt," *The Guardian,* June 9, 2011.

144. Most recently, this anger throughout the most affected countries has been directed at Germany and German diplomats, particularly in Greece. See, for example, Liz Alderman and Nicholas Koolish, "Greeks Pelt German Diplomat in Austerity Protest," *New York Times,* November 16, 2012. Indeed, a 2013 working paper copublished by IMF chief economist Olivier Blanchard seemed to acknowledge that the IMF underestimated the likely negative effect of austerity measures on growth during the European crisis. Olivier Blanchard and Daniel Leigh, "Growth Forecast Errors and Fiscal Multipliers," IMF Working Paper No. 13/1 (January 3, 2013).

145. See, for example, Jamie Smyth and Michael Steen, "Ireland Scrambles to Liquidate Anglo Irish," *Financial Times,* February 7, 2013.

146. Anglo Not Our Debt, www.notourdebt.ie (accessed 7/15/13).

147. See, for example, CAIC Report, 26. For a discussion of this "sucretization" policy, see Mansell and Openshaw, "Suturing the Open Veins," 170–172.

148. Excerpts of an interview with David Oddson, October 7, 2008, *Wall Street Journal,* October 17, 2008. For more on the events leading to the crisis, see Michael Waibel, "Iceland's Financial Crisis—Quo Vadis," *ASIL Insights* 14, no. 5 (March 1, 2010).

149. The UK and Netherlands governments decided to cover their residents' deposits in full, even above the amounts that the mandated deposit insurance scheme should have been designed to cover.

150. Simon Bowers, "Court Rules Against UK in £2.3bn Icesave Deposit Guarantees Battle," *The Guardian,* January 28, 2013.

151. In a surprise January 2013 decision, the European Free Trade Association court held that, under the relevant directive, a state party was obliged to establish a deposit-guarantee scheme, but it "does not lay down an obligation on the State and its authorities to ensure compensation if a deposit-guarantee scheme is unable to cope with its obligations in the event of a systemic crisis." EFTA Surveillance Authority v. Iceland, EFTA Case E-16/11 (January 28, 2013), Para. 144.

152. Ibid., Paras. 148, 150, 158.

Chapter 8. Politics and Prospects

1. Benedict Kingsbury points out that "a decline in the traditional sovereignty system weakens the relationship of mutual containment between sovereignty and inequality." Benedict Kingsbury, "Sovereignty and Inequality," in *Inequality, Globalization, and World Politics,* ed. Andrew Hurrell and Ngaire Woods (Oxford: Oxford University Press, 1999), 92.

2. An in-depth consideration of the facets and implications of the UNCTAD Principles is provided in Carlos Espósito, Yuefen Li, and Juan Pablo Bohoslavsky,

Sovereign Financing and International Law: The UNCTAD Principles on Responsible Sovereign Lending and Borrowing (Oxford: Oxford University Press, 2013).

3. Quoted from International Monetary Fund, "World Economic Outlook: Financial Crises: Causes and Indicators" (Washington DC: IMF, 1998), 8.

4. Jayachandran and Kremer note this concern as background for modeling an institutional mechanism that would determine odiousness *ex ante*. Seema Jayachandran and Michael Kremer, "Odious Debt," *American Economic Review* 96, no. 1 (2006): 82–92.

5. Quoted in Seema Jayachandran and Michael Kremer, "Odious Debt," in *Sovereign Debt at the Crossroads: Challenges and Proposals for Resolving the Third World Debt Crisis*, ed. Chris Jochnick and Fraser A. Preston (Oxford and New York: Oxford University Press, 2006), 215-225, 217.

6. Several economic studies have considered the evidence of creditor-side moral hazard associated with IMF support. See, for example, Olivier Jeanne and Jeromin Zettelmeyer, "International Bailouts, Moral Hazard, and Conditionality," *CESifo Working Paper Series*, no. 563 (2001); Andrew Haldane and Jorg Scheib, "IMF Lending and Creditor Moral Hazard," *Bank of England Working Paper*, no. 216 (2004). Many others discuss it as part of their larger research. See, for example, Kremer and Jayachandran, "Odious Debt," and Nouriel Roubini and Brad Setser, *Bail-outs or Bail-ins?: Responding to Financial Crises in Emerging Economies* (Washington, D.C.: Institute for International Economics, 2004).

7. This concern is expressed by Joseph Hanlon, *Dictators and Debt* (Oslo: Norwegian Church Aid, 1998).

8. Buchheit, Gulati, and Thompson call this the "intergenerational tension" in sovereign borrowing. Lee C. Buchheit, G. Mitu Gulati and Robert B. Thompson, "The Dilemma of Odious Debts," *Duke Law Journal* 56, no. 1 (2007): 1204–1208.

9. Patricia Adams points out that one problem of "loose lending" is that it severs the relationship that a ruling elite has with a state's population. In addition to providing elites with additional and often unaccountable funds (with which they can oppress the population), the government is not forced to deal with the oversight and accountability questions generally associated with raising taxes. Patricia Adams, *Odious Debts: Loose Lending, Corruption, and the Third World's Environmental Legacy* (Toronto: Earthscan, 1991), 151–156.

10. Statute of the International Court of Justice (1945), article 38(1)(b).

11. The volume on the UNCTAD Principles edited by Espósito, Li, and Bohoslavsky includes several pieces that consider the Principles in light of recent and related legal developments. See generally Espósito, Li, and Bohoslavsky, *Sovereign Financing and International Law*.

12. Jayachandran and Kremer, "Odious Debt," in Jochnick and Preston, *Sovereign Debt*, 215–225.

13. See, among others, the discussions in Adam Feibelman, "Equitable Subordination, Fraudulent Transfer, and Sovereign Debt," *Law and Contemporary Problems* 70, no. 4 (2007); Anna Gelpern, "Odious, Not Debt," *Law and Contemporary Problems* 70, no. 3 (2007); Robert Howse, "The Concept of Odious Debt in Public International Law," UNCTAD Discussion Paper No. 185 (July 2007).

Acknowledgments

This book would not have been possible without the support of many people. For their essential early guidance, I would like to thank Iain Johnston, Rawi Abdelal, Devesh Kapur, Benedict Kingsbury, Beth Simmons, and Richard Tuck. Their patient encouragement provided me with confidence in my arguments, and each offered insights and perspectives that immeasurably improved this book. Their commitment to scholarship and teaching is a model for what I hope to achieve in my own career.

I received incredibly helpful comments and criticisms at various stages from other colleagues, friends, and advisors, who graciously took time away from their own projects to think through portions (or in some cases all) of this work. I would especially like to thank Mark Blyth, Rachel Brewster, Chris Brummer, Lee Buchheit, Juan Pablo Bohoslavsky, Tai-Heng Cheng, Christine Desan, Nick Frayn, Jeffry Frieden, Stavros Gadinis, Anna Gelpern, David Grewal, Mitu Gulati, Andrew Guzman, Oddný Helgadóttir, Eric Helleiner, Robert Howse, Alex Gourevitch, Stanley Katz, Peter Katzenstein, Jonathan Kirshner, Mattias Kumm, Katerina Linos, Charles Maier, Tom McSweeney, Bernadette Meyler, Robert Post, Sabeel Rahman, Danya Reda, David Super, Chantal Thomas, Joseph Weiler, and Jason Yackee. This book also benefited from helpful feedback received at workshops held through Boston College, Georgetown University, George Washington University, Harvard Law School, NYU School of Law, University of California (Berkeley), University of Colorado (Boulder), University of Georgia (Athens), and the New York Area International Economic Law Working Group. I would also like to thank two anonymous reviewers for Harvard University Press, who provided excellent advice on the initial draft of this manuscript. Any remaining errors are of course my own.

While writing and revising, I benefited from the encouragement and friendship of Julian Blake, Asli Bali, Noah Dauber, Meera de Mel, Joy Ishii, Ariana Johnson, Sarah Kreps, Chung Hyun Lee, Kwang Hyun Lee, Darryl Li, Karuna Mantena, Jessica Ratcliff, Nico Silins, and Lori Wagner. I am also very grateful for the camaraderie of my former colleagues in the bankruptcy and restructuring department at Shearman & Sterling, LLP. I would like to acknowledge with gratitude Michael Aronson, my editor at Harvard University Press, for his faith in and commitment to this project. I am fortunate to have had his support and that of the team at Harvard University Press, including Kathi Drummy and

Heather Hughes. Marianna Vertullo shepherded the book through production with immense patience, and Deborah Jeppson copyedited the final manuscript with great care.

I was privileged to revise this manuscript during my first years of teaching at Cornell University Law School. My colleagues at the Law School have offered incredibly helpful feedback through several workshops. I owe much to their intellectual and personal support, and cannot imagine a more congenial setting in which to engage in scholarship and teaching. I would also like to thank my colleagues in the Government Department for welcoming me as their own, and for generously sharing with me their time and friendship. The resources of our wonderful library and the support of the Dean's Office and our administrative staff have been essential in completing this project. I benefited from excellent research assistance from Jim Bishop in making final revisions and additions.

Finally, I would like to thank my family, including my relatives in the United States, Indonesia, and Kenya. My parents-in-law, Phyllis Safiya Gabriel and Kip-korir Aly Azad Rana, have been loving and encouraging through every step of the project. My amazing sisters, Annette and Denette, have offered unfailing support, affection, and confidence, along with the occasional welcome distraction. I owe a huge debt of gratitude to my loving parents, Denny Lienau and Sri Setyaningsih Wiryopranoto Lienau. My father's conviction of history's continued relevance, manifest at the dinner table for as long as I can remember, has profoundly shaped my intellectual development. My mother's incredible generosity and warmth, demonstrated in many large and small acts, sustained me when my resolve faltered.

My wonderful daughter Navaz came into our family as I completed substantial edits for this book. Her smiles and laughter have become the highlight of my days, and they offered the gentle encouragement I needed to finally finish. I am most indebted to my husband, Aziz Rana, who has been my principal interlocutor and emotional support for many years. He has kept me company through long days and late nights, and read several complete drafts to improve this book in countless ways. His unconditional love and infinite faith in me have made this project possible and have immeasurably enriched my life. I dedicate this book to my parents, and to him.

Index

Note: Page numbers ending in "t" refer to tables.

Milton Keynes UK
Ingram Content Group UK Ltd.
UKHW010118280923
429503UK00002B/14/J